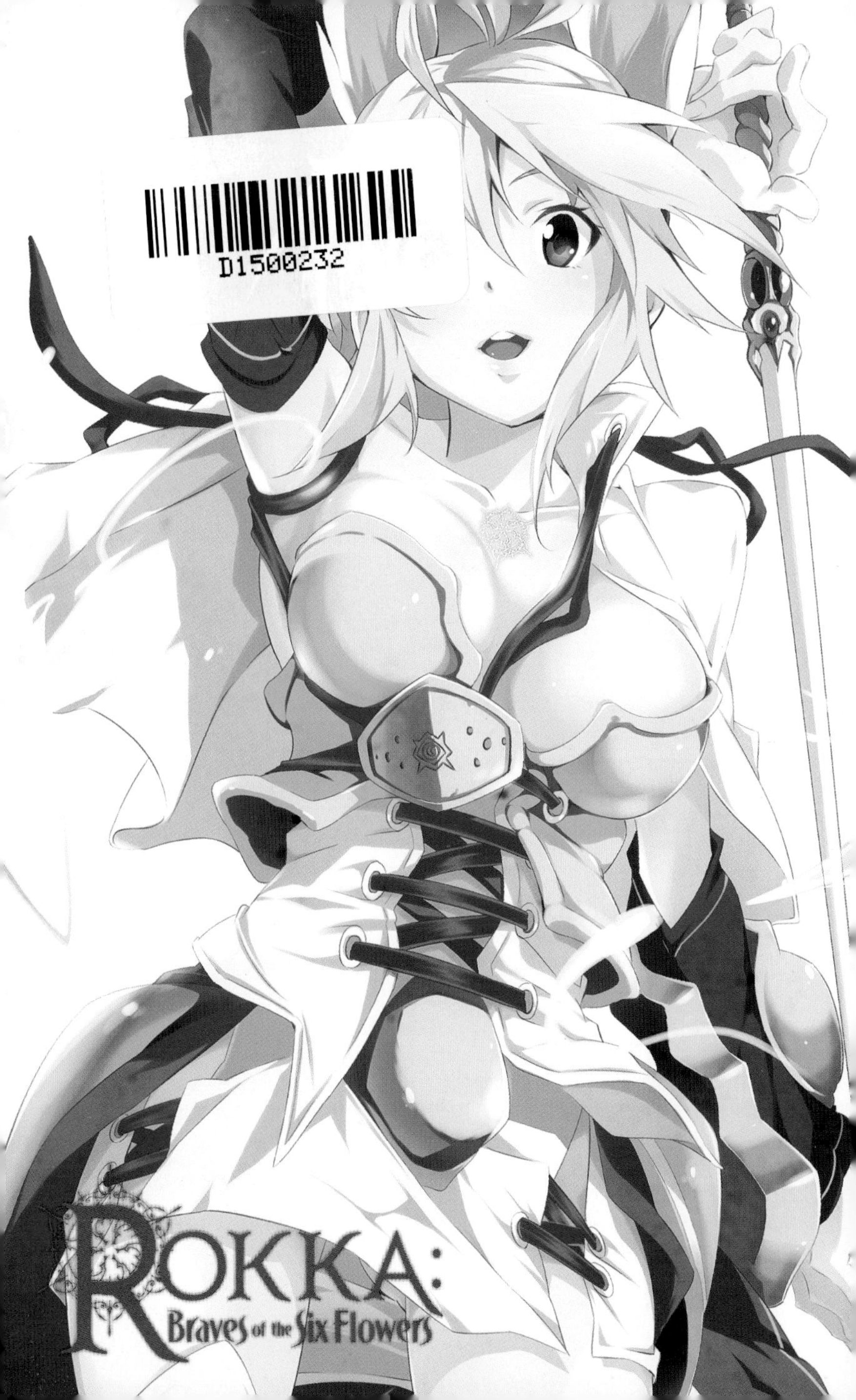
ROKKA:
Braves of the Six Flowers

CHARACTER INTRODUCTION

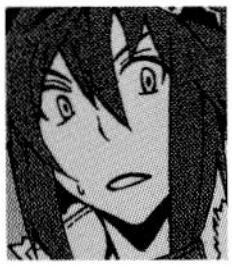

ADLET

A boy who declares that he is the strongest man in the world. Utilizes various hidden tools in battle.

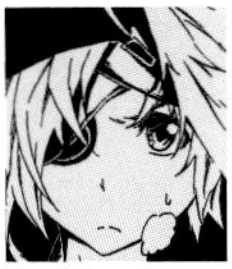

FREMY

The Saint of Gunpowder.
A cold girl who tends to keep others at a distance.

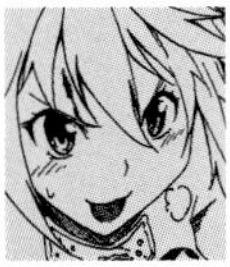

NASHETANIA

The Saint of Blades.
The freewheeling and mischievous princess of the powerful country of Piena.

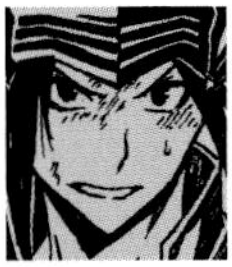

GOLDOF

A young knight of Piena who loyally serves Nashetania.

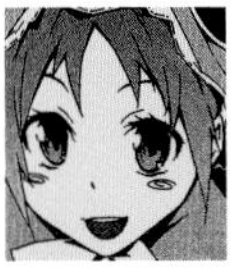

CHAMO

The Saint of Swamps.
An arrogant girl said to be the most powerful warrior alive.

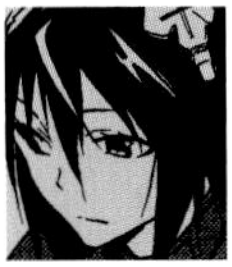

MORA

The Saint of Mountains.
Serves as the elder in charge of the saints.

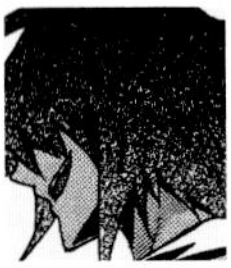

HANS

An assassin who uses an otherworldly style of swordplay.
Speaks in a catlike manner.

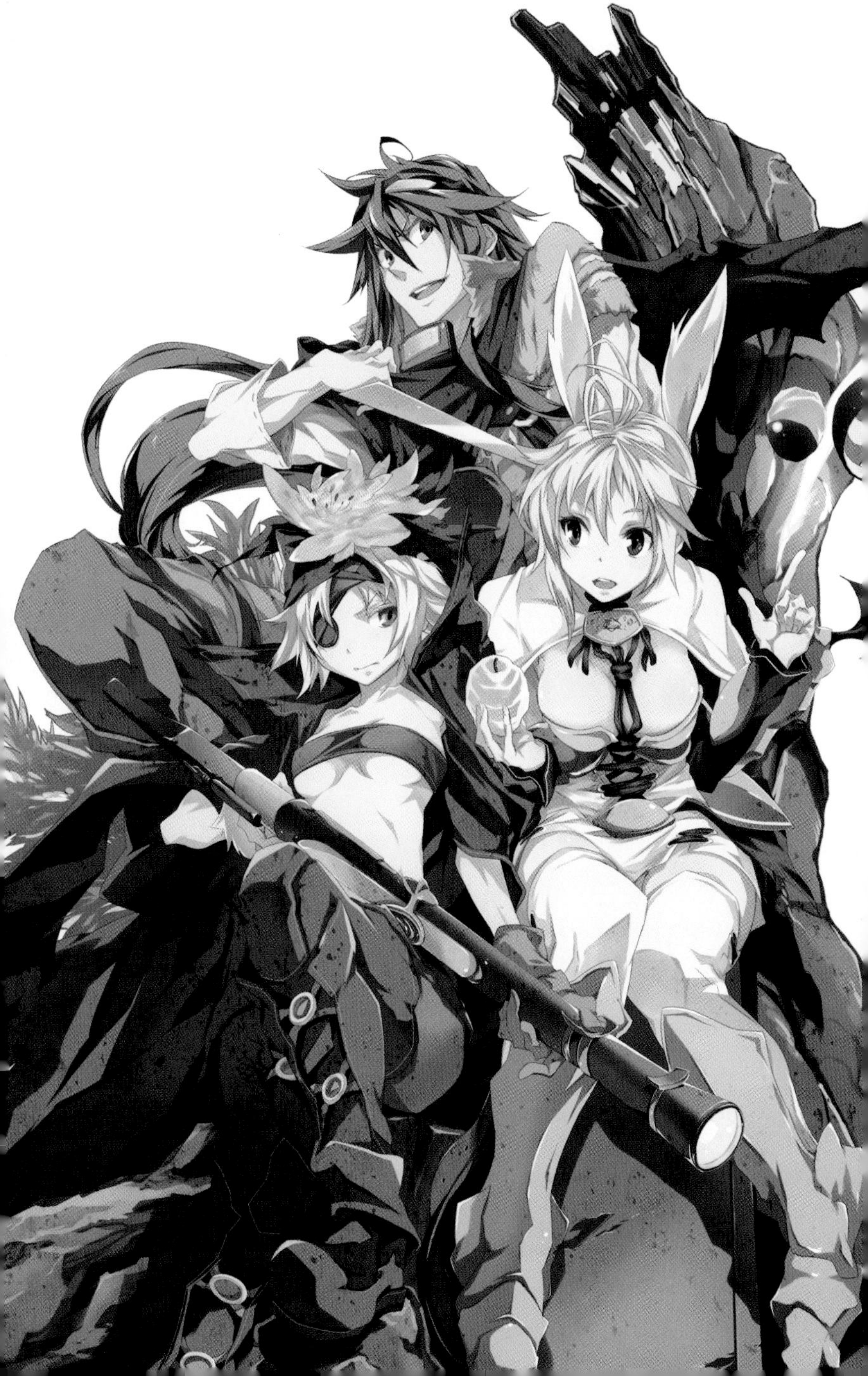

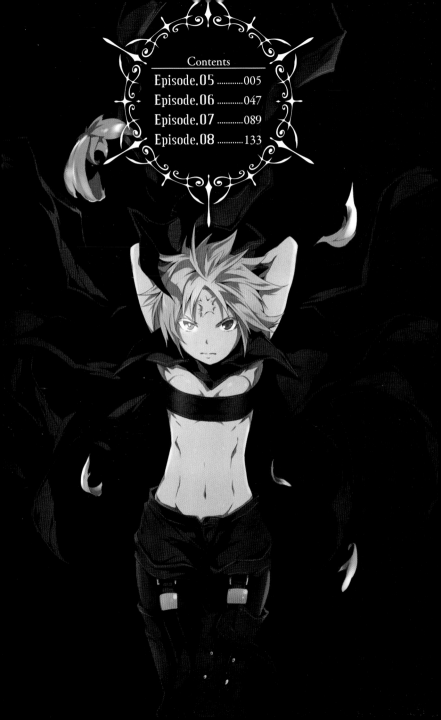

Contents

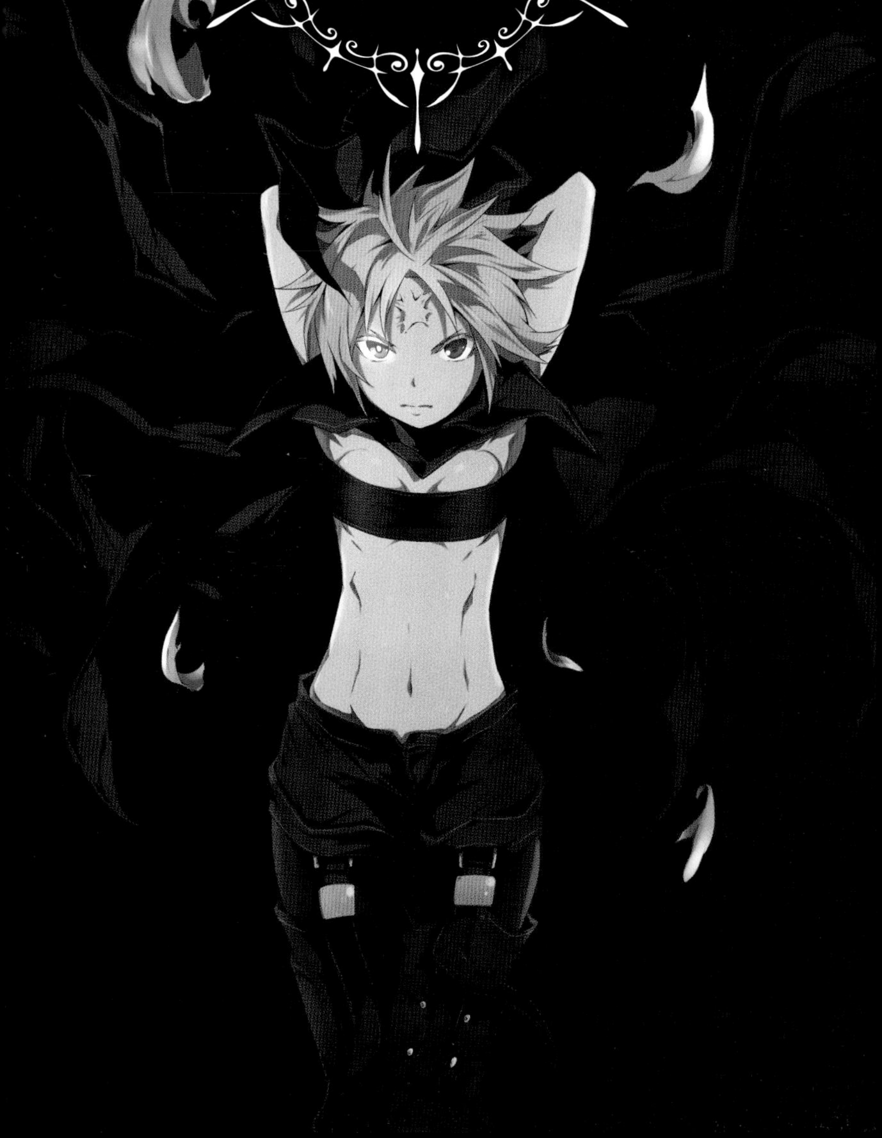

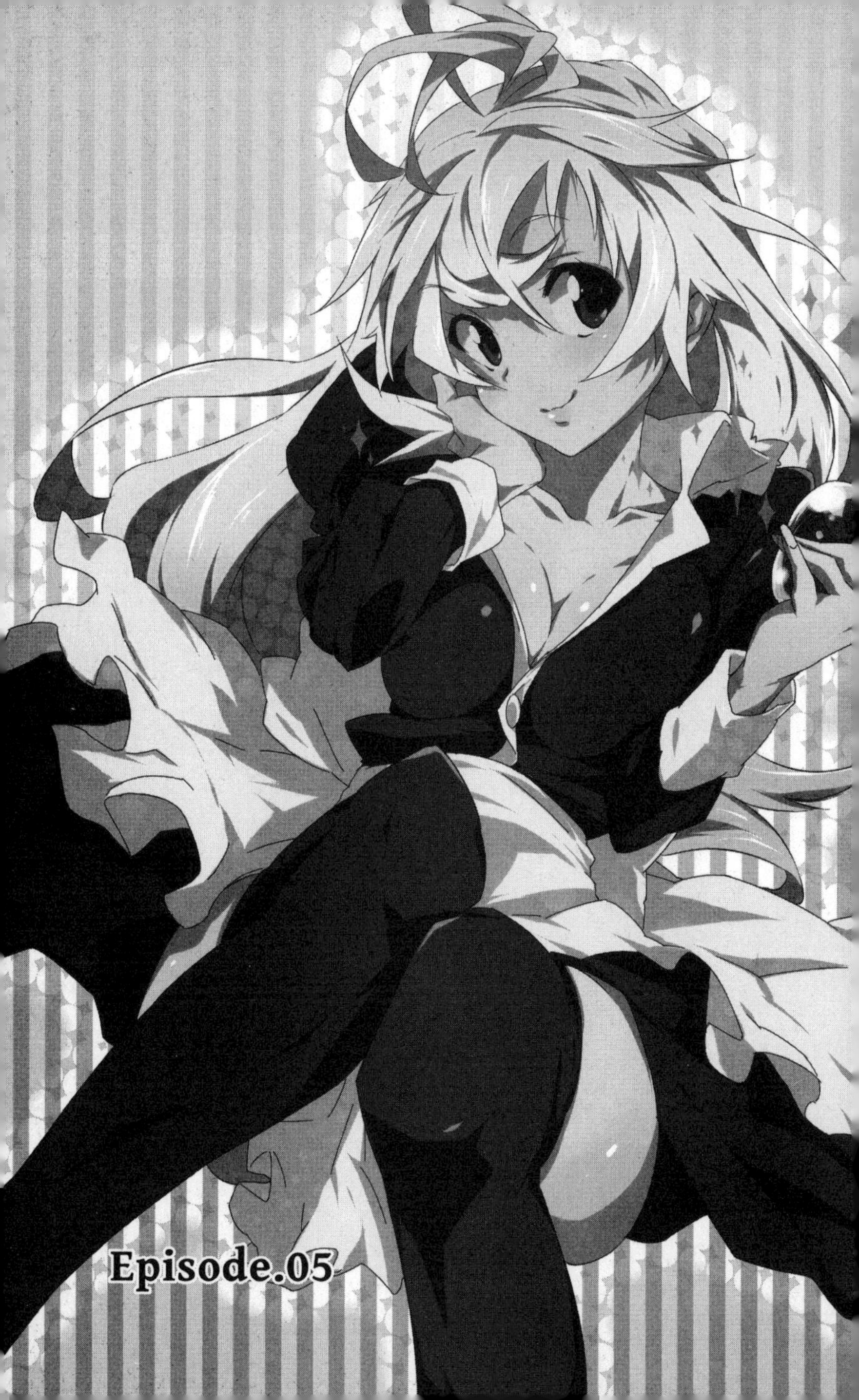
Episode.05

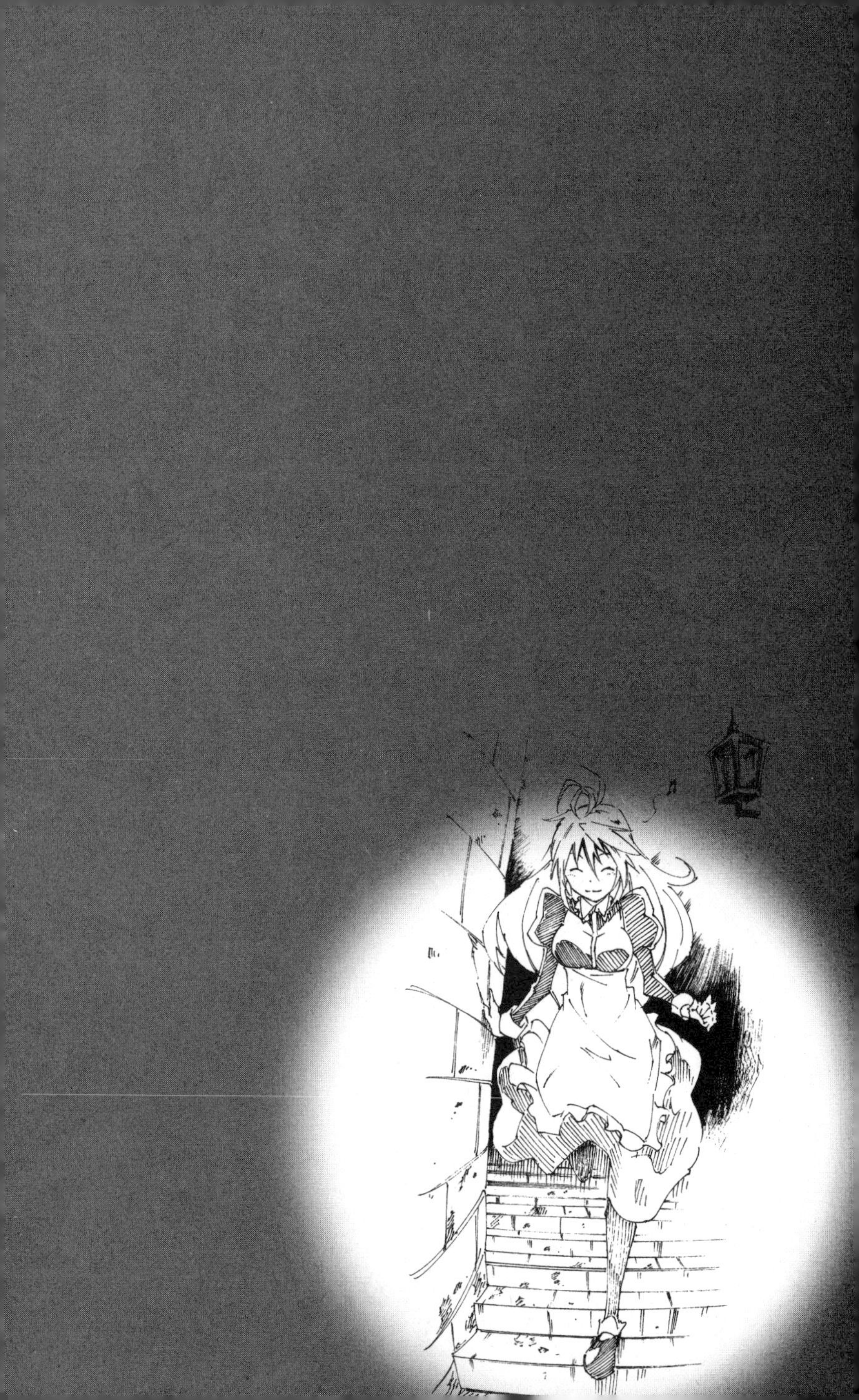

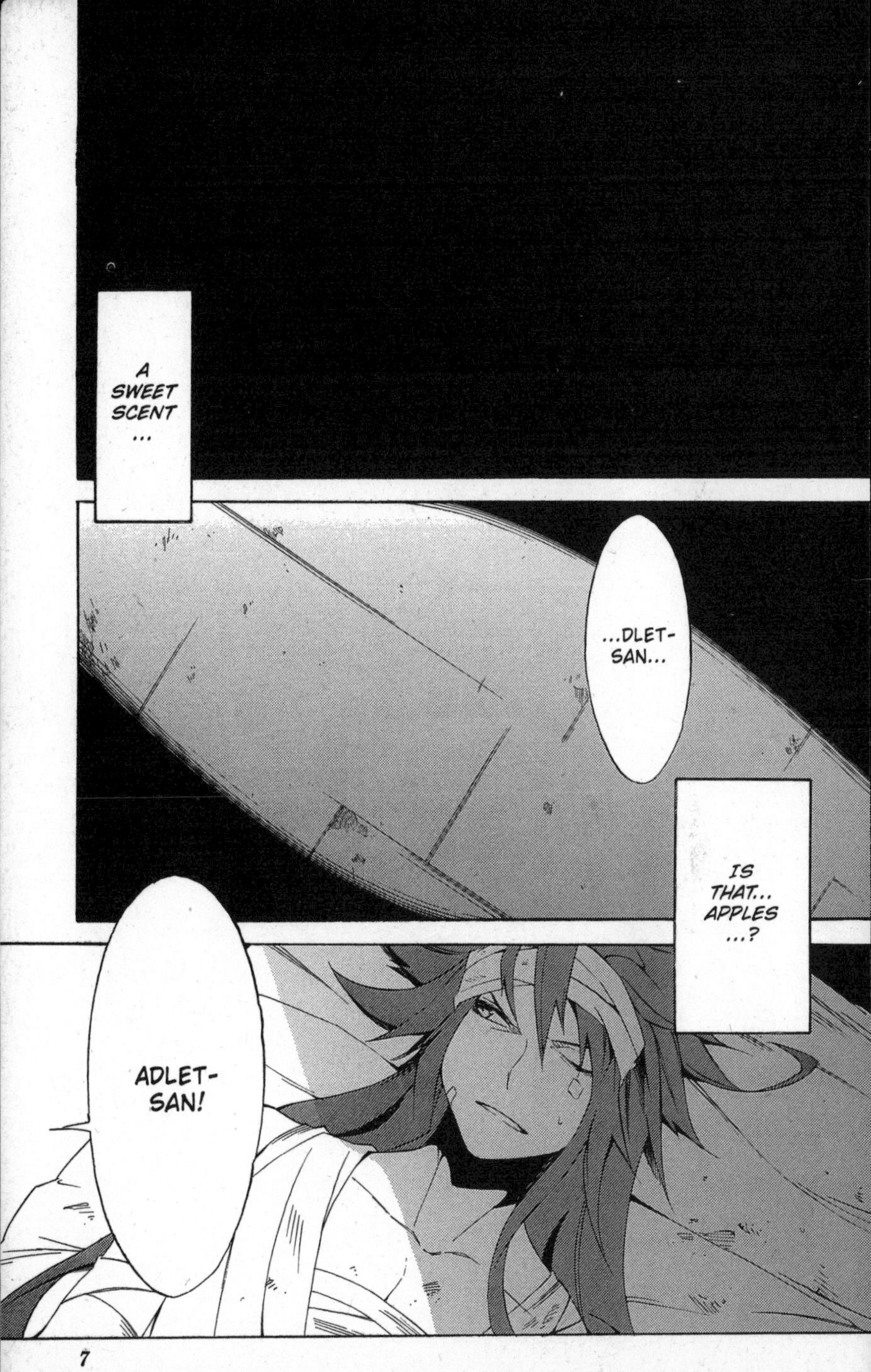
A SWEET SCENT...
...DLET-SAN...
IS THAT... APPLES...?
ADLET-SAN!

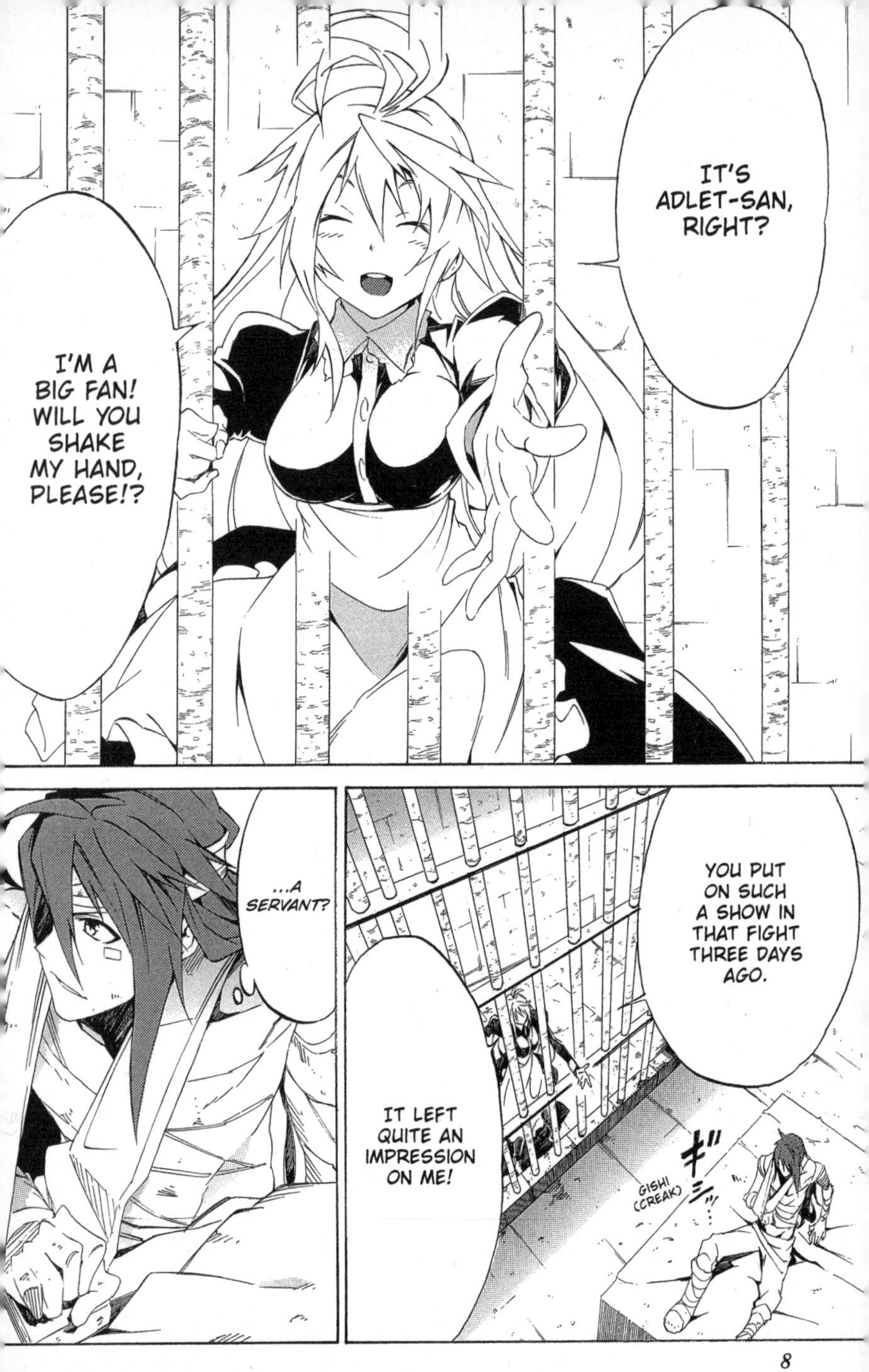
IT'S ADLET-SAN, RIGHT?
I'M A BIG FAN! WILL YOU SHAKE MY HAND, PLEASE!?
YOU PUT ON SUCH A SHOW IN THAT FIGHT THREE DAYS AGO.
IT LEFT QUITE AN IMPRESSION ON ME!
GISHI (CREAK)
...A SERVANT?

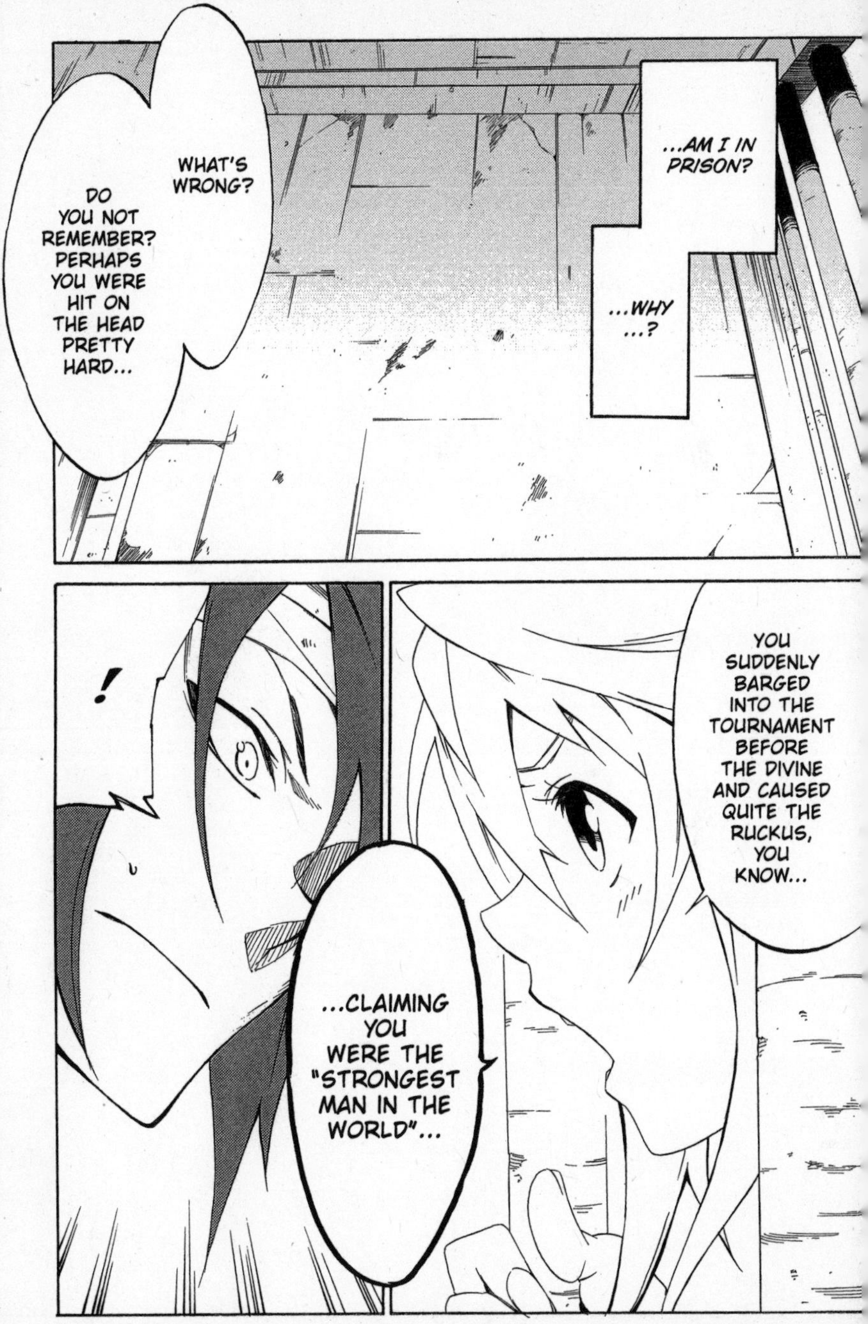
...AM I IN PRISON?
...WHY ...?
WHAT'S WRONG?
DO YOU NOT REMEMBER? PERHAPS YOU WERE HIT ON THE HEAD PRETTY HARD...
YOU SUDDENLY BARGED INTO THE TOURNAMENT BEFORE THE DIVINE AND CAUSED QUITE THE RUCKUS, YOU KNOW...
...CLAIMING YOU WERE THE "STRONGEST MAN IN THE WORLD"...
!

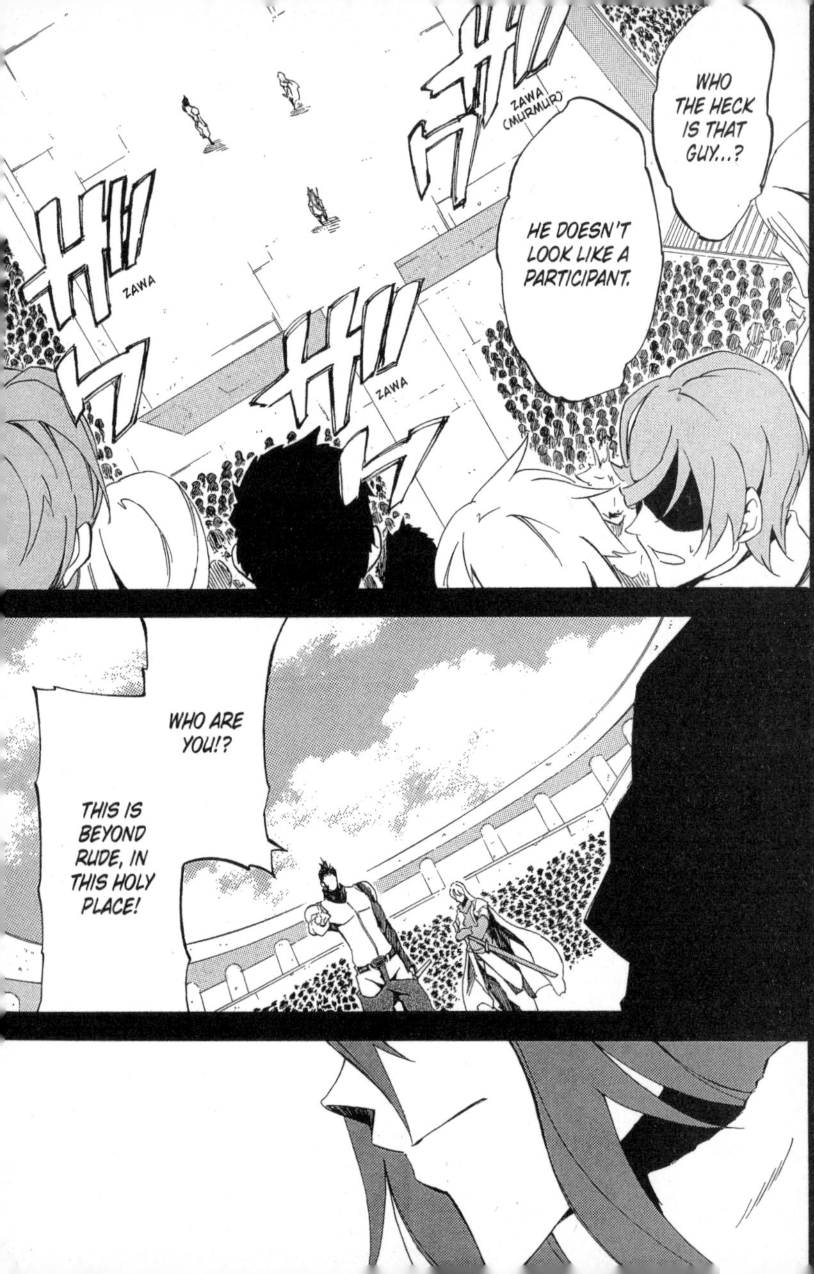
WHO THE HECK IS THAT GUY...?
HE DOESN'T LOOK LIKE A PARTICIPANT.
ZAWA (MURMUR)
ZAWA
ZAWA
WHO ARE YOU!?
THIS IS BEYOND RUDE, IN THIS HOLY PLACE!

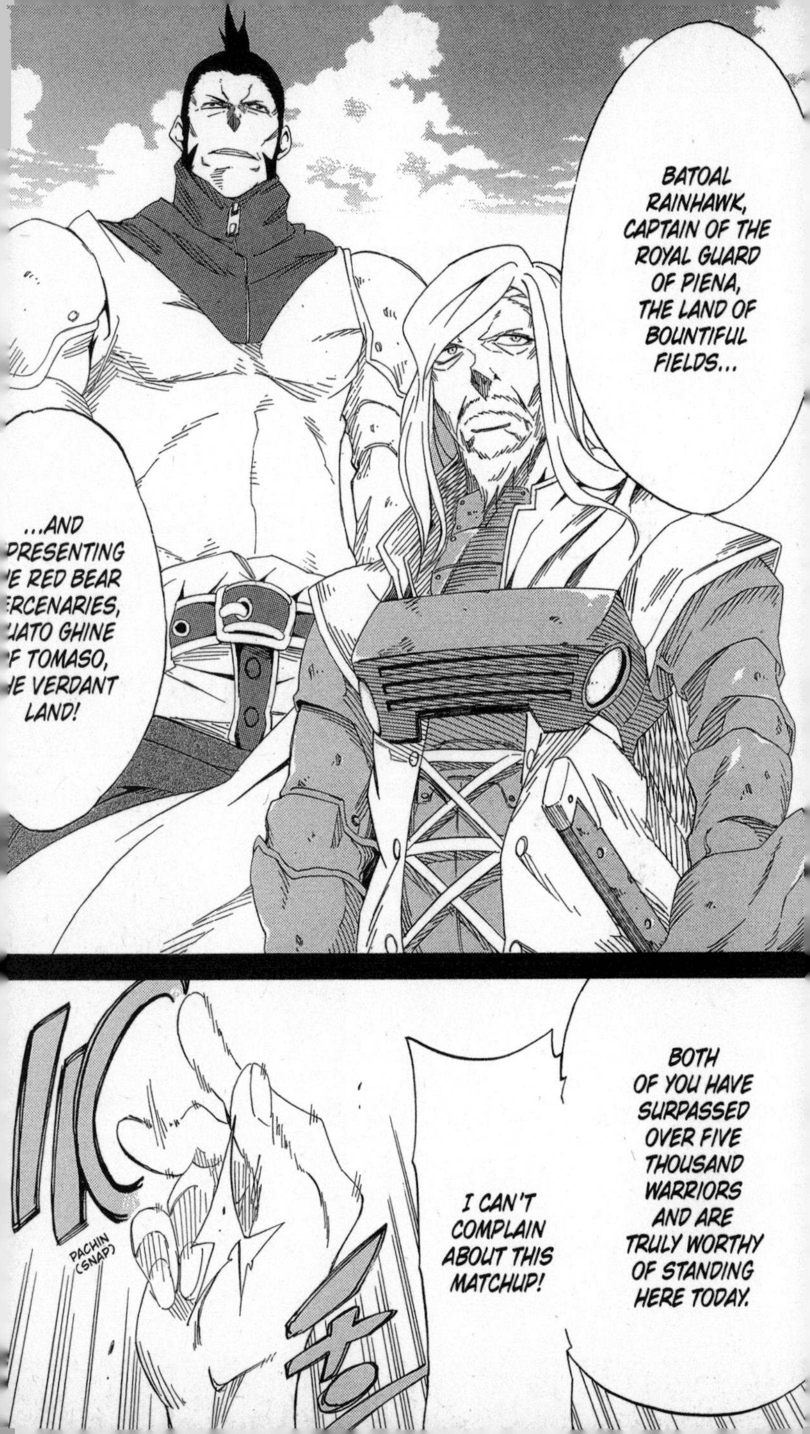
BATOAL RAINHAWK, CAPTAIN OF THE ROYAL GUARD OF PIENA, THE LAND OF BOUNTIFUL FIELDS...
...AND PRESENTING E RED BEAR ERCENARIES, HATO GHINE F TOMASO, HE VERDANT LAND!
BOTH OF YOU HAVE SURPASSED OVER FIVE THOUSAND WARRIORS AND ARE TRULY WORTHY OF STANDING HERE TODAY.
I CAN'T COMPLAIN ABOUT THIS MATCHUP!
PACHIN (SNAP)

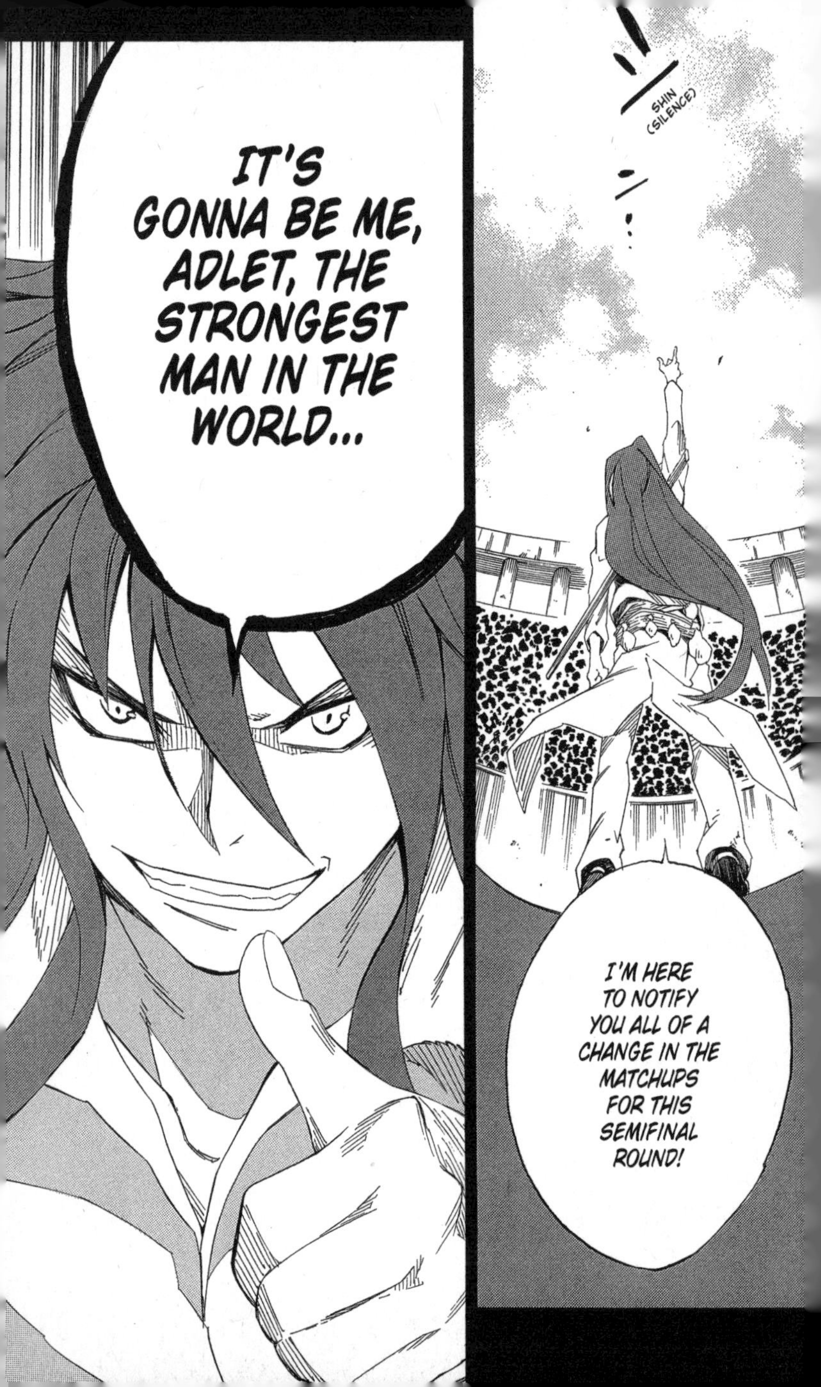
SHIN (SILENCE)
I'M HERE TO NOTIFY YOU ALL OF A CHANGE IN THE MATCHUPS FOR THIS SEMIFINAL ROUND!
IT'S GONNA BE ME, ADLET, THE STRONGEST MAN IN THE WORLD...

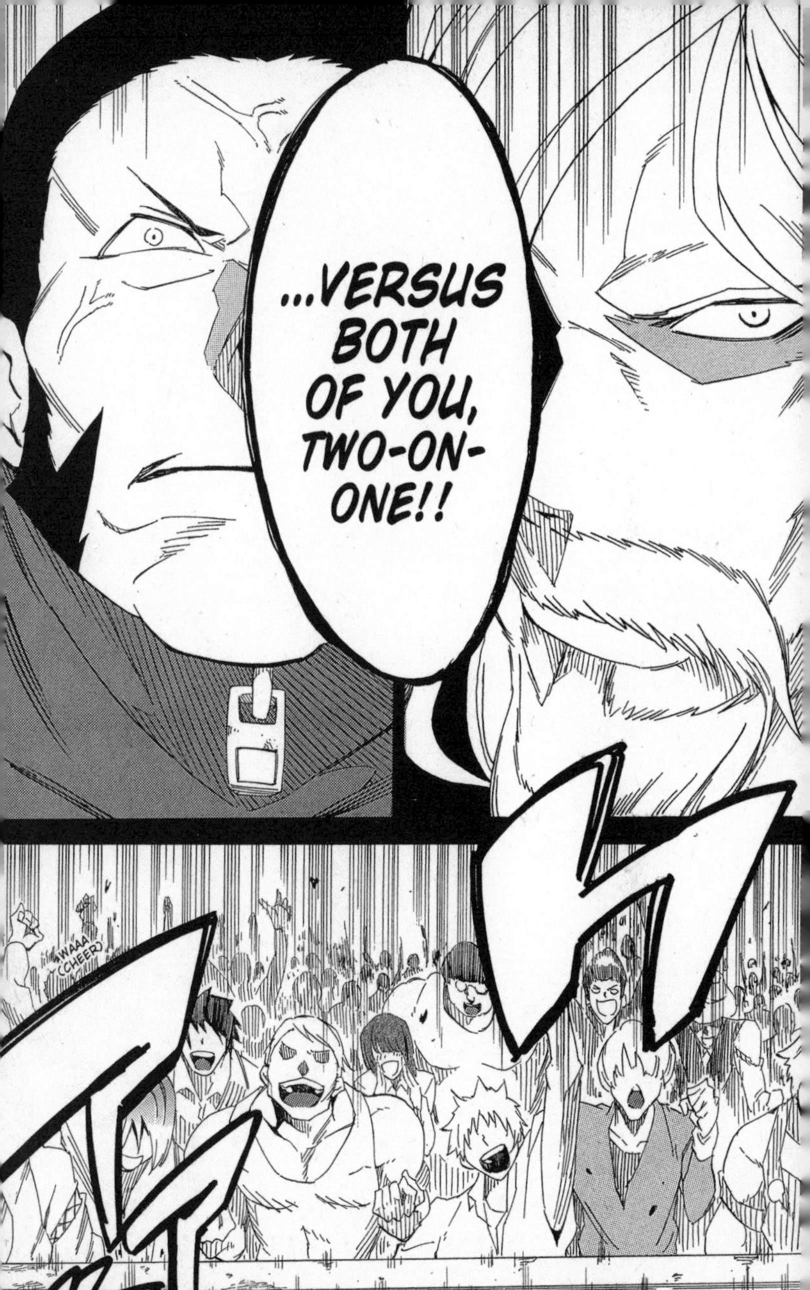
...VERSUS BOTH OF YOU, TWO-ON-ONE!!
WAAA (CHEER)

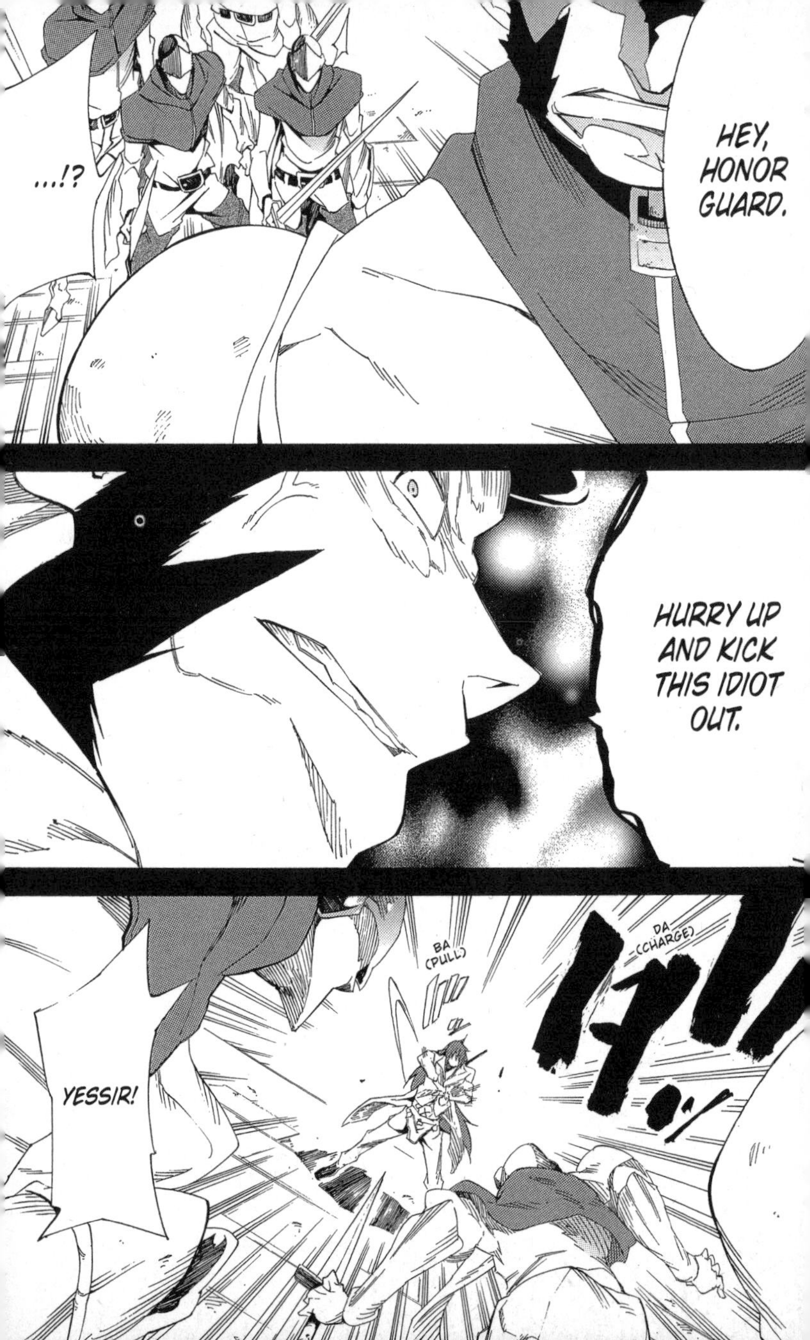
HEY, HONOR GUARD.
...!?
HURRY UP AND KICK THIS IDIOT OUT.
DA (CHARGE)
BA (PULL)
YESSIR!

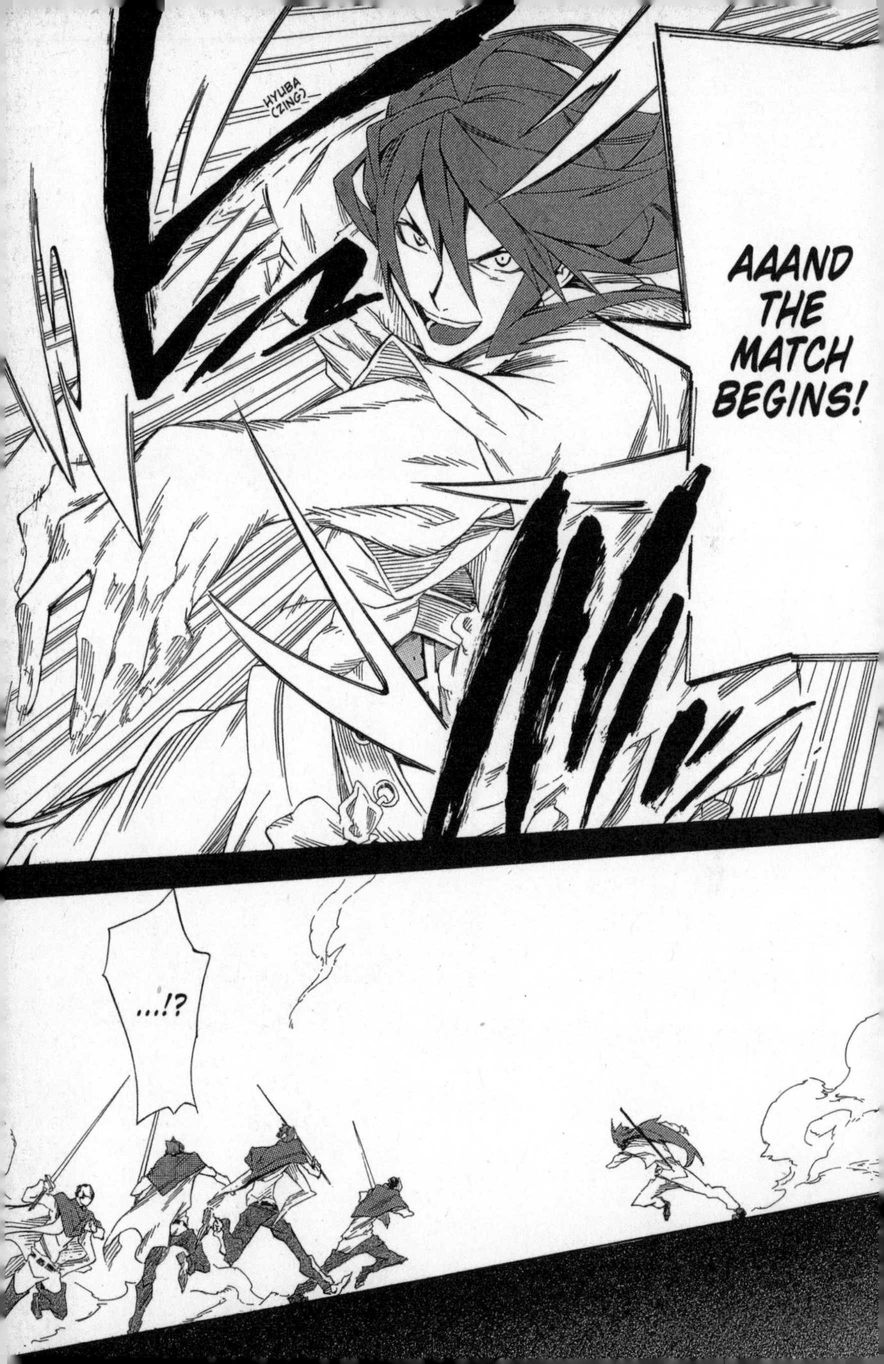
HYUBA
(ZING)
AAAND THE MATCH BEGINS!
...!?

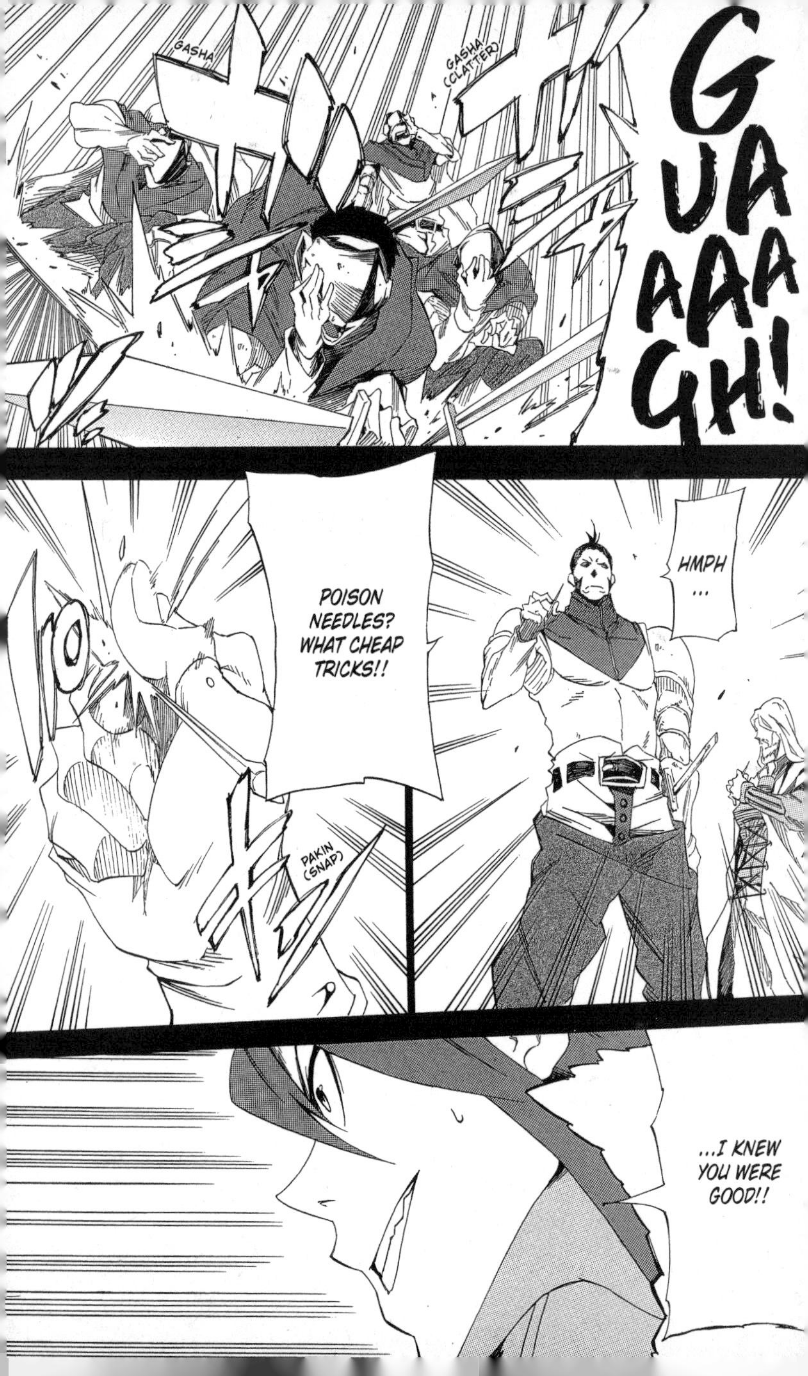
GUAAAAAGH!
GASHA (CLATTER)
GASHA
HMPH...
POISON NEEDLES? WHAT CHEAP TRICKS!!
PAKIN (SNAP)
...I KNEW YOU WERE GOOD!!

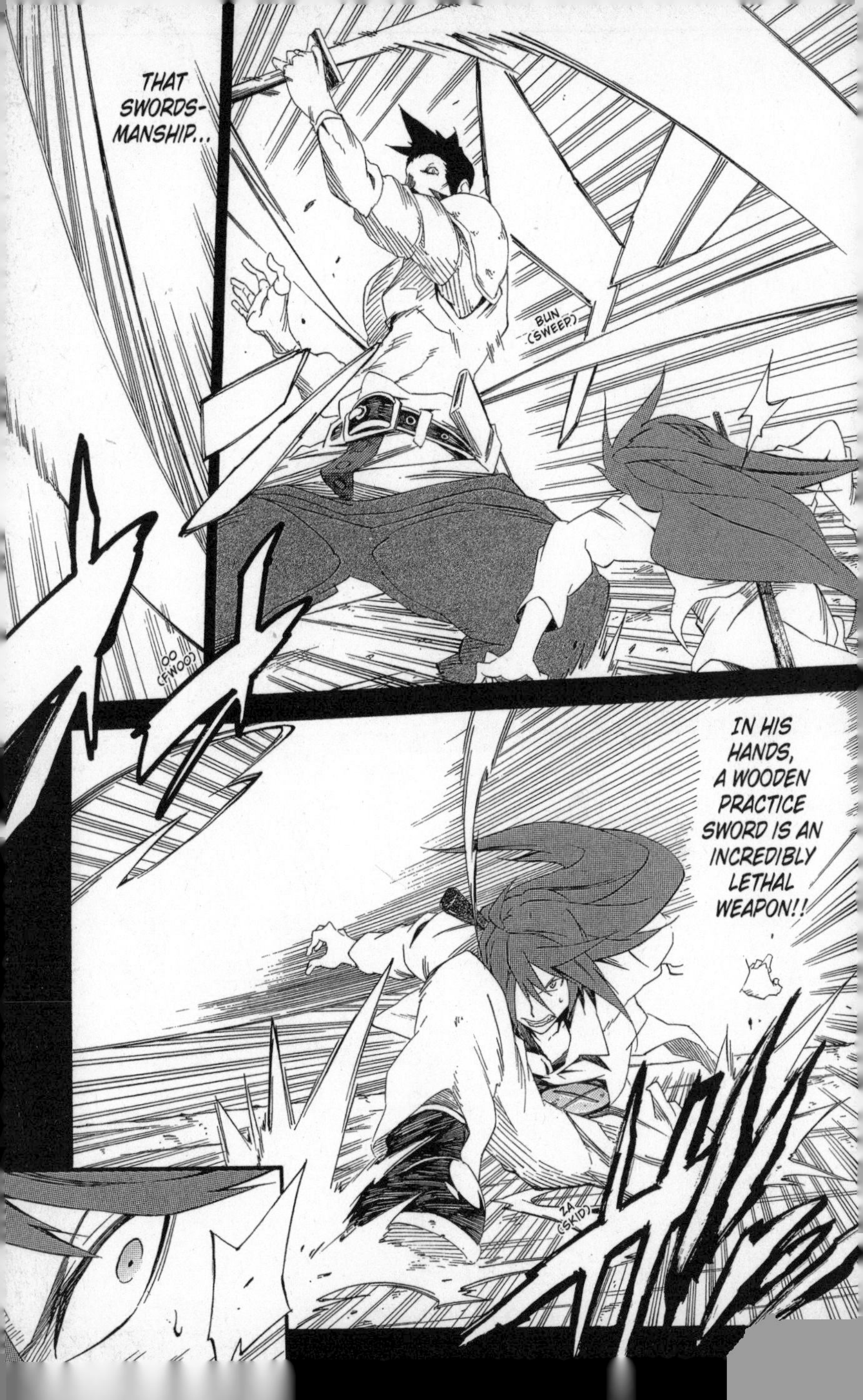
THAT SWORDS-MANSHIP...
BUN (SWEEP)
OO (FWOO)
IN HIS HANDS, A WOODEN PRACTICE SWORD IS AN INCREDIBLY LETHAL WEAPON!!
ZA (SKID)

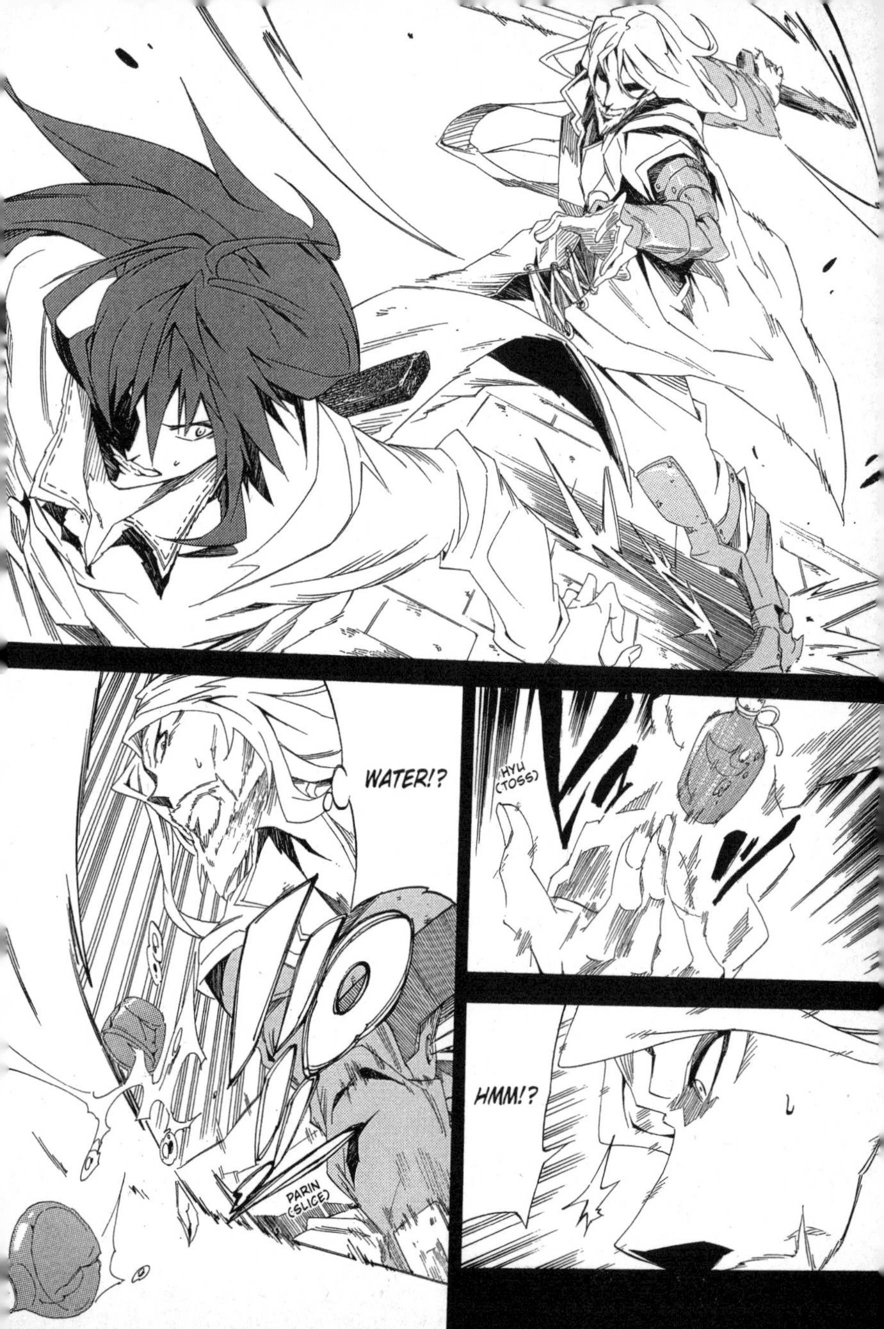
HYU (TOSS)
HMM!?
WATER!?
PARIN (SLICE)

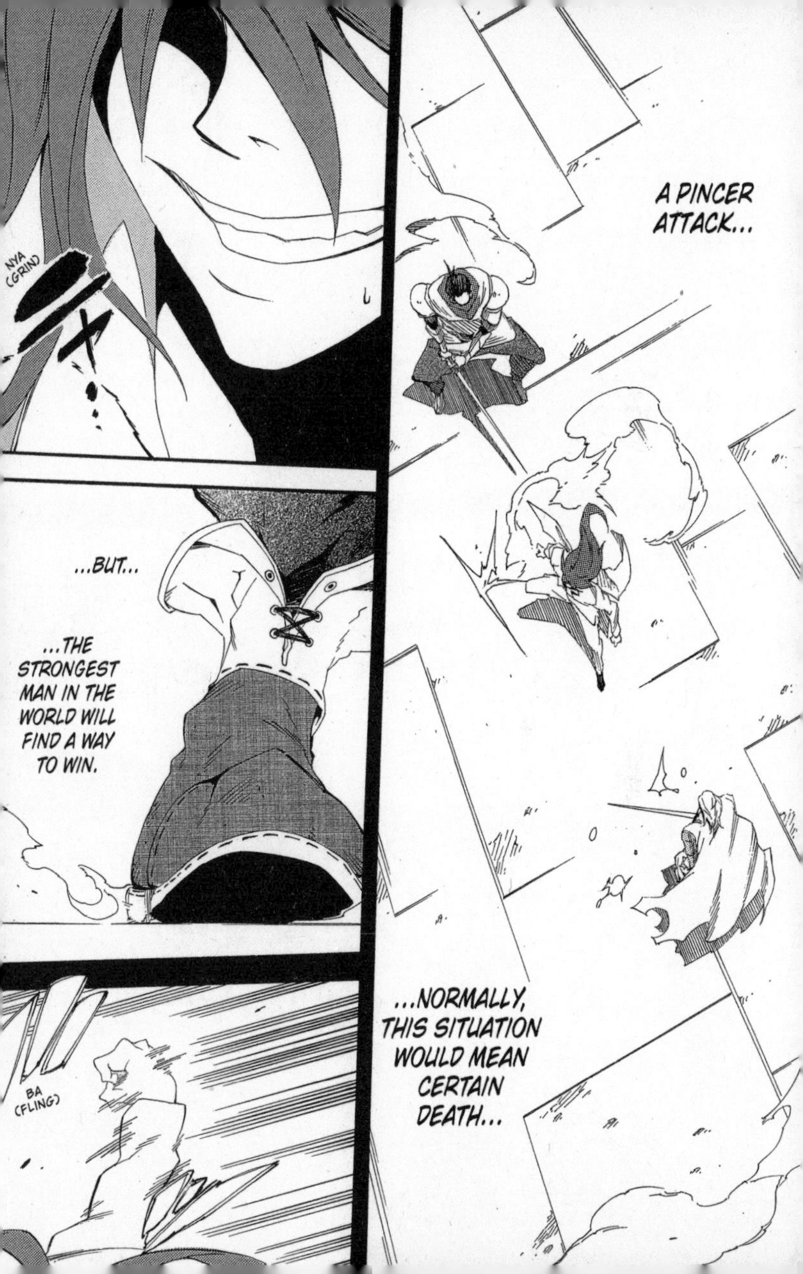
A PINCER ATTACK...
...NORMALLY, THIS SITUATION WOULD MEAN CERTAIN DEATH...
NYA (GRIN)
...BUT...
...THE STRONGEST MAN IN THE WORLD WILL FIND A WAY TO WIN.
BA (FLING)

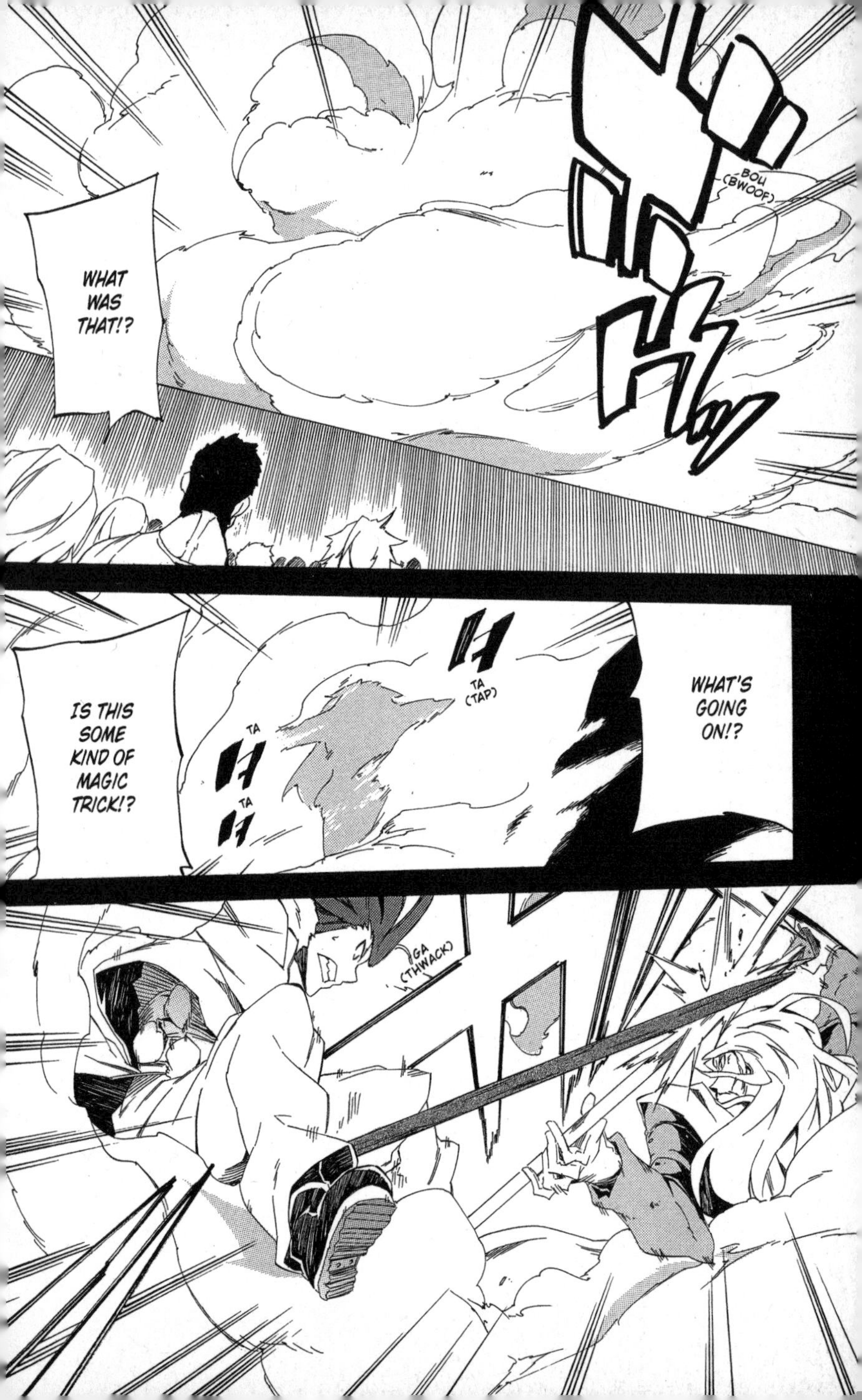
BOU (BWOOF)
WHAT WAS THAT!?
WHAT'S GOING ON!?
TA (TAP)
TA
TA
IS THIS SOME KIND OF MAGIC TRICK!?
GA (THWACK)

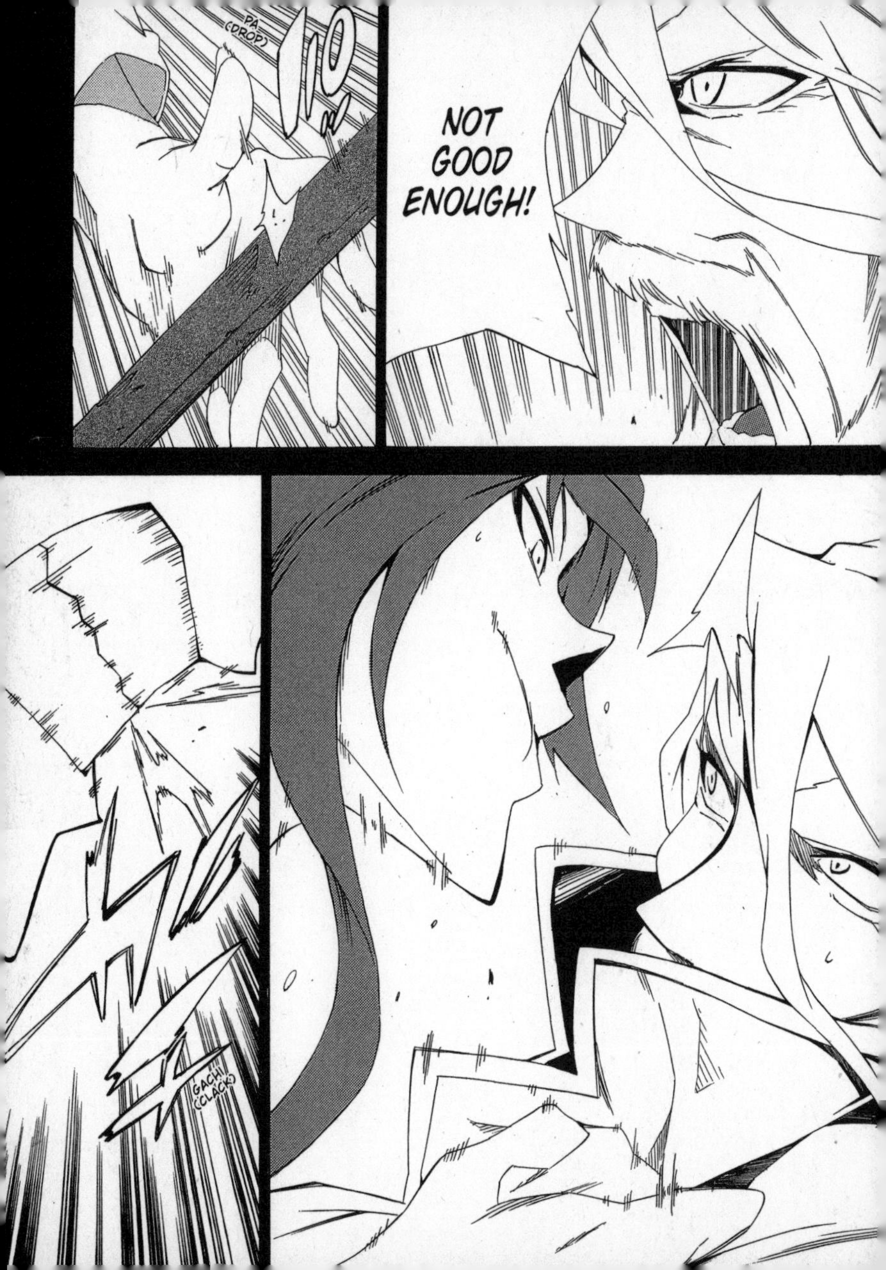
NOT GOOD ENOUGH!
PA (DROP)
GACHI (CLACK)

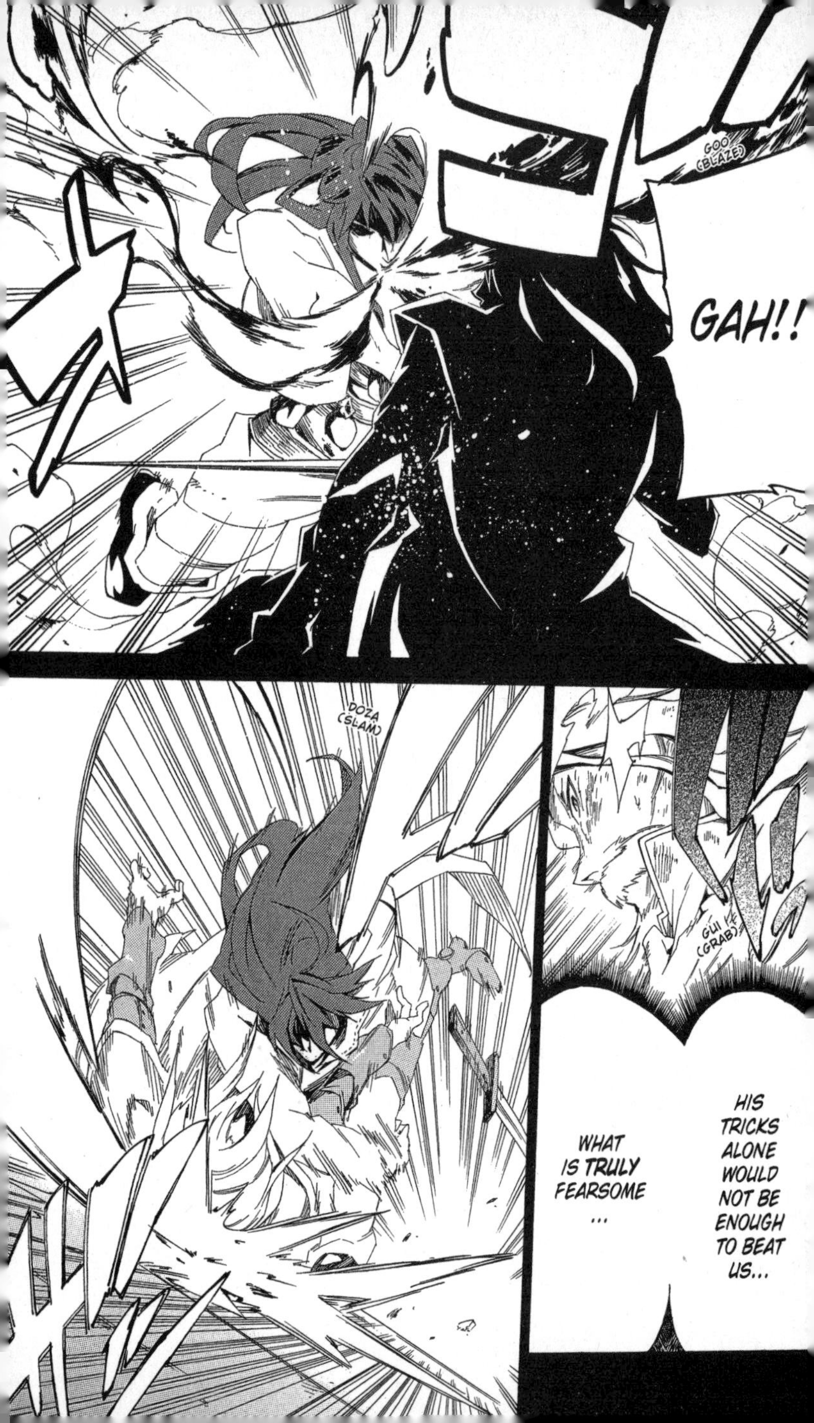
GOO (BLAZE)
GAH!!
GUI (GRAB)
HIS TRICKS ALONE WOULD NOT BE ENOUGH TO BEAT US...
WHAT IS TRULY FEARSOME ...
DOZA (SLAM)

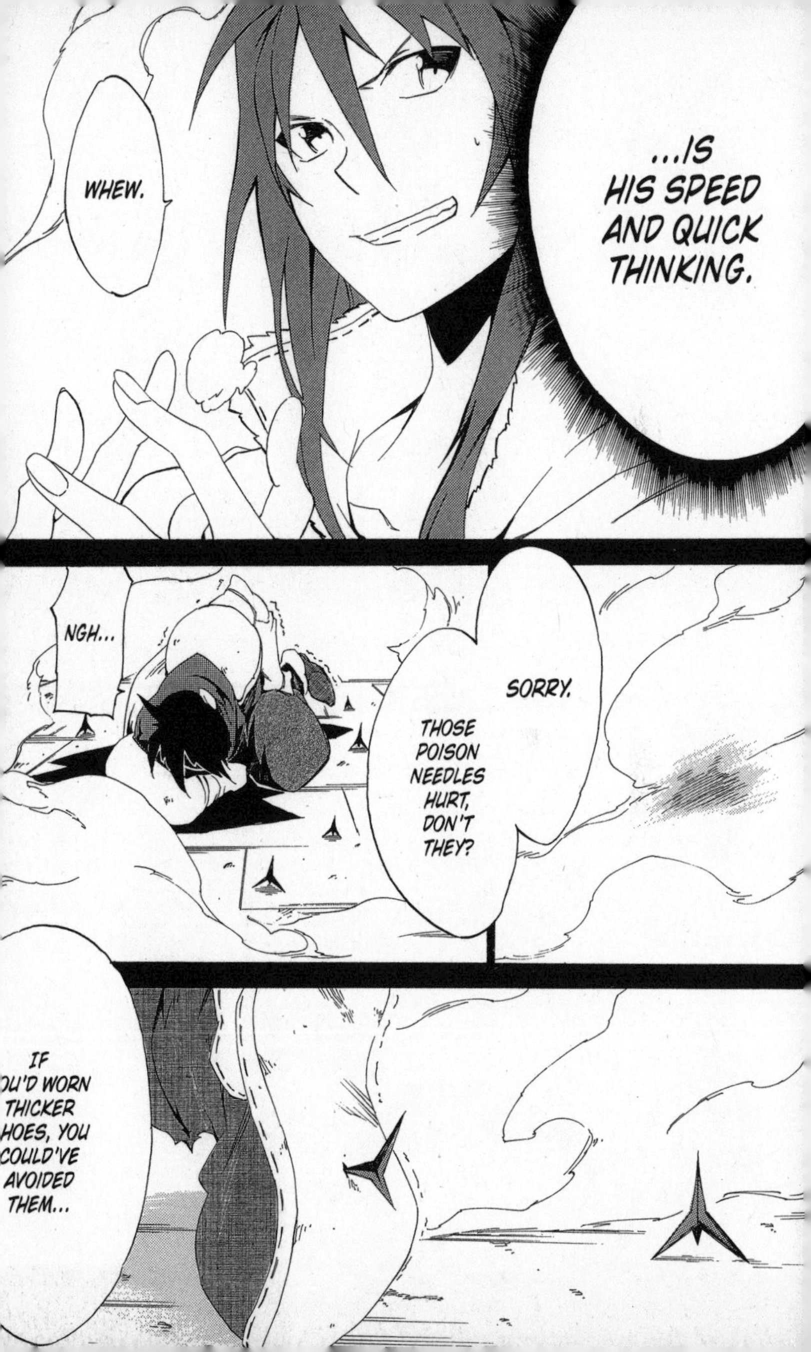
...IS HIS SPEED AND QUICK THINKING.
WHEW.
SORRY.
THOSE POISON NEEDLES HURT, DON'T THEY?
NGH...
IF OU'D WORN THICKER HOES, YOU COULD'VE AVOIDED THEM...

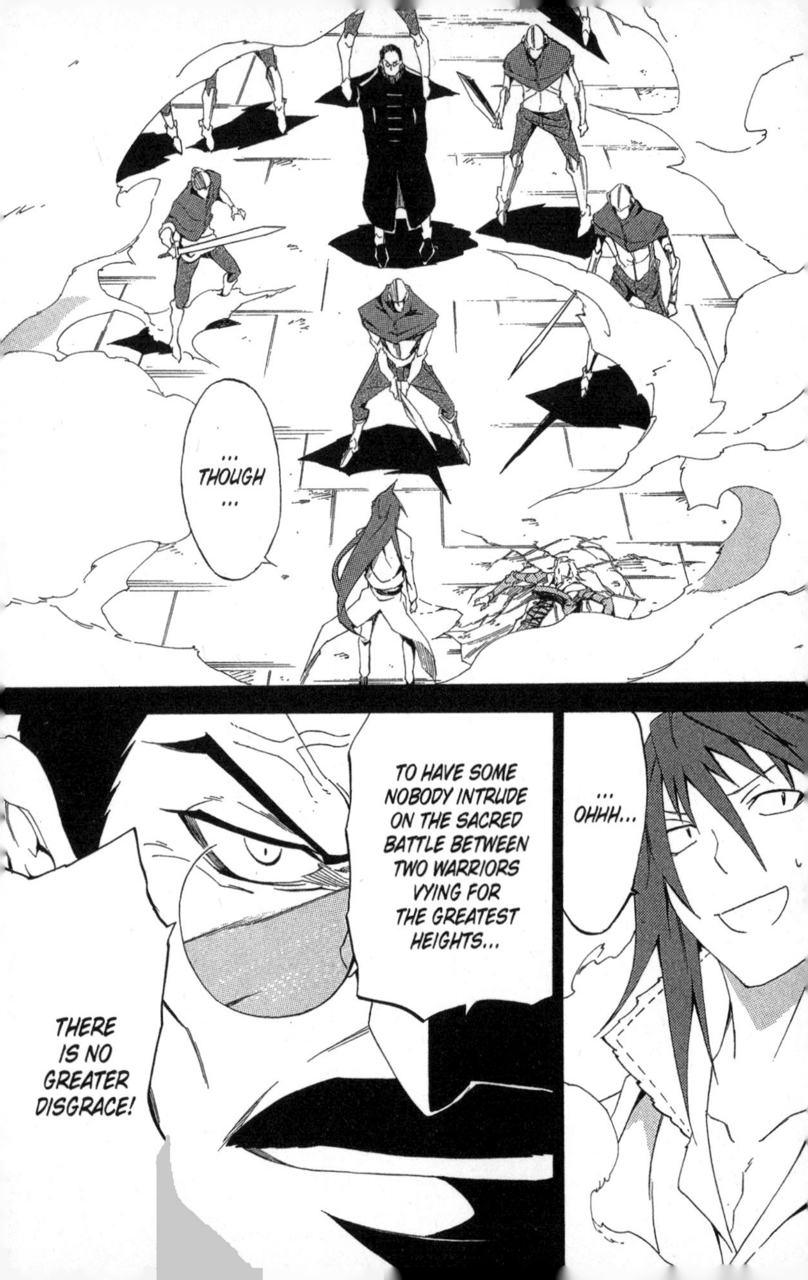
... THOUGH ...
... OHHH...
TO HAVE SOME NOBODY INTRUDE ON THE SACRED BATTLE BETWEEN TWO WARRIORS VYING FOR THE GREATEST HEIGHTS...
THERE IS NO GREATER DISGRACE!

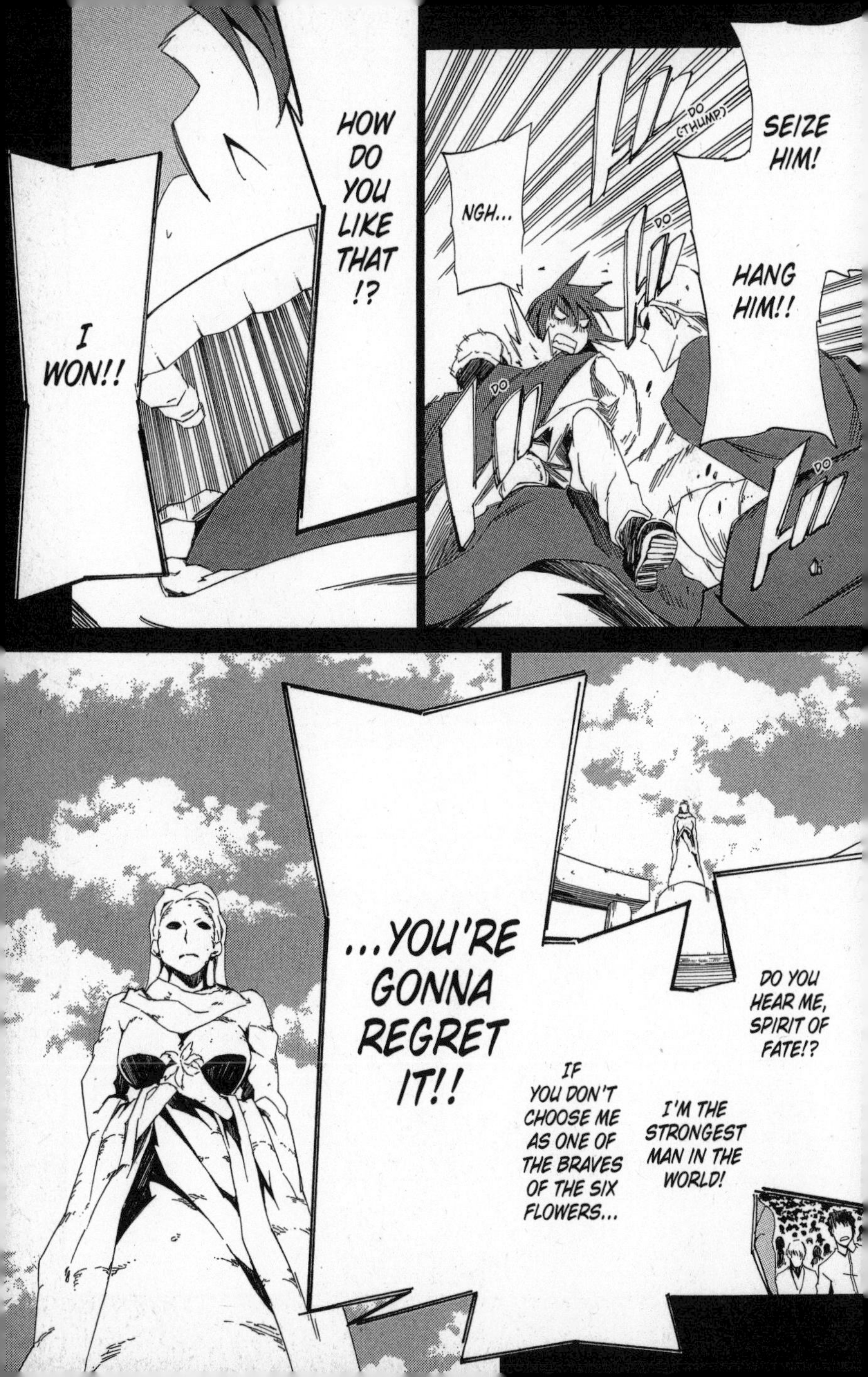

SEIZE HIM!
HANG HIM!!
DO (THUMP)
DO
NGH...
DO
DO
HOW DO YOU LIKE THAT!?
I WON!!
DO YOU HEAR ME, SPIRIT OF FATE!?
I'M THE STRONGEST MAN IN THE WORLD!
IF YOU DON'T CHOOSE ME AS ONE OF THE BRAVES OF THE SIX FLOWERS...
...YOU'RE GONNA REGRET IT!!

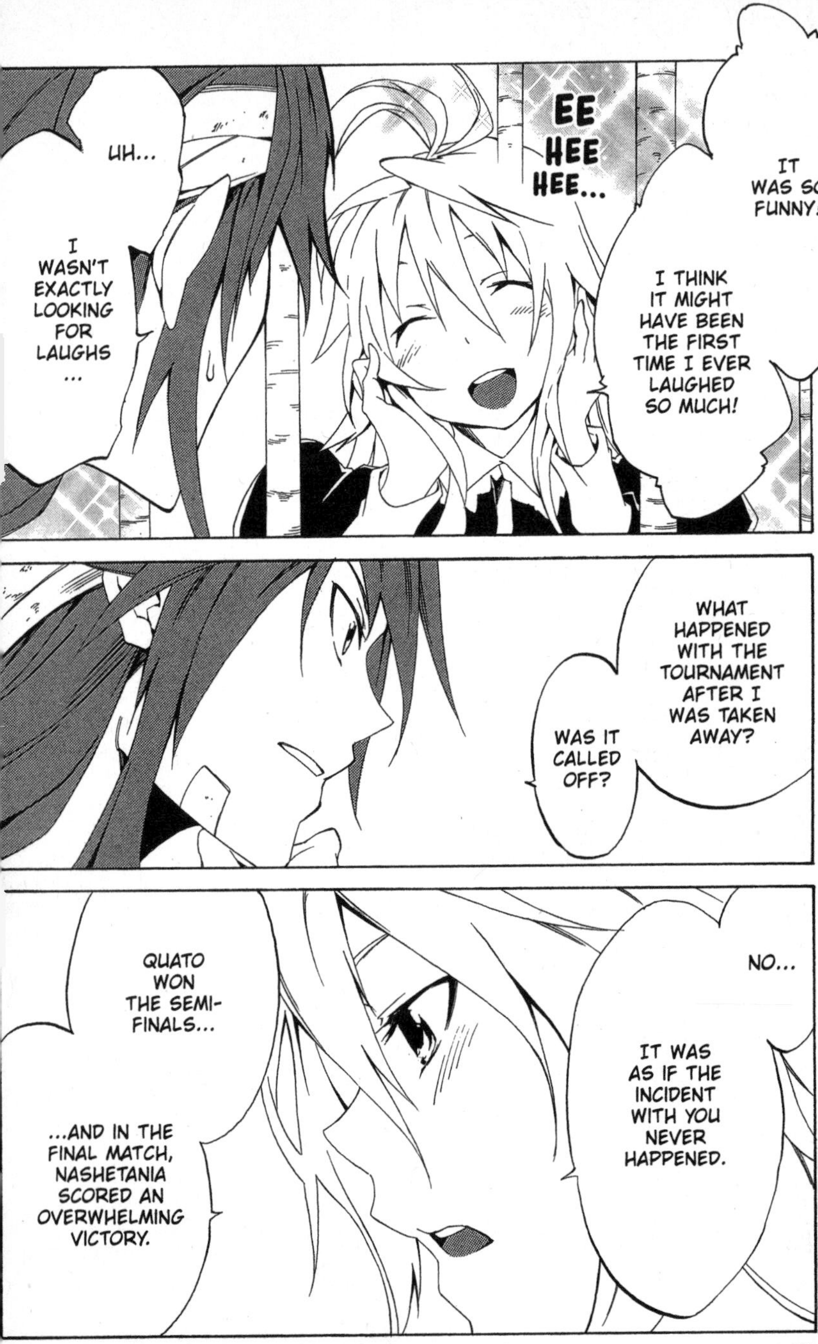
IT WAS SO FUNNY!
EE HEE HEE...
I THINK IT MIGHT HAVE BEEN THE FIRST TIME I EVER LAUGHED SO MUCH!
UH...
I WASN'T EXACTLY LOOKING FOR LAUGHS ...
WHAT HAPPENED WITH THE TOURNAMENT AFTER I WAS TAKEN AWAY?
WAS IT CALLED OFF?
NO...
IT WAS AS IF THE INCIDENT WITH YOU NEVER HAPPENED.
QUATO WON THE SEMI-FINALS...
...AND IN THE FINAL MATCH, NASHETANIA SCORED AN OVERWHELMING VICTORY.

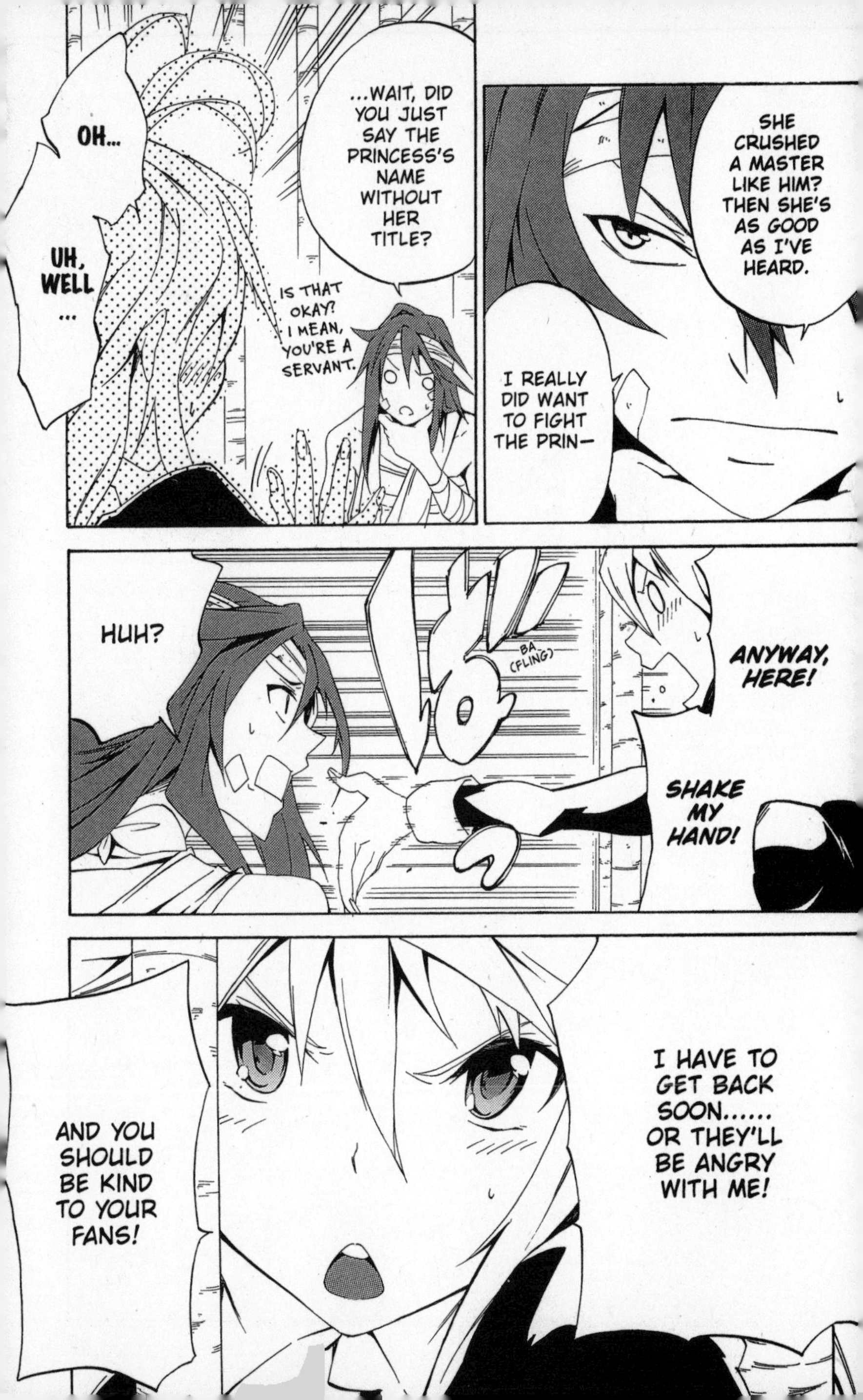
SHE CRUSHED A MASTER LIKE HIM? THEN SHE'S AS GOOD AS I'VE HEARD.
I REALLY DID WANT TO FIGHT THE PRIN—
...WAIT, DID YOU JUST SAY THE PRINCESS'S NAME WITHOUT HER TITLE?
IS THAT OKAY? I MEAN, YOU'RE A SERVANT.
OH...
UH, WELL ...
ANYWAY, HERE!
SHAKE MY HAND!
BA (FLING)
HUH?
I HAVE TO GET BACK SOON...... OR THEY'LL BE ANGRY WITH ME!
AND YOU SHOULD BE KIND TO YOUR FANS!

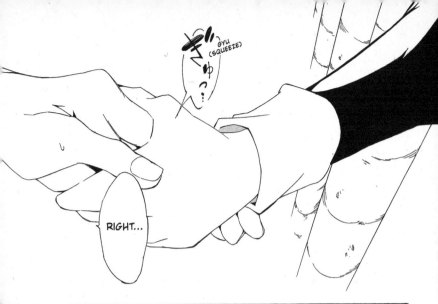

GYU (SQUEEZE)

RIGHT...

...SO SOFT.

ADLET-SAN...

I CAN TELL YOUR HEART'S RACING.

GUI (TUG)

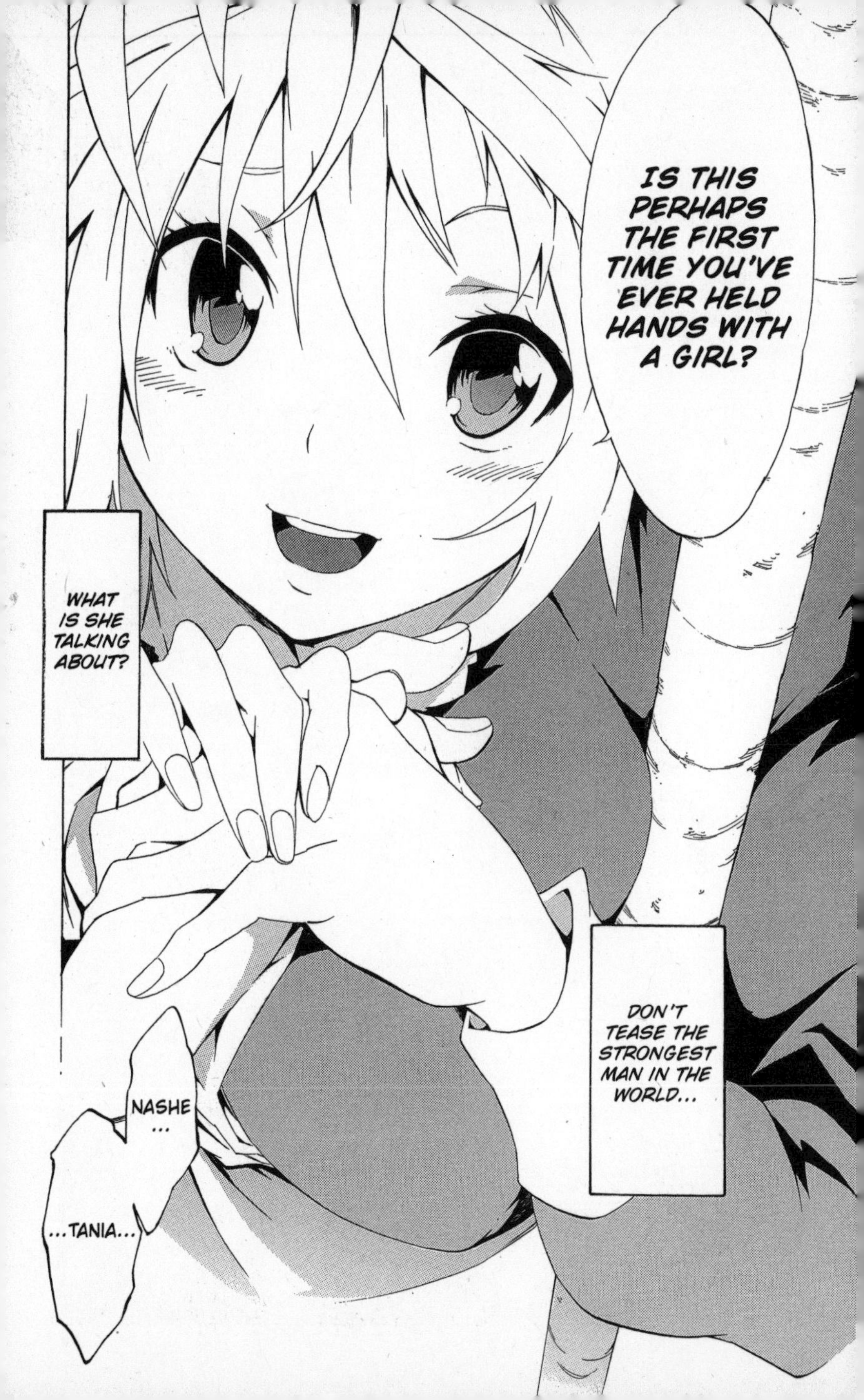
IS THIS PERHAPS THE FIRST TIME YOU'VE EVER HELD HANDS WITH A GIRL?
WHAT IS SHE TALKING ABOUT?
DON'T TEASE THE STRONGEST MAN IN THE WORLD...
NASHE...
...TANIA...

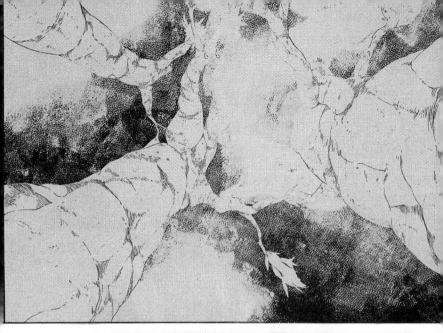

ZUKI
(THROB)

UGH...

DIDN'T I COLLAPSE FACE-DOWN...?

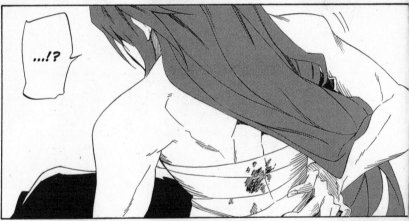

....!?

IT MISSED YOUR VITALS.

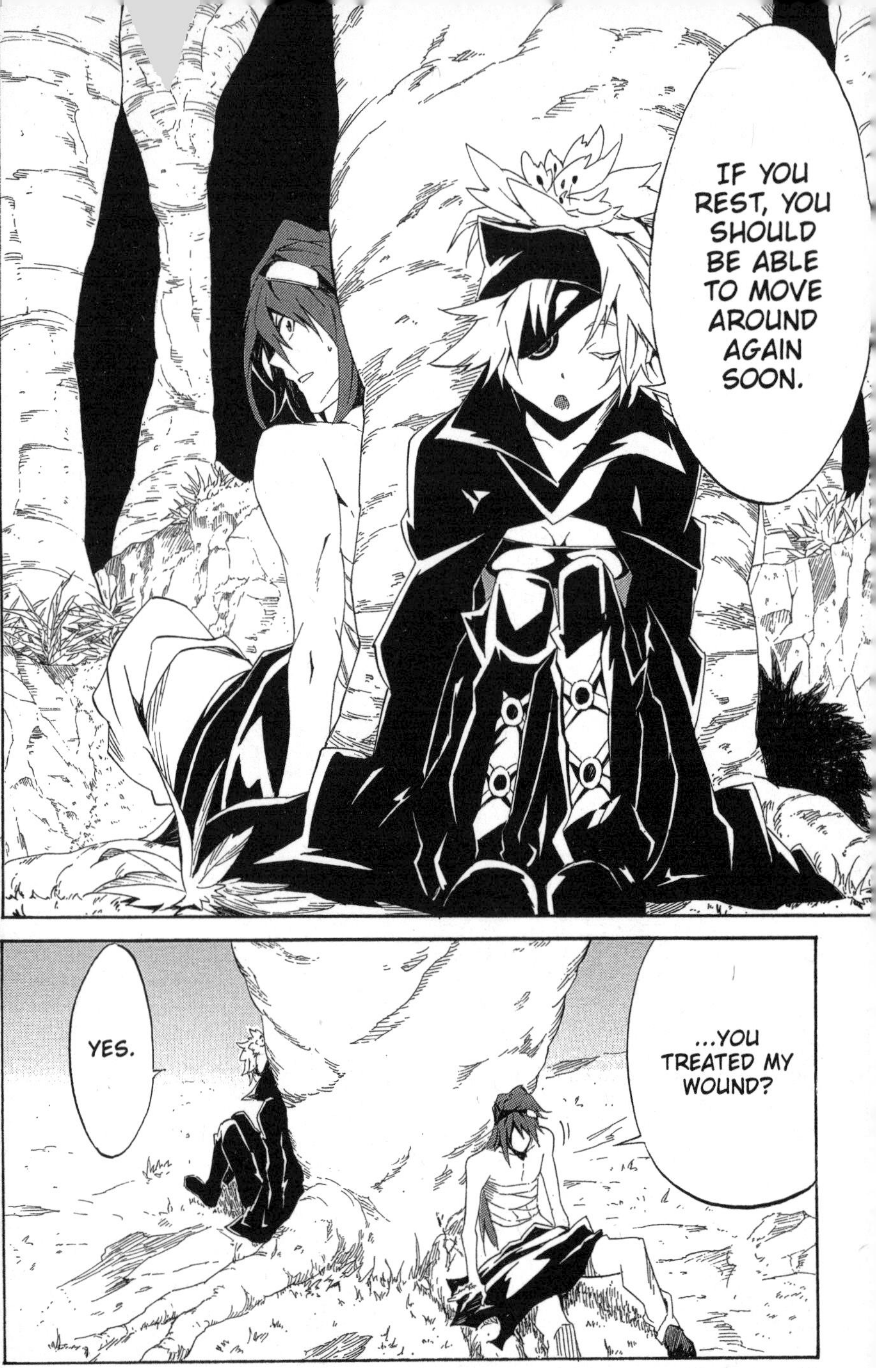
IF YOU REST, YOU SHOULD BE ABLE TO MOVE AROUND AGAIN SOON.
...YOU TREATED MY WOUND?
YES.

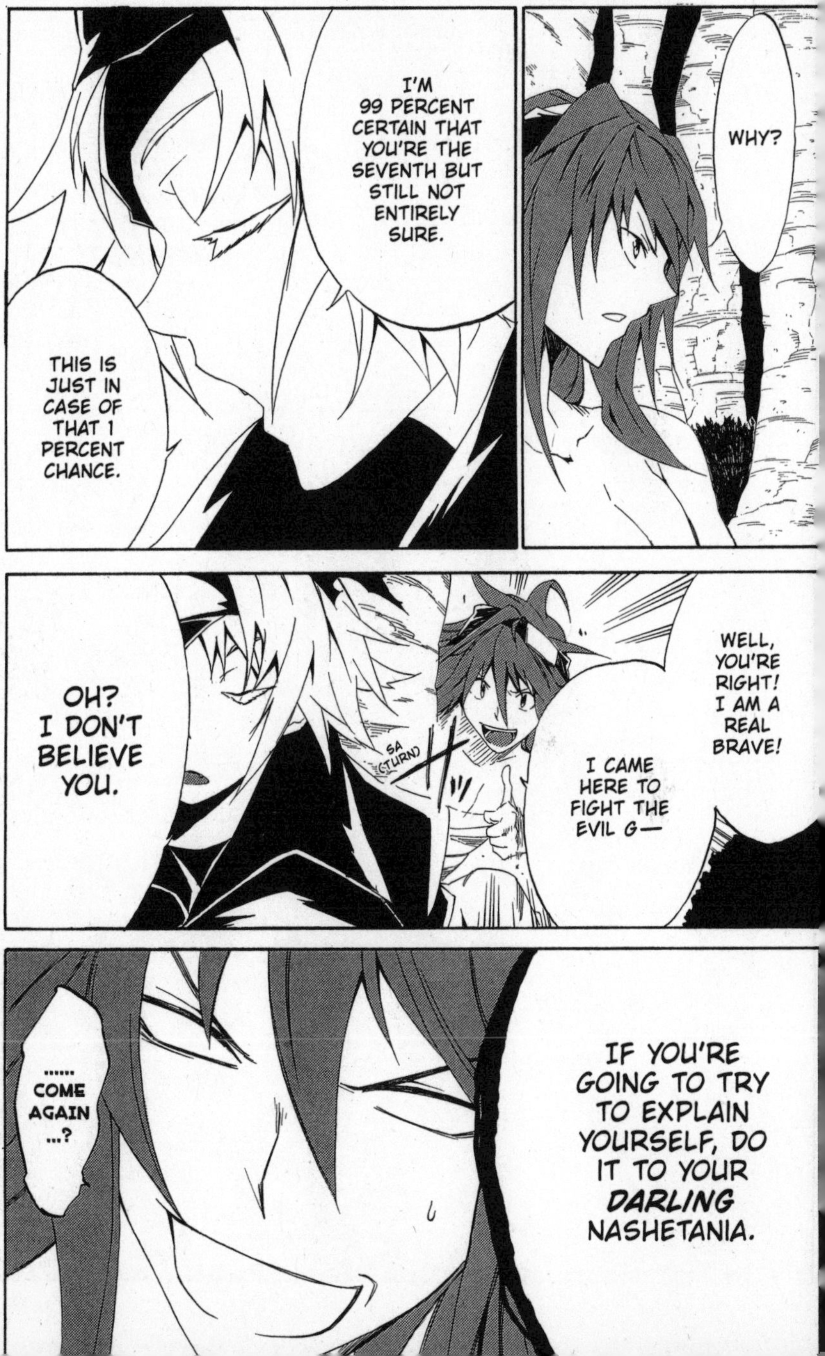
WHY?
I'M 99 PERCENT CERTAIN THAT YOU'RE THE SEVENTH BUT STILL NOT ENTIRELY SURE.
THIS IS JUST IN CASE OF THAT 1 PERCENT CHANCE.
WELL, YOU'RE RIGHT! I AM A REAL BRAVE!
I CAME HERE TO FIGHT THE EVIL G—
SA (TURN)
OH? I DON'T BELIEVE YOU.
IF YOU'RE GOING TO TRY TO EXPLAIN YOURSELF, DO IT TO YOUR DARLING NASHETANIA.
...... COME AGAIN ...?

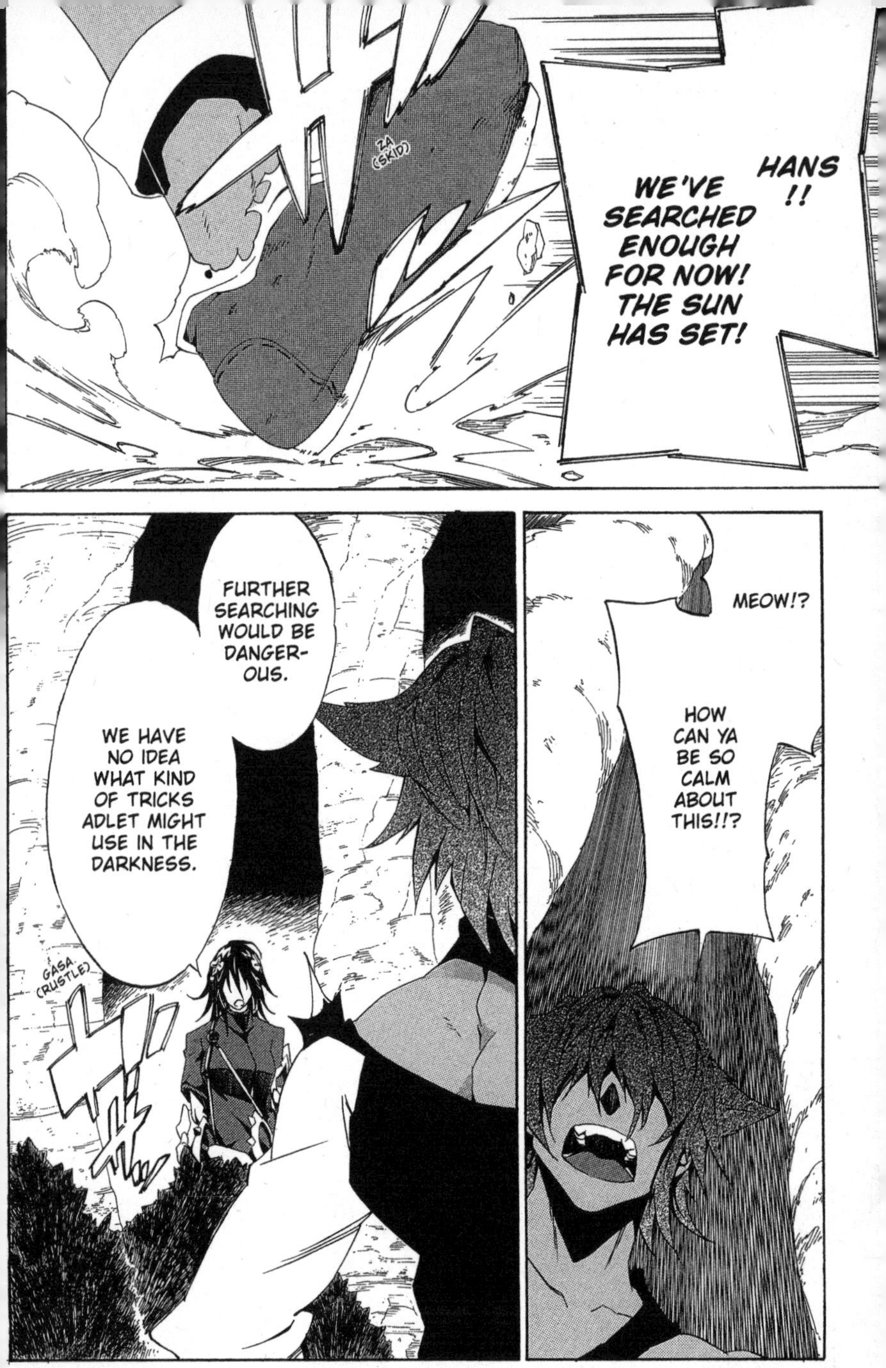
HANS!! WE'VE SEARCHED ENOUGH FOR NOW! THE SUN HAS SET!
ZA (SKID)
MEOW!?
HOW CAN YA BE SO CALM ABOUT THIS!!?
FURTHER SEARCHING WOULD BE DANGER-OUS.
WE HAVE NO IDEA WHAT KIND OF TRICKS ADLET MIGHT USE IN THE DARKNESS.
GASA (RUSTLE)

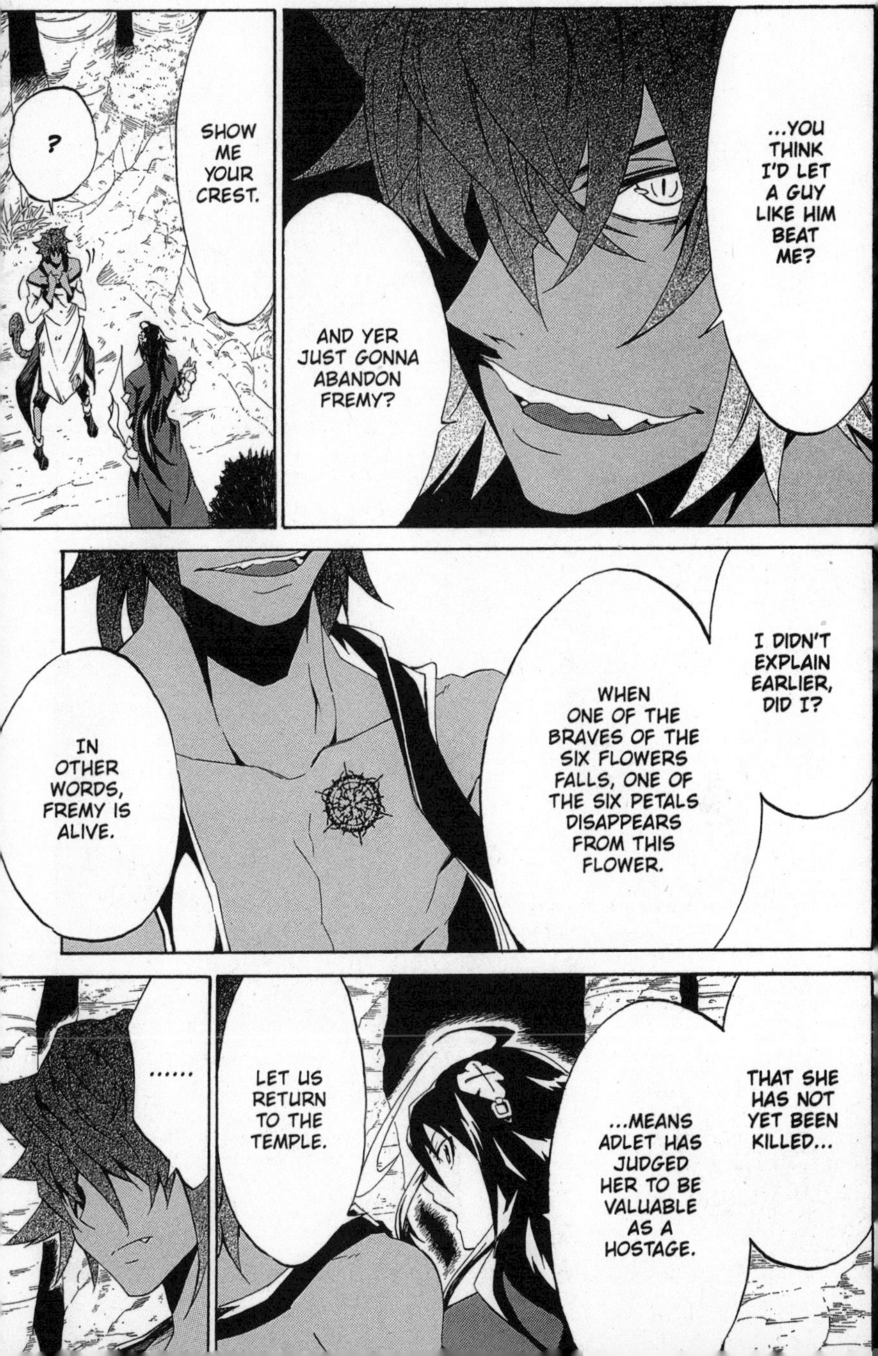
...YOU THINK I'D LET A GUY LIKE HIM BEAT ME?
AND YER JUST GONNA ABANDON FREMY?
SHOW ME YOUR CREST.
?
I DIDN'T EXPLAIN EARLIER, DID I?
WHEN ONE OF THE BRAVES OF THE SIX FLOWERS FALLS, ONE OF THE SIX PETALS DISAPPEARS FROM THIS FLOWER.
IN OTHER WORDS, FREMY IS ALIVE.
THAT SHE HAS NOT YET BEEN KILLED...
...MEANS ADLET HAS JUDGED HER TO BE VALUABLE AS A HOSTAGE.
LET US RETURN TO THE TEMPLE.
......

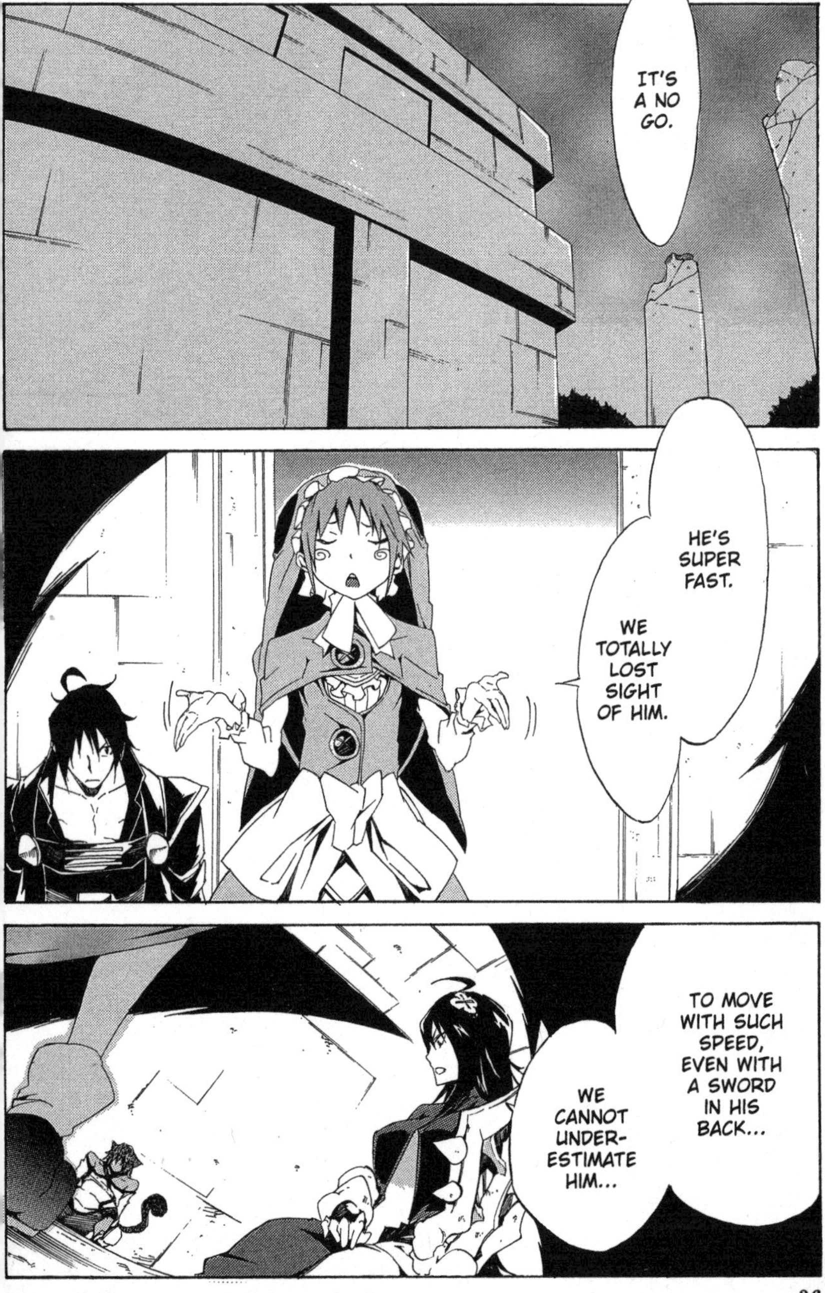
IT'S A NO GO.
HE'S SUPER FAST.
WE TOTALLY LOST SIGHT OF HIM.
TO MOVE WITH SUCH SPEED, EVEN WITH A SWORD IN HIS BACK...
WE CANNOT UNDER-ESTIMATE HIM...

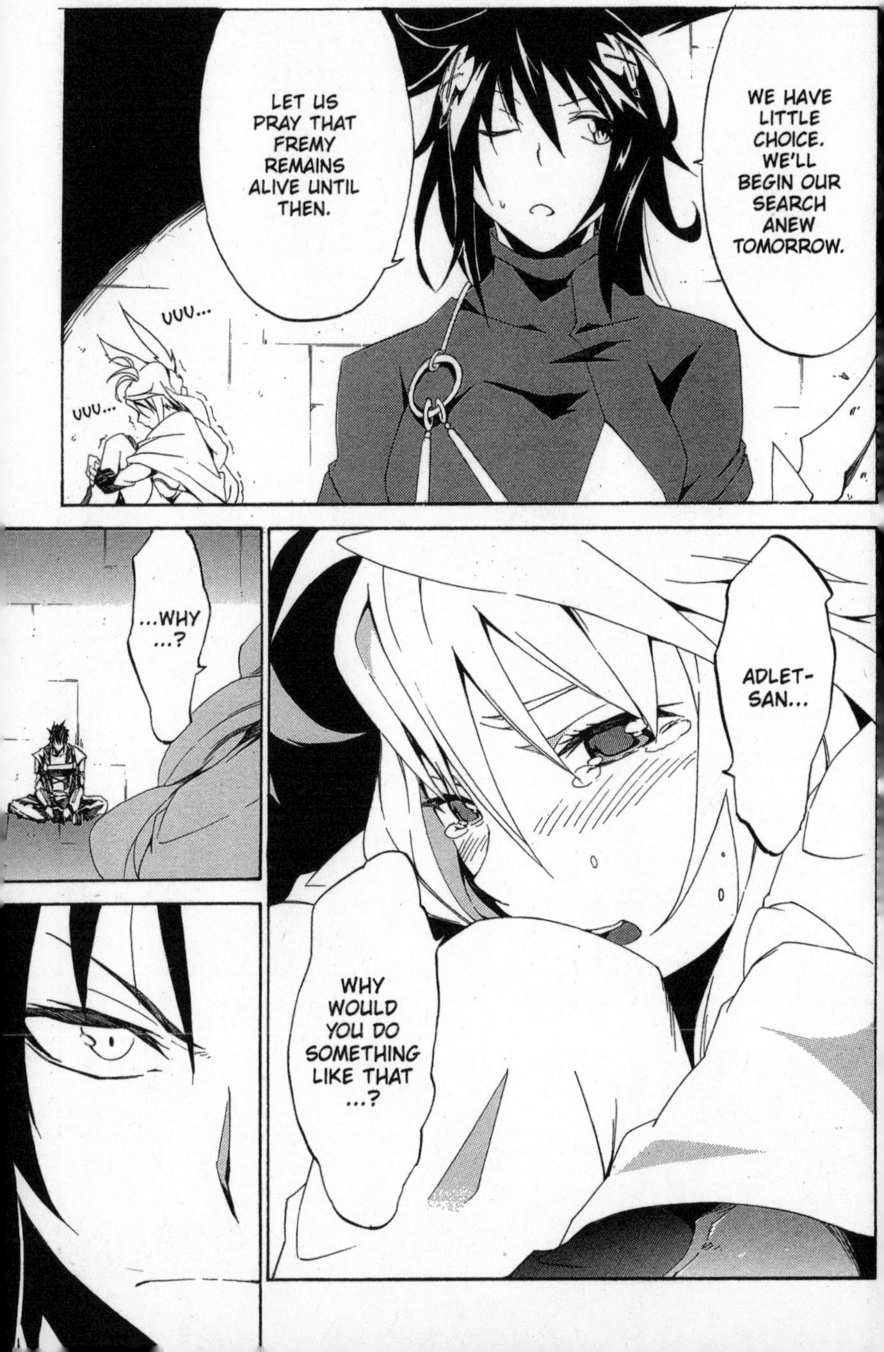
WE HAVE LITTLE CHOICE. WE'LL BEGIN OUR SEARCH ANEW TOMORROW.
LET US PRAY THAT FREMY REMAINS ALIVE UNTIL THEN.
UUU...
UUU...
ADLET-SAN...
WHY WOULD YOU DO SOMETHING LIKE THAT ...?
...WHY ...?

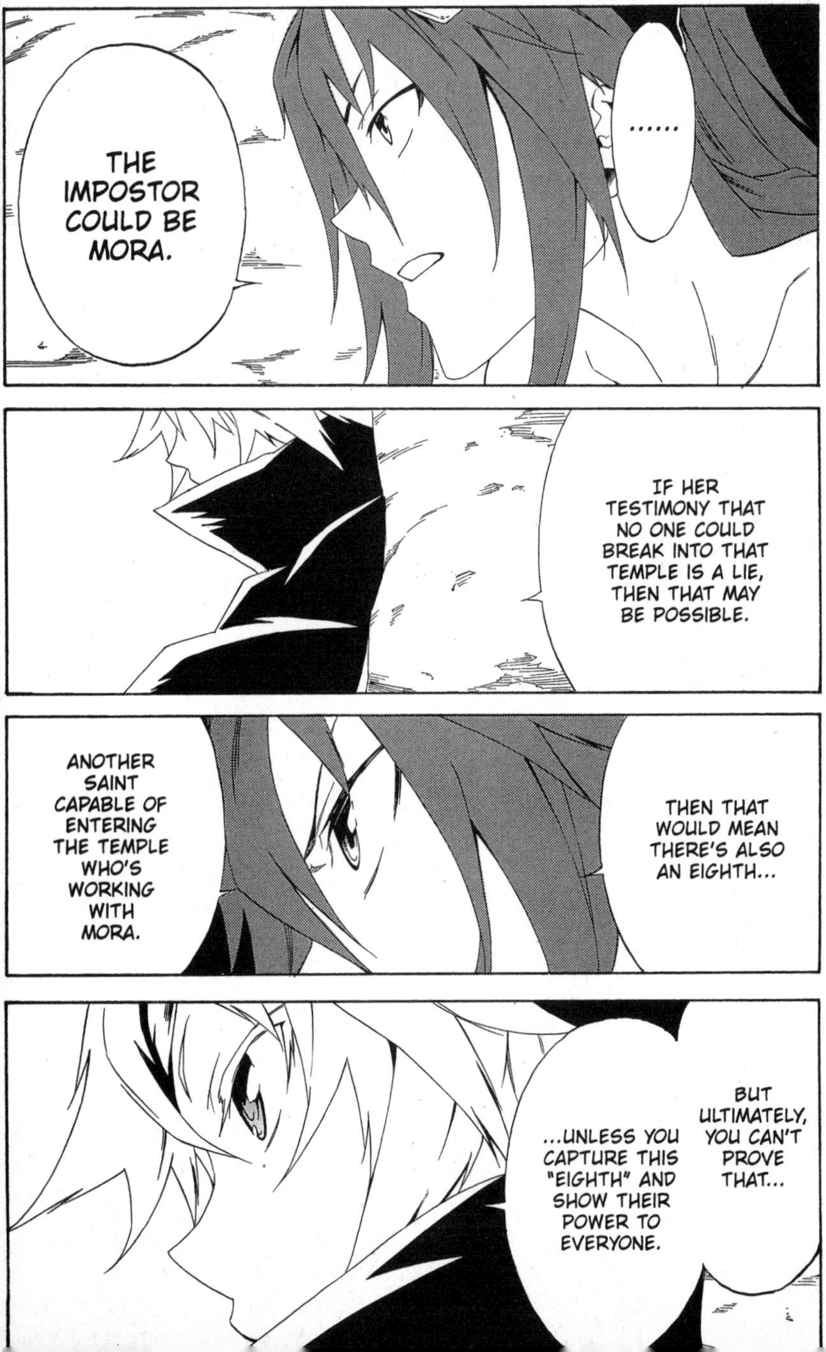
......
THE IMPOSTOR COULD BE MORA.
IF HER TESTIMONY THAT NO ONE COULD BREAK INTO THAT TEMPLE IS A LIE, THEN THAT MAY BE POSSIBLE.
THEN THAT WOULD MEAN THERE'S ALSO AN EIGHTH...
ANOTHER SAINT CAPABLE OF ENTERING THE TEMPLE WHO'S WORKING WITH MORA.
BUT ULTIMATELY, YOU CAN'T PROVE THAT...
...UNLESS YOU CAPTURE THIS "EIGHTH" AND SHOW THEIR POWER TO EVERYONE.

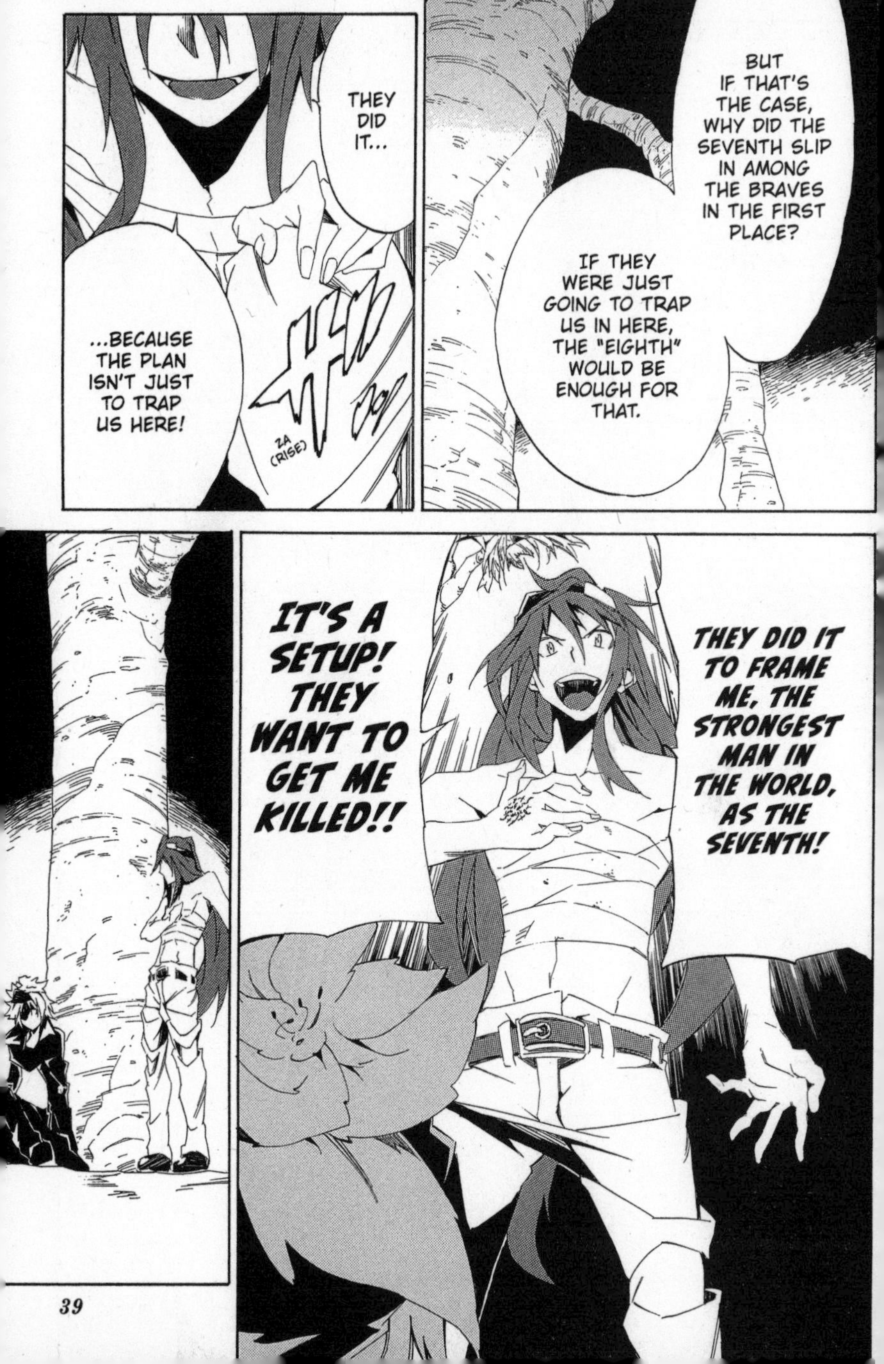
BUT IF THAT'S THE CASE, WHY DID THE SEVENTH SLIP IN AMONG THE BRAVES IN THE FIRST PLACE?
IF THEY WERE JUST GOING TO TRAP US IN HERE, THE "EIGHTH" WOULD BE ENOUGH FOR THAT.
THEY DID IT...
...BECAUSE THE PLAN ISN'T JUST TO TRAP US HERE!
ZA (RISE)
THEY DID IT TO FRAME ME, THE STRONGEST MAN IN THE WORLD, AS THE SEVENTH!
IT'S A SETUP! THEY WANT TO GET ME KILLED!!

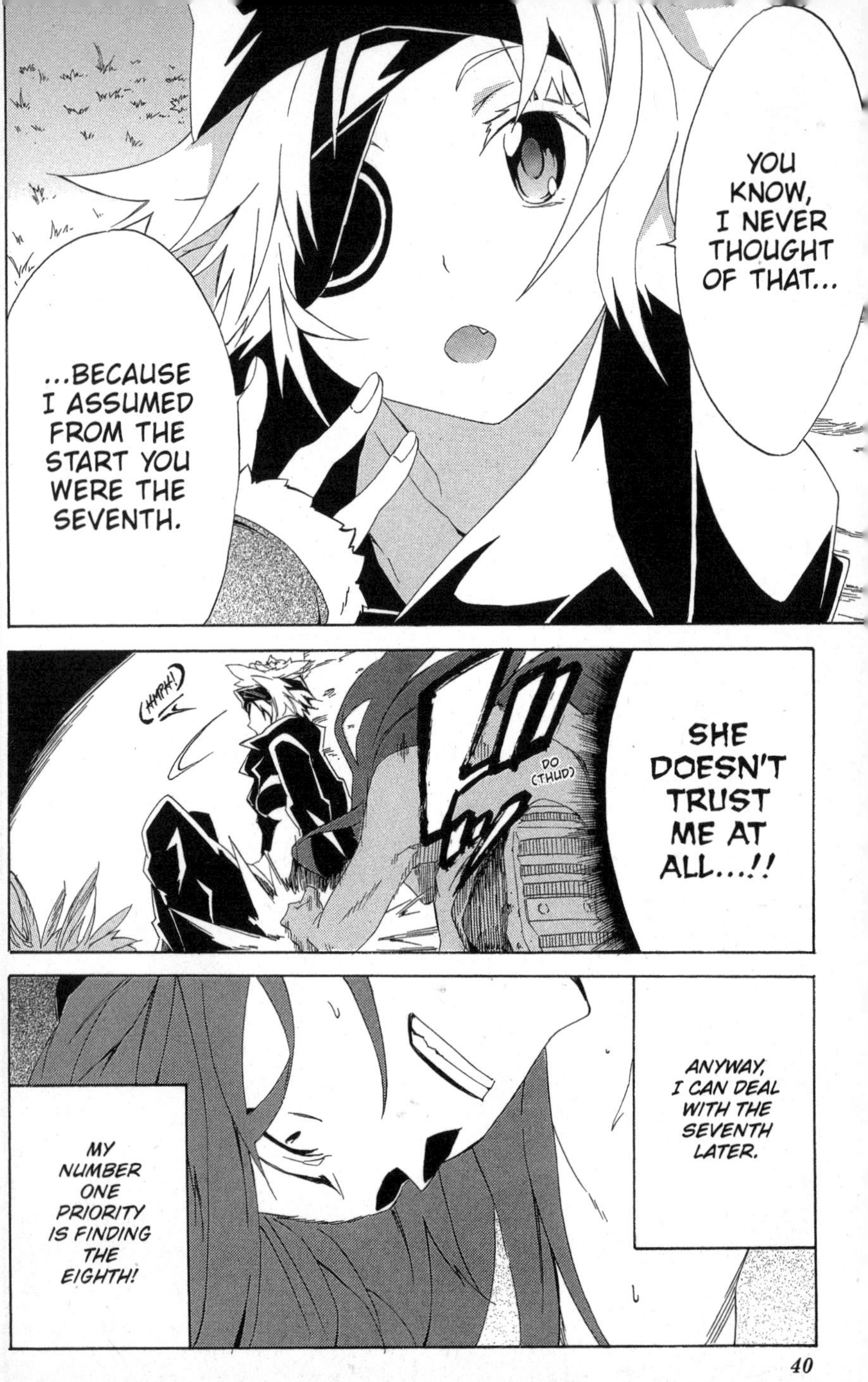

YOU KNOW, I NEVER THOUGHT OF THAT...
...BECAUSE I ASSUMED FROM THE START YOU WERE THE SEVENTH.
SHE DOESN'T TRUST ME AT ALL...!!
DO (THUD)
(HMPH!)
ANYWAY, I CAN DEAL WITH THE SEVENTH LATER.
MY NUMBER ONE PRIORITY IS FINDING THE EIGHTH!

CAN I DO THIS ALL ALONE?

...I CAN'T EXPECT HELP FROM HER.

JUDGING FROM FREMY'S ATTITUDE...

...WHILE EVADING THE REST OF THEM...?

AND CAN I FERRET OUT AN "EIGHTH" WITH UNKNOWN POWERS WHO'S HIDING...

......I CAN'T.

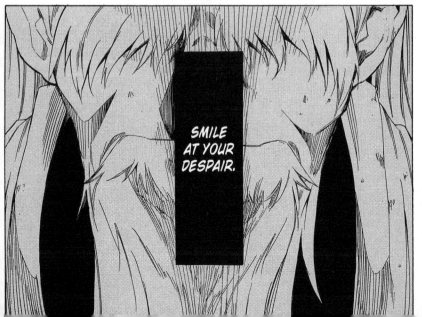

SMILE
AT YOUR
DESPAIR.

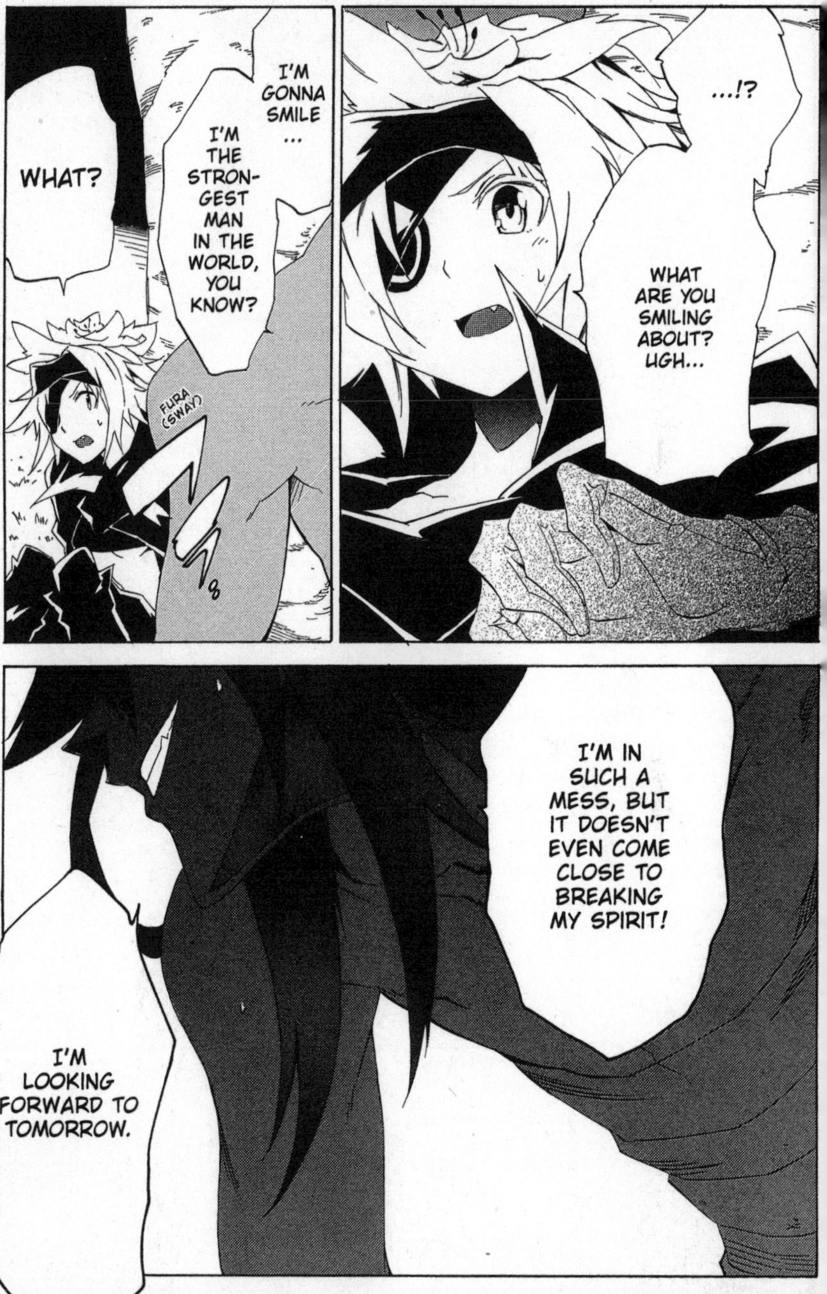
...!?
WHAT ARE YOU SMILING ABOUT? UGH...
I'M GONNA SMILE ...
I'M THE STRON-GEST MAN IN THE WORLD, YOU KNOW?
WHAT?
FURA (SWAY)
I'M IN SUCH A MESS, BUT IT DOESN'T EVEN COME CLOSE TO BREAKING MY SPIRIT!
I'M LOOKING FORWARD TO TOMORROW.

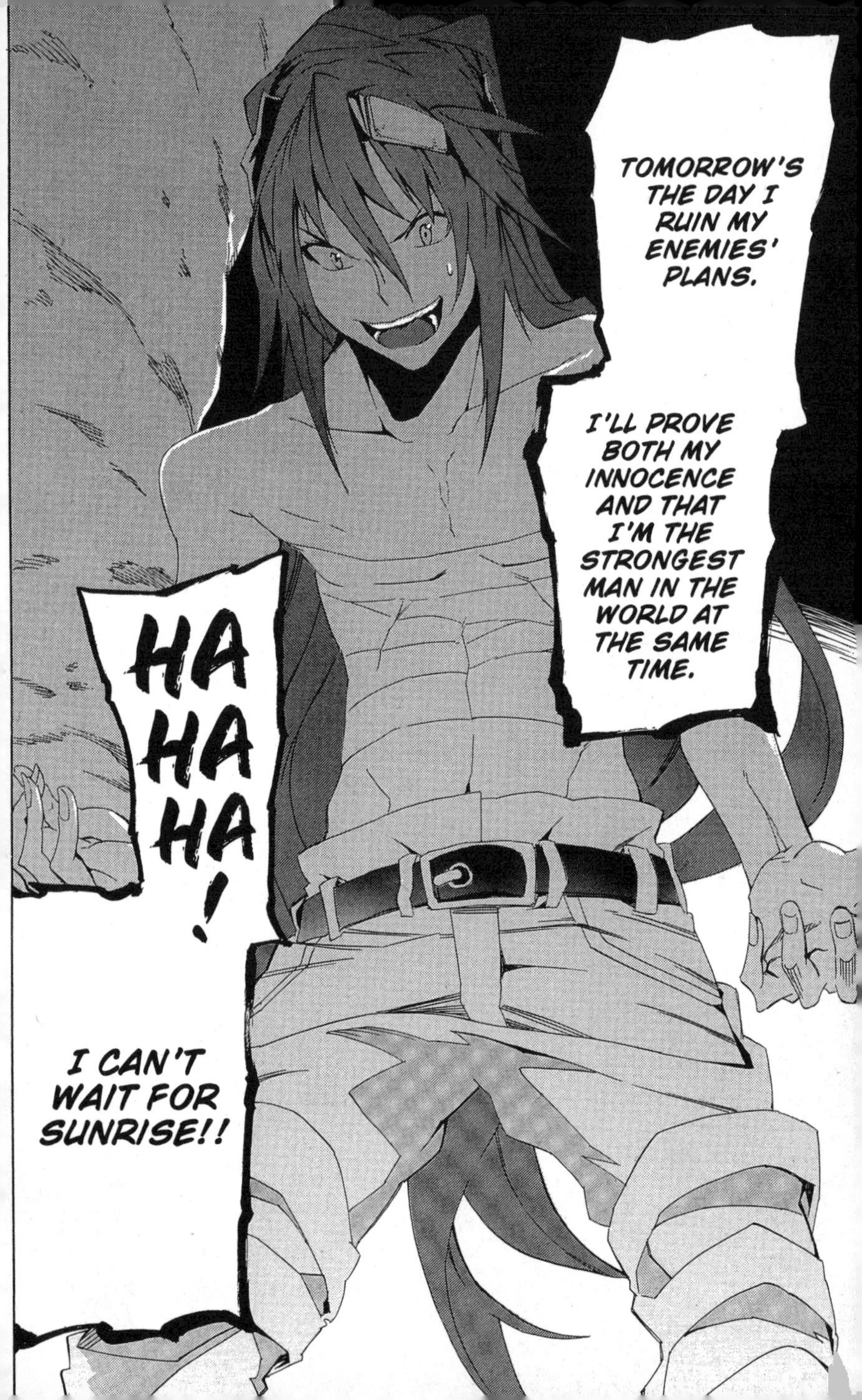
TOMORROW'S THE DAY I RUIN MY ENEMIES' PLANS.
I'LL PROVE BOTH MY INNOCENCE AND THAT I'M THE STRONGEST MAN IN THE WORLD AT THE SAME TIME.
HA HA HA HA!
I CAN'T WAIT FOR SUNRISE!!

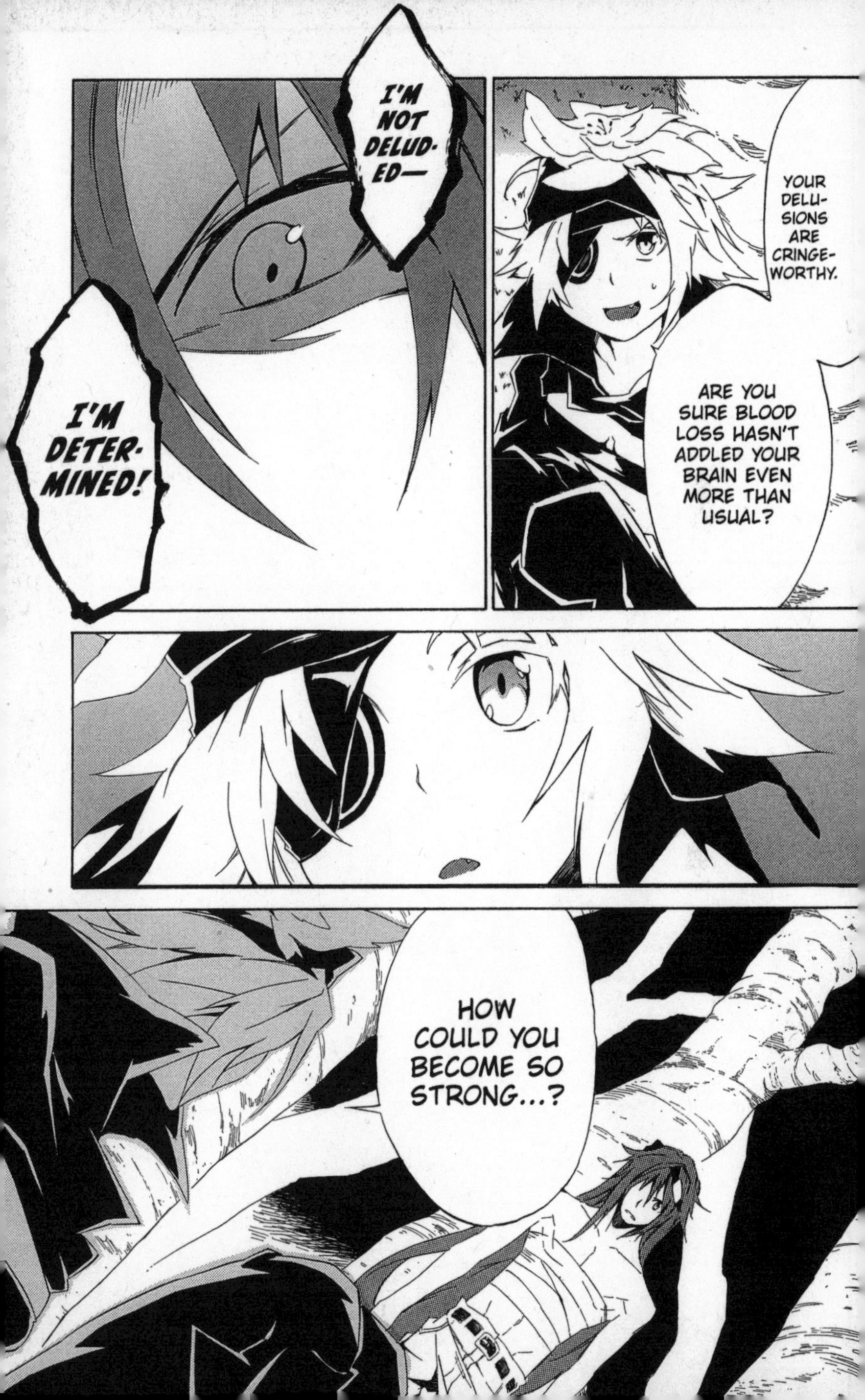
YOUR DELUSIONS ARE CRINGE-WORTHY.
ARE YOU SURE BLOOD LOSS HASN'T ADDLED YOUR BRAIN EVEN MORE THAN USUAL?
I'M NOT DELUD-ED—
I'M DETER-MINED!
HOW COULD YOU BECOME SO STRONG...?

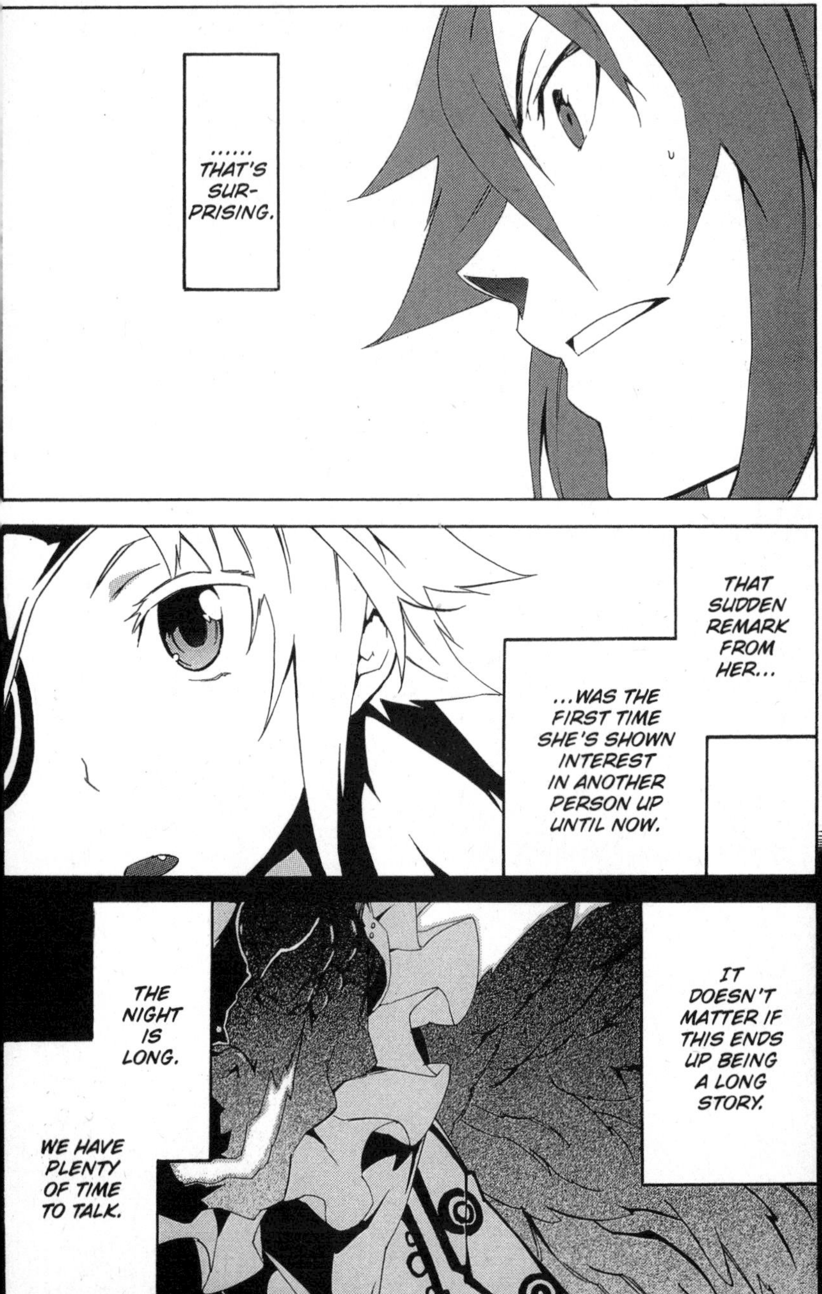
......
THAT'S SUR-PRISING.
THAT SUDDEN REMARK FROM HER...
...WAS THE FIRST TIME SHE'S SHOWN INTEREST IN ANOTHER PERSON UP UNTIL NOW.
IT DOESN'T MATTER IF THIS ENDS UP BEING A LONG STORY.
THE NIGHT IS LONG.
WE HAVE PLENTY OF TIME TO TALK.

Episode.06

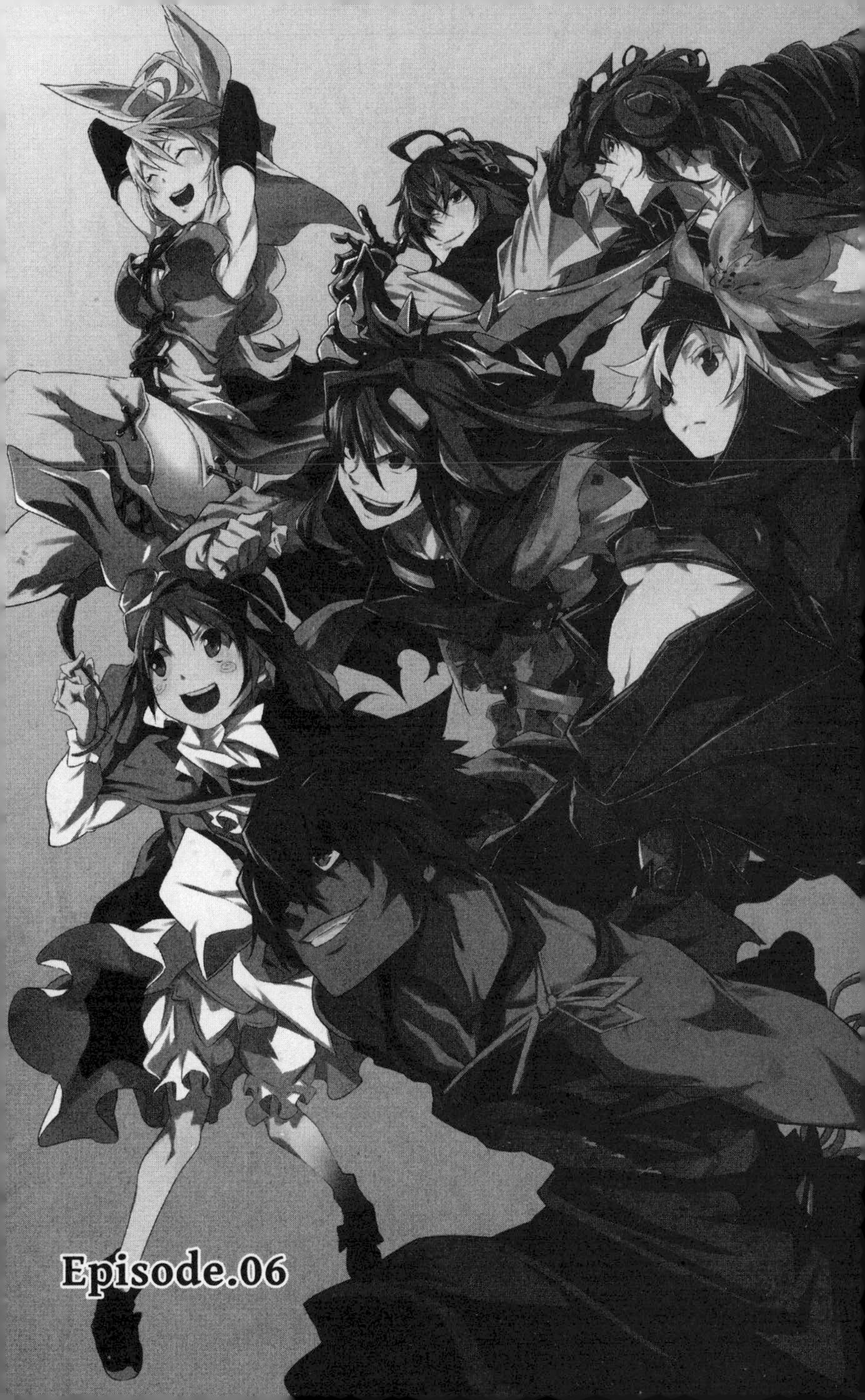

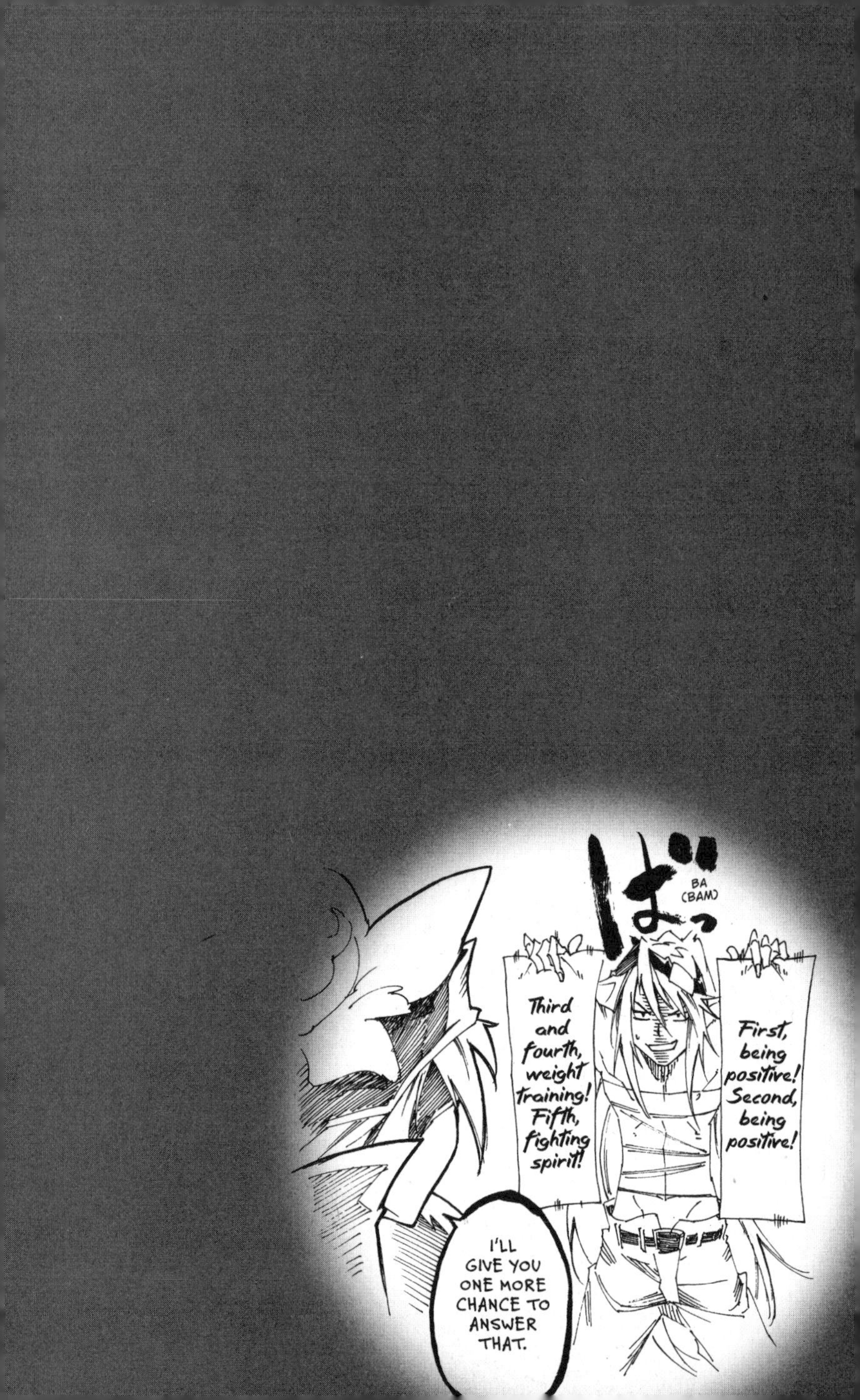
ばっ
BA (BAM)
First, being positive! Second, being positive!
Third and fourth, weight training! Fifth, fighting spirit!
I'LL GIVE YOU ONE MORE CHANCE TO ANSWER THAT.

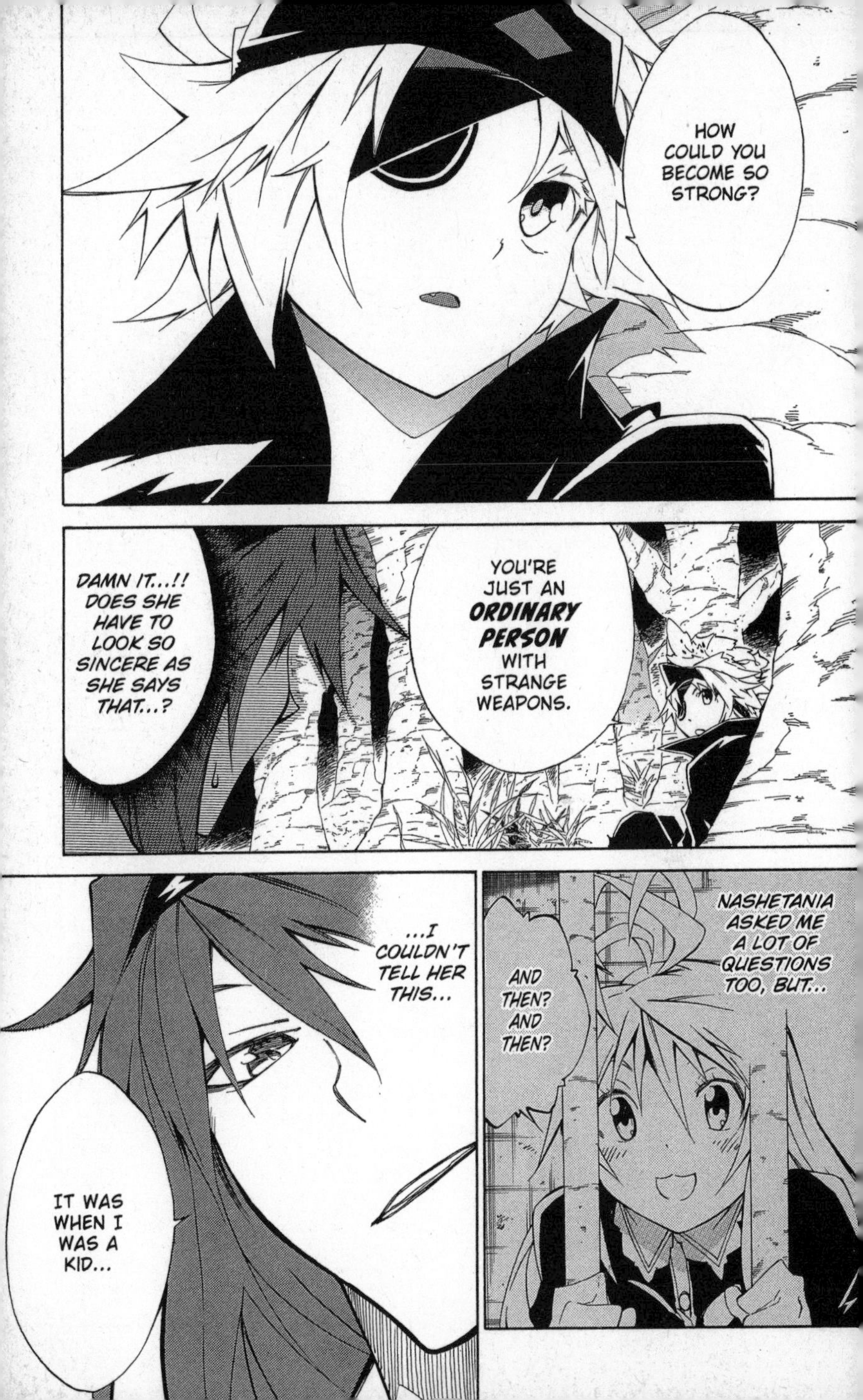
HOW COULD YOU BECOME SO STRONG?
YOU'RE JUST AN **ORDINARY PERSON** WITH STRANGE WEAPONS.
DAMN IT...!! DOES SHE HAVE TO LOOK SO SINCERE AS SHE SAYS THAT...?
NASHETANIA ASKED ME A LOT OF QUESTIONS TOO, BUT...
AND THEN? AND THEN?
...I COULDN'T TELL HER THIS...
IT WAS WHEN I WAS A KID...

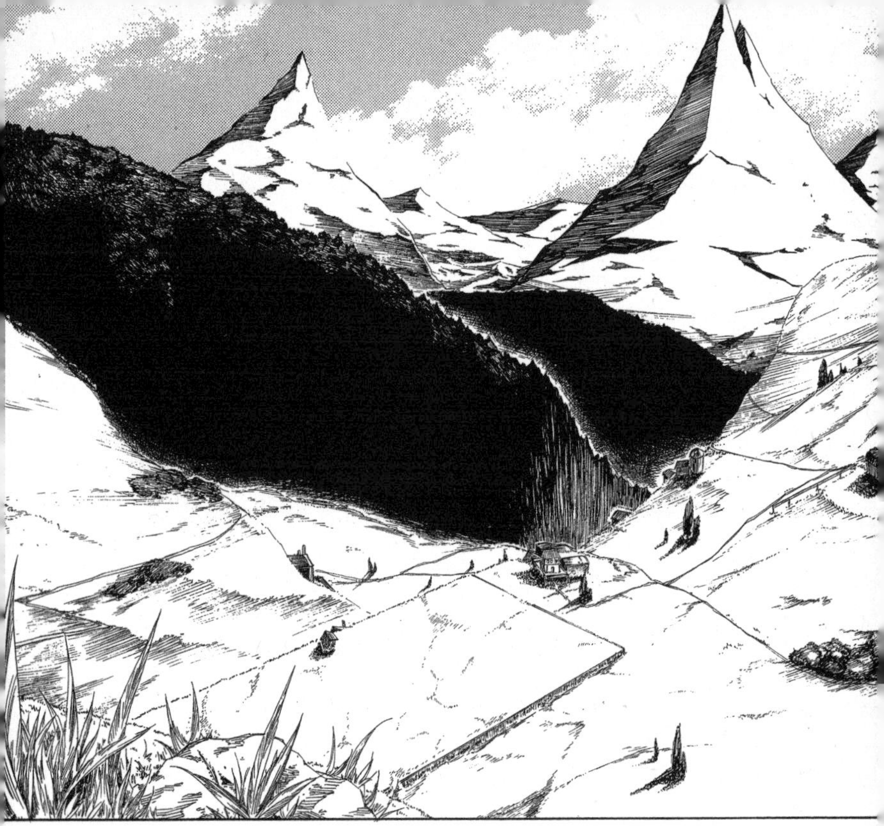

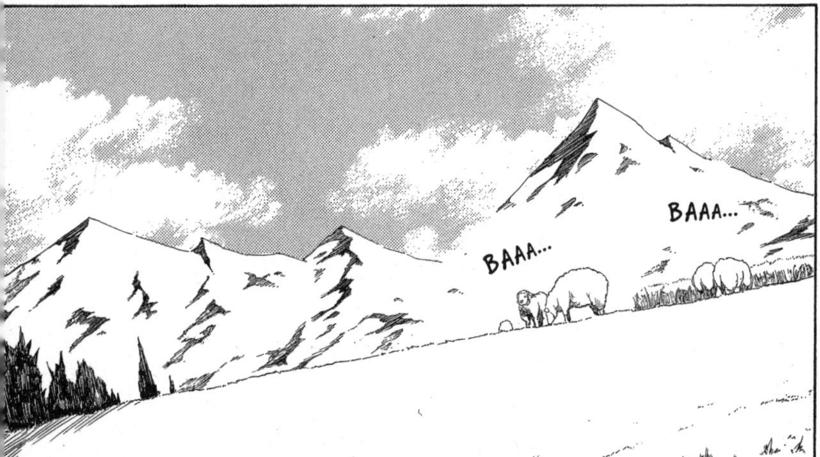
BAAA...
BAAA...

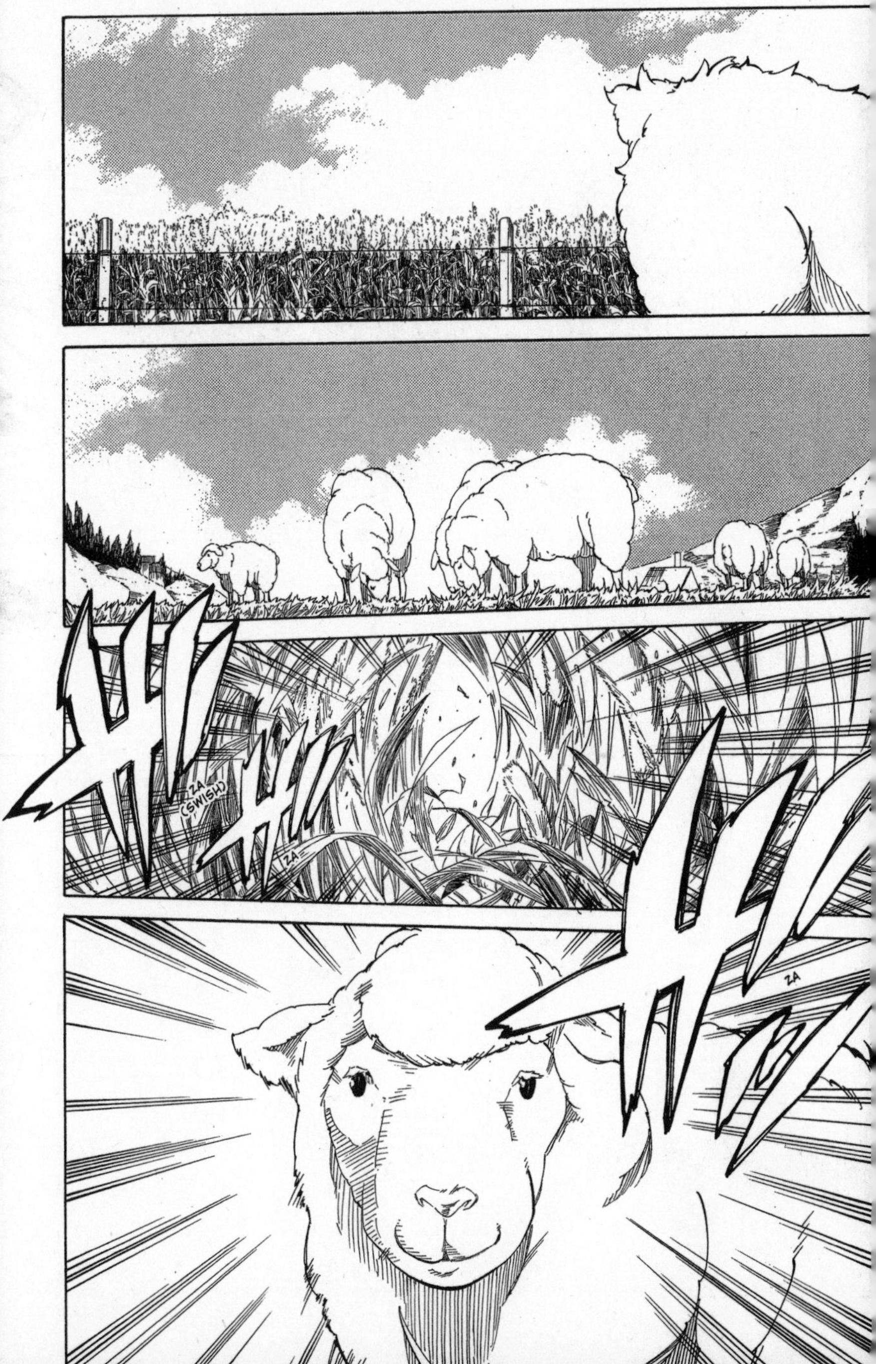
ZA (SWISH)
ZA
ZA

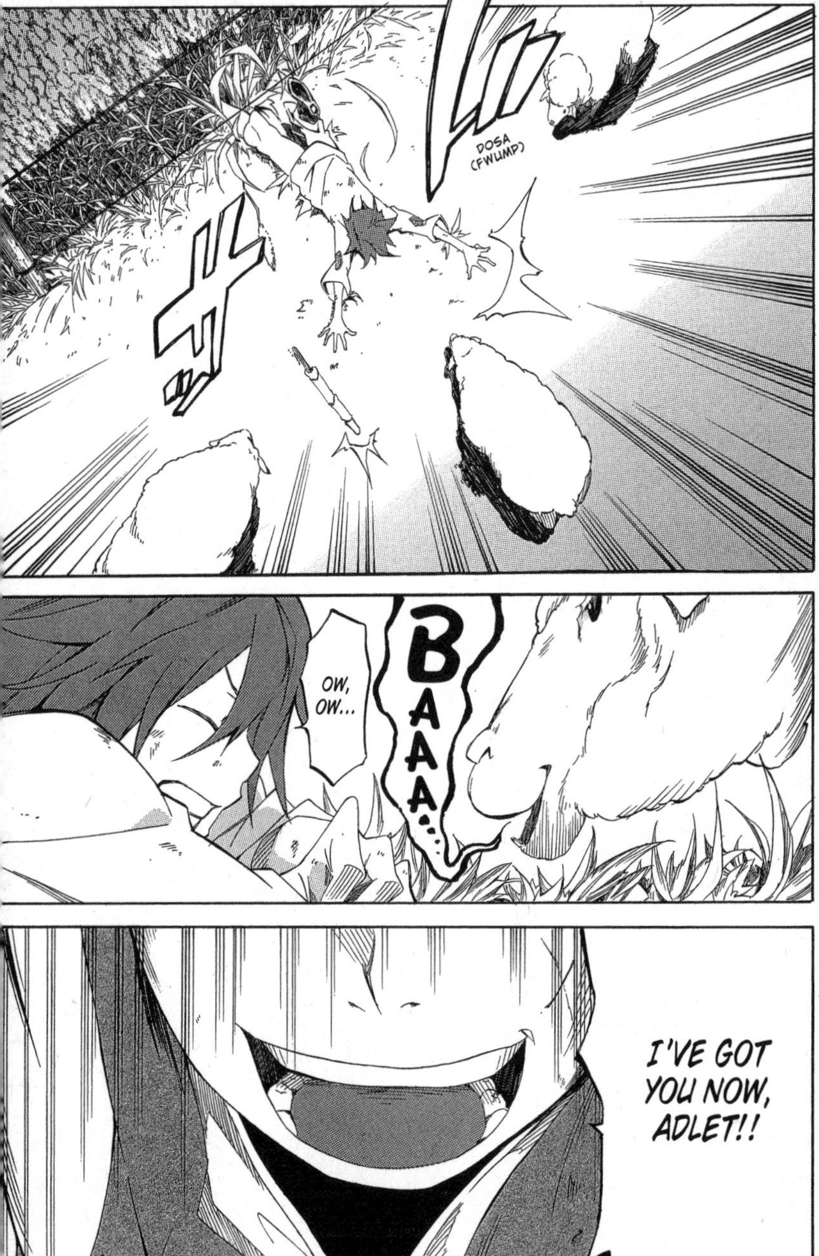
DOSA
(FWUMP)
BAAAA...
OW, OW...
I'VE GOT YOU NOW, ADLET!!

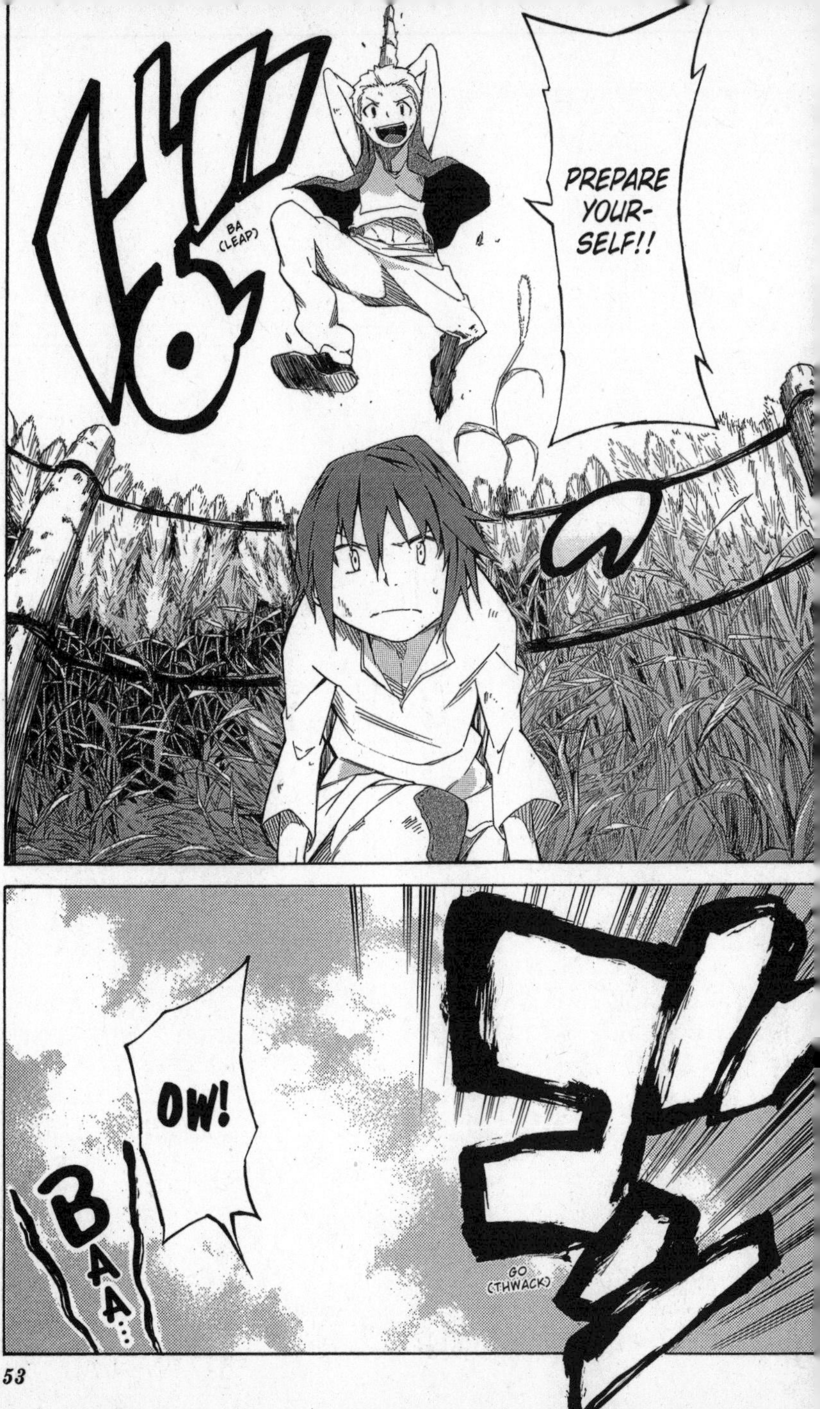
PREPARE YOUR-SELF!!
BA (LEAP)
GO (THWACK)
OW!
BAA...

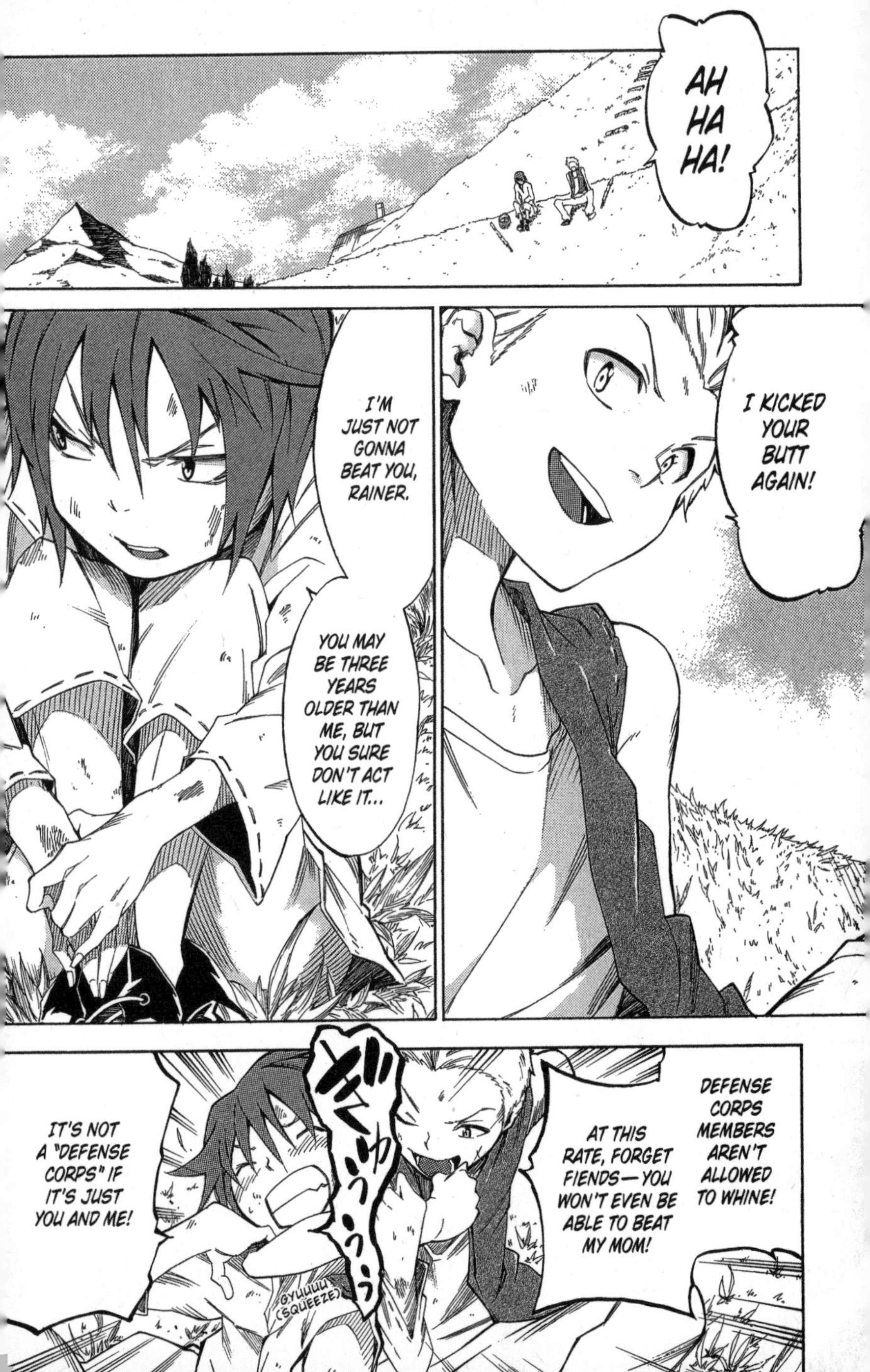
AH HA HA!
I KICKED YOUR BUTT AGAIN!
I'M JUST NOT GONNA BEAT YOU, RAINER.
YOU MAY BE THREE YEARS OLDER THAN ME, BUT YOU SURE DON'T ACT LIKE IT...
DEFENSE CORPS MEMBERS AREN'T ALLOWED TO WHINE!
AT THIS RATE, FORGET FIENDS—YOU WON'T EVEN BE ABLE TO BEAT MY MOM!
GYUUUU (SQUEEZE)
IT'S NOT A "DEFENSE CORPS" IF IT'S JUST YOU AND ME!

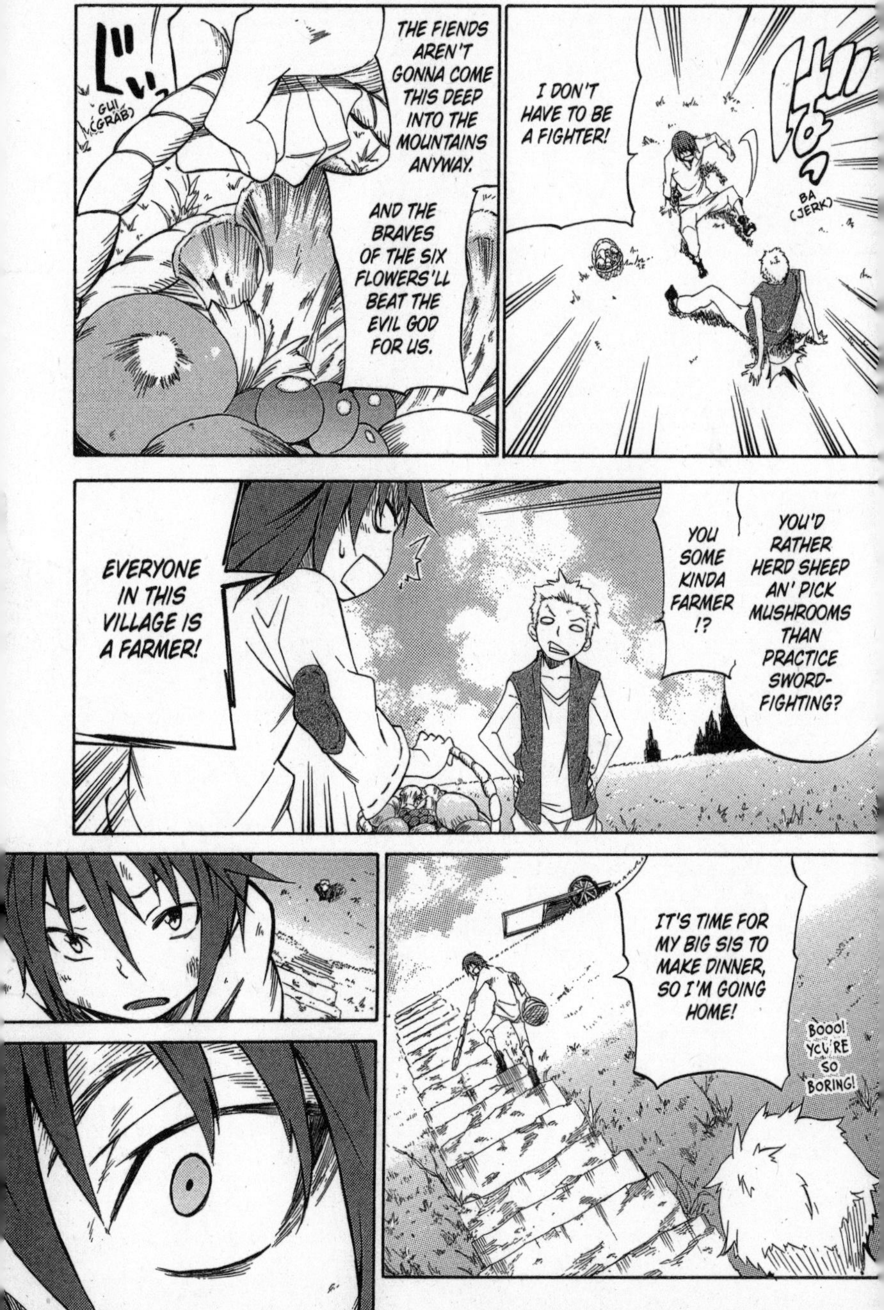
I DON'T HAVE TO BE A FIGHTER!
BA (JERK)
GUI (GRAB)
THE FIENDS AREN'T GONNA COME THIS DEEP INTO THE MOUNTAINS ANYWAY.
AND THE BRAVES OF THE SIX FLOWERS'LL BEAT THE EVIL GOD FOR US.
YOU'D RATHER HERD SHEEP AN' PICK MUSHROOMS THAN PRACTICE SWORD-FIGHTING?
YOU SOME KINDA FARMER!?
EVERYONE IN THIS VILLAGE IS A FARMER!
IT'S TIME FOR MY BIG SIS TO MAKE DINNER, SO I'M GOING HOME!
BOOO! YOU'RE SO BORING!

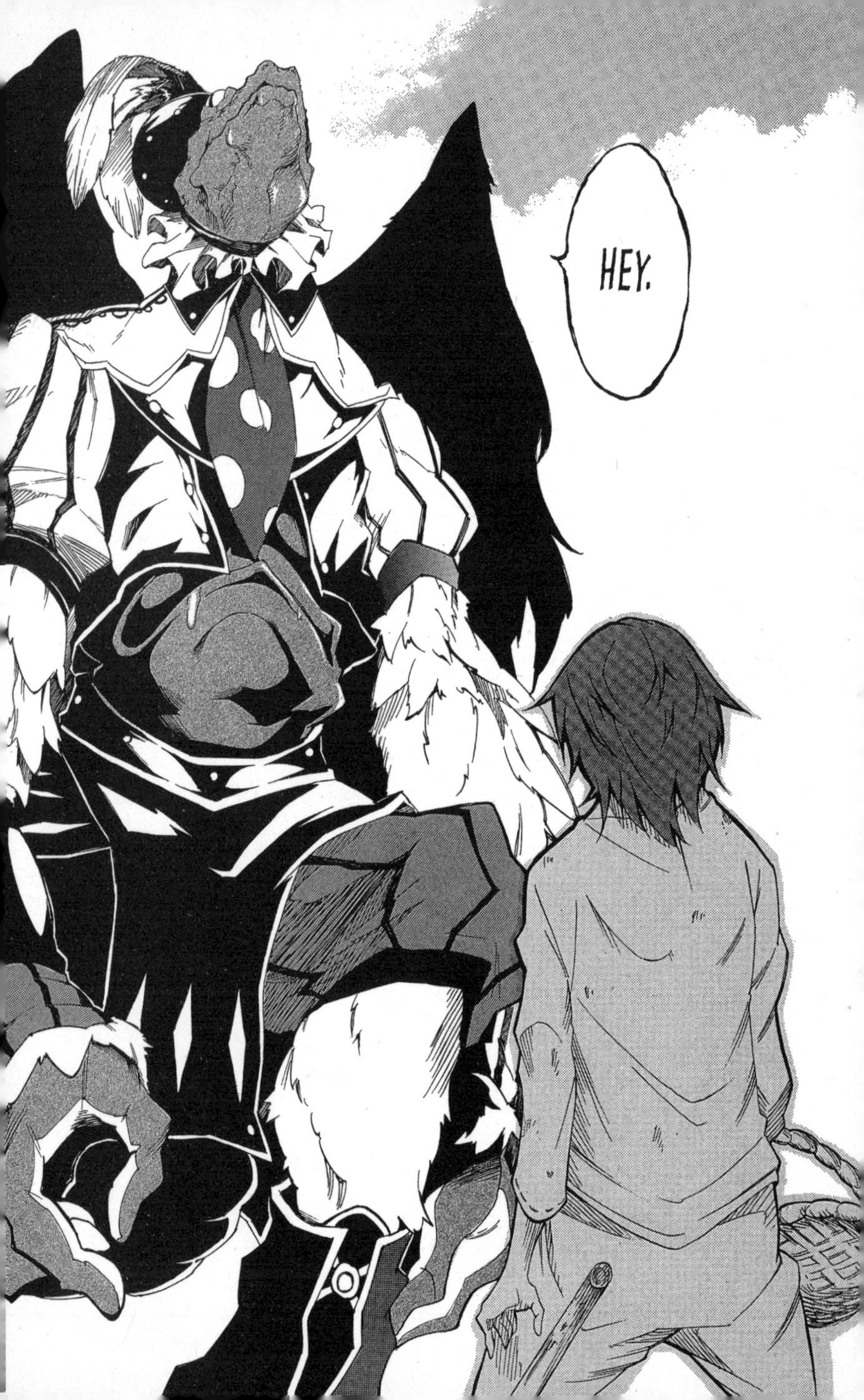
HEY.

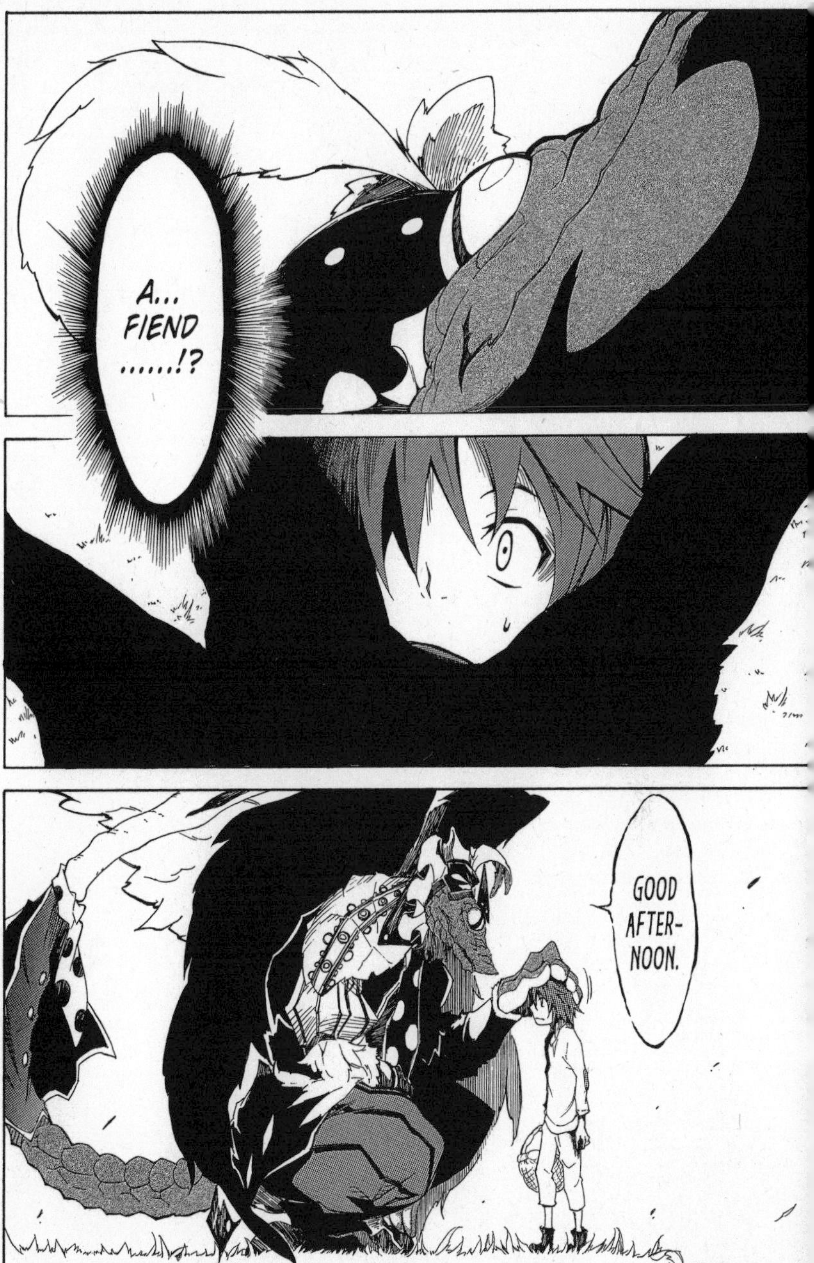
A... FIEND ......!?
GOOD AFTER-NOON.

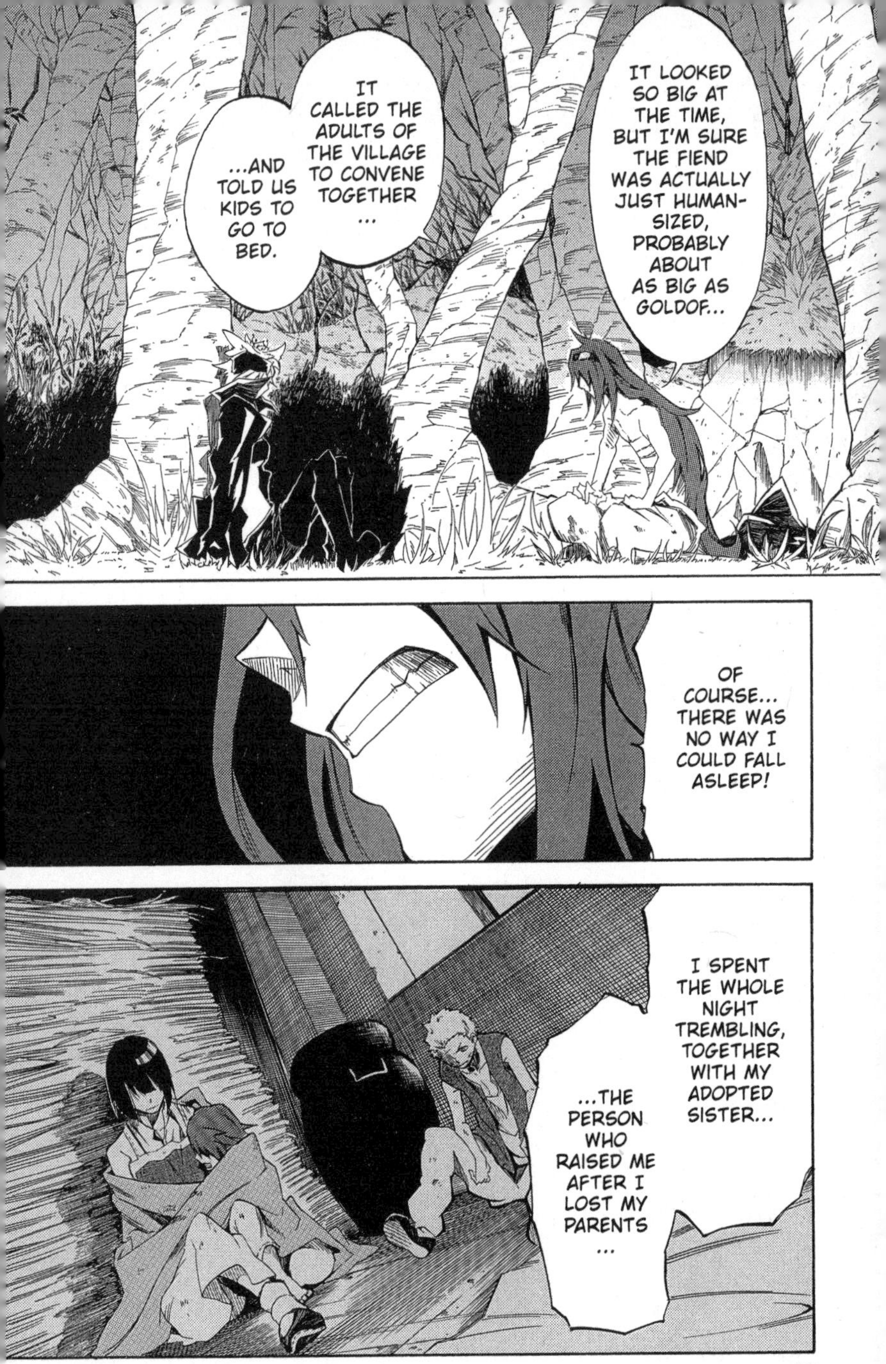
IT LOOKED SO BIG AT THE TIME, BUT I'M SURE THE FIEND WAS ACTUALLY JUST HUMAN-SIZED, PROBABLY ABOUT AS BIG AS GOLDOF...
IT CALLED THE ADULTS OF THE VILLAGE TO CONVENE TOGETHER...
...AND TOLD US KIDS TO GO TO BED.
OF COURSE... THERE WAS NO WAY I COULD FALL ASLEEP!
I SPENT THE WHOLE NIGHT TREMBLING, TOGETHER WITH MY ADOPTED SISTER...
...THE PERSON WHO RAISED ME AFTER I LOST MY PARENTS...

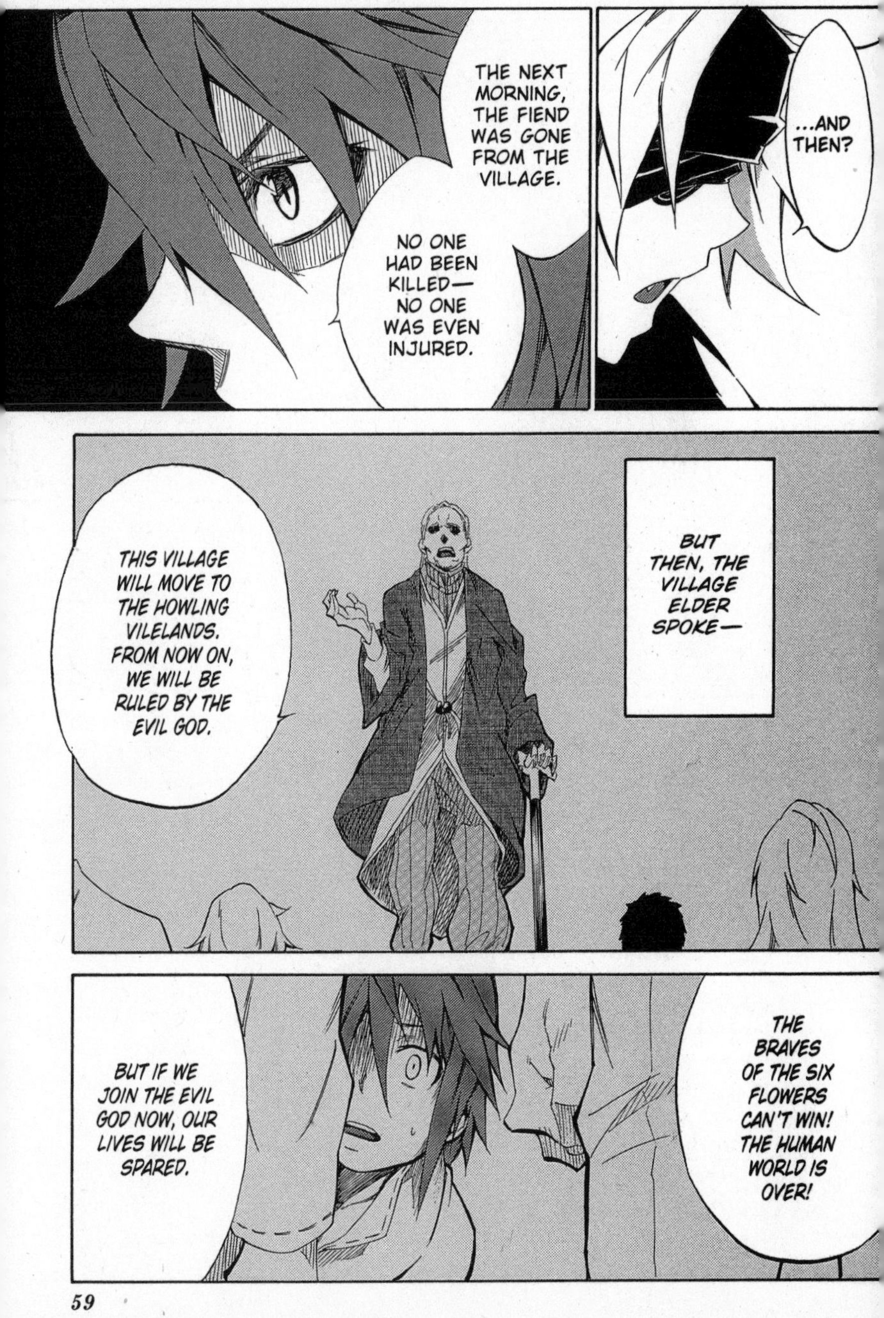
...AND THEN?
THE NEXT MORNING, THE FIEND WAS GONE FROM THE VILLAGE.
NO ONE HAD BEEN KILLED—NO ONE WAS EVEN INJURED.
BUT THEN, THE VILLAGE ELDER SPOKE—
THIS VILLAGE WILL MOVE TO THE HOWLING VILELANDS. FROM NOW ON, WE WILL BE RULED BY THE EVIL GOD.
THE BRAVES OF THE SIX FLOWERS CAN'T WIN! THE HUMAN WORLD IS OVER!
BUT IF WE JOIN THE EVIL GOD NOW, OUR LIVES WILL BE SPARED.

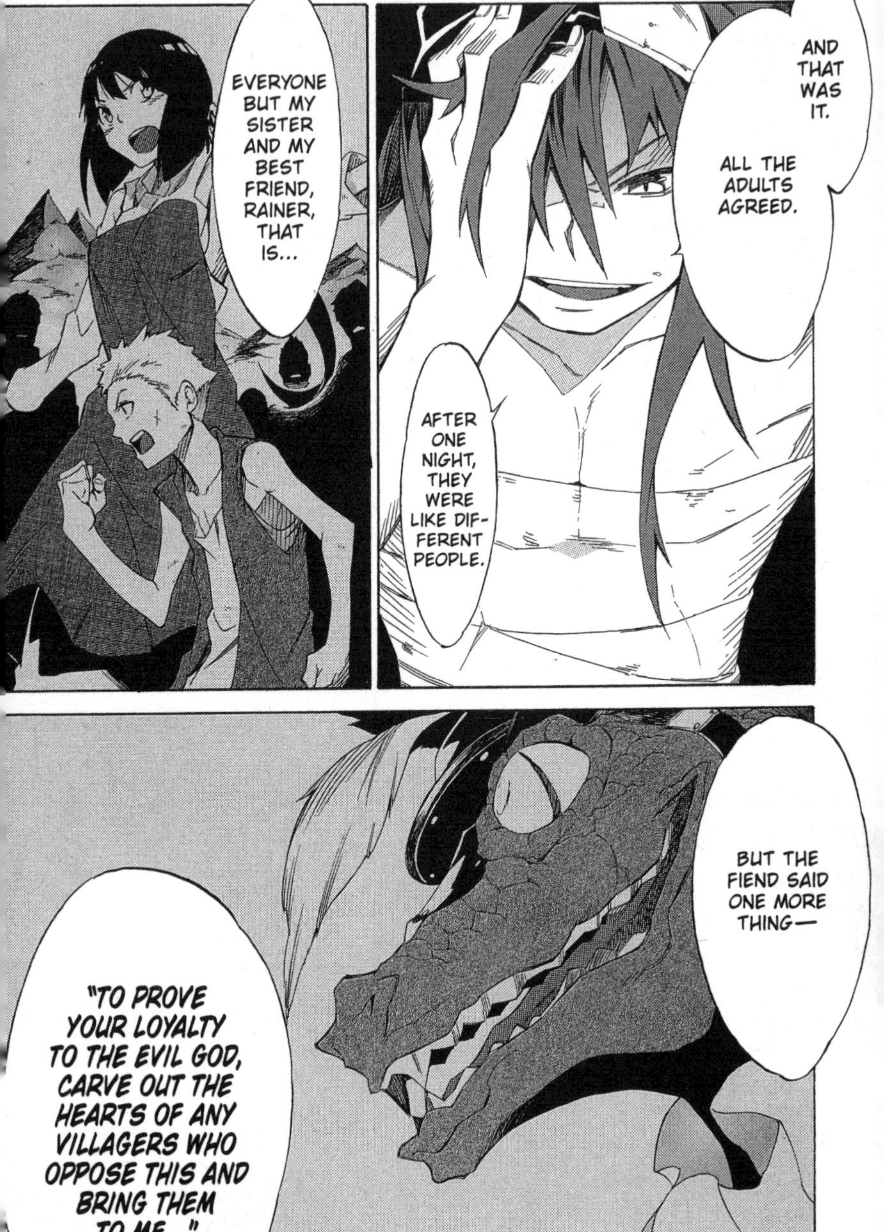
AND THAT WAS IT.
ALL THE ADULTS AGREED.
AFTER ONE NIGHT, THEY WERE LIKE DIFFERENT PEOPLE.
EVERYONE BUT MY SISTER AND MY BEST FRIEND, RAINER, THAT IS...
BUT THE FIEND SAID ONE MORE THING—
"TO PROVE YOUR LOYALTY TO THE EVIL GOD, CARVE OUT THE HEARTS OF ANY VILLAGERS WHO OPPOSE THIS AND BRING THEM TO ME..."

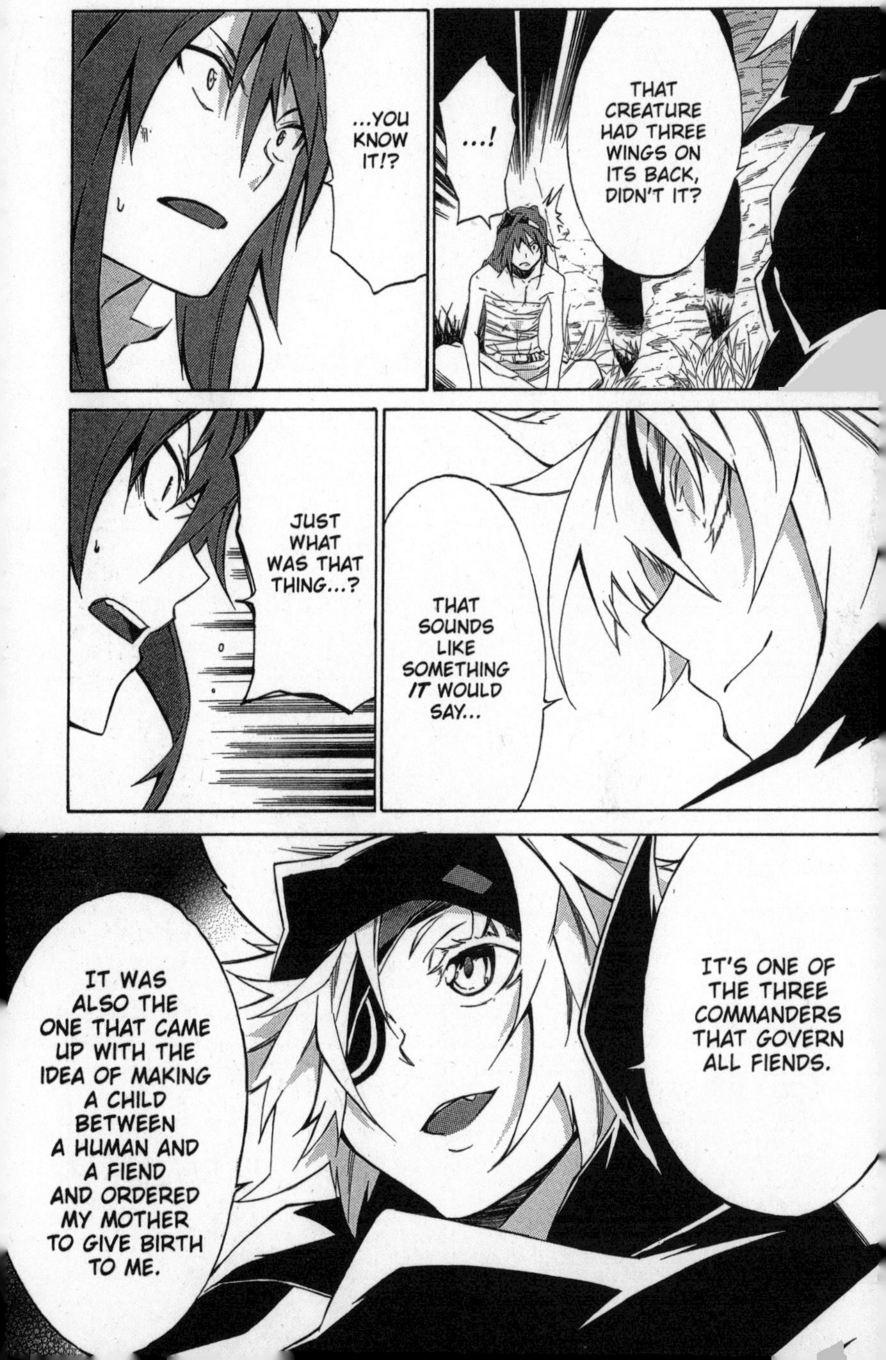
THAT CREATURE HAD THREE WINGS ON ITS BACK, DIDN'T IT?
...!
...YOU KNOW IT!?
THAT SOUNDS LIKE SOMETHING *IT* WOULD SAY...
JUST WHAT WAS THAT THING...?
IT'S ONE OF THE THREE COMMANDERS THAT GOVERN ALL FIENDS.
IT WAS ALSO THE ONE THAT CAME UP WITH THE IDEA OF MAKING A CHILD BETWEEN A HUMAN AND A FIEND AND ORDERED MY MOTHER TO GIVE BIRTH TO ME.

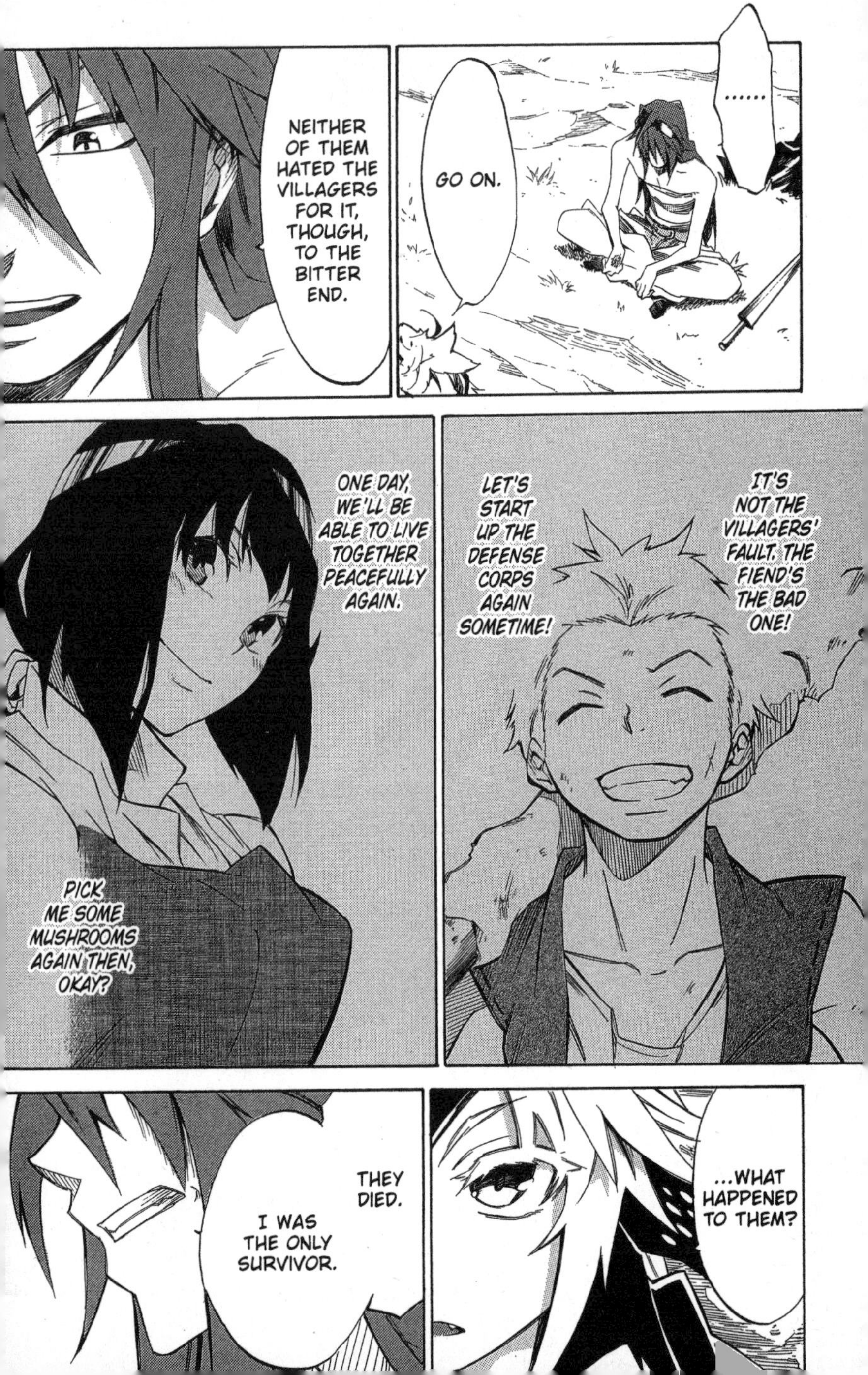
......
GO ON.
NEITHER OF THEM HATED THE VILLAGERS FOR IT, THOUGH, TO THE BITTER END.
IT'S NOT THE VILLAGERS' FAULT. THE FIEND'S THE BAD ONE!
LET'S START UP THE DEFENSE CORPS AGAIN SOMETIME!
ONE DAY, WE'LL BE ABLE TO LIVE TOGETHER PEACEFULLY AGAIN.
PICK ME SOME MUSHROOMS AGAIN THEN, OKAY?
...WHAT HAPPENED TO THEM?
THEY DIED.
I WAS THE ONLY SURVIVOR.

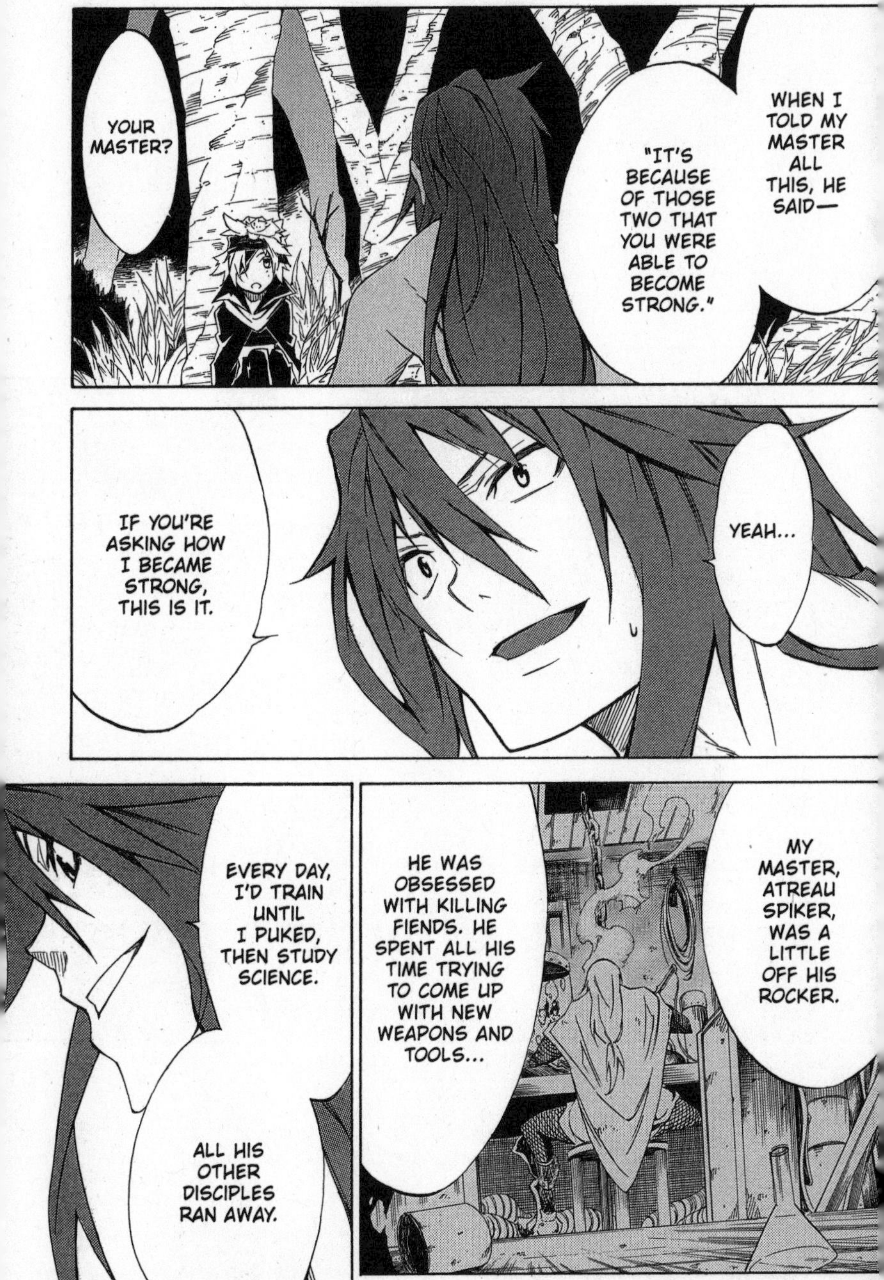
WHEN I TOLD MY MASTER ALL THIS, HE SAID—
"IT'S BECAUSE OF THOSE TWO THAT YOU WERE ABLE TO BECOME STRONG."
YOUR MASTER?
YEAH...
IF YOU'RE ASKING HOW I BECAME STRONG, THIS IS IT.
MY MASTER, ATREAU SPIKER, WAS A LITTLE OFF HIS ROCKER.
HE WAS OBSESSED WITH KILLING FIENDS. HE SPENT ALL HIS TIME TRYING TO COME UP WITH NEW WEAPONS AND TOOLS...
EVERY DAY, I'D TRAIN UNTIL I PUKED, THEN STUDY SCIENCE.
ALL HIS OTHER DISCIPLES RAN AWAY.

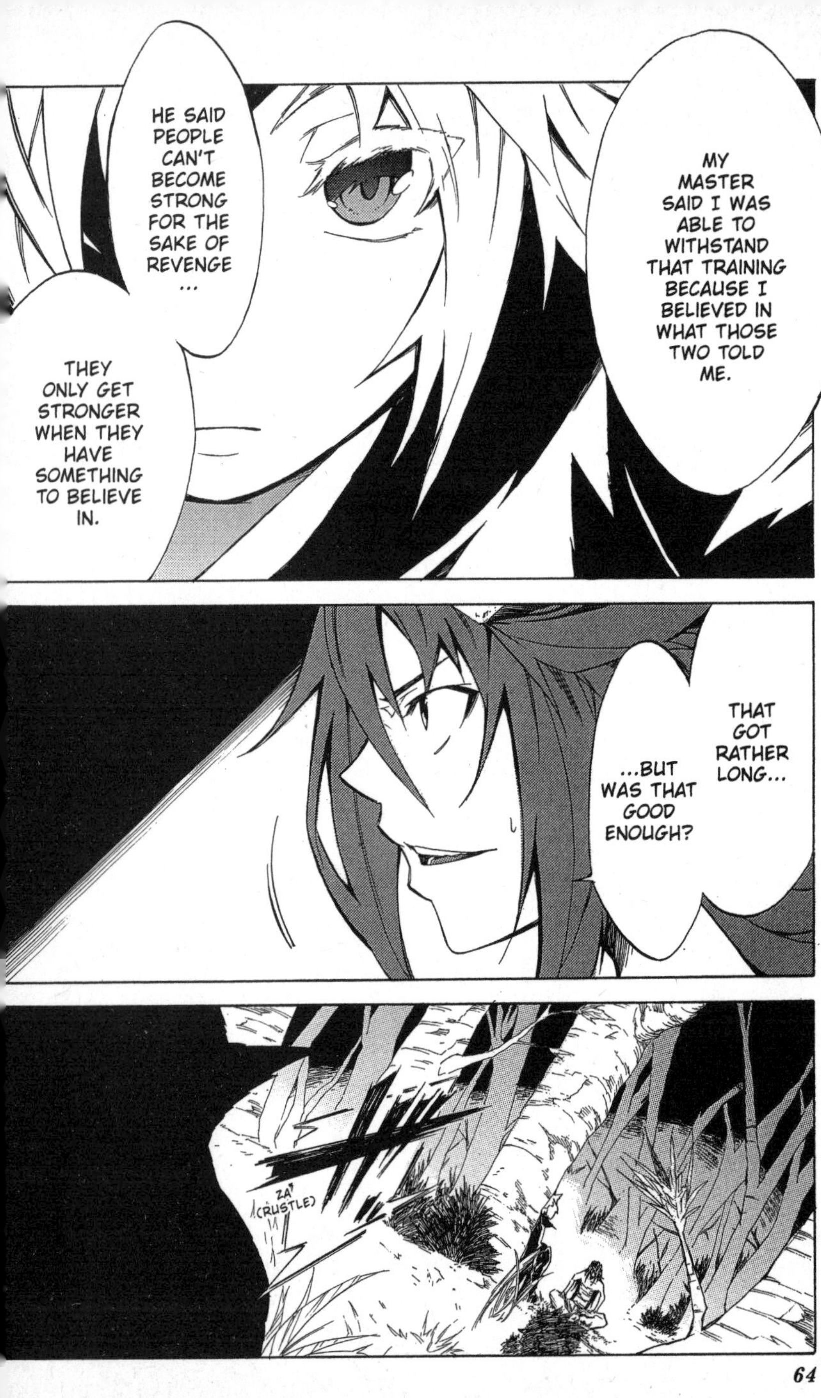
MY MASTER SAID I WAS ABLE TO WITHSTAND THAT TRAINING BECAUSE I BELIEVED IN WHAT THOSE TWO TOLD ME.
HE SAID PEOPLE CAN'T BECOME STRONG FOR THE SAKE OF REVENGE ...
THEY ONLY GET STRONGER WHEN THEY HAVE SOMETHING TO BELIEVE IN.
THAT GOT RATHER LONG...
...BUT WAS THAT GOOD ENOUGH?
ZA (CRUSTLE)

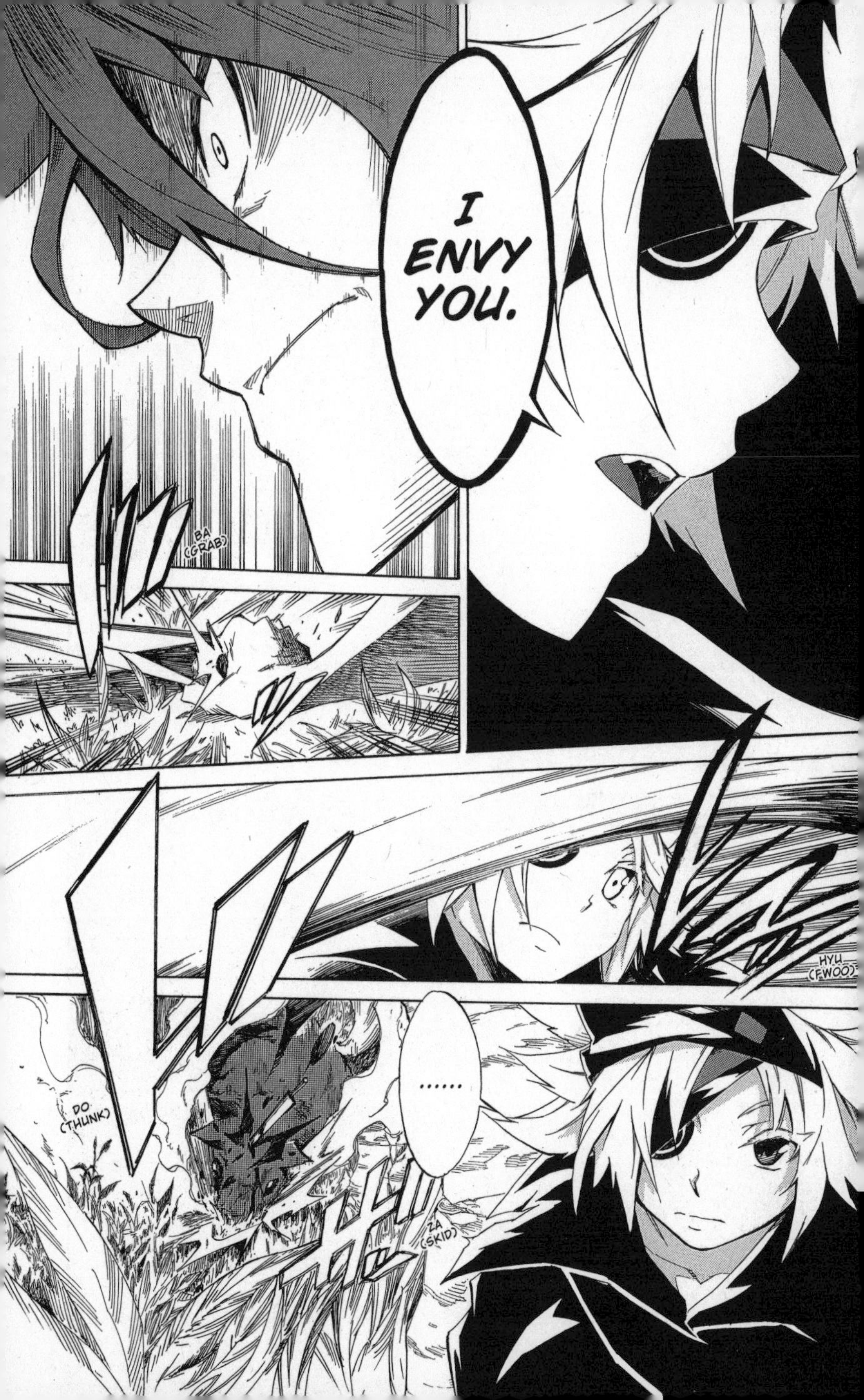
I ENVY YOU.
BA (GRAB)
HYU (FWOO)
......
ZA (SKID)
DO (THUNK)

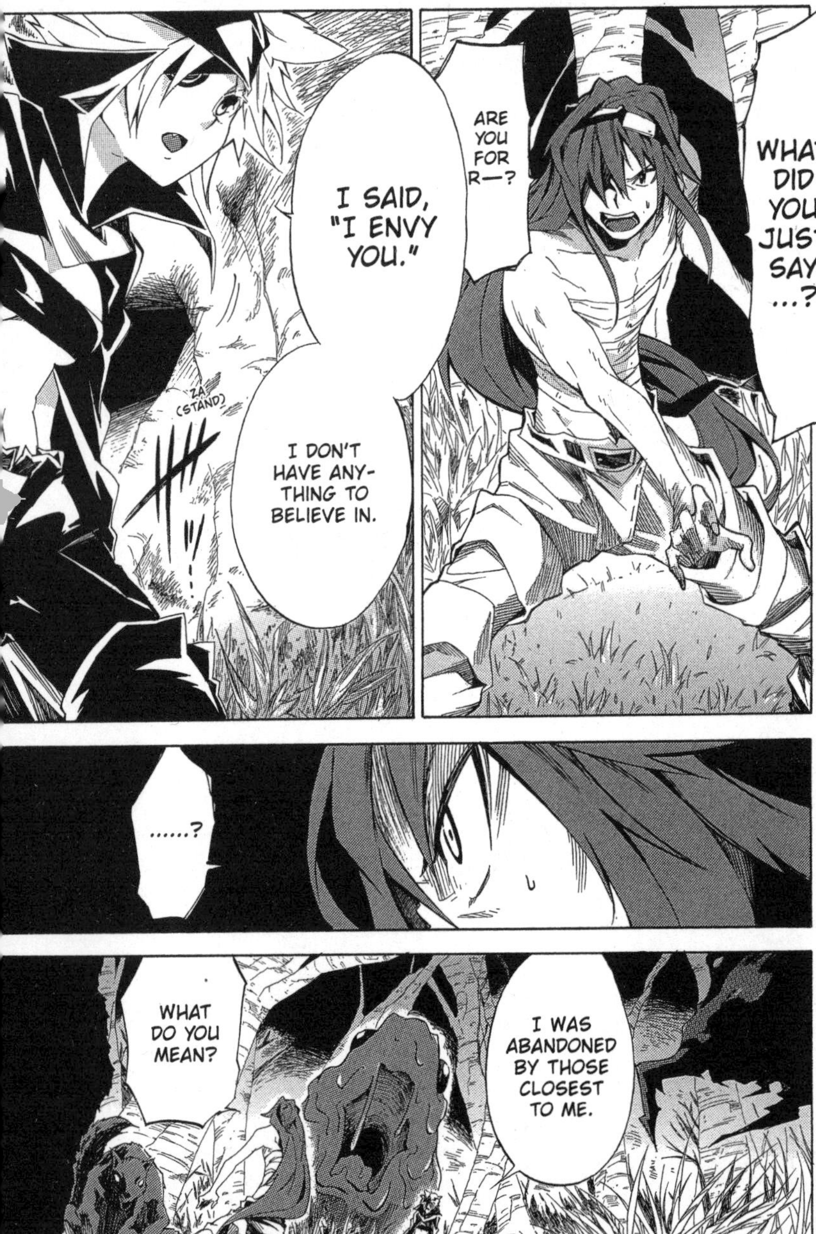
WHAT DID YOU JUST SAY ...?
ARE YOU FOR R—?
I SAID, "I ENVY YOU."
ZA (STAND)
I DON'T HAVE ANY-THING TO BELIEVE IN.
......?
WHAT DO YOU MEAN?
I WAS ABANDONED BY THOSE CLOSEST TO ME.

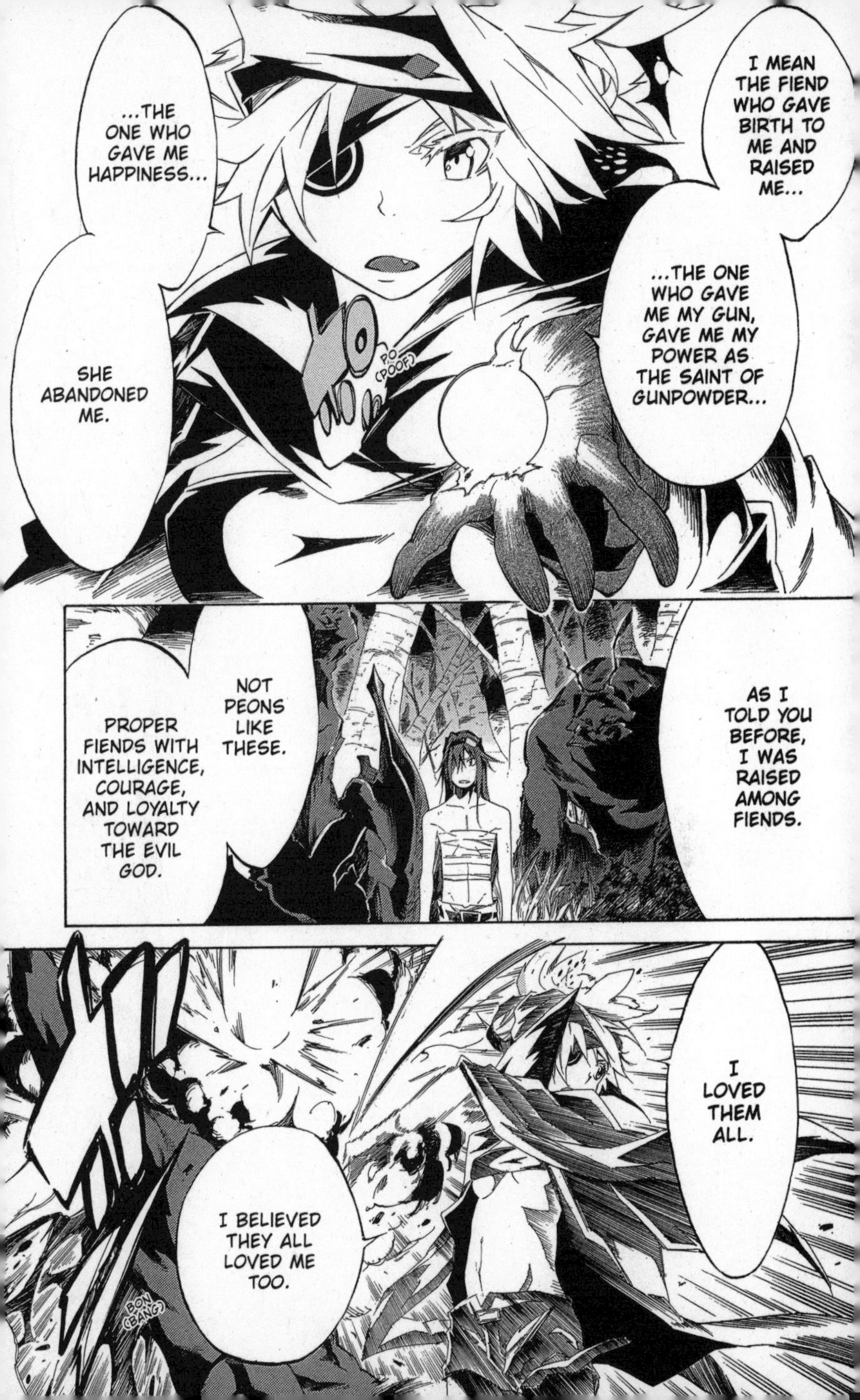
I MEAN THE FIEND WHO GAVE BIRTH TO ME AND RAISED ME...
...THE ONE WHO GAVE ME MY GUN, GAVE ME MY POWER AS THE SAINT OF GUNPOWDER...
PO (POOF)
...THE ONE WHO GAVE ME HAPPINESS...
SHE ABANDONED ME.
AS I TOLD YOU BEFORE, I WAS RAISED AMONG FIENDS.
NOT PEONS LIKE THESE.
PROPER FIENDS WITH INTELLIGENCE, COURAGE, AND LOYALTY TOWARD THE EVIL GOD.
I LOVED THEM ALL.
I BELIEVED THEY ALL LOVED ME TOO.
BON (BANG)

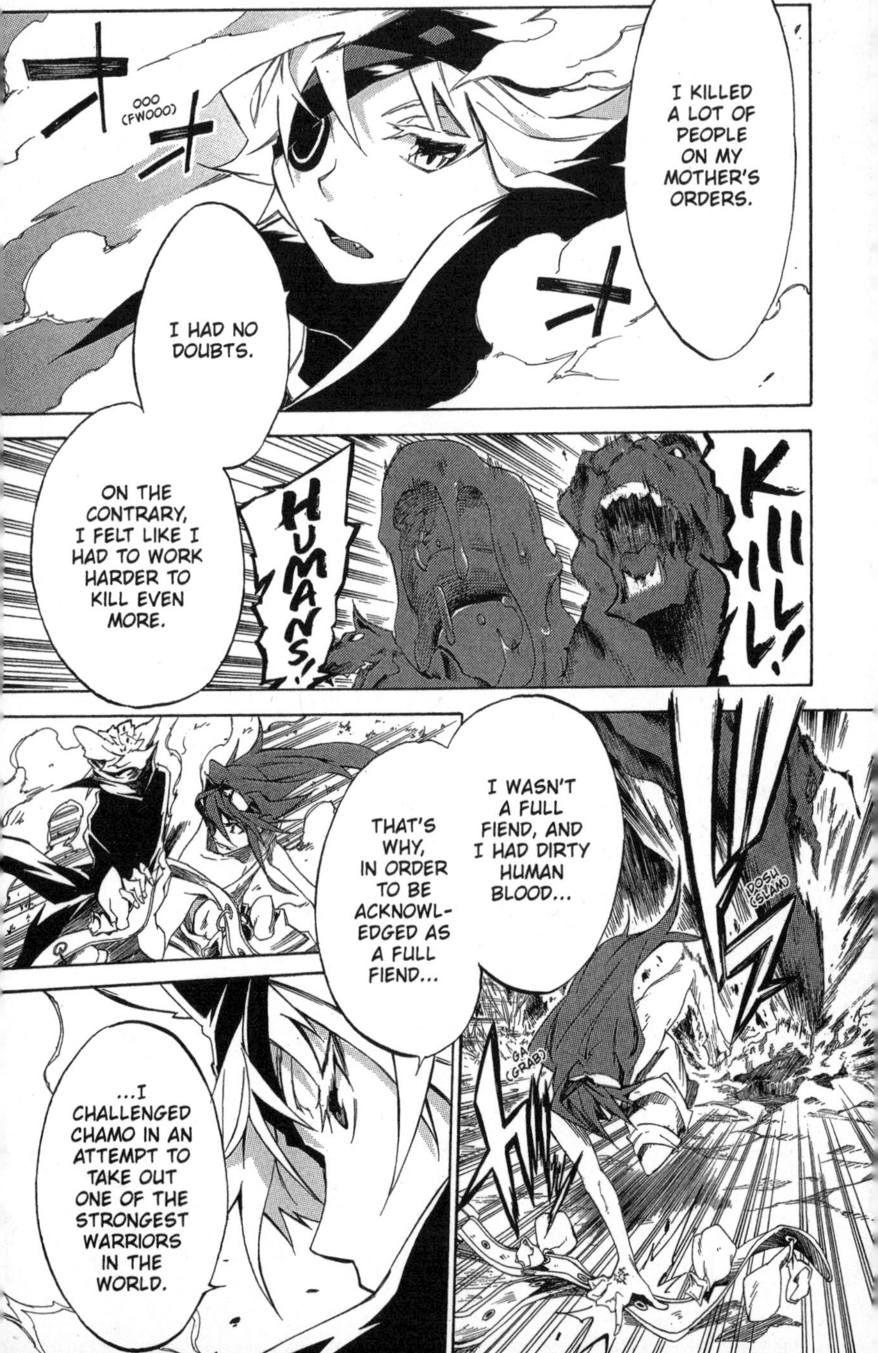
I KILLED A LOT OF PEOPLE ON MY MOTHER'S ORDERS.
OOO (FWOOO)
I HAD NO DOUBTS.
KIIILLL!
HUMANS!!
ON THE CONTRARY, I FELT LIKE I HAD TO WORK HARDER TO KILL EVEN MORE.
DOSH (SLAM)
I WASN'T A FULL FIEND, AND I HAD DIRTY HUMAN BLOOD...
THAT'S WHY, IN ORDER TO BE ACKNOWL-EDGED AS A FULL FIEND...
GA (GRAB)
...I CHALLENGED CHAMO IN AN ATTEMPT TO TAKE OUT ONE OF THE STRONGEST WARRIORS IN THE WORLD.

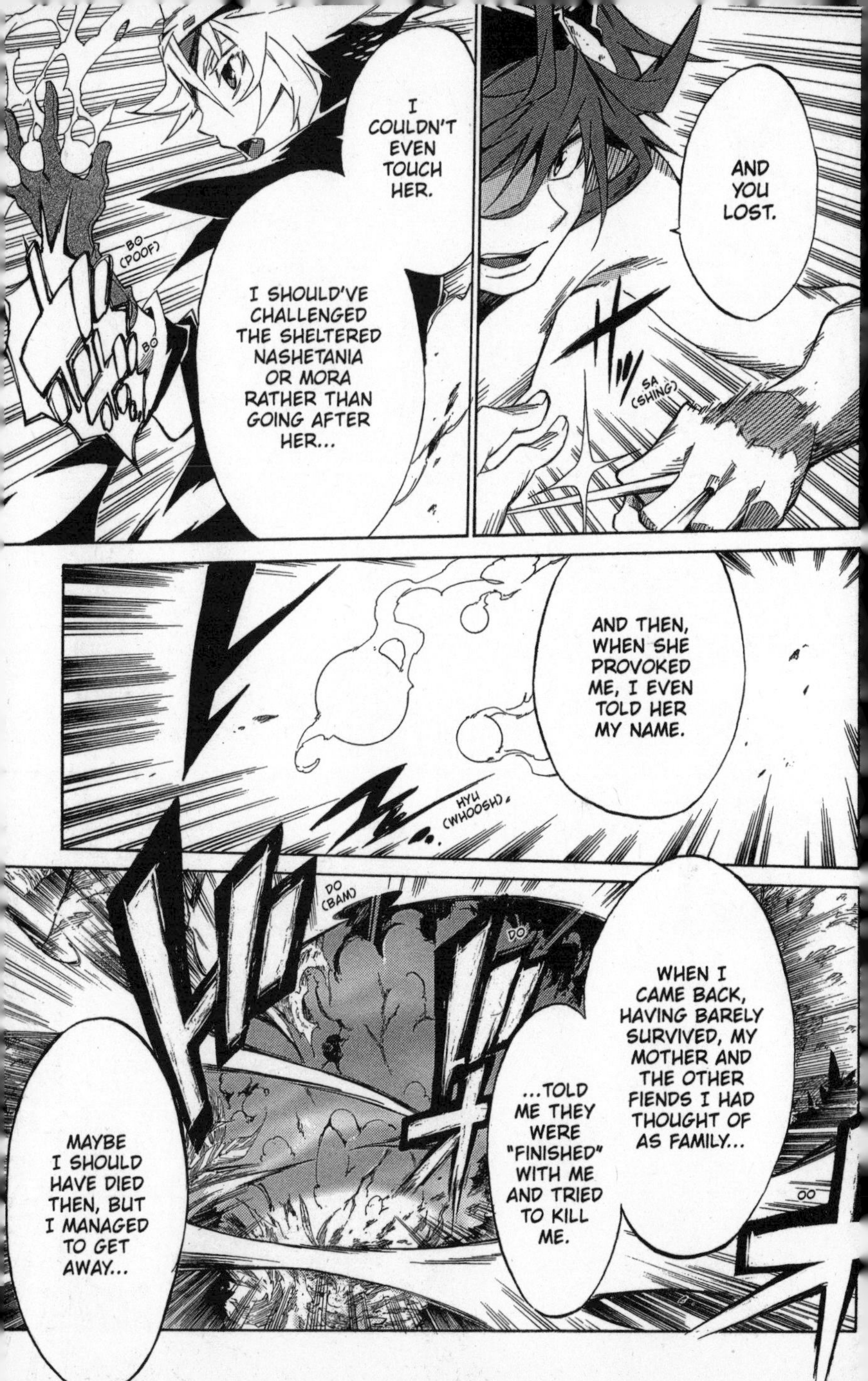
AND YOU LOST.
SA (SHING)
I COULDN'T EVEN TOUCH HER.
I SHOULD'VE CHALLENGED THE SHELTERED NASHETANIA OR MORA RATHER THAN GOING AFTER HER...
BO (POOF)
BO
AND THEN, WHEN SHE PROVOKED ME, I EVEN TOLD HER MY NAME.
HYU (WHOOSH)
WHEN I CAME BACK, HAVING BARELY SURVIVED, MY MOTHER AND THE OTHER FIENDS I HAD THOUGHT OF AS FAMILY...
...TOLD ME THEY WERE "FINISHED" WITH ME AND TRIED TO KILL ME.
DO (BAM)
DO
OO
MAYBE I SHOULD HAVE DIED THEN, BUT I MANAGED TO GET AWAY...

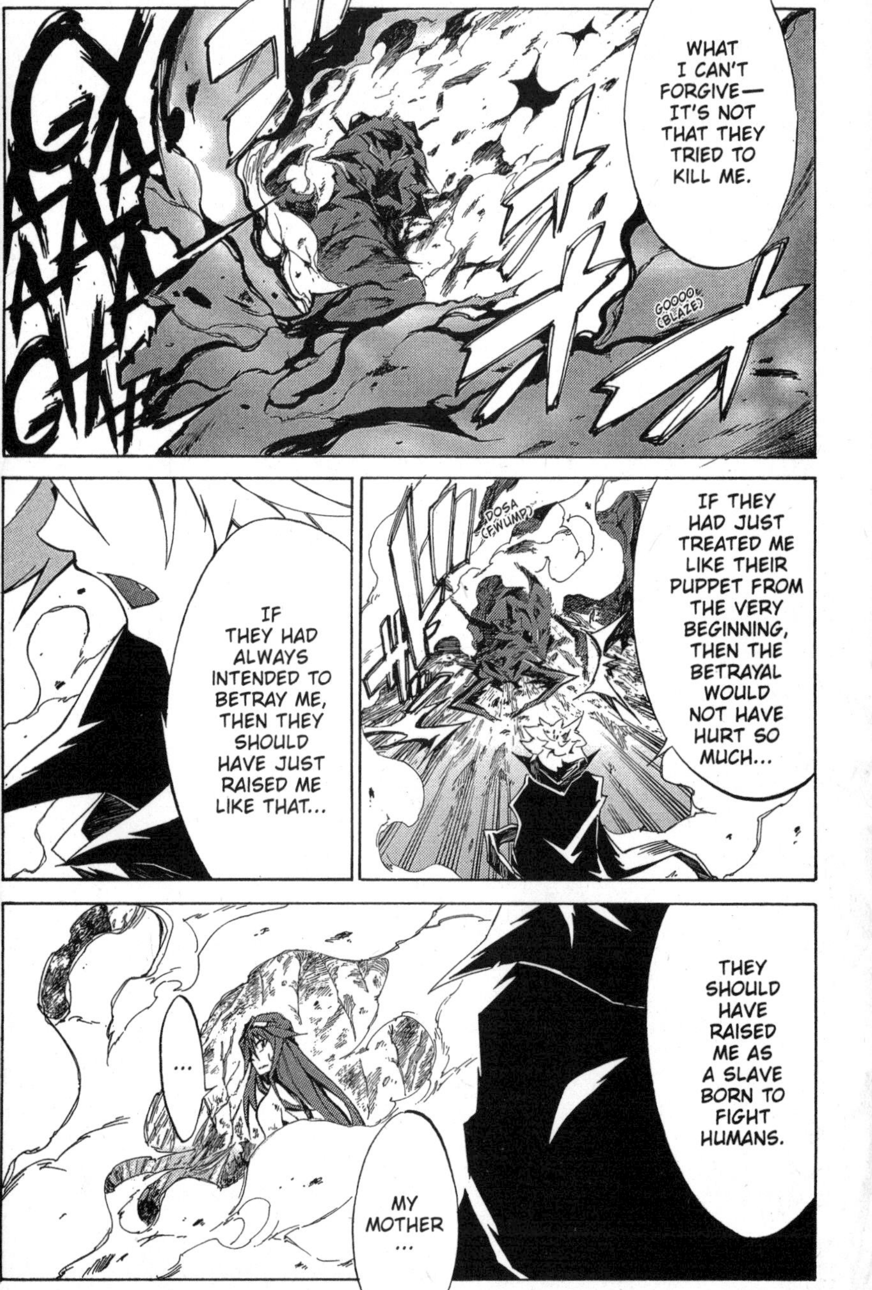
WHAT I CAN'T FORGIVE— IT'S NOT THAT THEY TRIED TO KILL ME.
GOOOO (BLAZE)
IF THEY HAD JUST TREATED ME LIKE THEIR PUPPET FROM THE VERY BEGINNING, THEN THE BETRAYAL WOULD NOT HAVE HURT SO MUCH...
DOSA (FWUMP)
IF THEY HAD ALWAYS INTENDED TO BETRAY ME, THEN THEY SHOULD HAVE JUST RAISED ME LIKE THAT...
THEY SHOULD HAVE RAISED ME AS A SLAVE BORN TO FIGHT HUMANS.
...
MY MOTHER ...

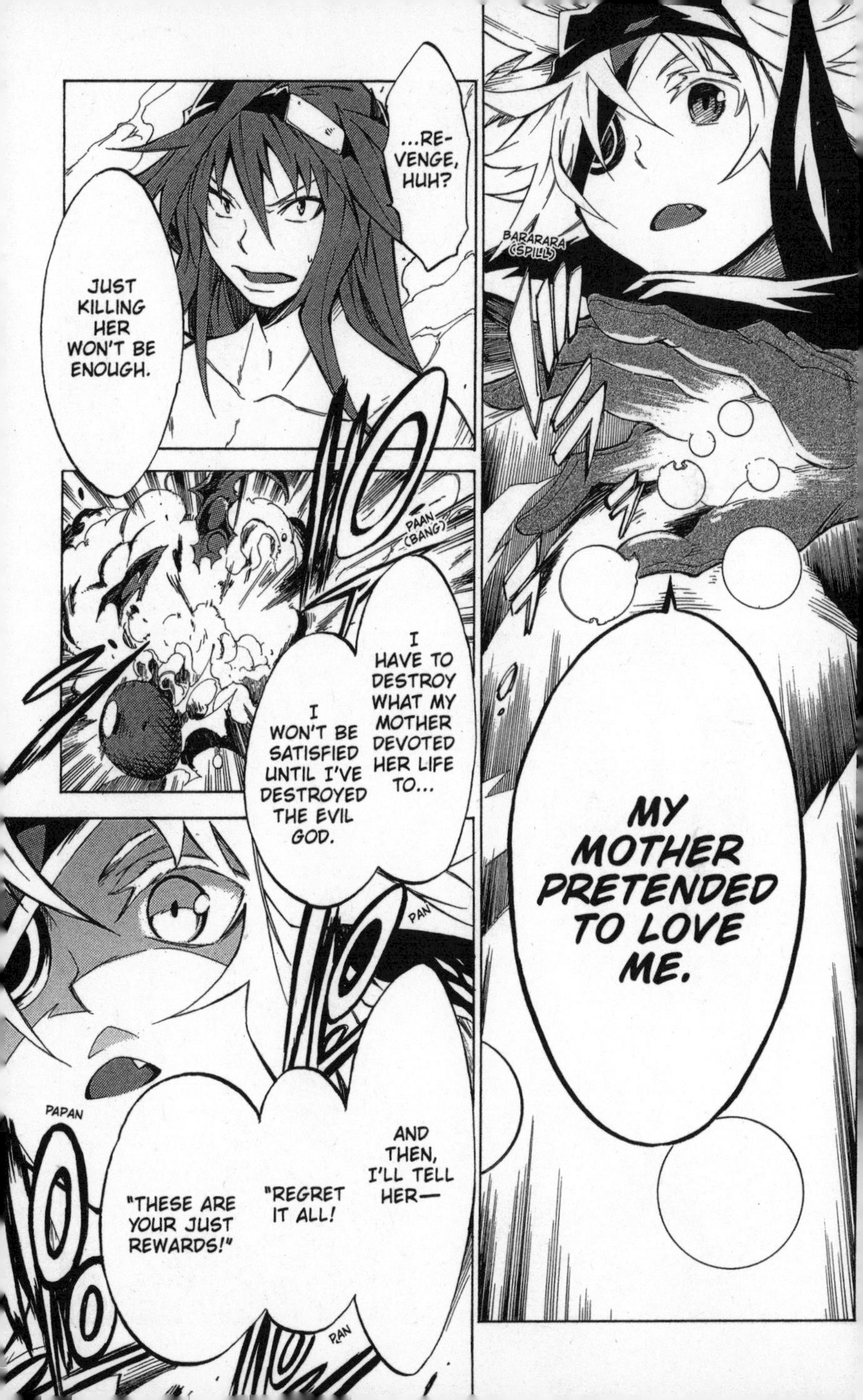
BARARARA (SPILLS)
MY MOTHER PRETENDED TO LOVE ME.
...RE-VENGE, HUH?
JUST KILLING HER WON'T BE ENOUGH.
PAAN (BANG)
I HAVE TO DESTROY WHAT MY MOTHER DEVOTED HER LIFE TO...
I WON'T BE SATISFIED UNTIL I'VE DESTROYED THE EVIL GOD.
PAN
AND THEN, I'LL TELL HER—
"REGRET IT ALL!
"THESE ARE YOUR JUST REWARDS!"
PAPAN
PAN

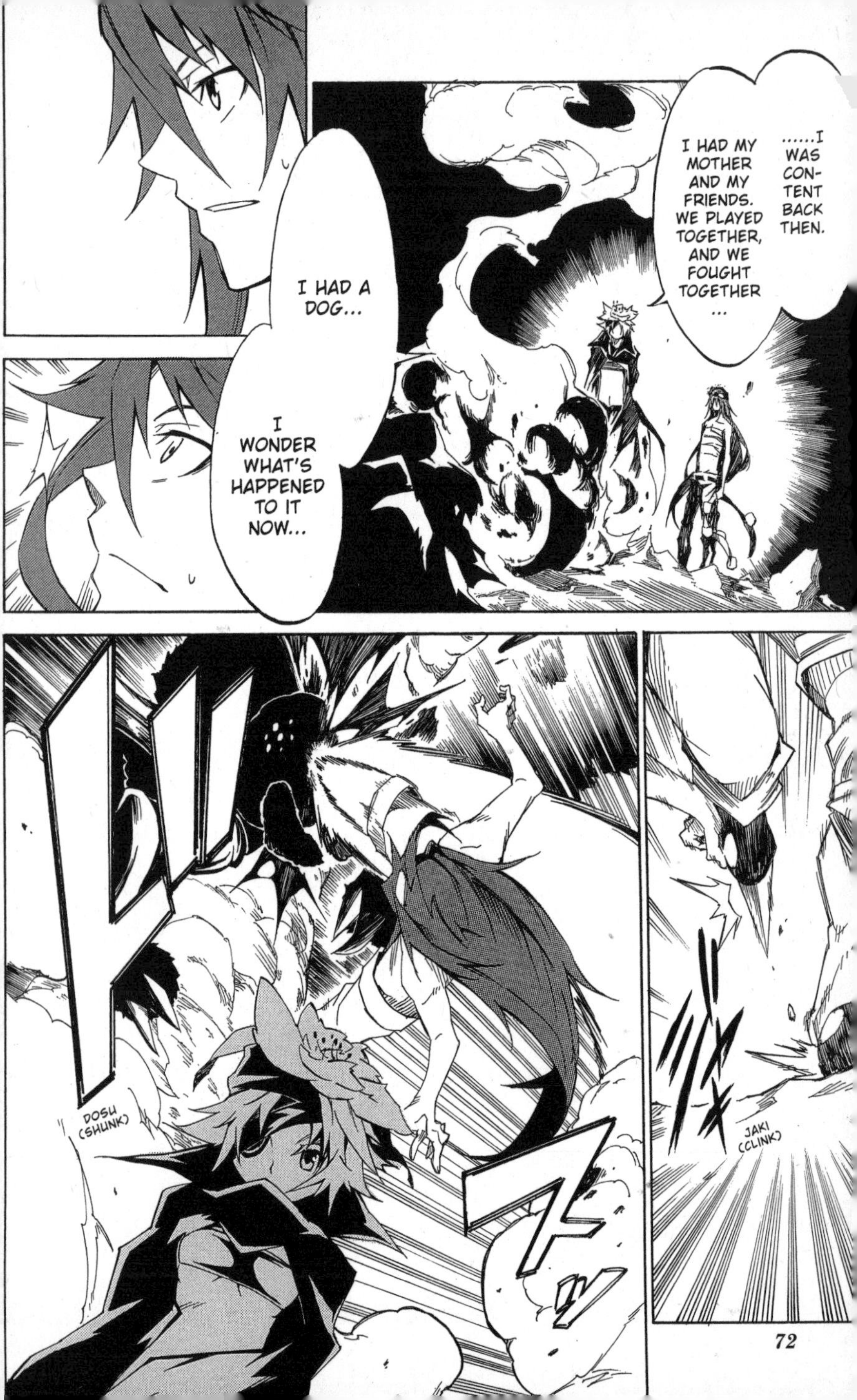
......I WAS CON-TENT BACK THEN.
I HAD MY MOTHER AND MY FRIENDS. WE PLAYED TOGETHER, AND WE FOUGHT TOGETHER...
I HAD A DOG...
I WONDER WHAT'S HAPPENED TO IT NOW...
JAKI (CLINK)
DOSU (SHUNK)

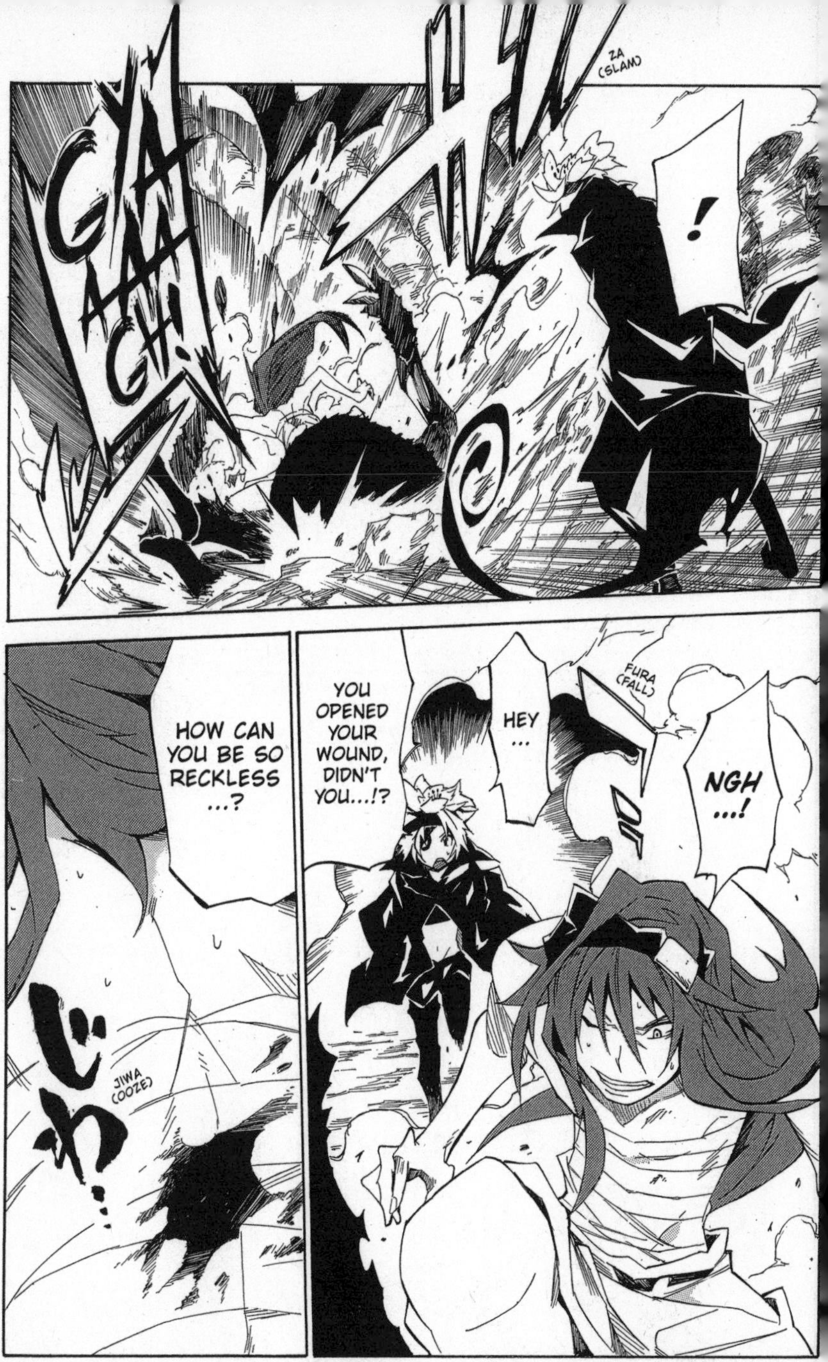
ZA (SLAM)
!
GAAACH!
NGH...!
FURA (FALL)
HEY...
YOU OPENED YOUR WOUND, DIDN'T YOU...!?
HOW CAN YOU BE SO RECKLESS...?
JIWA (OOZE)

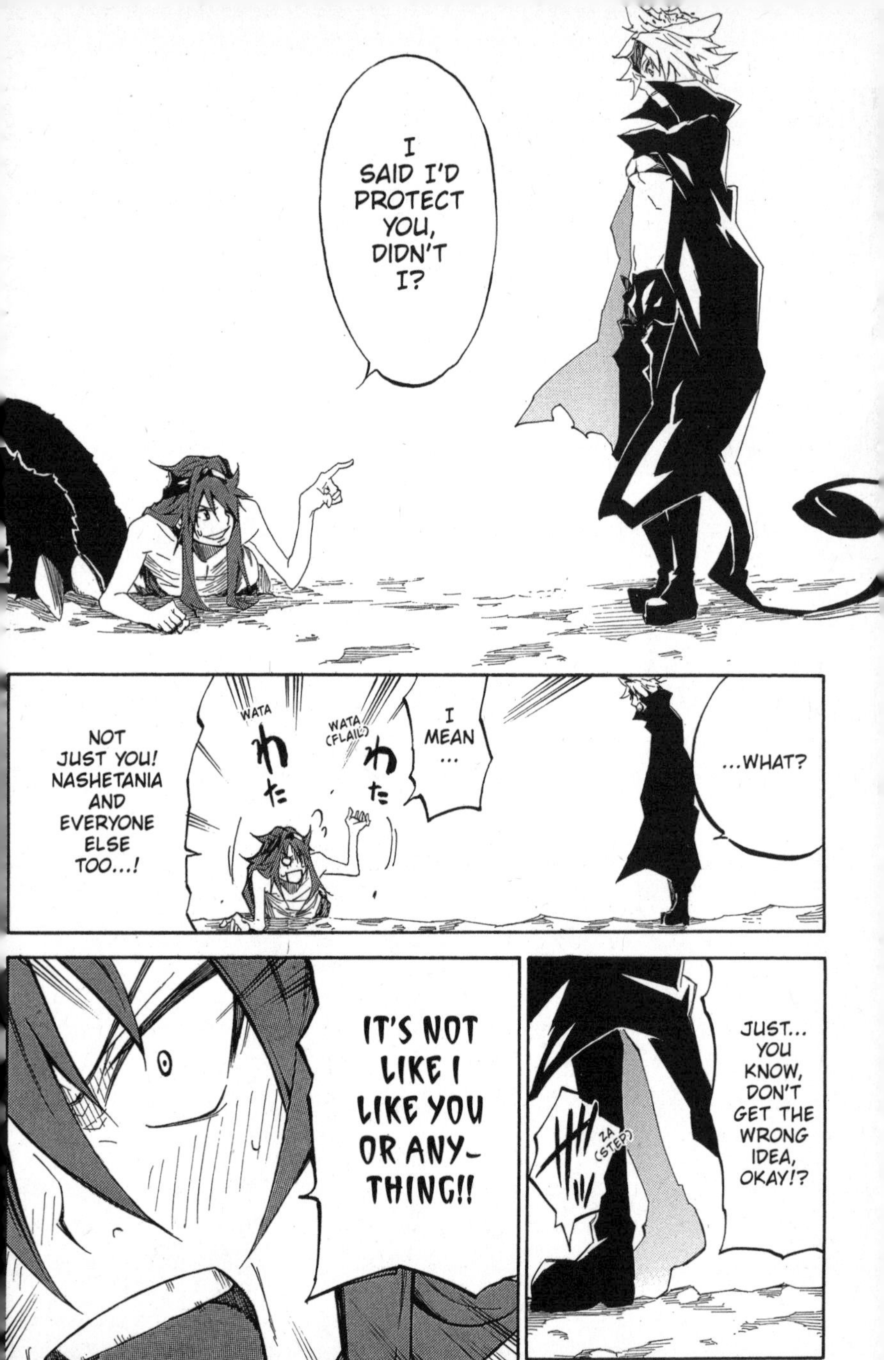
I SAID I'D PROTECT YOU, DIDN'T I?
...WHAT?
I MEAN ...
WATA (FLAIL)
わた
WATA
わた
NOT JUST YOU! NASHETANIA AND EVERYONE ELSE TOO...!
JUST... YOU KNOW, DON'T GET THE WRONG IDEA, OKAY!?
ZA (STEP)
IT'S NOT LIKE I LIKE YOU OR ANY-THING!!

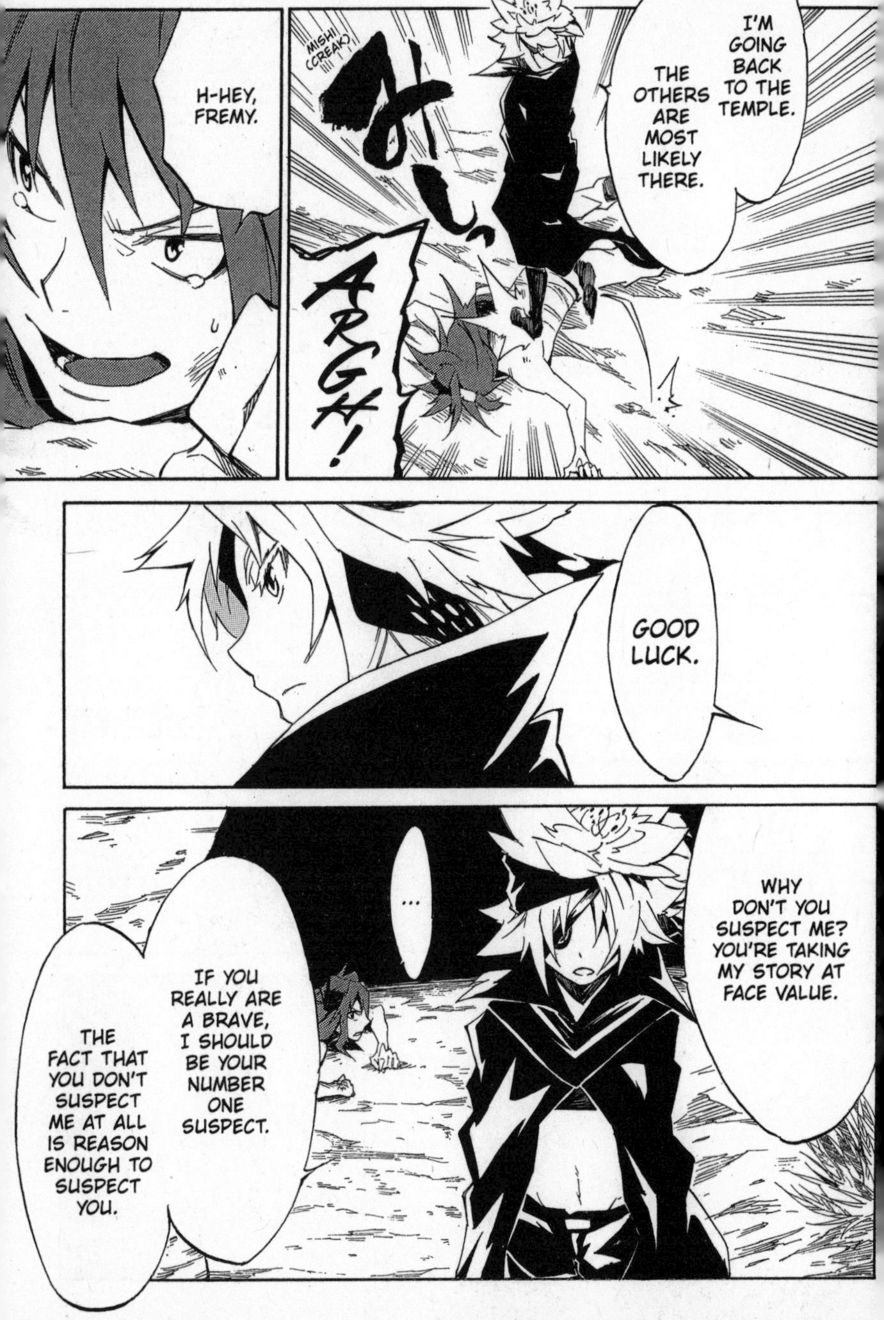
I'M GOING BACK TO THE TEMPLE.
THE OTHERS ARE MOST LIKELY THERE.
MISHI (CREAK)
ARGH!
H-HEY, FREMY.
GOOD LUCK.
WHY DON'T YOU SUSPECT ME? YOU'RE TAKING MY STORY AT FACE VALUE.
...
IF YOU REALLY ARE A BRAVE, I SHOULD BE YOUR NUMBER ONE SUSPECT.
THE FACT THAT YOU DON'T SUSPECT ME AT ALL IS REASON ENOUGH TO SUSPECT YOU.

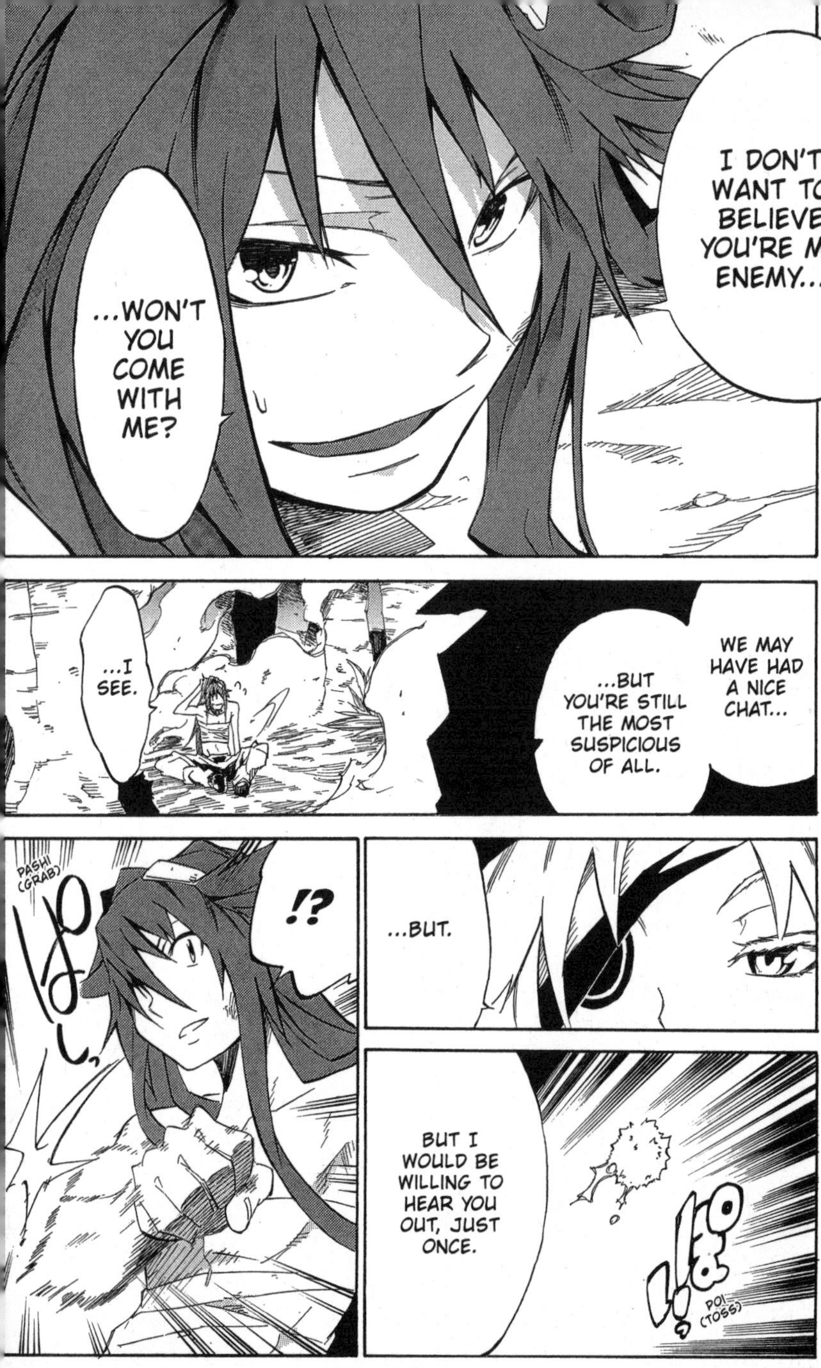
I DON'T WANT TO BELIEVE YOU'RE MY ENEMY...
...WON'T YOU COME WITH ME?
WE MAY HAVE HAD A NICE CHAT...
...BUT YOU'RE STILL THE MOST SUSPICIOUS OF ALL.
...I SEE.
...BUT.
BUT I WOULD BE WILLING TO HEAR YOU OUT, JUST ONCE.
POI (TOSS)
!?
PASHI (GRAB)

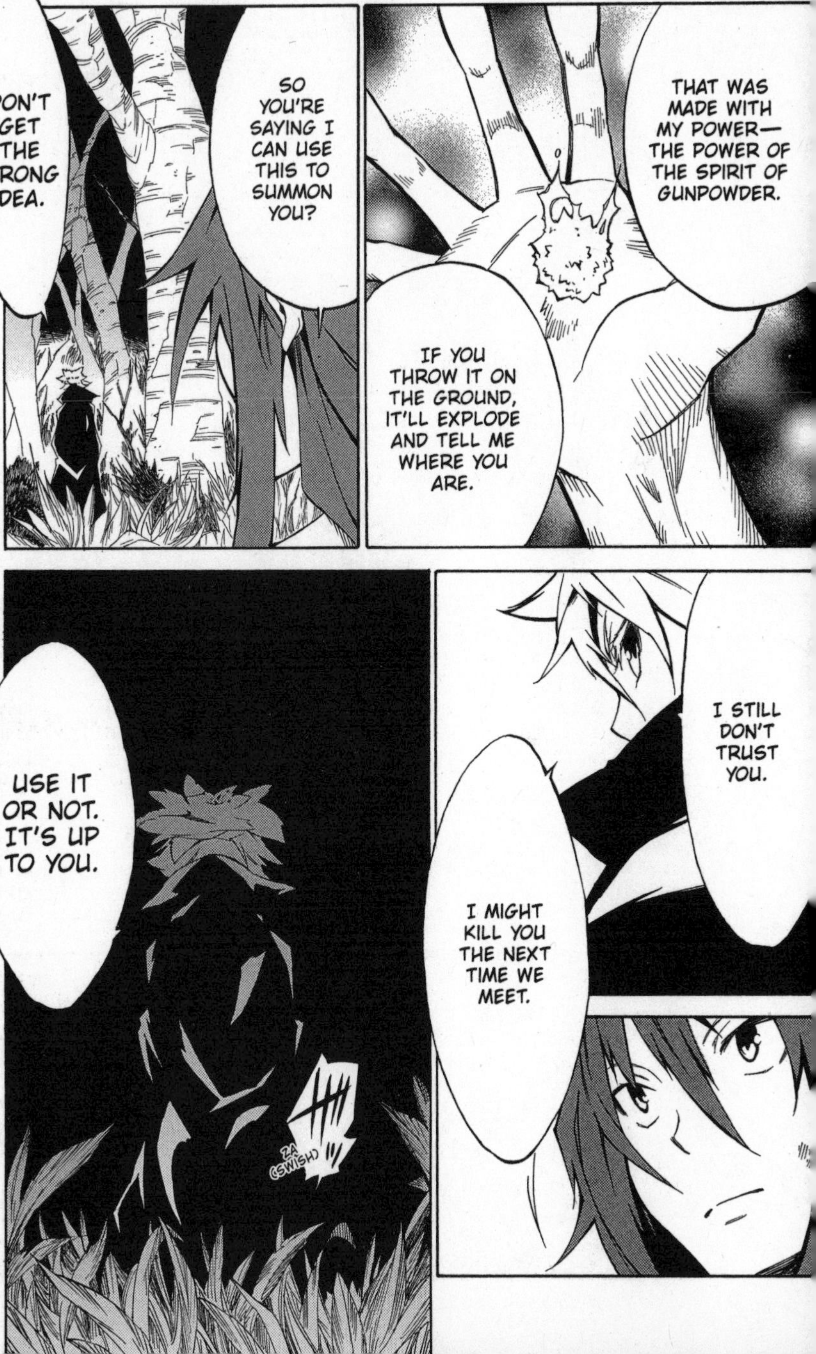
THAT WAS MADE WITH MY POWER—THE POWER OF THE SPIRIT OF GUNPOWDER.
IF YOU THROW IT ON THE GROUND, IT'LL EXPLODE AND TELL ME WHERE YOU ARE.
SO YOU'RE SAYING I CAN USE THIS TO SUMMON YOU?
DON'T GET THE WRONG IDEA.
I STILL DON'T TRUST YOU.
I MIGHT KILL YOU THE NEXT TIME WE MEET.
USE IT OR NOT. IT'S UP TO YOU.
ZA (SWISH)

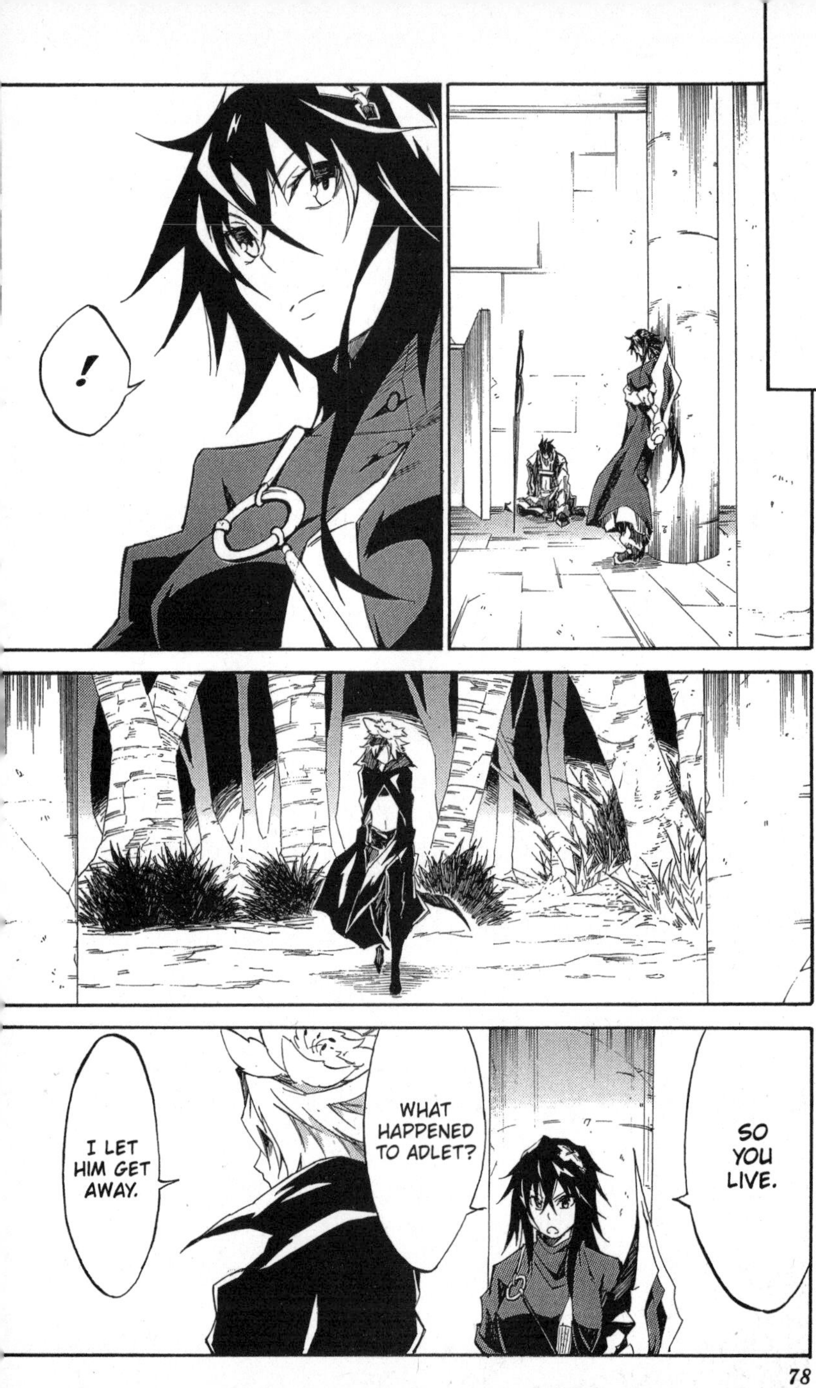
!
SO YOU LIVE.
WHAT HAPPENED TO ADLET?
I LET HIM GET AWAY.

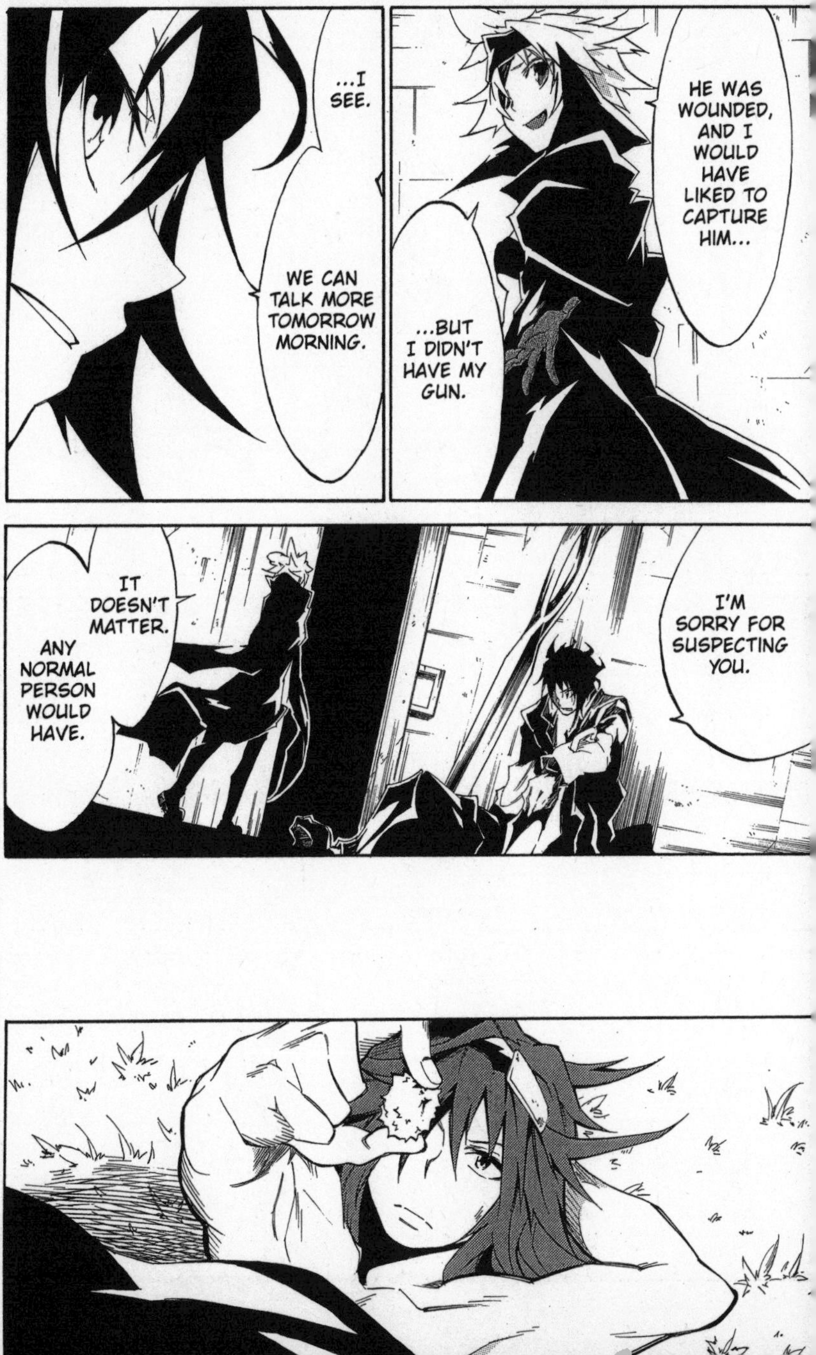
HE WAS WOUNDED, AND I WOULD HAVE LIKED TO CAPTURE HIM...
...BUT I DIDN'T HAVE MY GUN.
...I SEE.
WE CAN TALK MORE TOMORROW MORNING.
I'M SORRY FOR SUSPECTING YOU.
IT DOESN'T MATTER.
ANY NORMAL PERSON WOULD HAVE.

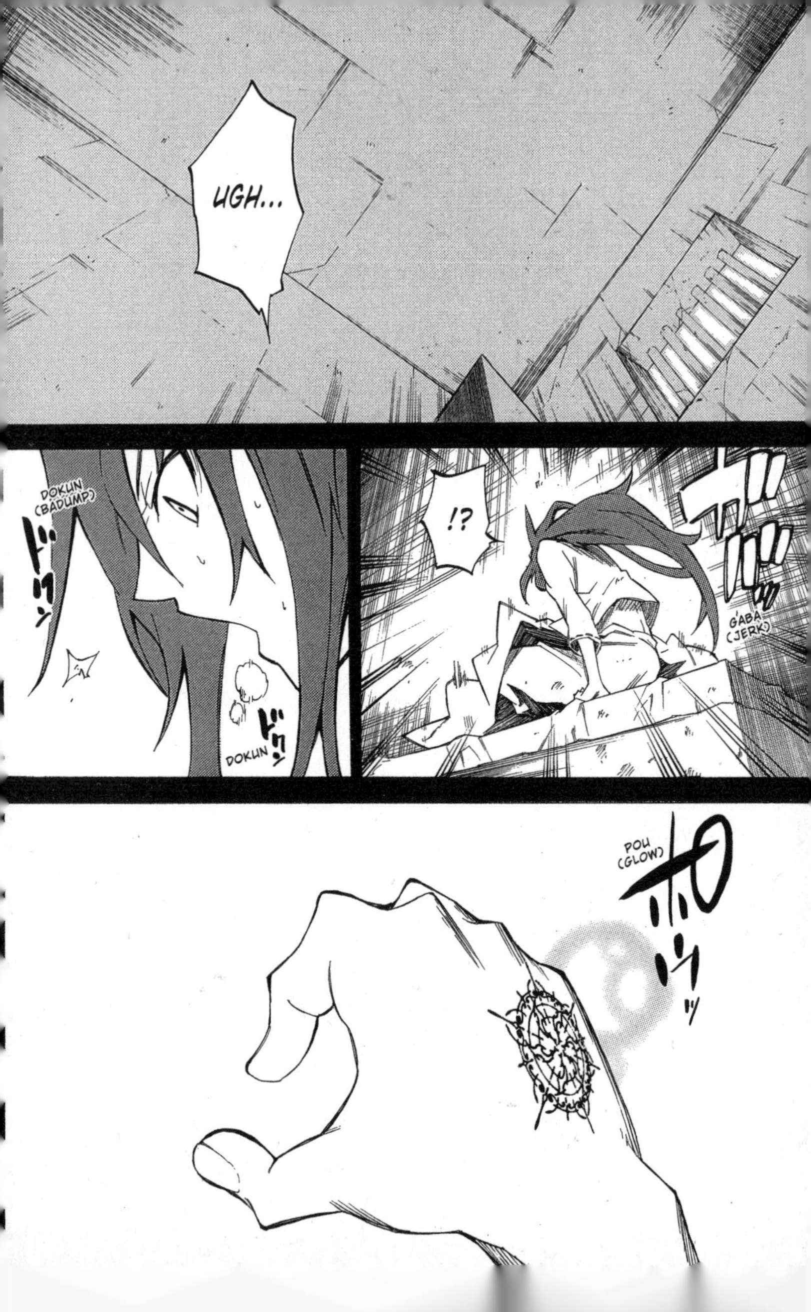
UGH...
!?
GABA (JERK)
DOKUN (BADUMP)
DOKUN
POU (GLOW)

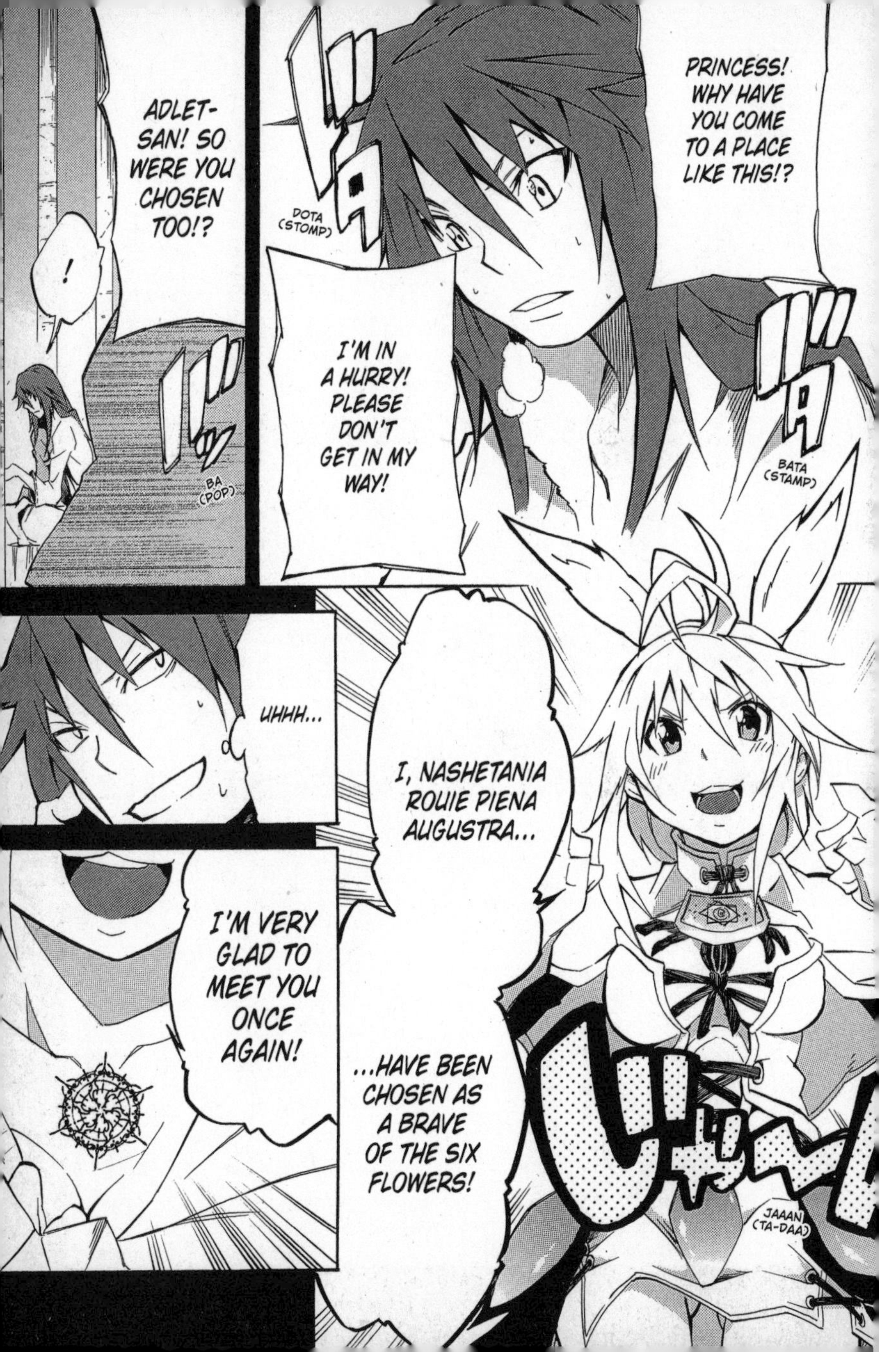
PRINCESS! WHY HAVE YOU COME TO A PLACE LIKE THIS!?
BATA (STAMP)
I'M IN A HURRY! PLEASE DON'T GET IN MY WAY!
DOTA (STOMP)
ADLET-SAN! SO WERE YOU CHOSEN TOO!?
!
BA (POP)
I, NASHETANIA ROUIE PIENA AUGUSTRA...
...HAVE BEEN CHOSEN AS A BRAVE OF THE SIX FLOWERS!
JAAAN (TA-DAA)
UHHH...
I'M VERY GLAD TO MEET YOU ONCE AGAIN!

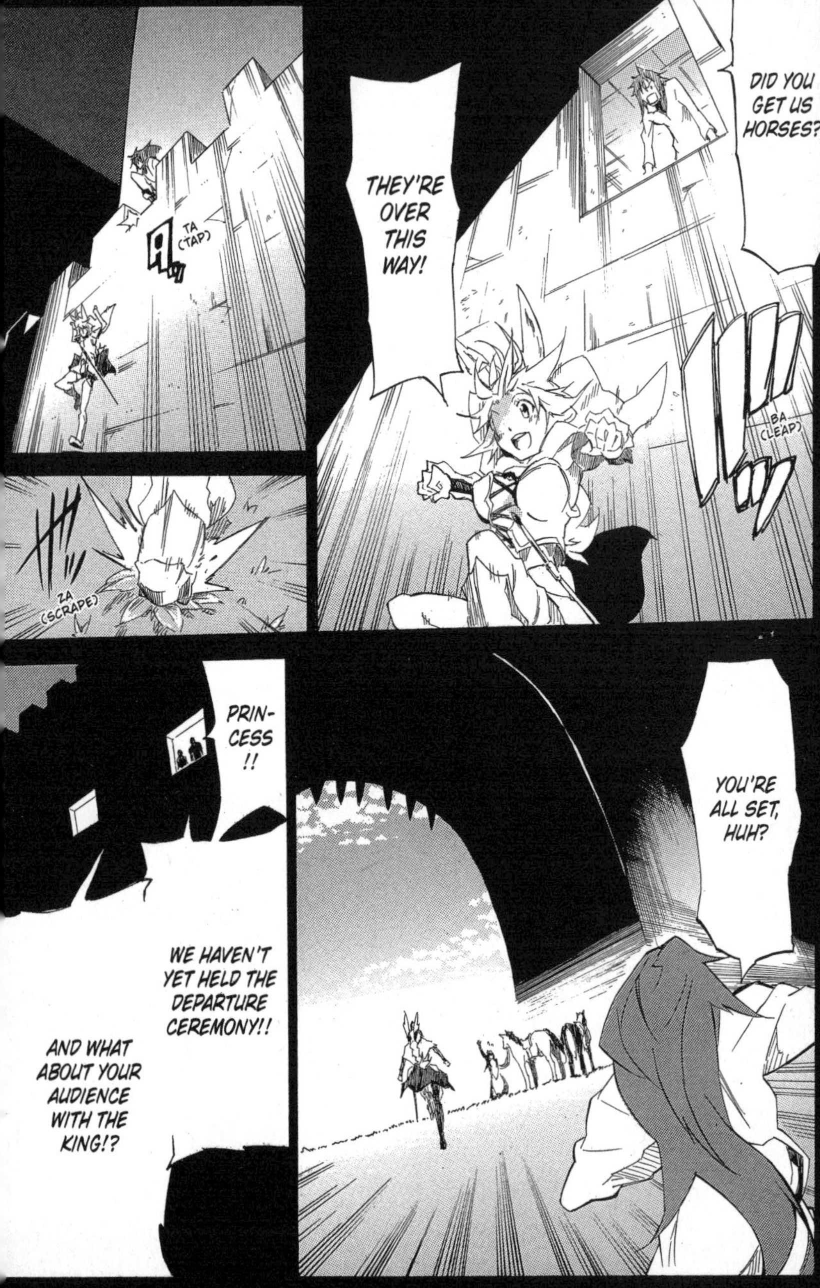
DID YOU GET US HORSES?
THEY'RE OVER THIS WAY!
BA (LEAP)
TA (TAP)
ZA (SCRAPE)
YOU'RE ALL SET, HUH?
PRIN-CESS!!
WE HAVEN'T YET HELD THE DEPARTURE CEREMONY!!
AND WHAT ABOUT YOUR AUDIENCE WITH THE KING!?

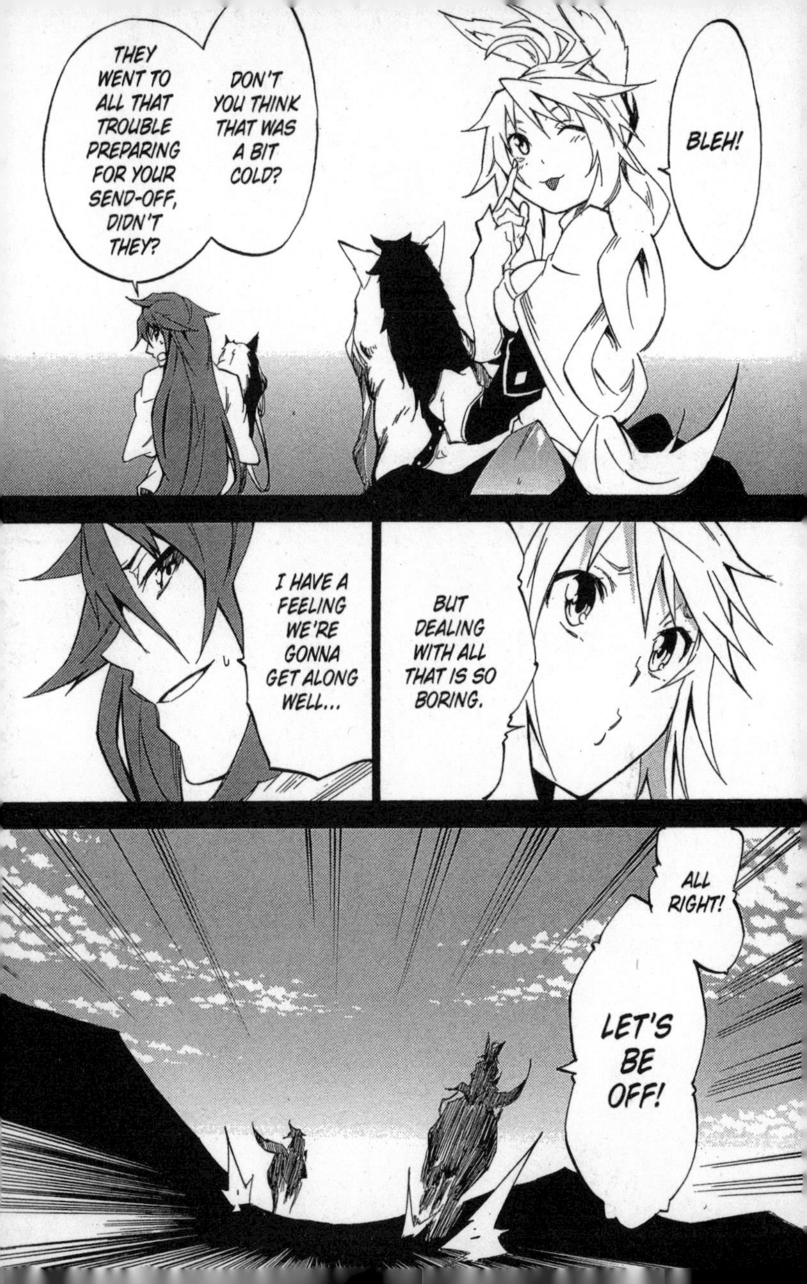
BLEH!
DON'T YOU THINK THAT WAS A BIT COLD?
THEY WENT TO ALL THAT TROUBLE PREPARING FOR YOUR SEND-OFF, DIDN'T THEY?
BUT DEALING WITH ALL THAT IS SO BORING.
I HAVE A FEELING WE'RE GONNA GET ALONG WELL...
ALL RIGHT!
LET'S BE OFF!

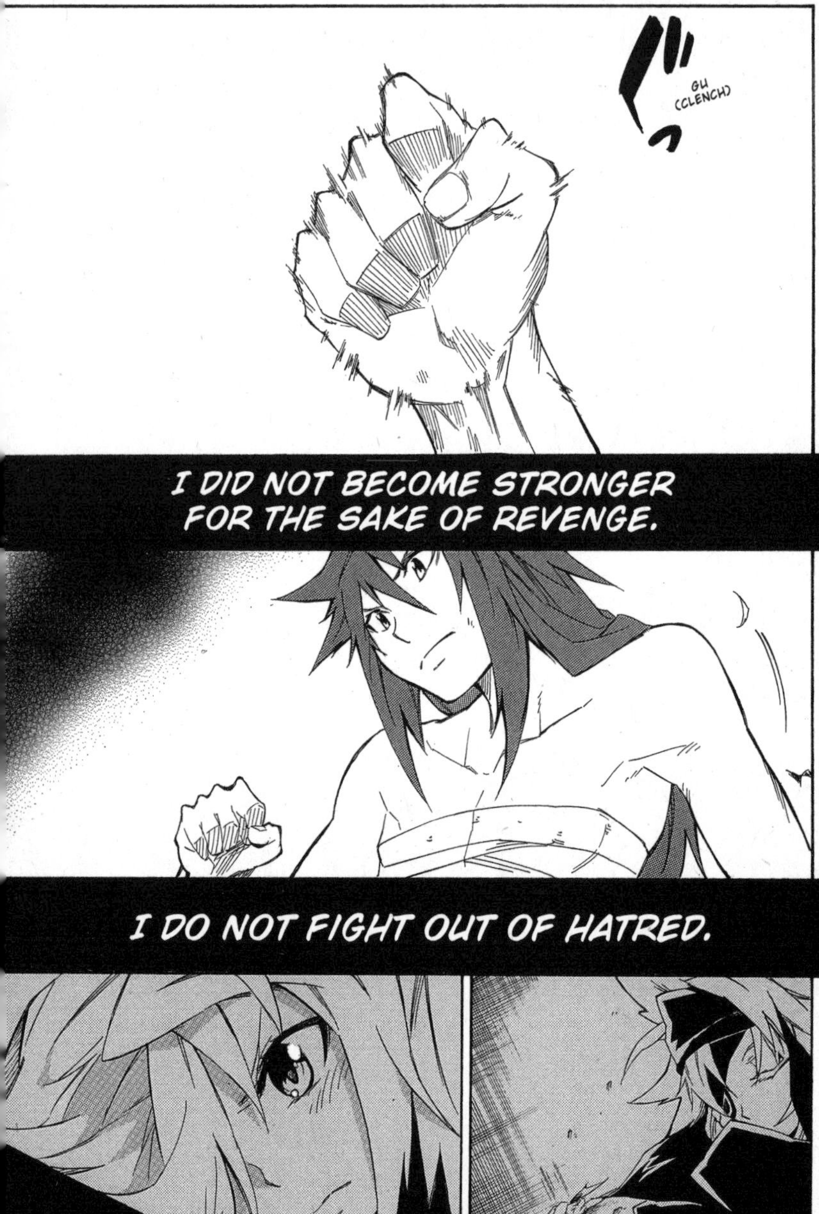
GU
(CLENCH)
I DID NOT BECOME STRONGER
FOR THE SAKE OF REVENGE.
I DO NOT FIGHT OUT OF HATRED.

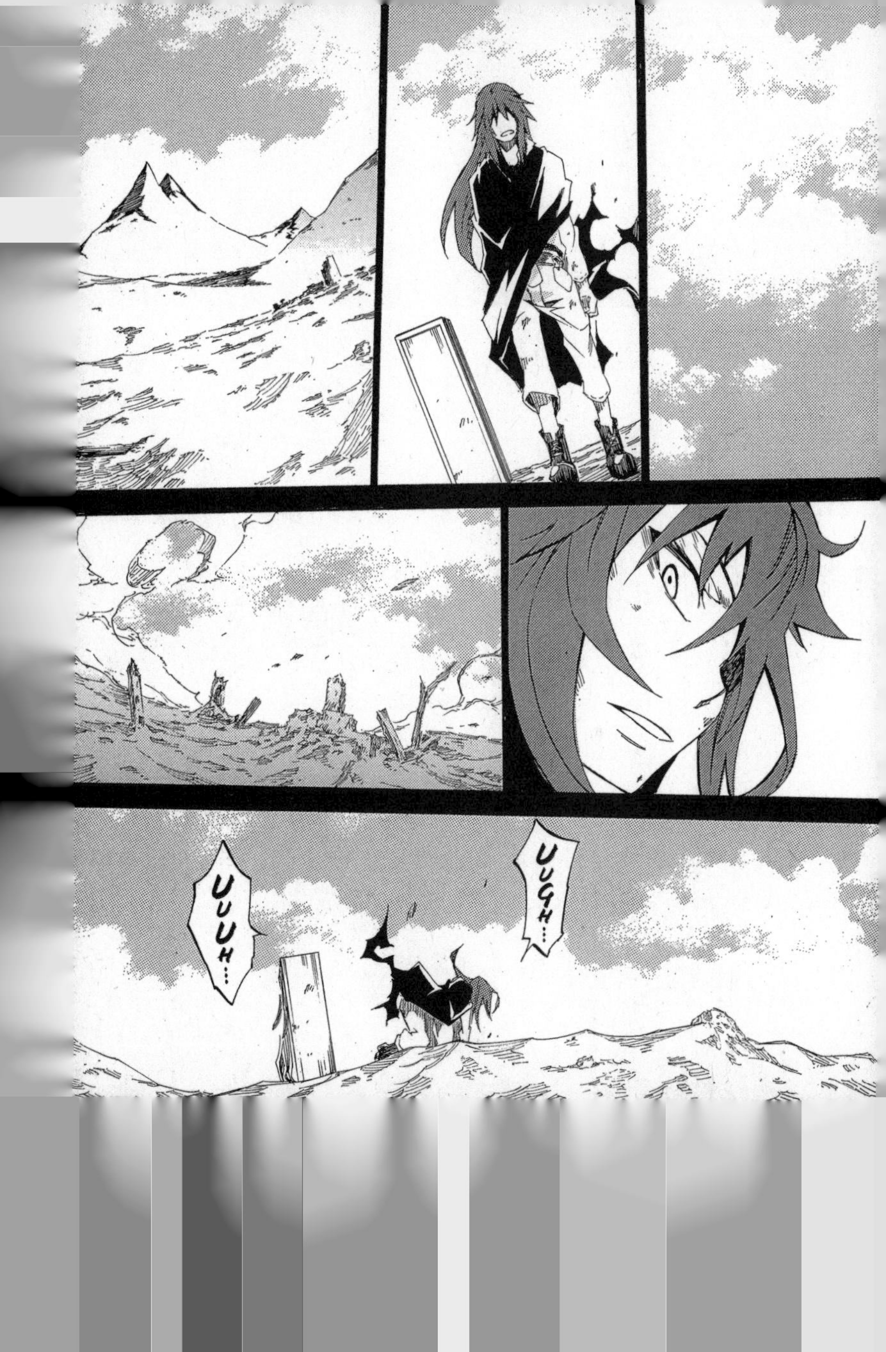
UUGH...
UUUH...

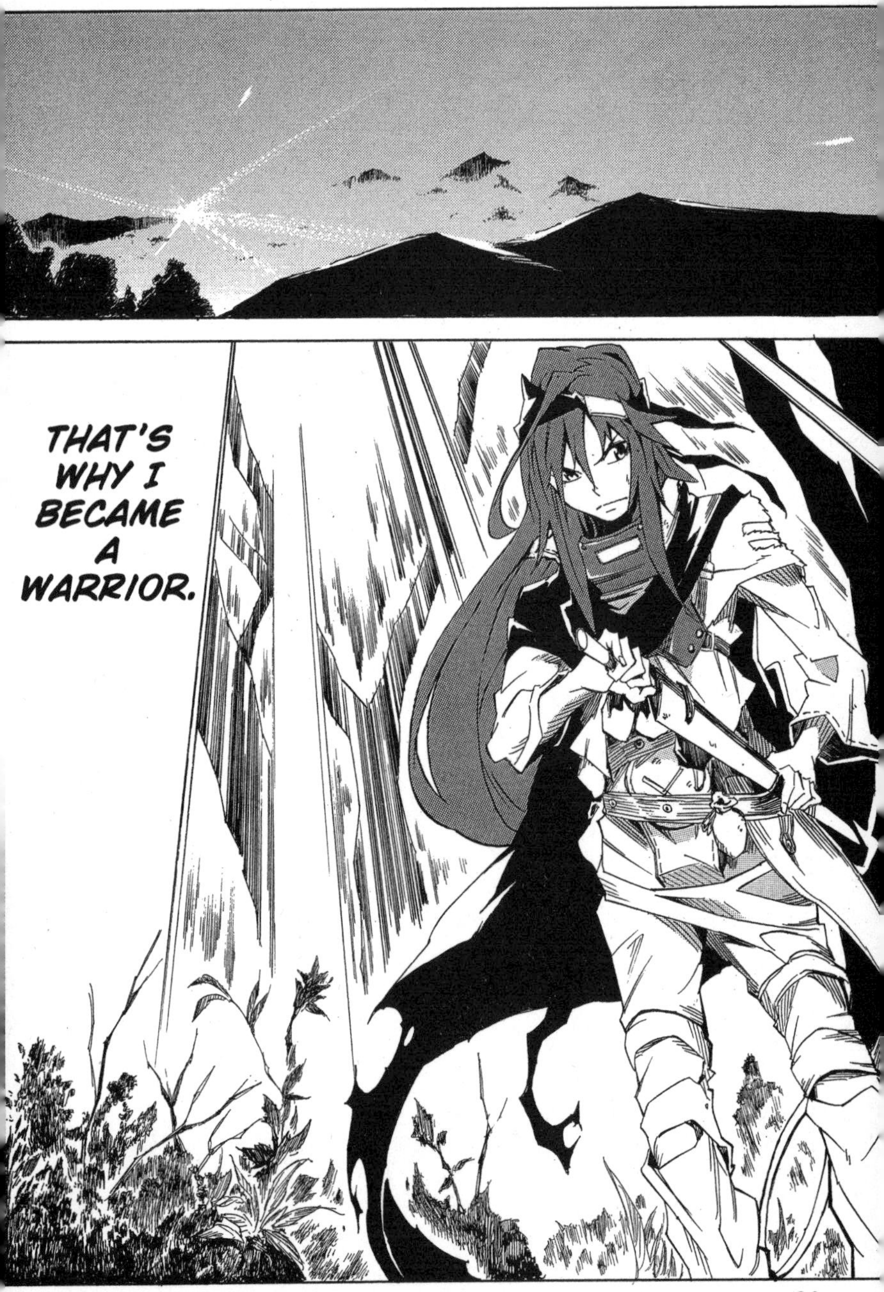
THAT'S WHY I BECAME A WARRIOR.

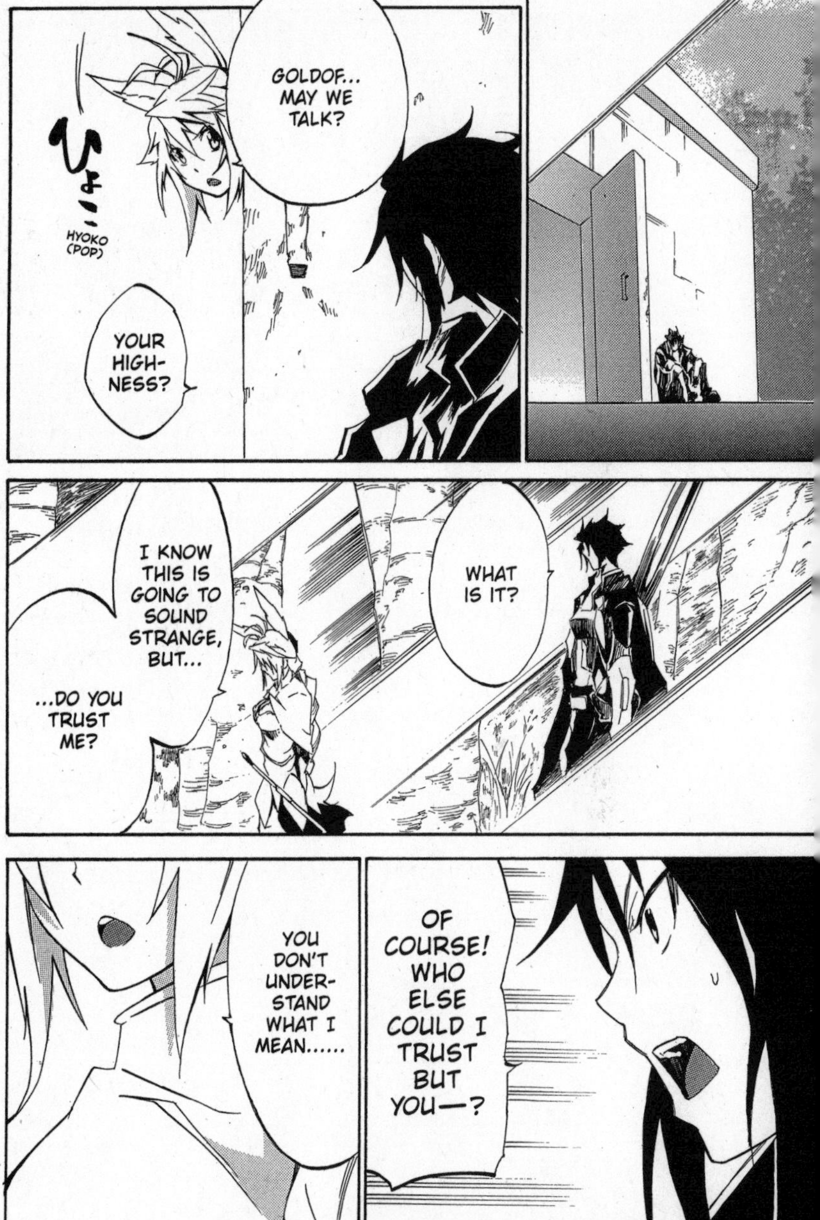
GOLDOF... MAY WE TALK?
ひょこ
HYOKO (POP)
YOUR HIGH-NESS?
WHAT IS IT?
I KNOW THIS IS GOING TO SOUND STRANGE, BUT...
...DO YOU TRUST ME?
OF COURSE! WHO ELSE COULD I TRUST BUT YOU—?
YOU DON'T UNDER-STAND WHAT I MEAN......

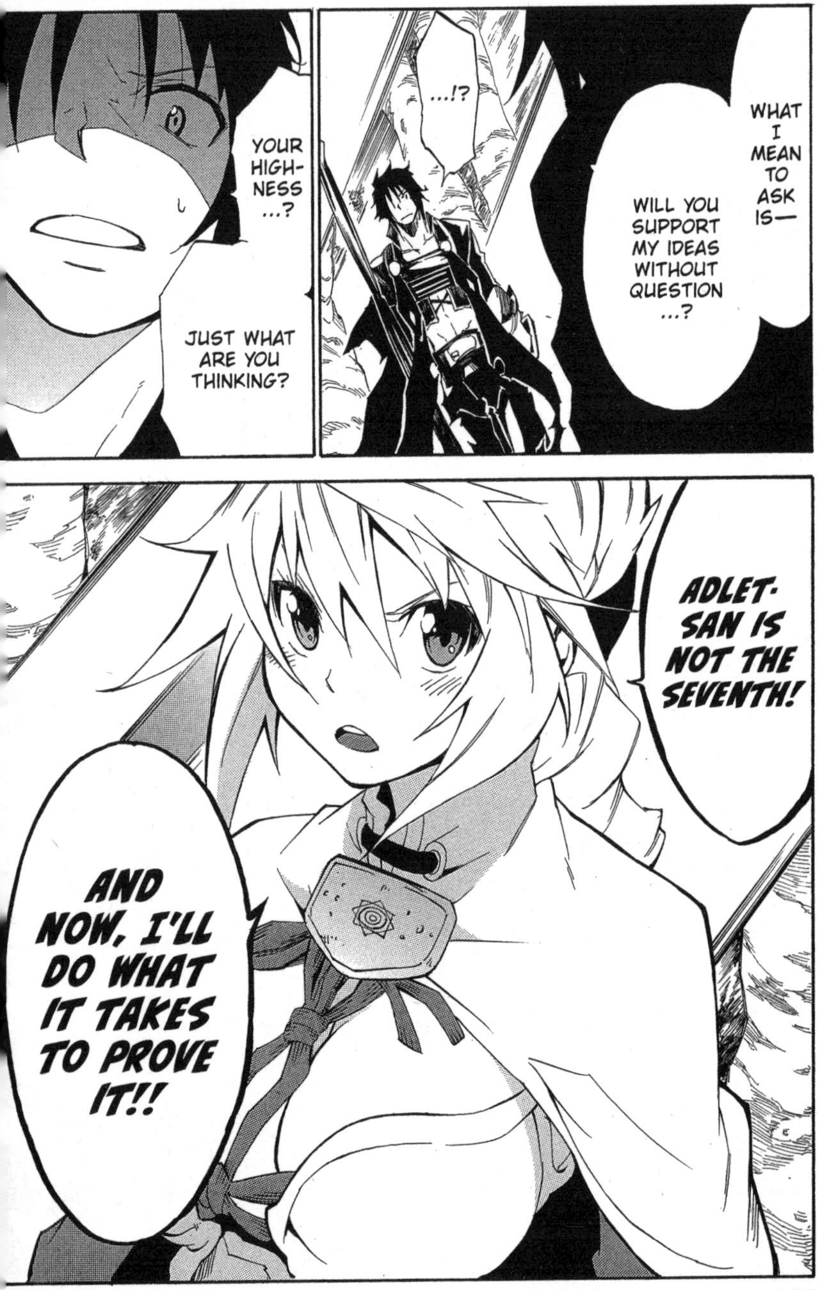
WHAT I MEAN TO ASK IS—
WILL YOU SUPPORT MY IDEAS WITHOUT QUESTION ...?
...!?
YOUR HIGHNESS ...?
JUST WHAT ARE YOU THINKING?
ADLET-SAN IS NOT THE SEVENTH!
AND NOW, I'LL DO WHAT IT TAKES TO PROVE IT!!

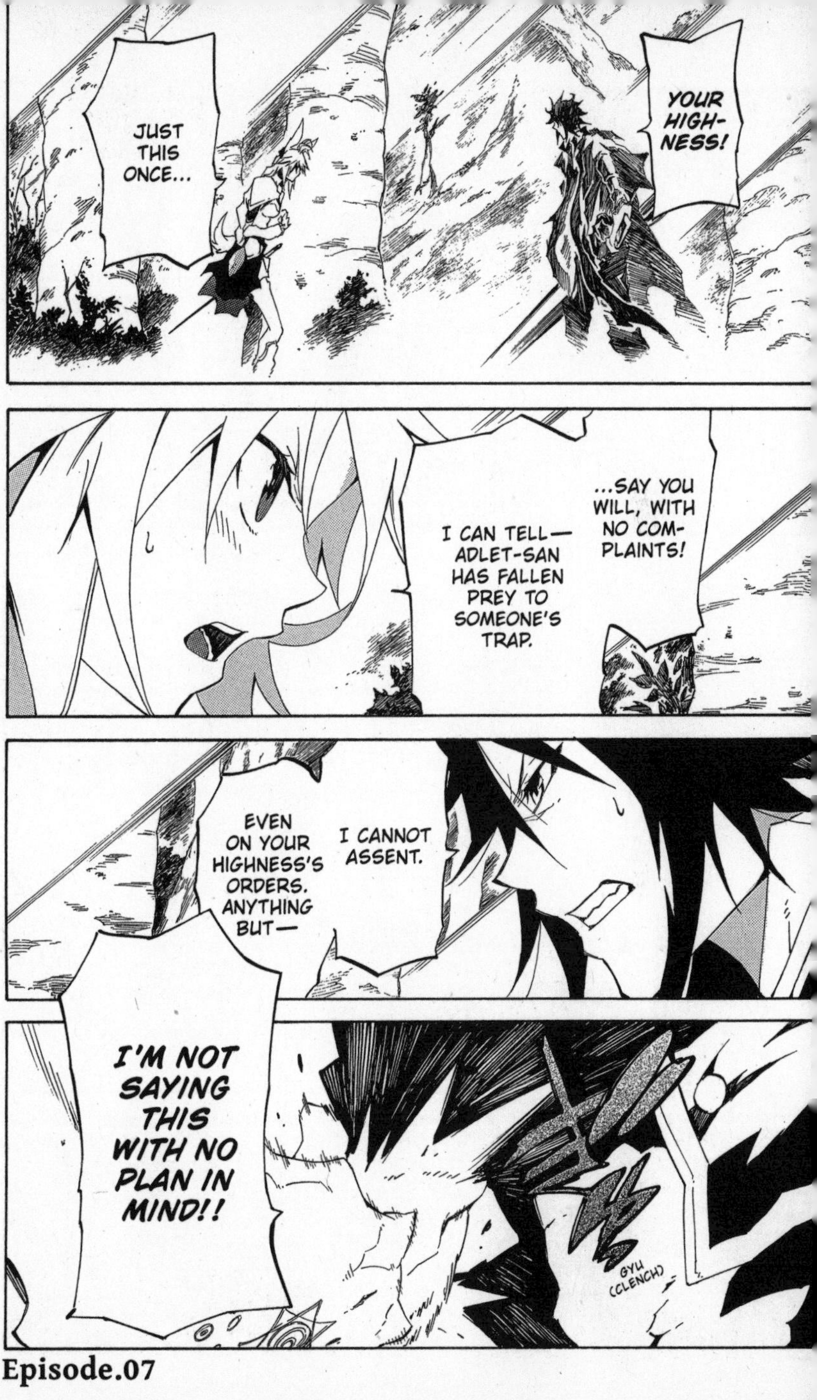
YOUR HIGH- NESS!
JUST THIS ONCE...
...SAY YOU WILL, WITH NO COM- PLAINTS!
I CAN TELL— ADLET-SAN HAS FALLEN PREY TO SOMEONE'S TRAP.
I CANNOT ASSENT.
EVEN ON YOUR HIGHNESS'S ORDERS. ANYTHING BUT—
I'M NOT SAYING THIS WITH NO PLAN IN MIND!!
GYU (CLENCH)

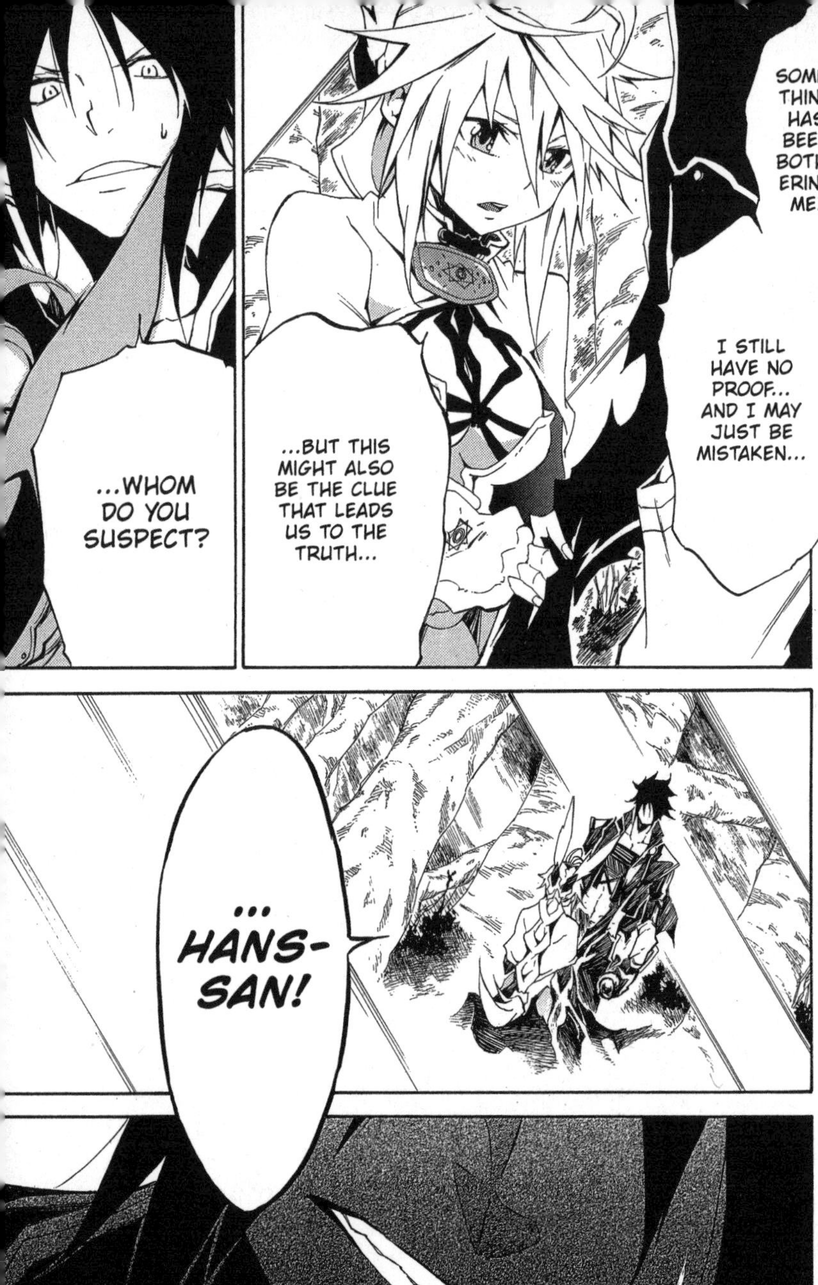
SOMETHING HAS BEEN BOTHERING ME.
I STILL HAVE NO PROOF... AND I MAY JUST BE MISTAKEN...
...BUT THIS MIGHT ALSO BE THE CLUE THAT LEADS US TO THE TRUTH...
...WHOM DO YOU SUSPECT?
... HANS-SAN!

Episode.07

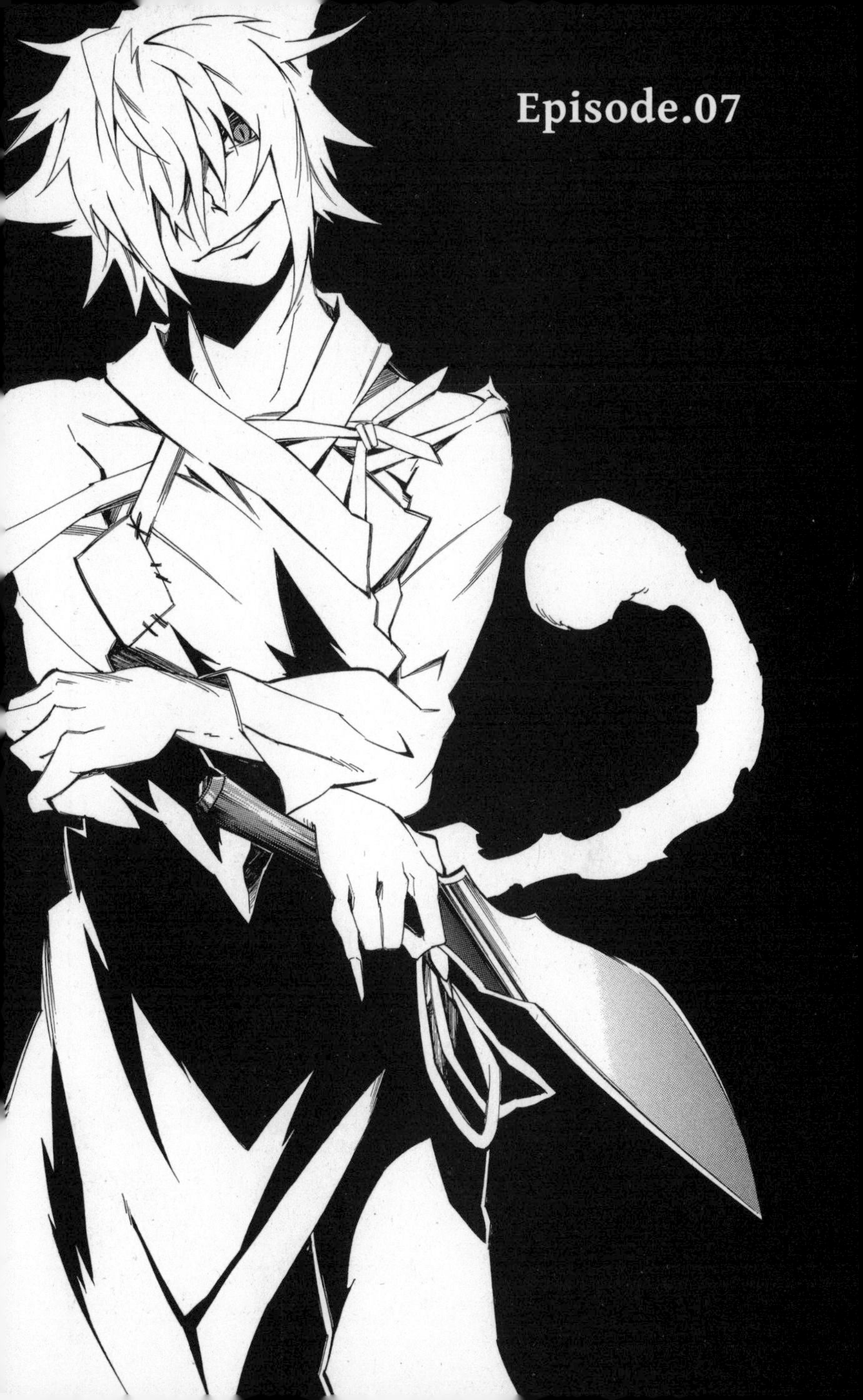

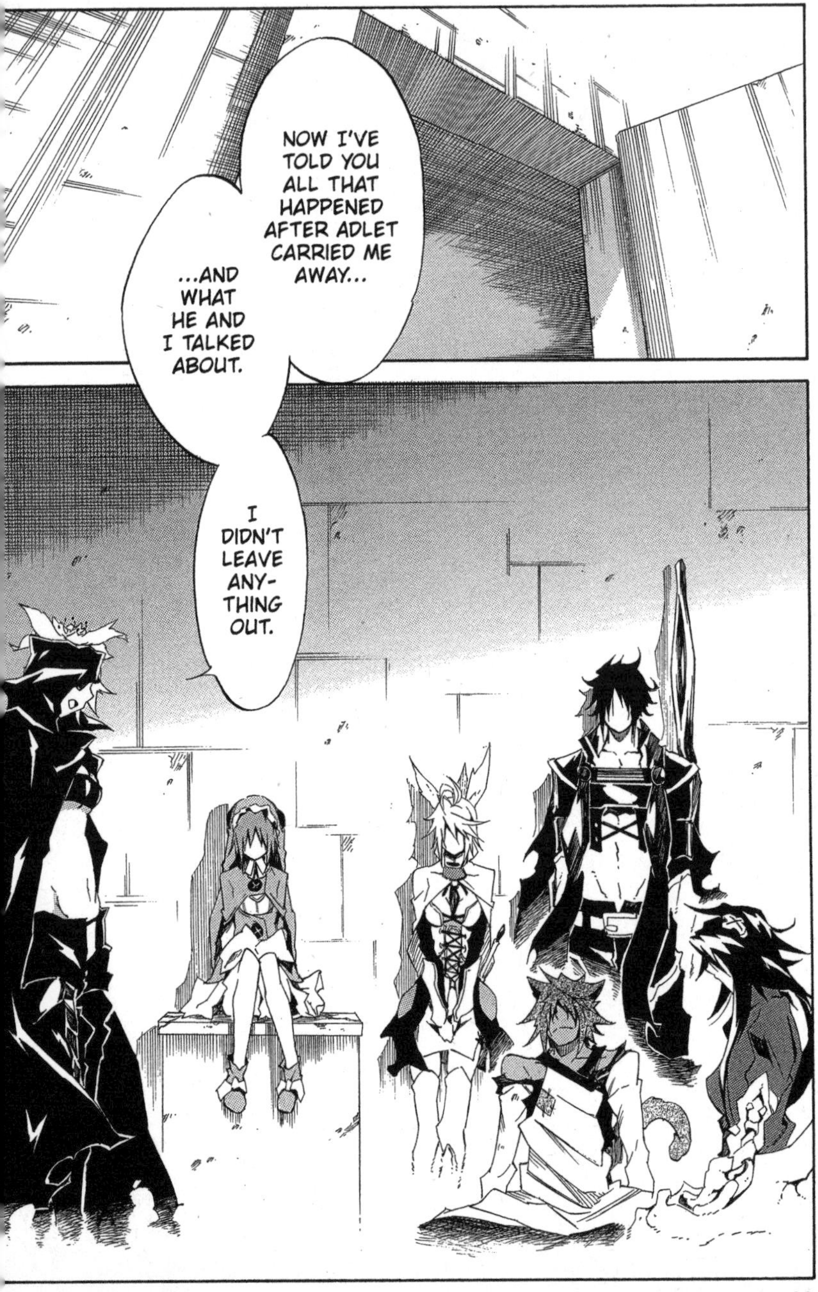
NOW I'VE TOLD YOU ALL THAT HAPPENED AFTER ADLET CARRIED ME AWAY...
...AND WHAT HE AND I TALKED ABOUT.
I DIDN'T LEAVE ANY-THING OUT.

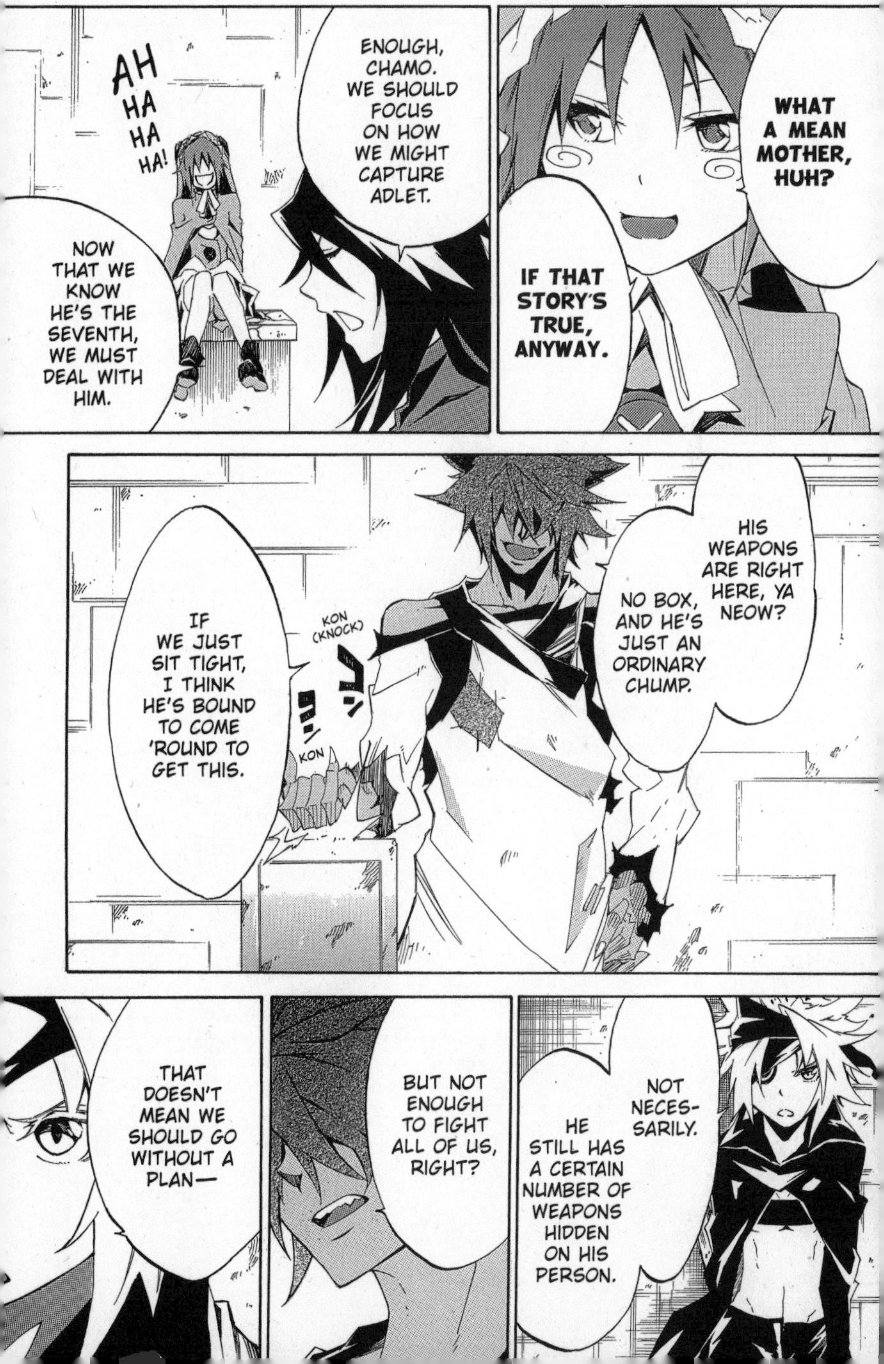
WHAT A MEAN MOTHER, HUH?
IF THAT STORY'S TRUE, ANYWAY.
ENOUGH, CHAMO. WE SHOULD FOCUS ON HOW WE MIGHT CAPTURE ADLET.
AH HA HA HA!
NOW THAT WE KNOW HE'S THE SEVENTH, WE MUST DEAL WITH HIM.
HIS WEAPONS ARE RIGHT HERE, YA NEOW?
NO BOX, AND HE'S JUST AN ORDINARY CHUMP.
KON (KNOCK)
KON
IF WE JUST SIT TIGHT, I THINK HE'S BOUND TO COME 'ROUND TO GET THIS.
NOT NECES-SARILY.
HE STILL HAS A CERTAIN NUMBER OF WEAPONS HIDDEN ON HIS PERSON.
BUT NOT ENOUGH TO FIGHT ALL OF US, RIGHT?
THAT DOESN'T MEAN WE SHOULD GO WITHOUT A PLAN—

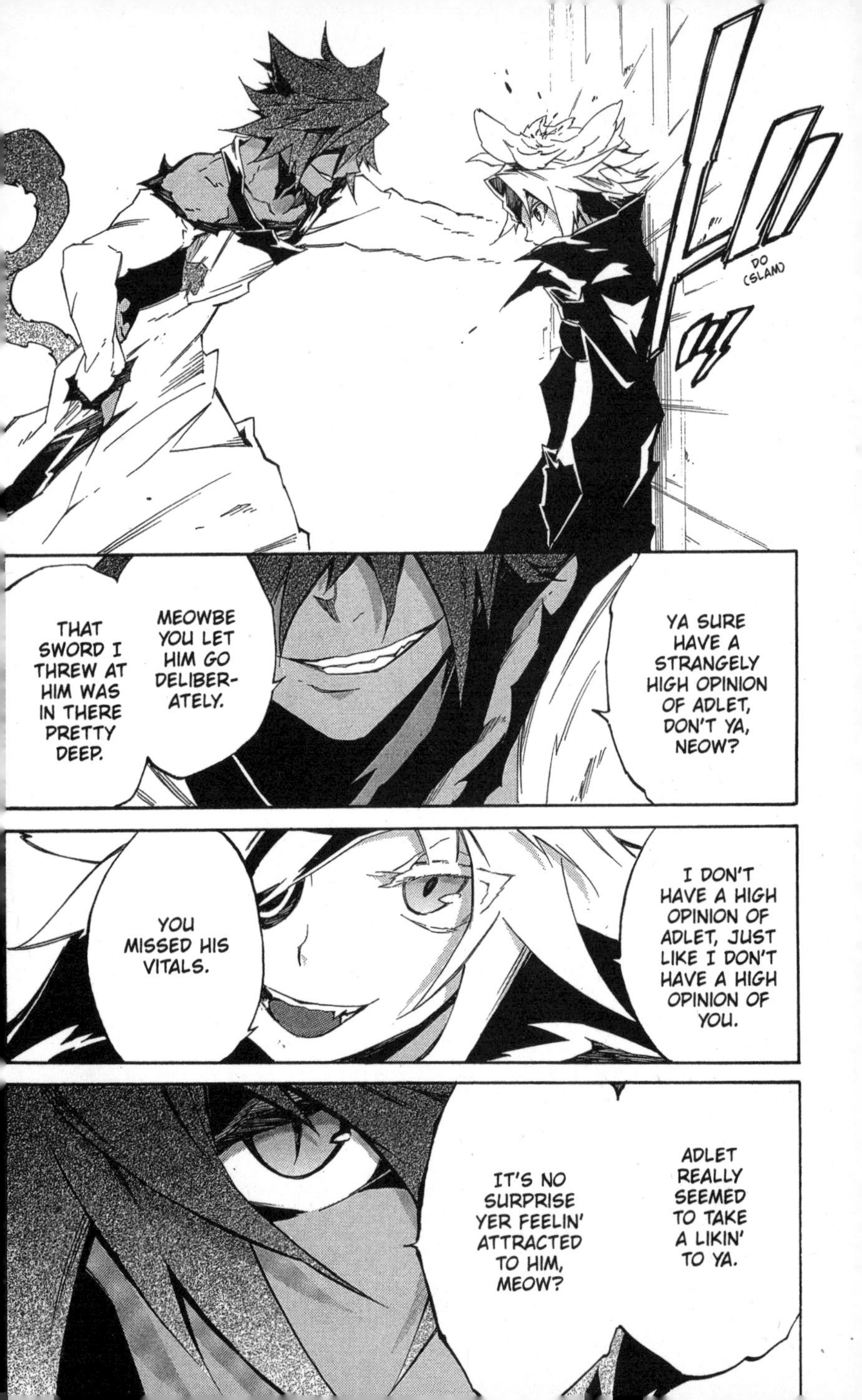
DO (SLAM)
YA SURE HAVE A STRANGELY HIGH OPINION OF ADLET, DON'T YA, NEOW?
MEOWBE YOU LET HIM GO DELIBER-ATELY.
THAT SWORD I THREW AT HIM WAS IN THERE PRETTY DEEP.
I DON'T HAVE A HIGH OPINION OF ADLET, JUST LIKE I DON'T HAVE A HIGH OPINION OF YOU.
YOU MISSED HIS VITALS.
ADLET REALLY SEEMED TO TAKE A LIKIN' TO YA.
IT'S NO SURPRISE YER FEELIN' ATTRACTED TO HIM, MEOW?

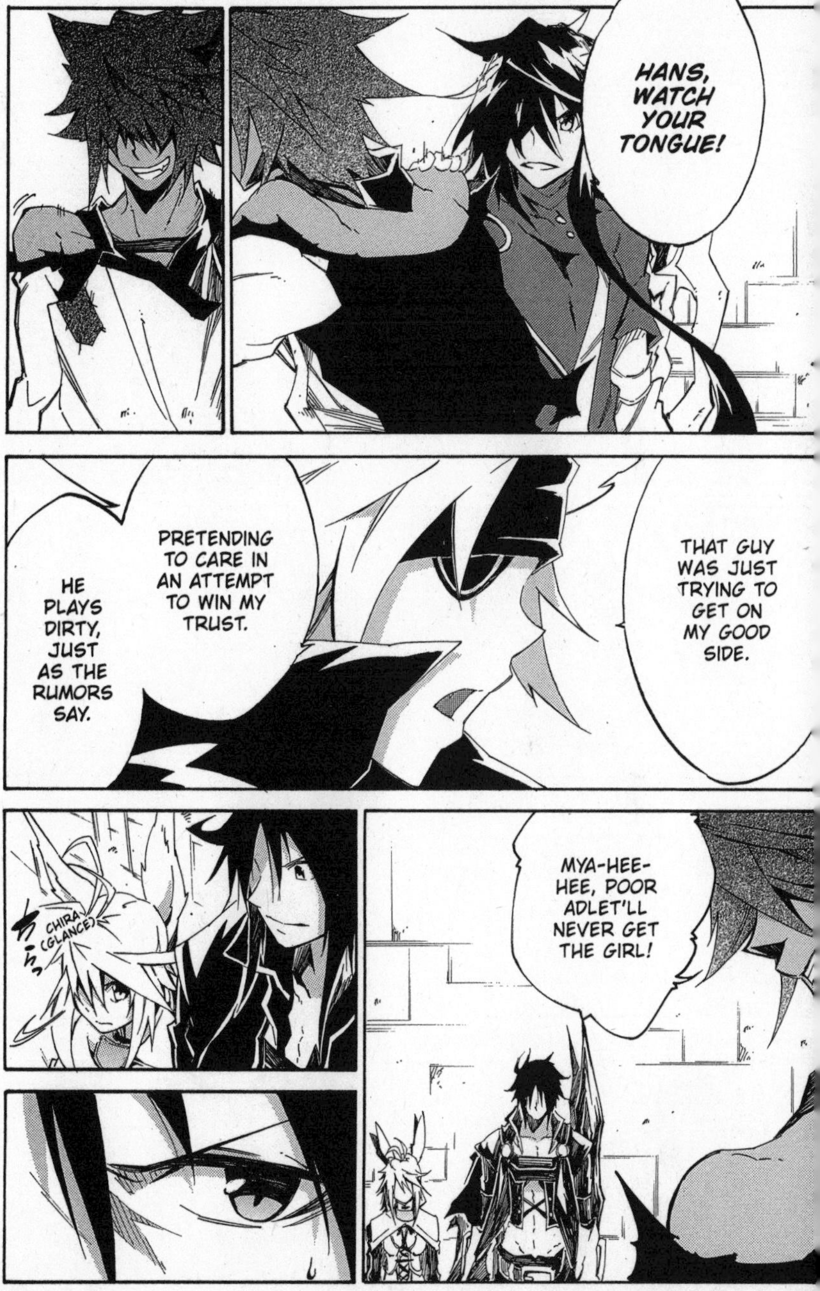
HANS, WATCH YOUR TONGUE!
THAT GUY WAS JUST TRYING TO GET ON MY GOOD SIDE.
PRETENDING TO CARE IN AN ATTEMPT TO WIN MY TRUST.
HE PLAYS DIRTY, JUST AS THE RUMORS SAY.
MYA-HEE-HEE, POOR ADLET'LL NEVER GET THE GIRL!
CHIRA (GLANCE)

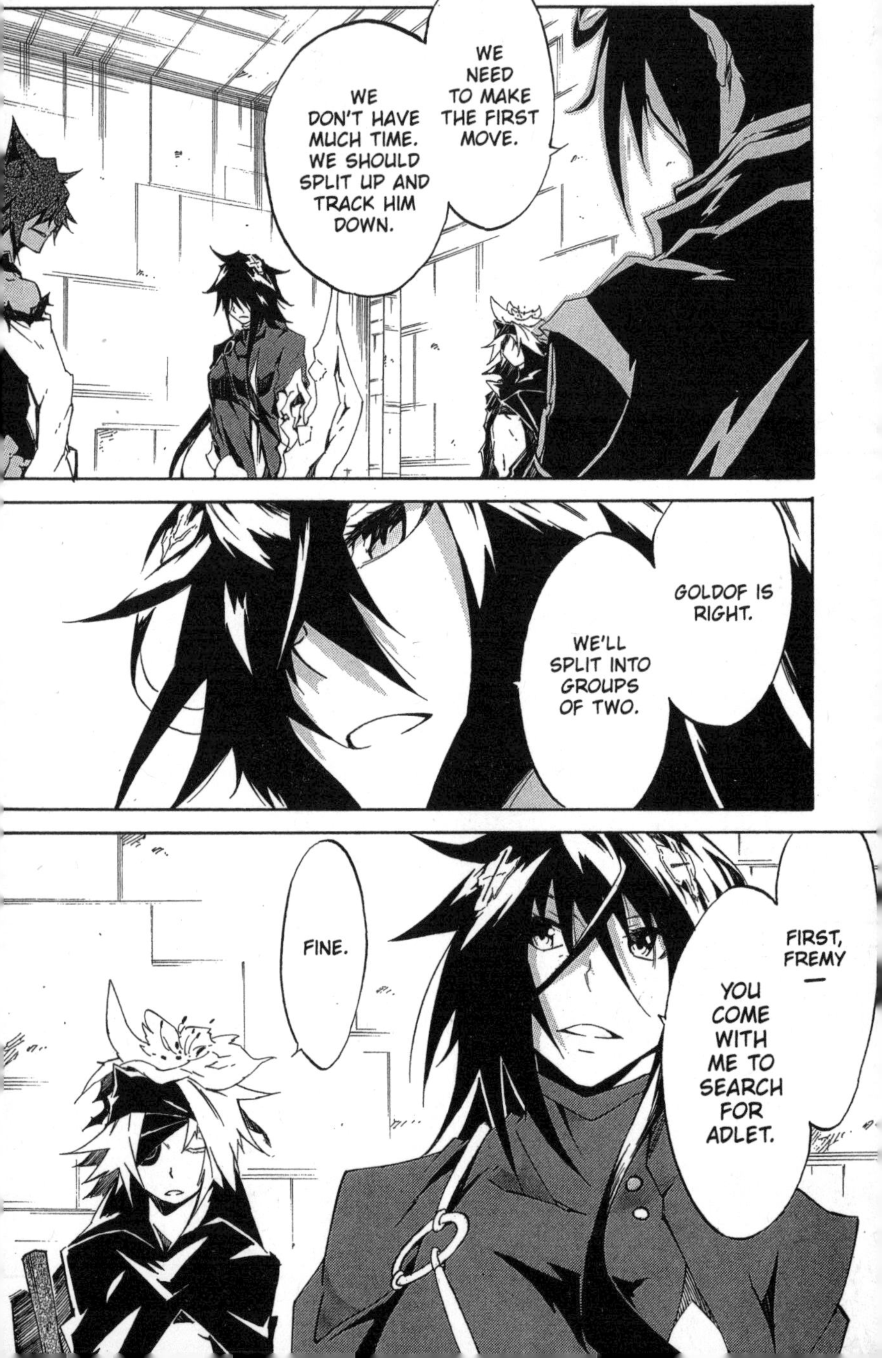
WE NEED TO MAKE THE FIRST MOVE.
WE DON'T HAVE MUCH TIME. WE SHOULD SPLIT UP AND TRACK HIM DOWN.
GOLDOF IS RIGHT.
WE'LL SPLIT INTO GROUPS OF TWO.
FIRST, FREMY—
YOU COME WITH ME TO SEARCH FOR ADLET.
FINE.

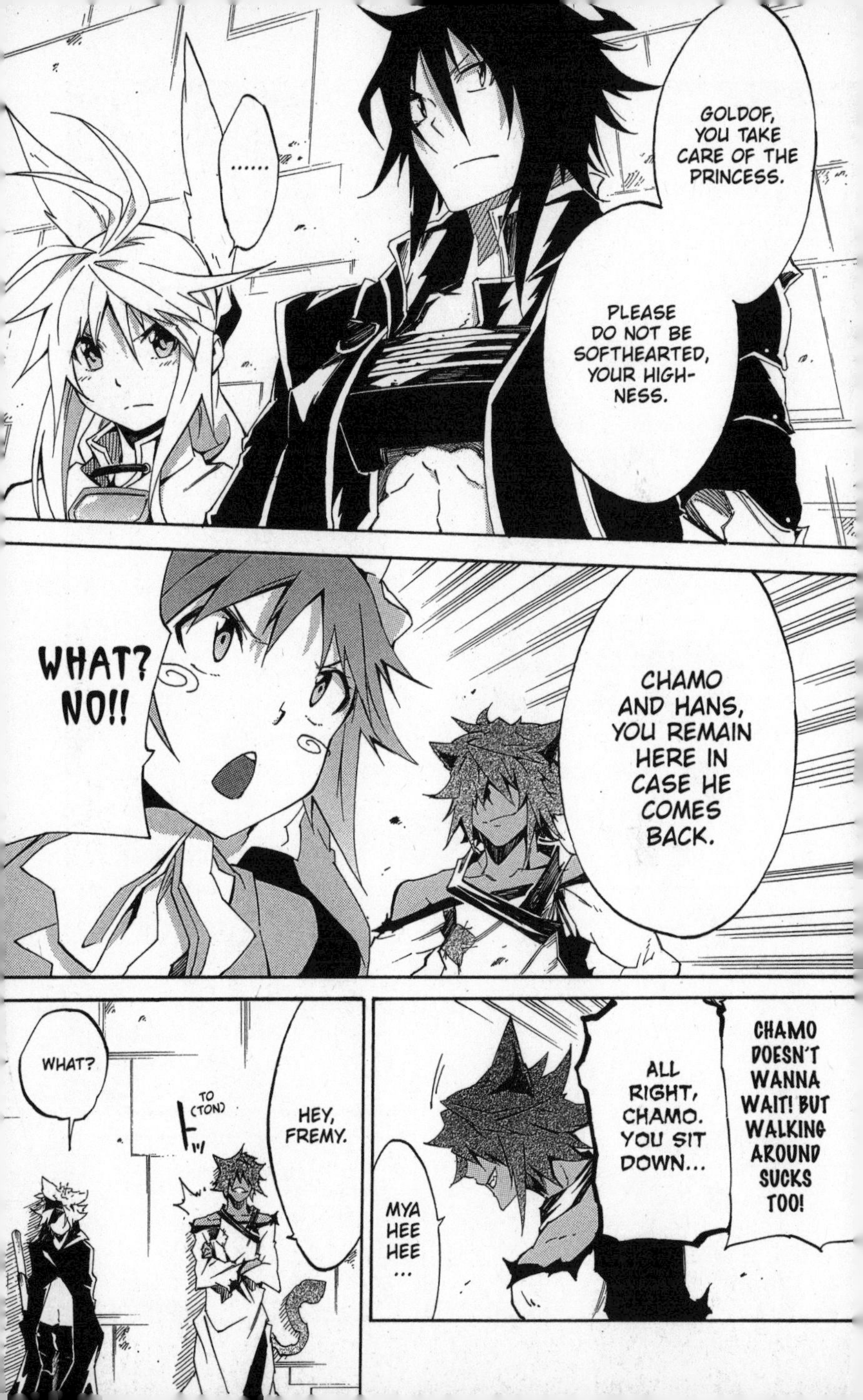
GOLDOF, YOU TAKE CARE OF THE PRINCESS.
......
PLEASE DO NOT BE SOFTHEARTED, YOUR HIGH-NESS.
CHAMO AND HANS, YOU REMAIN HERE IN CASE HE COMES BACK.
WHAT? NO!!
CHAMO DOESN'T WANNA WAIT! BUT WALKING AROUND SUCKS TOO!
ALL RIGHT, CHAMO. YOU SIT DOWN...
MYA HEE HEE ...
HEY, FREMY.
TO (TON)
WHAT?

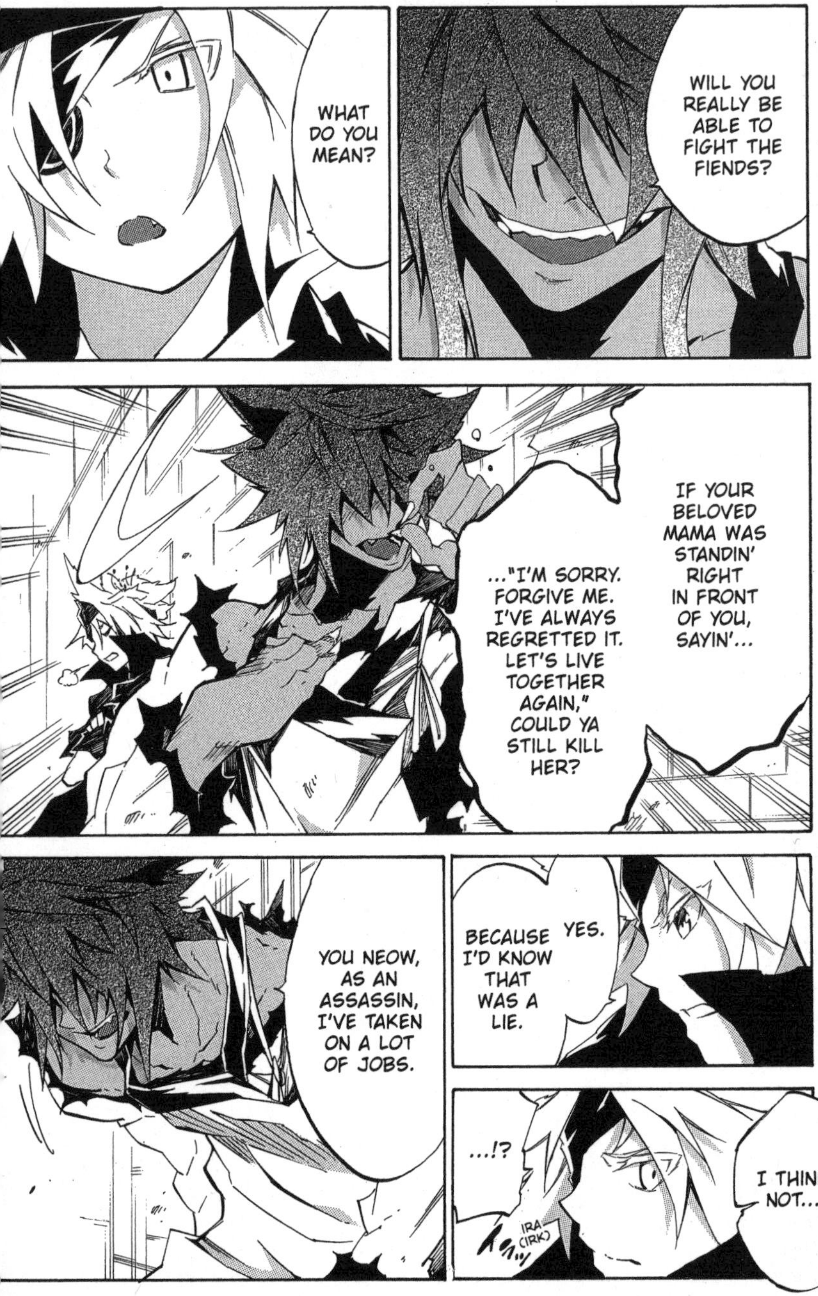
WILL YOU REALLY BE ABLE TO FIGHT THE FIENDS?
WHAT DO YOU MEAN?
IF YOUR BELOVED MAMA WAS STANDIN' RIGHT IN FRONT OF YOU, SAYIN'...
..."I'M SORRY. FORGIVE ME. I'VE ALWAYS REGRETTED IT. LET'S LIVE TOGETHER AGAIN," COULD YA STILL KILL HER?
YES.
BECAUSE I'D KNOW THAT WAS A LIE.
I THINK NOT...
...!?
IRA (IRK)
YOU NEOW, AS AN ASSASSIN, I'VE TAKEN ON A LOT OF JOBS.

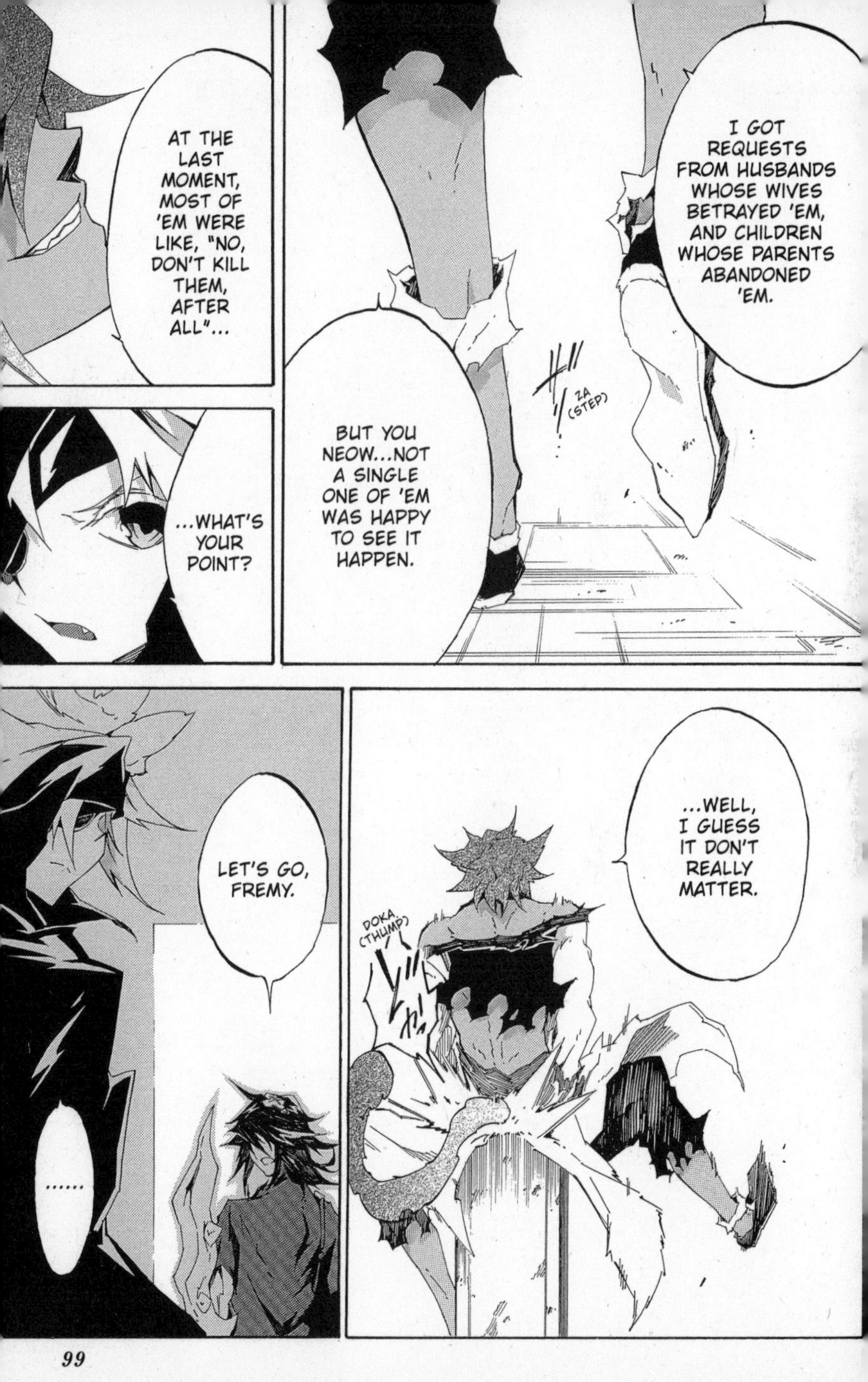
I GOT REQUESTS FROM HUSBANDS WHOSE WIVES BETRAYED 'EM, AND CHILDREN WHOSE PARENTS ABANDONED 'EM.
BUT YOU NEOW...NOT A SINGLE ONE OF 'EM WAS HAPPY TO SEE IT HAPPEN.
ZA (STEP)
AT THE LAST MOMENT, MOST OF 'EM WERE LIKE, "NO, DON'T KILL THEM, AFTER ALL"...
...WHAT'S YOUR POINT?
...WELL, I GUESS IT DON'T REALLY MATTER.
DOKA (THUMP)
LET'S GO, FREMY.
......

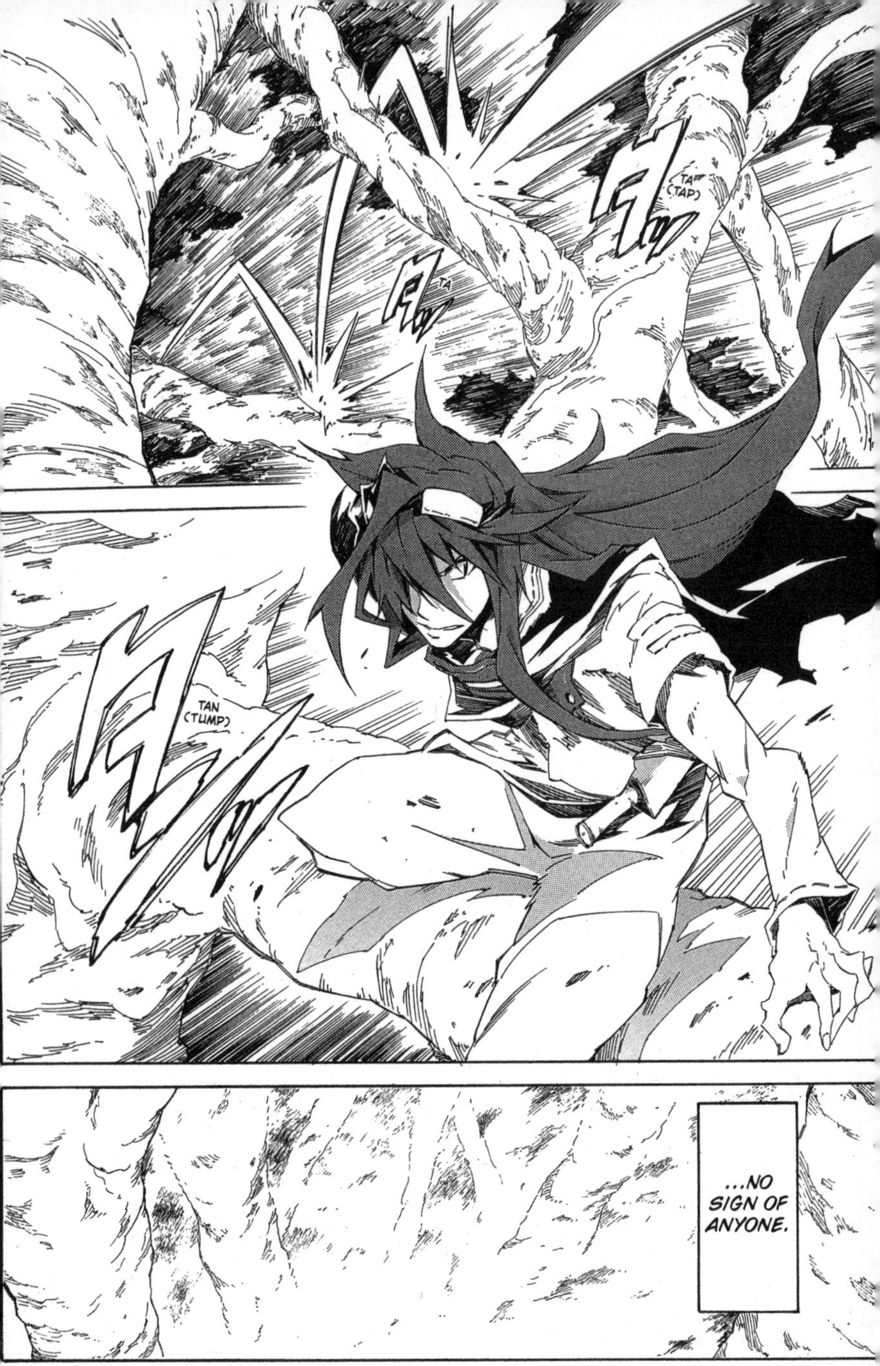
TA (TAP)
TA
TAN (TUMP)
...NO SIGN OF ANYONE.

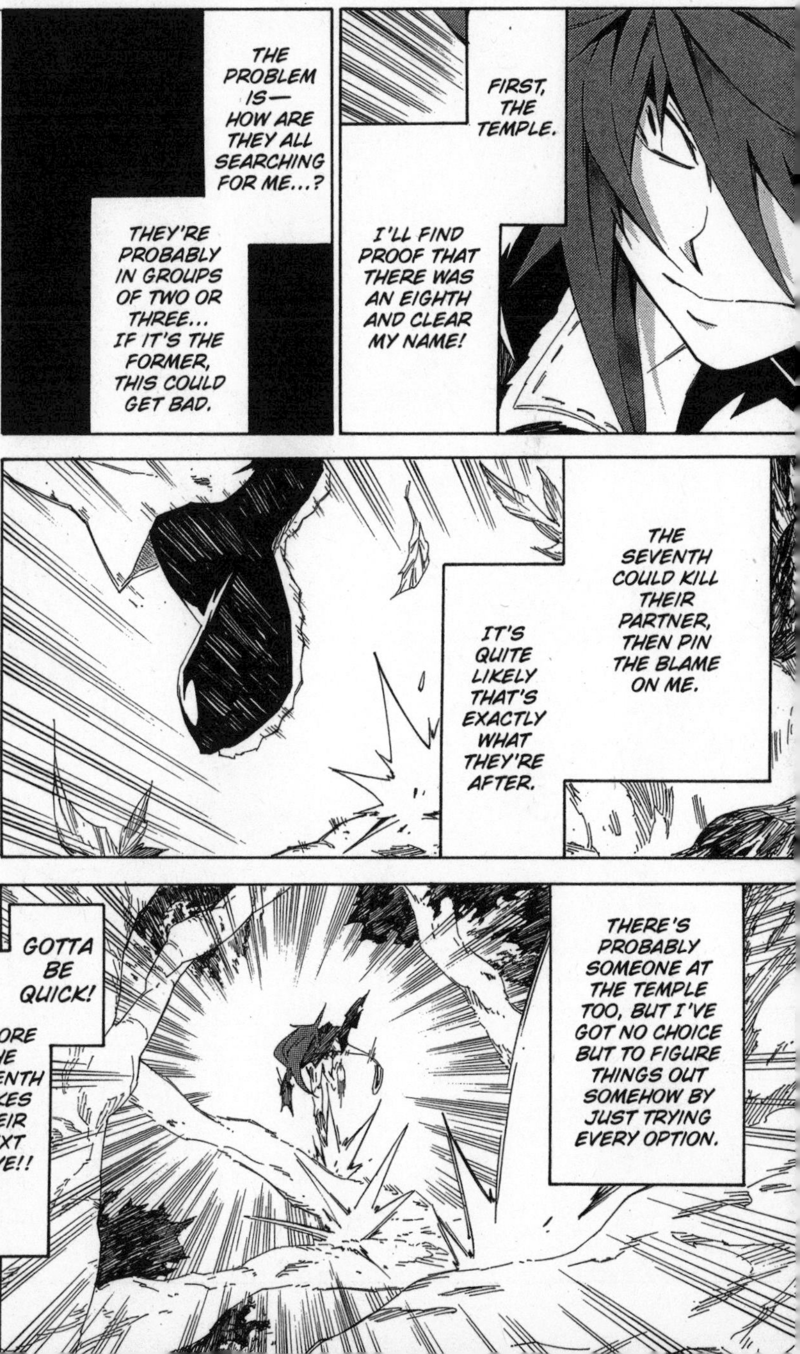
FIRST, THE TEMPLE.
I'LL FIND PROOF THAT THERE WAS AN EIGHTH AND CLEAR MY NAME!
THE PROBLEM IS— HOW ARE THEY ALL SEARCHING FOR ME...?
THEY'RE PROBABLY IN GROUPS OF TWO OR THREE... IF IT'S THE FORMER, THIS COULD GET BAD.
THE SEVENTH COULD KILL THEIR PARTNER, THEN PIN THE BLAME ON ME.
IT'S QUITE LIKELY THAT'S EXACTLY WHAT THEY'RE AFTER.
THERE'S PROBABLY SOMEONE AT THE TEMPLE TOO, BUT I'VE GOT NO CHOICE BUT TO FIGURE THINGS OUT SOMEHOW BY JUST TRYING EVERY OPTION.
GOTTA BE QUICK!
BEFORE THE SEVENTH MAKES THEIR NEXT MOVE!!

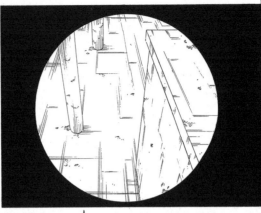

NO SIGN OF ANYONE HERE AT THE TEMPLE...

OOO
(FWOO)

TA
(TAP)

(GASA)
(RUSTLE)

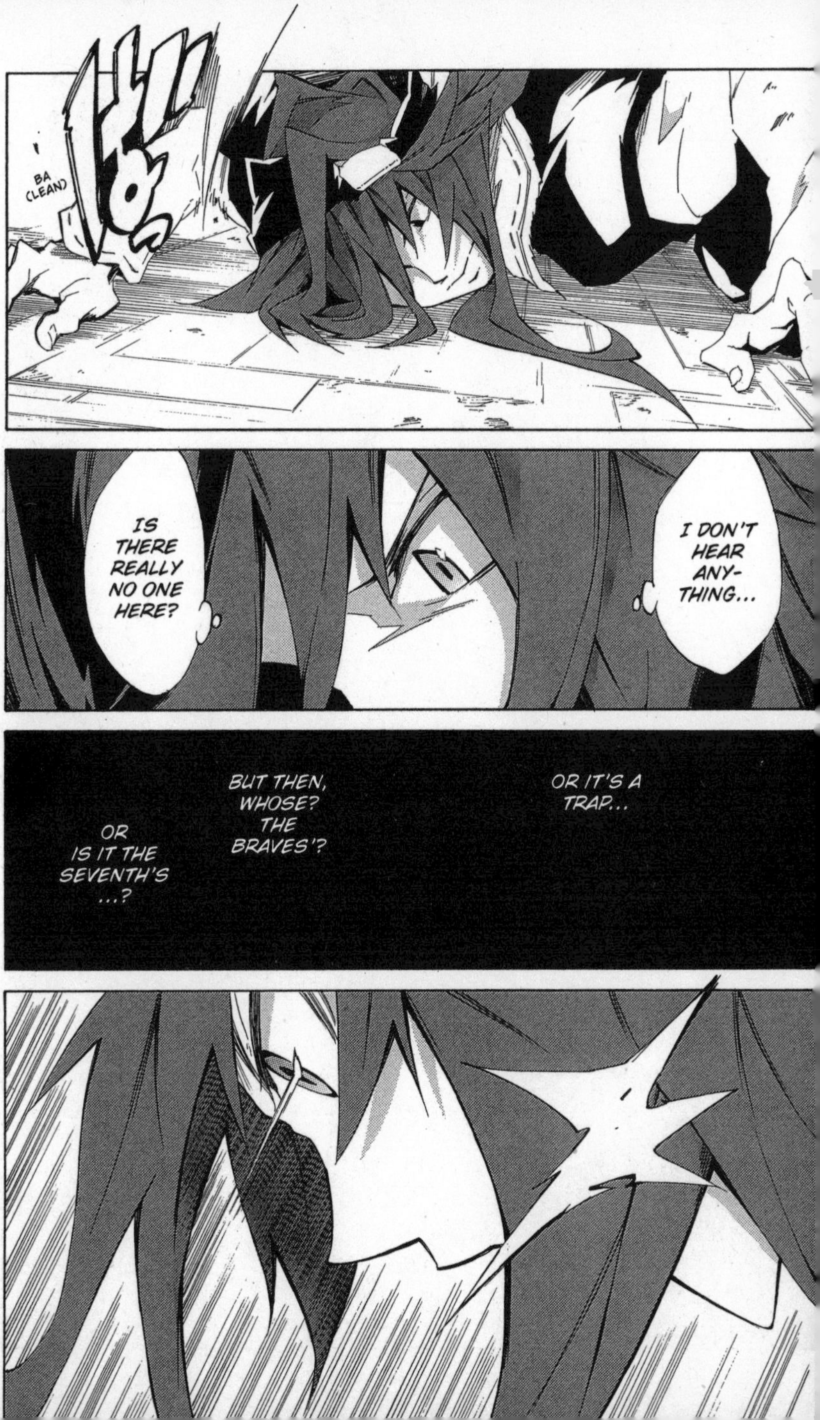
BA (CLEAN)
I DON'T HEAR ANYTHING...
IS THERE REALLY NO ONE HERE?
OR IT'S A TRAP...
BUT THEN, WHOSE? THE BRAVES'?
OR IS IT THE SEVENTH'S ...?

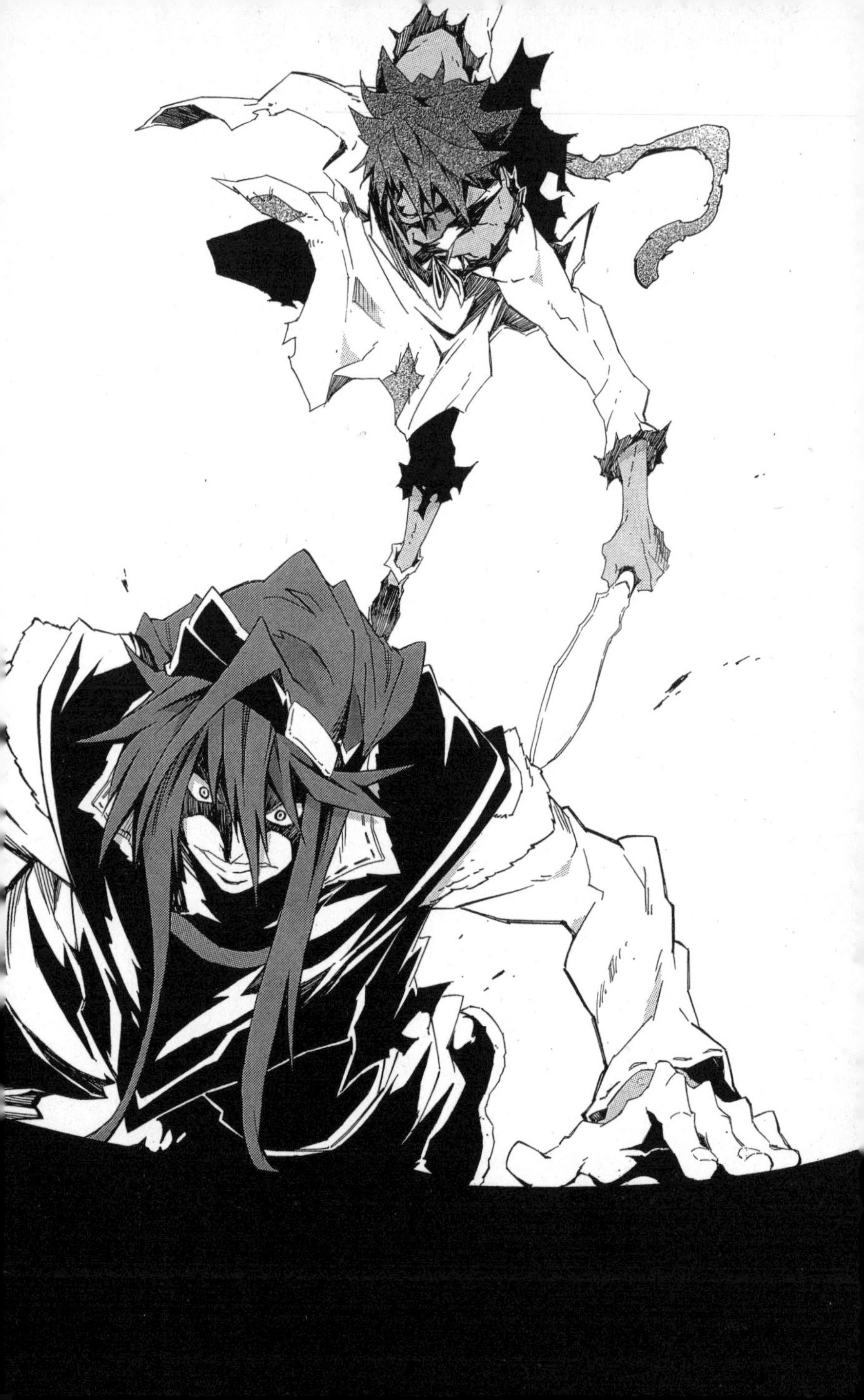

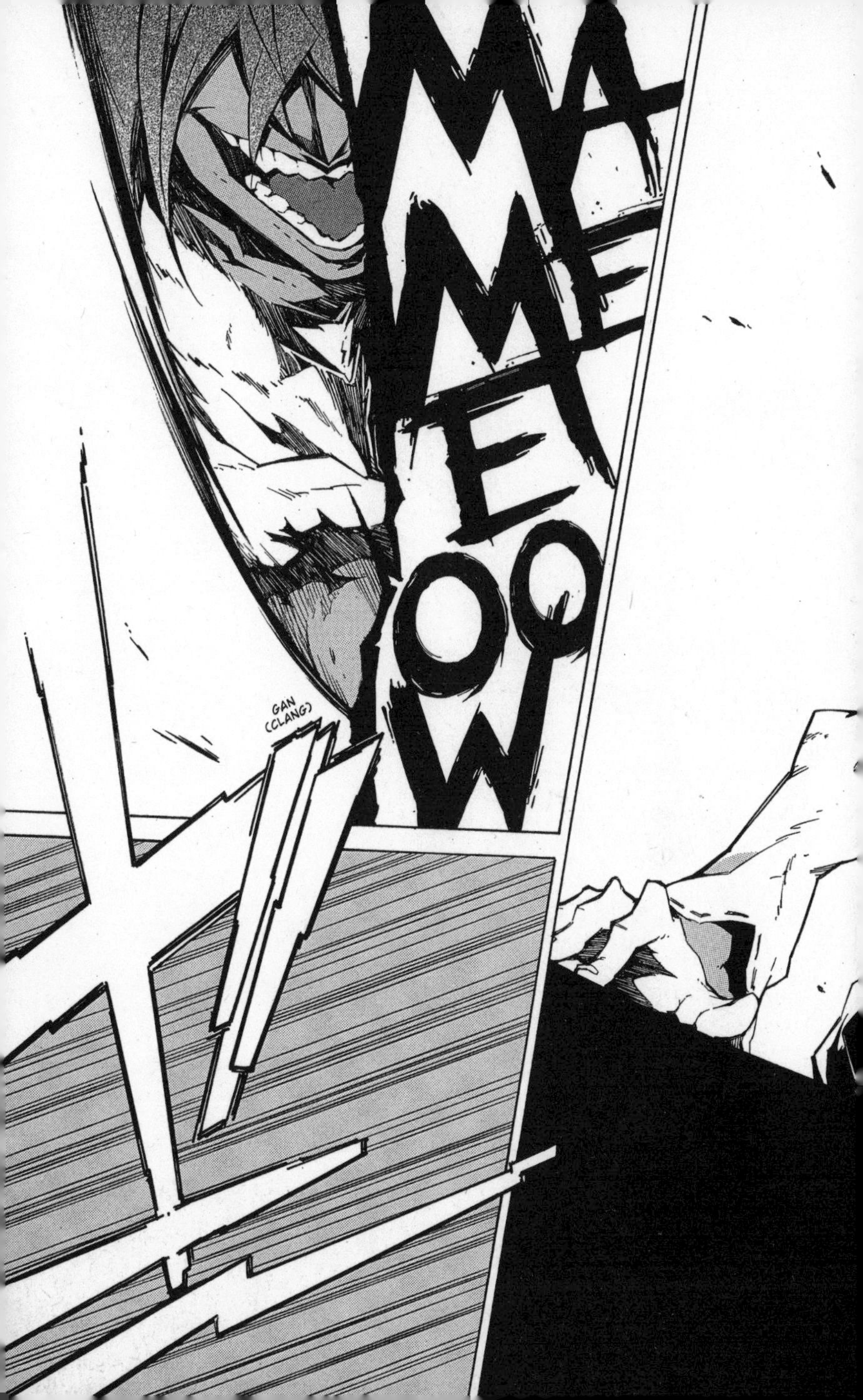
MAMEEOOW
GAN
(CLANG)

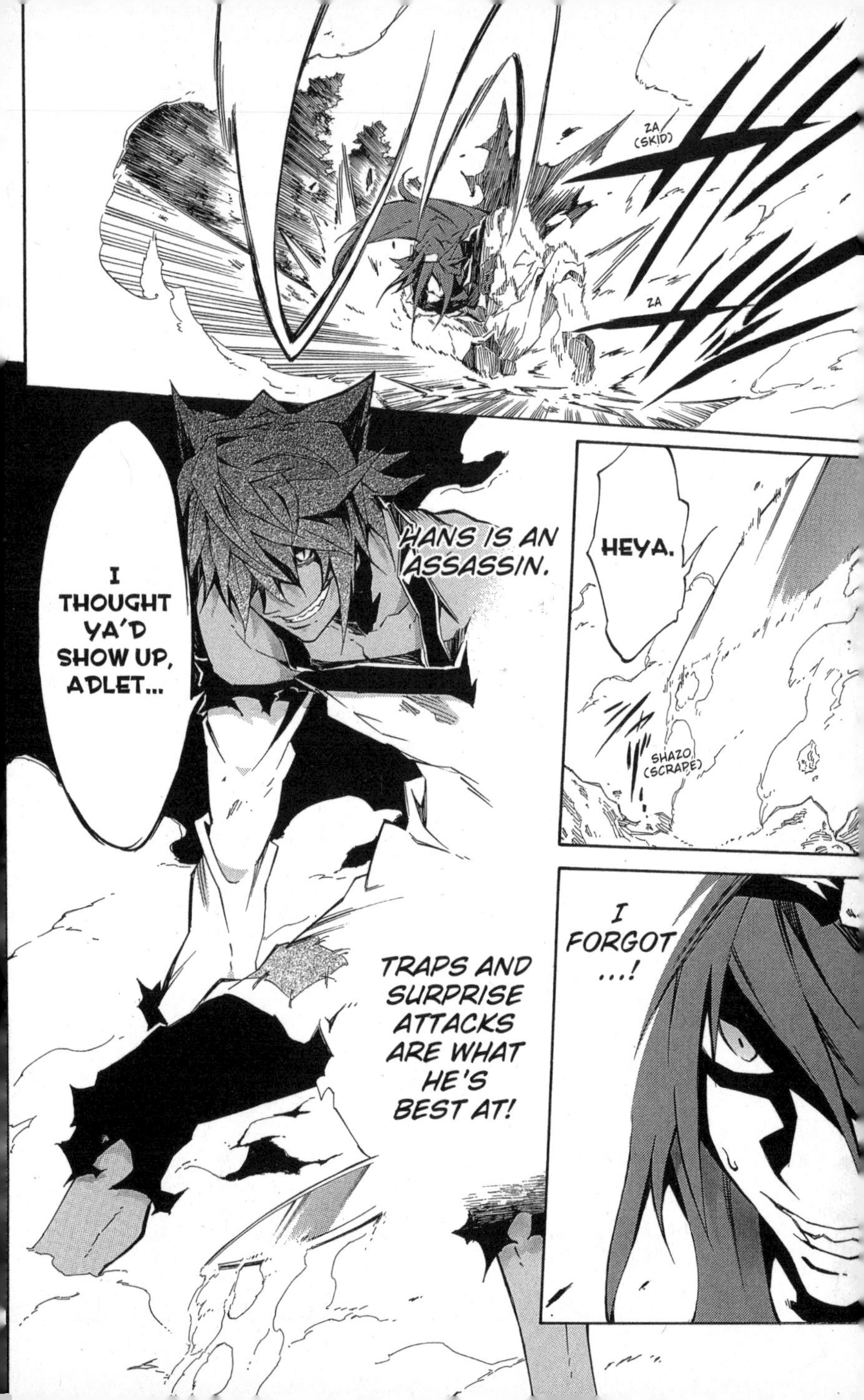
ZA
(SKID)
ZA
HEYA.
SHAZO
(SCRAPE)
I FORGOT ...!
HANS IS AN ASSASSIN.
I THOUGHT YA'D SHOW UP, ADLET...
TRAPS AND SURPRISE ATTACKS ARE WHAT HE'S BEST AT!

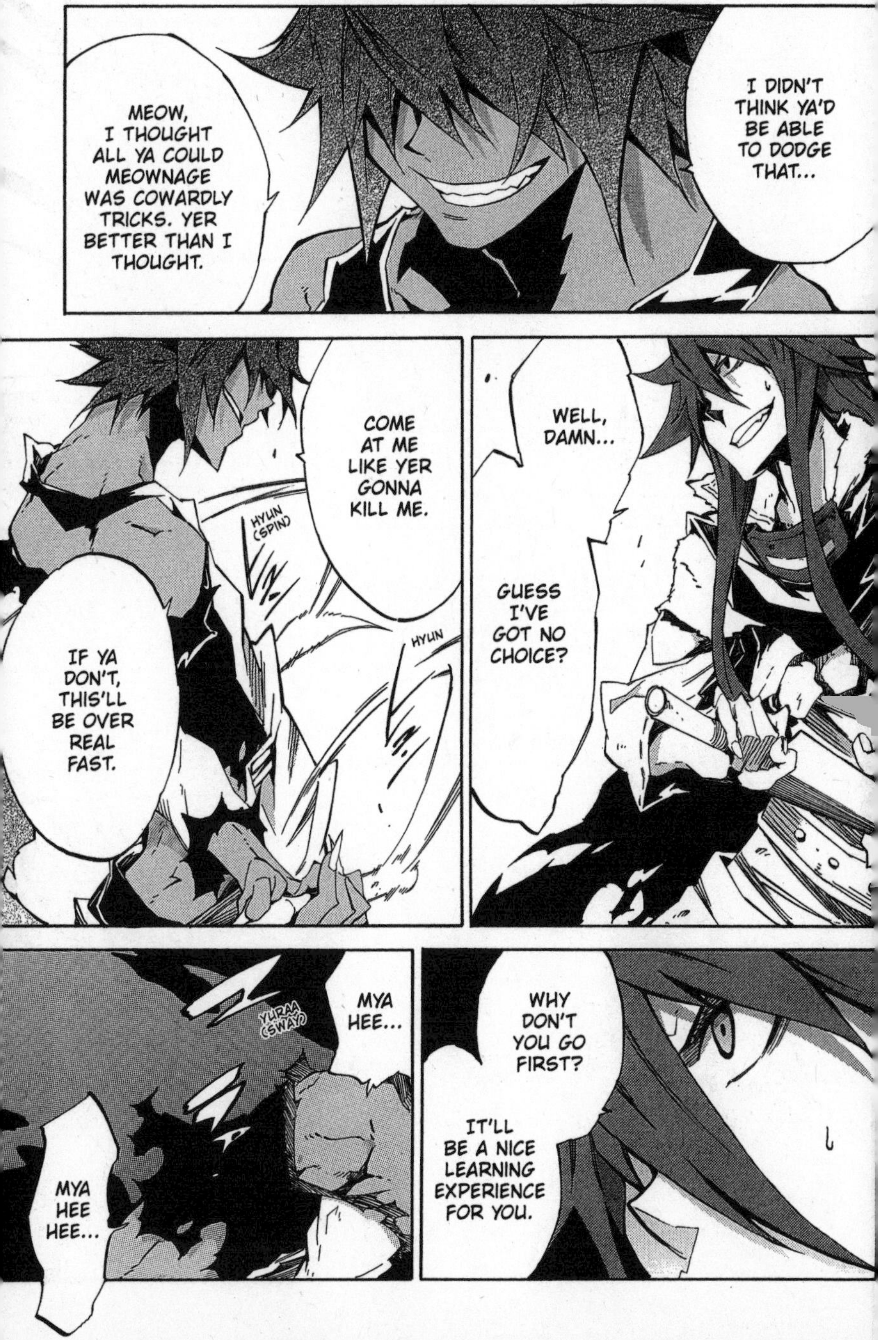
I DIDN'T THINK YA'D BE ABLE TO DODGE THAT...
MEOW, I THOUGHT ALL YA COULD MEOWNAGE WAS COWARDLY TRICKS. YER BETTER THAN I THOUGHT.
WELL, DAMN...
GUESS I'VE GOT NO CHOICE?
COME AT ME LIKE YER GONNA KILL ME.
HYUN (SPIN)
HYUN
IF YA DON'T, THIS'LL BE OVER REAL FAST.
WHY DON'T YOU GO FIRST?
IT'LL BE A NICE LEARNING EXPERIENCE FOR YOU.
MYA HEE...
YURAA (SWAY)
MYA HEE HEE...

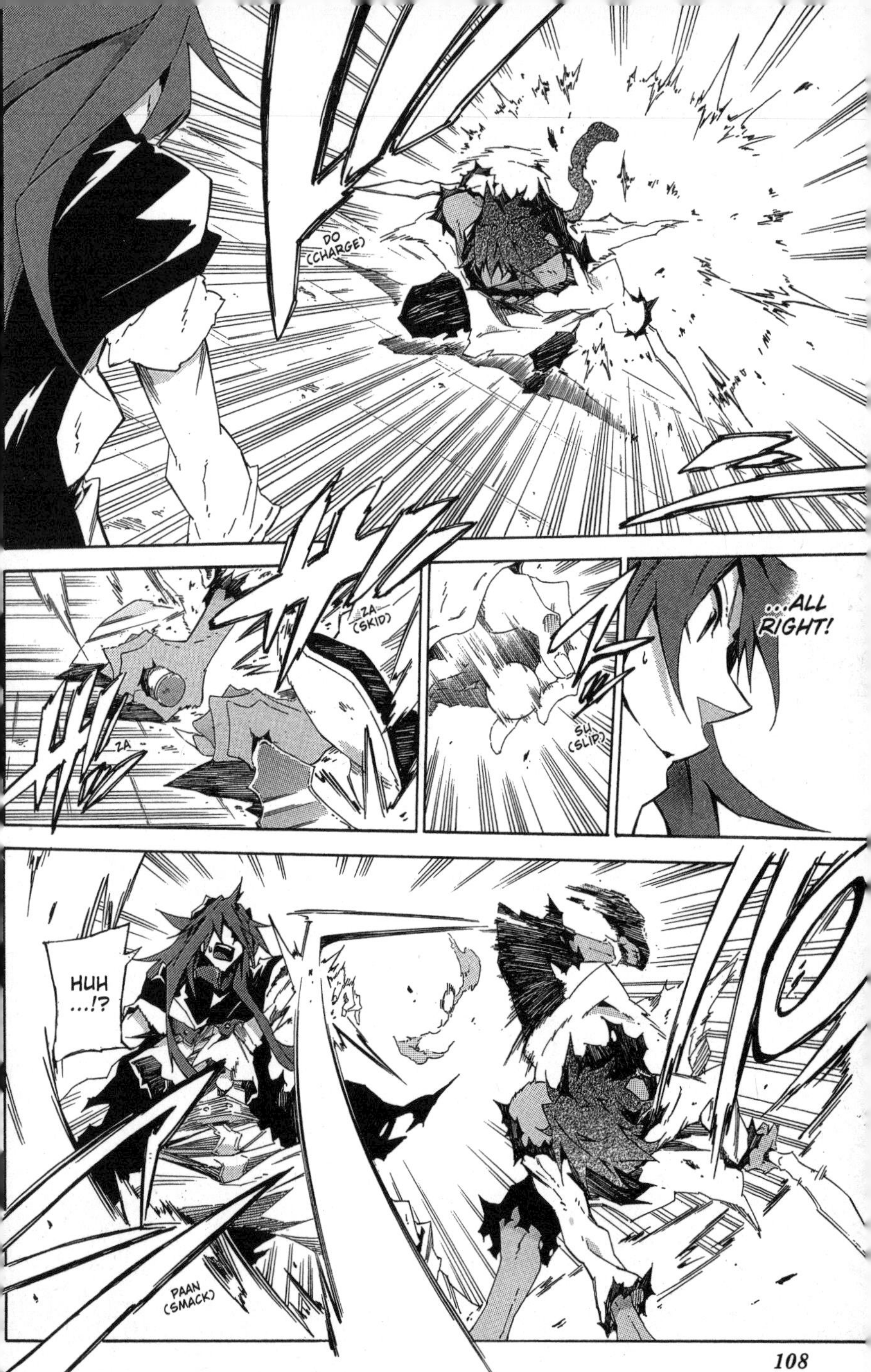
DO
(CHARGE)
...ALL RIGHT!
SU
(SLIP)
ZA
(SKID)
ZA
HUH
...!?
PAAN
(SMACK)

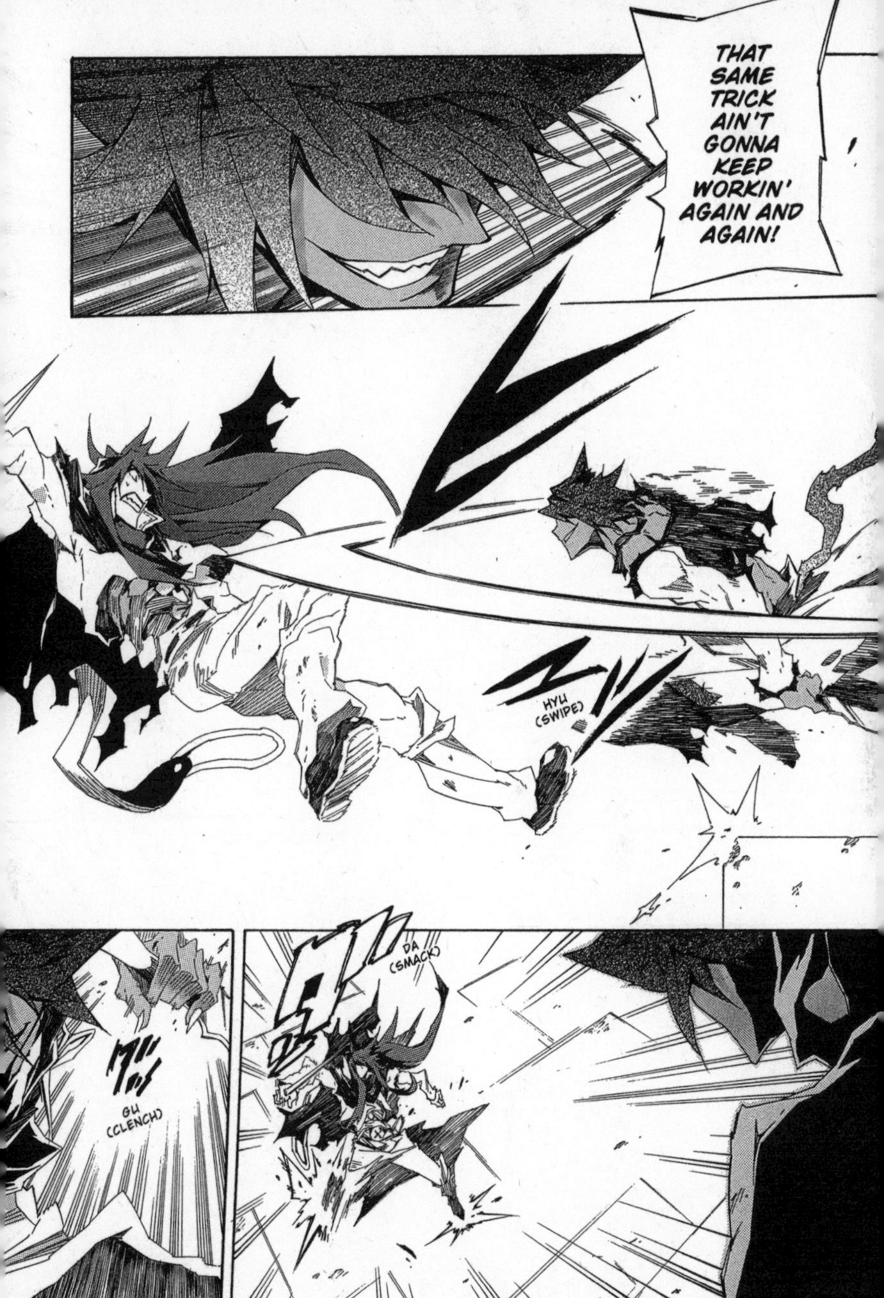
THAT SAME TRICK AIN'T GONNA KEEP WORKIN' AGAIN AND AGAIN!
HYU (SWIPE)
DA (SMACK)
GU (CLENCH)

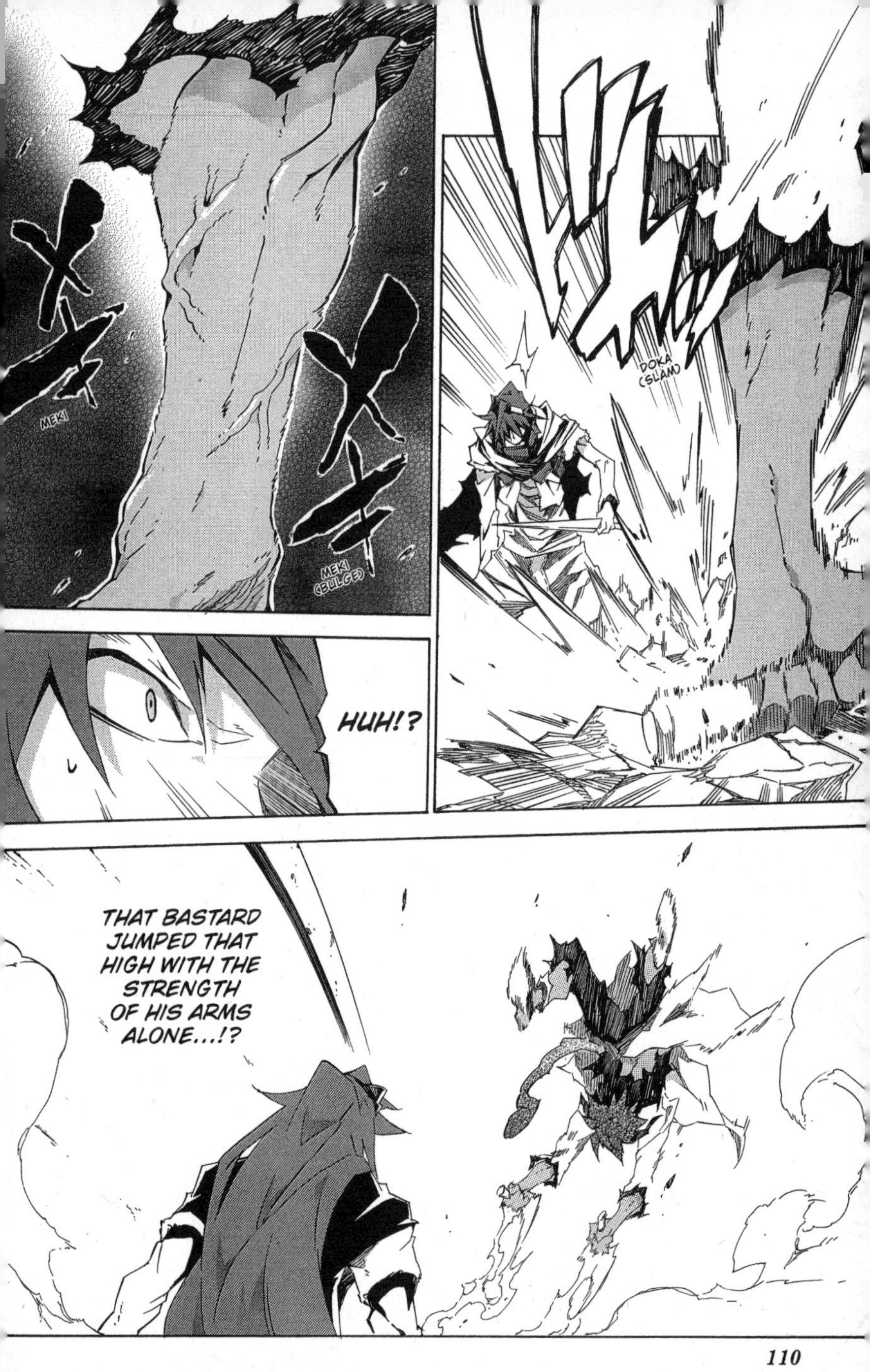
DOKA (SLAM)
MEKI
MEKI (BULGE)
HUH!?
THAT BASTARD JUMPED THAT HIGH WITH THE STRENGTH OF HIS ARMS ALONE...!?

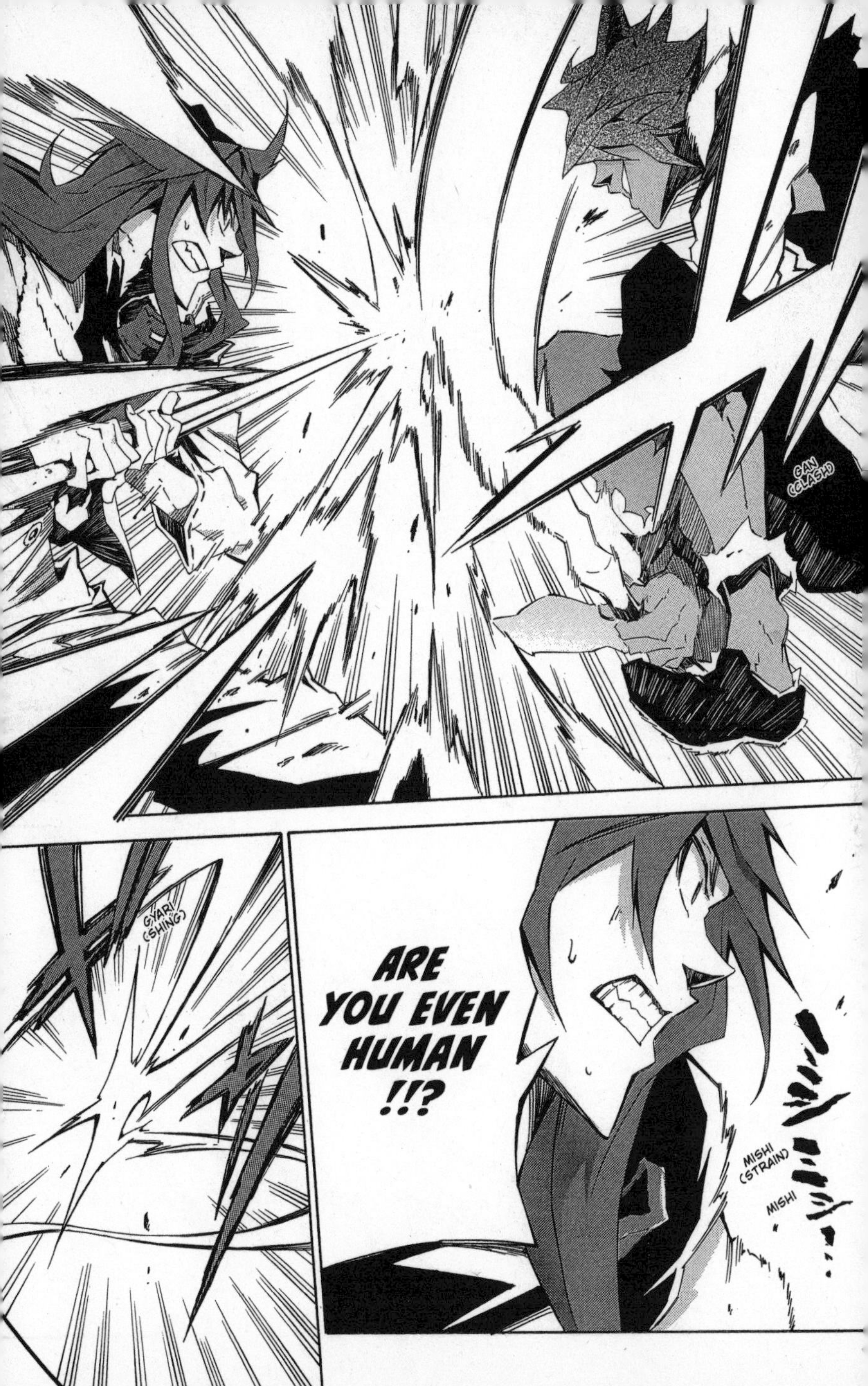
GAN (CLASH)
ARE YOU EVEN HUMAN !!?
MISHI (STRAIN)
MISHI
GYARI (SHING)

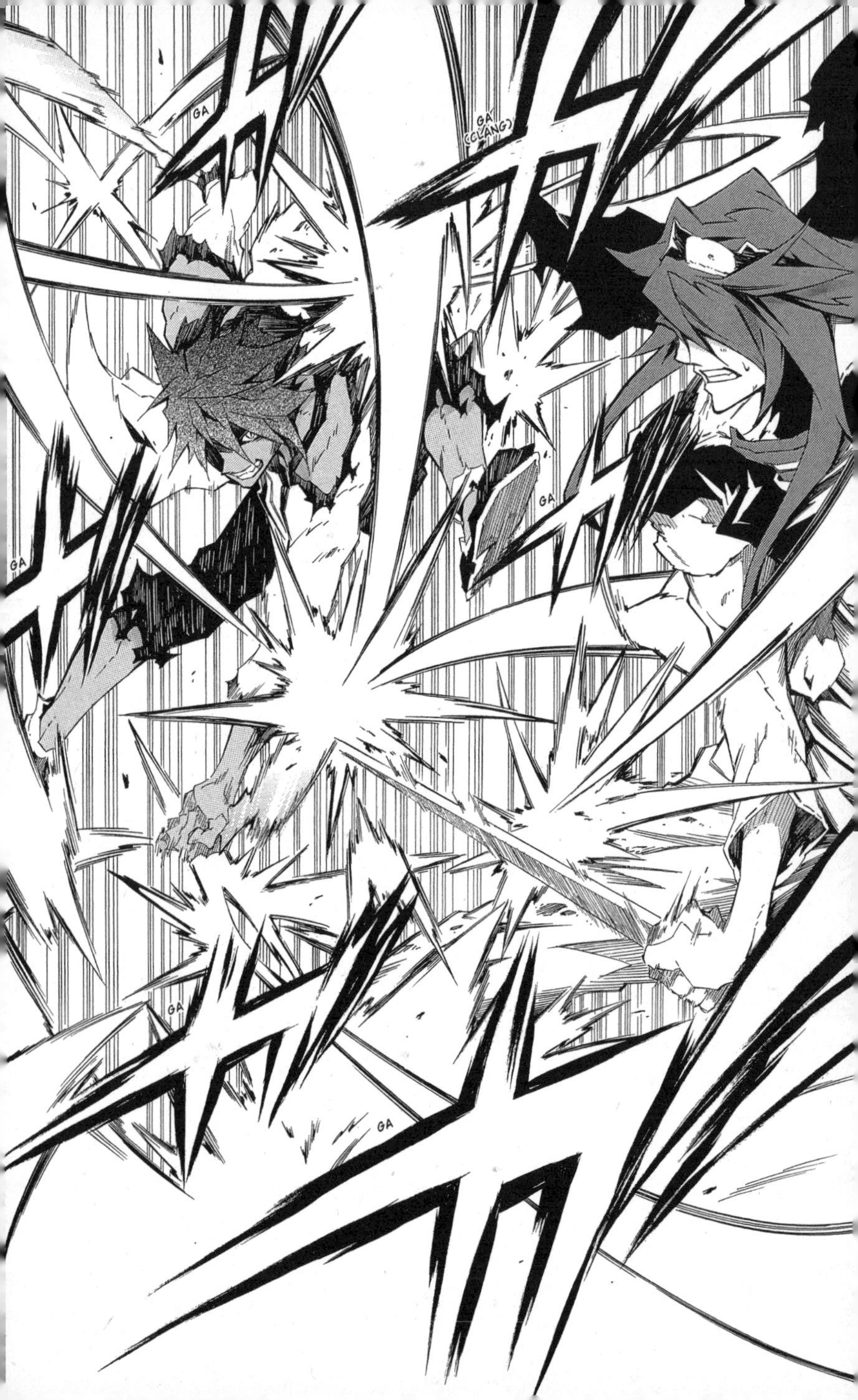

GA
(CLANG)
GA
GA
GA
GA
GA

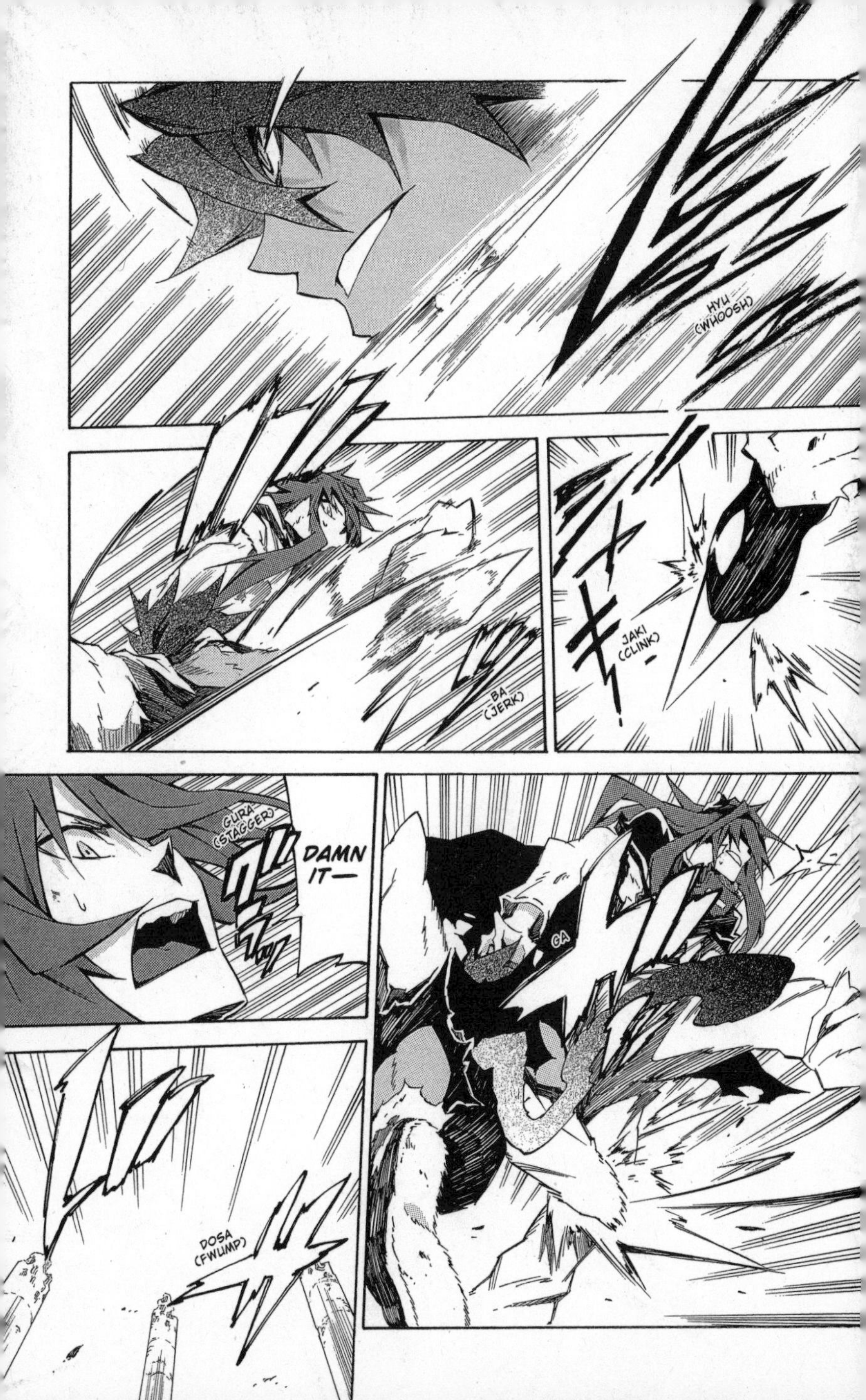
HYU (WHOOSH)
JAKI (CLINK)
BA (JERK)
GA
GURA (STAGGER)
DAMN IT—
DOSA (FWUMP)

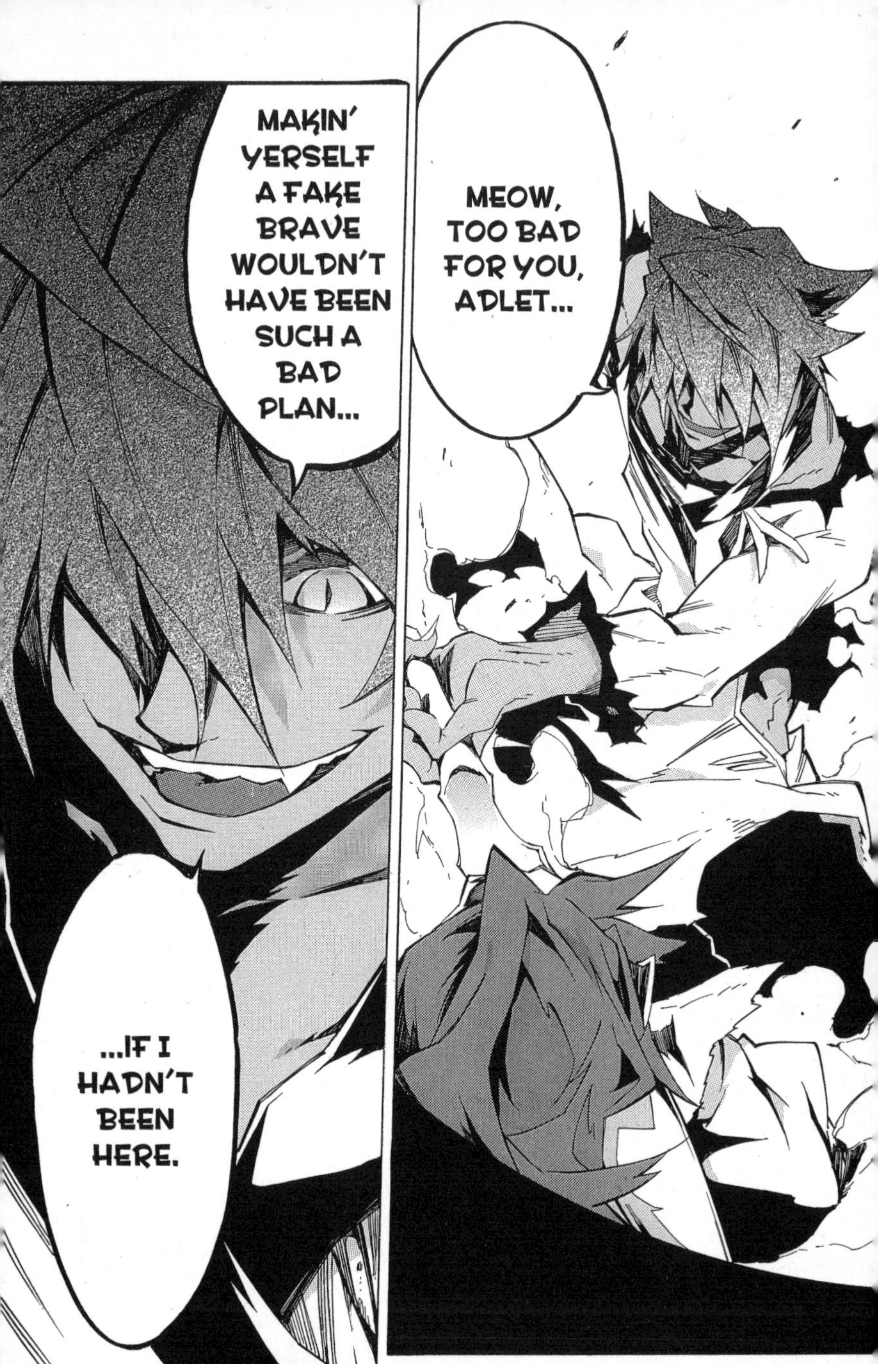
MEOW, TOO BAD FOR YOU, ADLET...
MAKIN' YERSELF A FAKE BRAVE WOULDN'T HAVE BEEN SUCH A BAD PLAN...
...IF I HADN'T BEEN HERE.

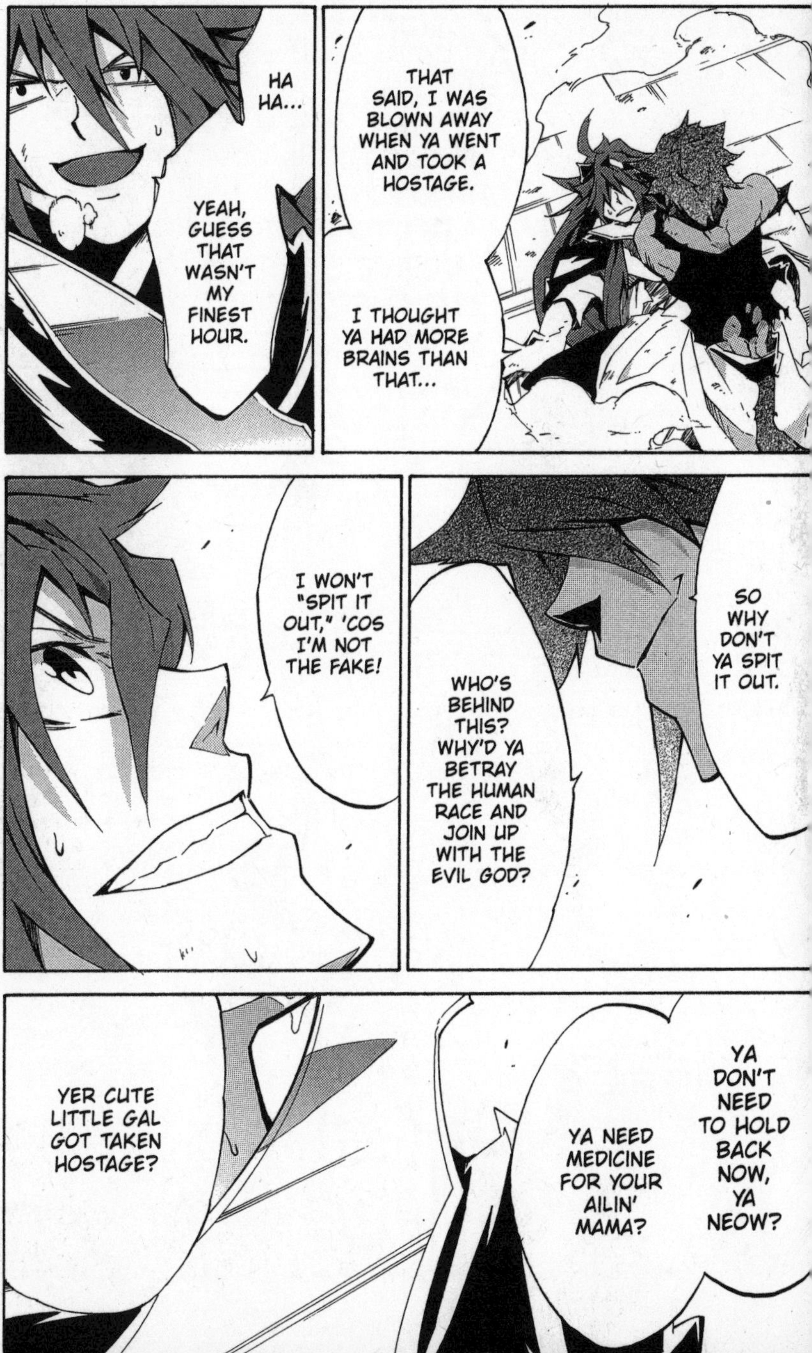
THAT SAID, I WAS BLOWN AWAY WHEN YA WENT AND TOOK A HOSTAGE.
I THOUGHT YA HAD MORE BRAINS THAN THAT...
HA HA...
YEAH, GUESS THAT WASN'T MY FINEST HOUR.
SO WHY DON'T YA SPIT IT OUT.
WHO'S BEHIND THIS? WHY'D YA BETRAY THE HUMAN RACE AND JOIN UP WITH THE EVIL GOD?
I WON'T "SPIT IT OUT," 'COS I'M NOT THE FAKE!
YA DON'T NEED TO HOLD BACK NOW, YA NEOW?
YA NEED MEDICINE FOR YOUR AILIN' MAMA?
YER CUTE LITTLE GAL GOT TAKEN HOSTAGE?

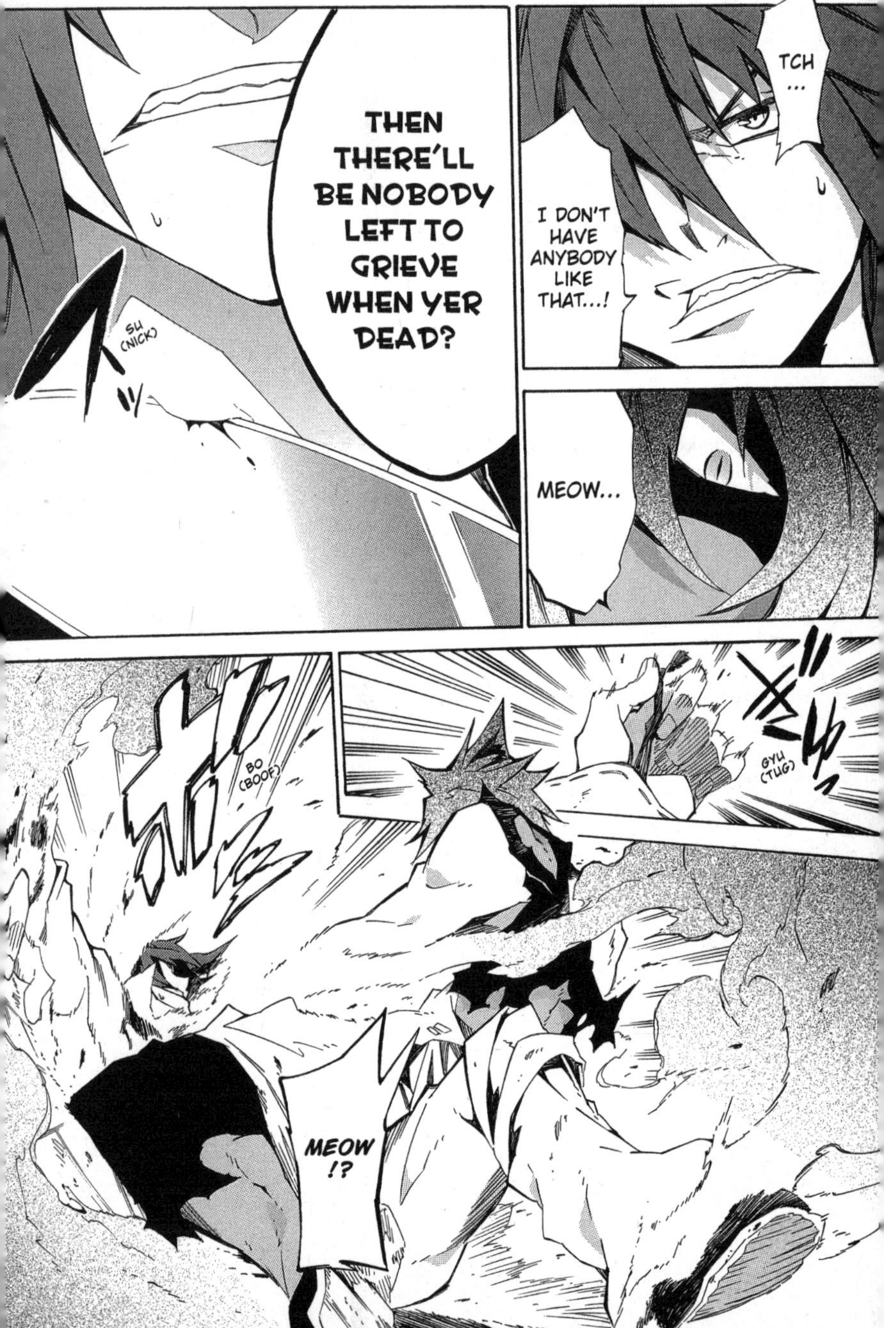
TCH ...
I DON'T HAVE ANYBODY LIKE THAT...!
MEOW...
THEN THERE'LL BE NOBODY LEFT TO GRIEVE WHEN YER DEAD?
SU (NICK)
GYU (TUG)
BO (BOOF)
MEOW !?

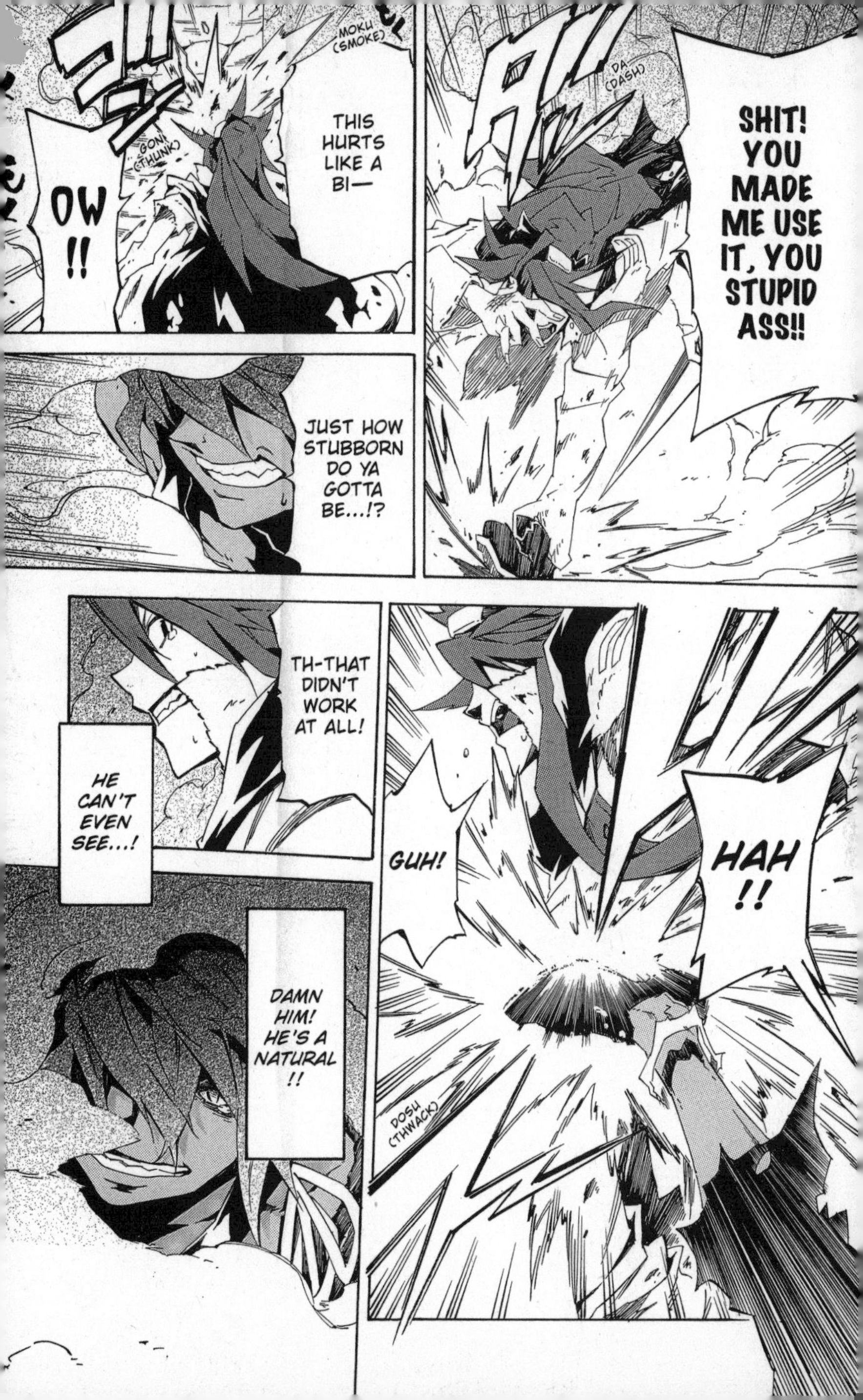
DA (DASH)
SHIT! YOU MADE ME USE IT, YOU STUPID ASS!!
MOKU (SMOKE)
THIS HURTS LIKE A BI—
GON (THUNK)
OW !!
JUST HOW STUBBORN DO YA GOTTA BE...!?
HAH !!
GUH!
DOSU (THWACK)
TH-THAT DIDN'T WORK AT ALL!
HE CAN'T EVEN SEE...!
DAMN HIM! HE'S A NATURAL !!

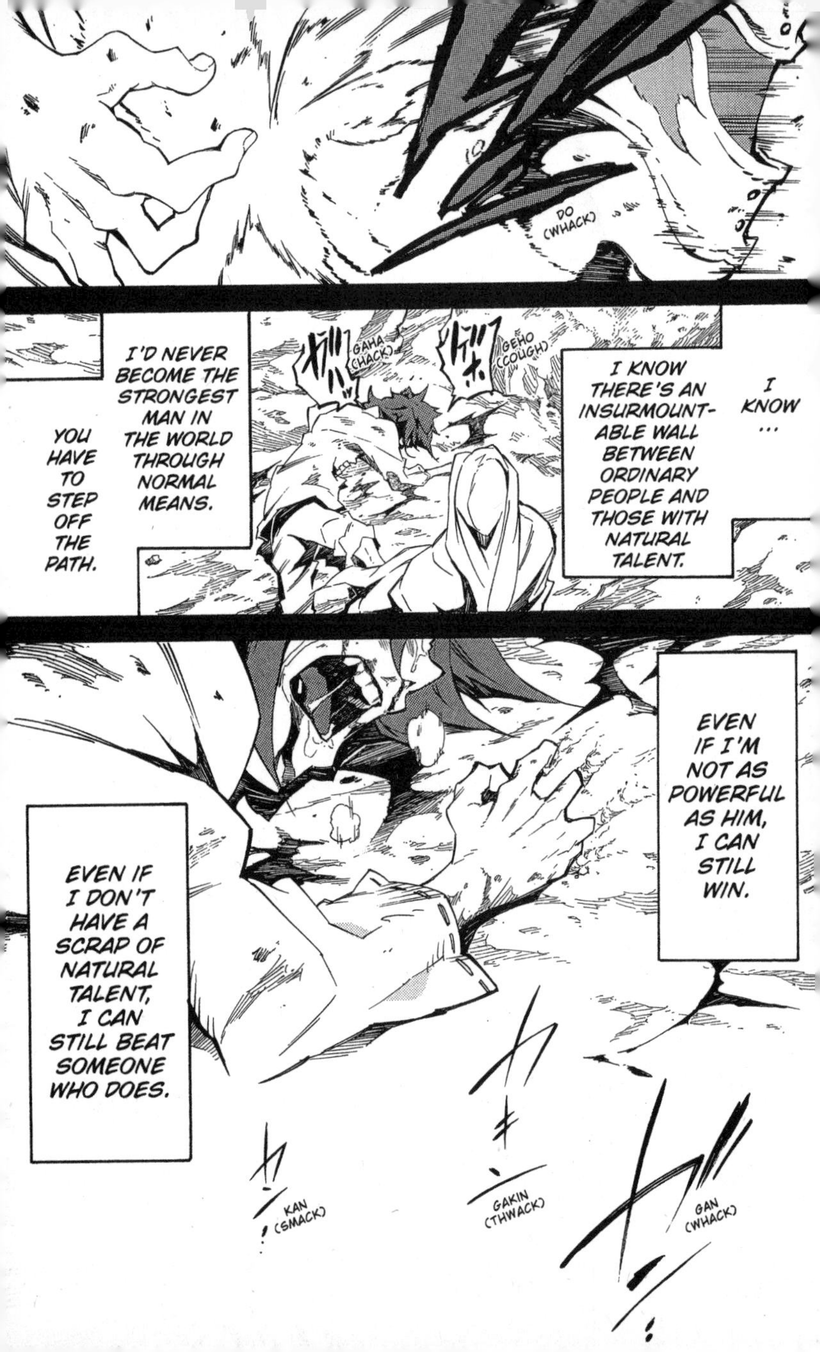
DO (WHACK)
I KNOW...
I KNOW THERE'S AN INSURMOUNT-ABLE WALL BETWEEN ORDINARY PEOPLE AND THOSE WITH NATURAL TALENT.
GEHO (COUGH)
GAHA (HACK)
I'D NEVER BECOME THE STRONGEST MAN IN THE WORLD THROUGH NORMAL MEANS.
YOU HAVE TO STEP OFF THE PATH.
EVEN IF I'M NOT AS POWERFUL AS HIM, I CAN STILL WIN.
EVEN IF I DON'T HAVE A SCRAP OF NATURAL TALENT, I CAN STILL BEAT SOMEONE WHO DOES.
GAN (WHACK)
GAKIN (THWACK)
KAN (SMACK)

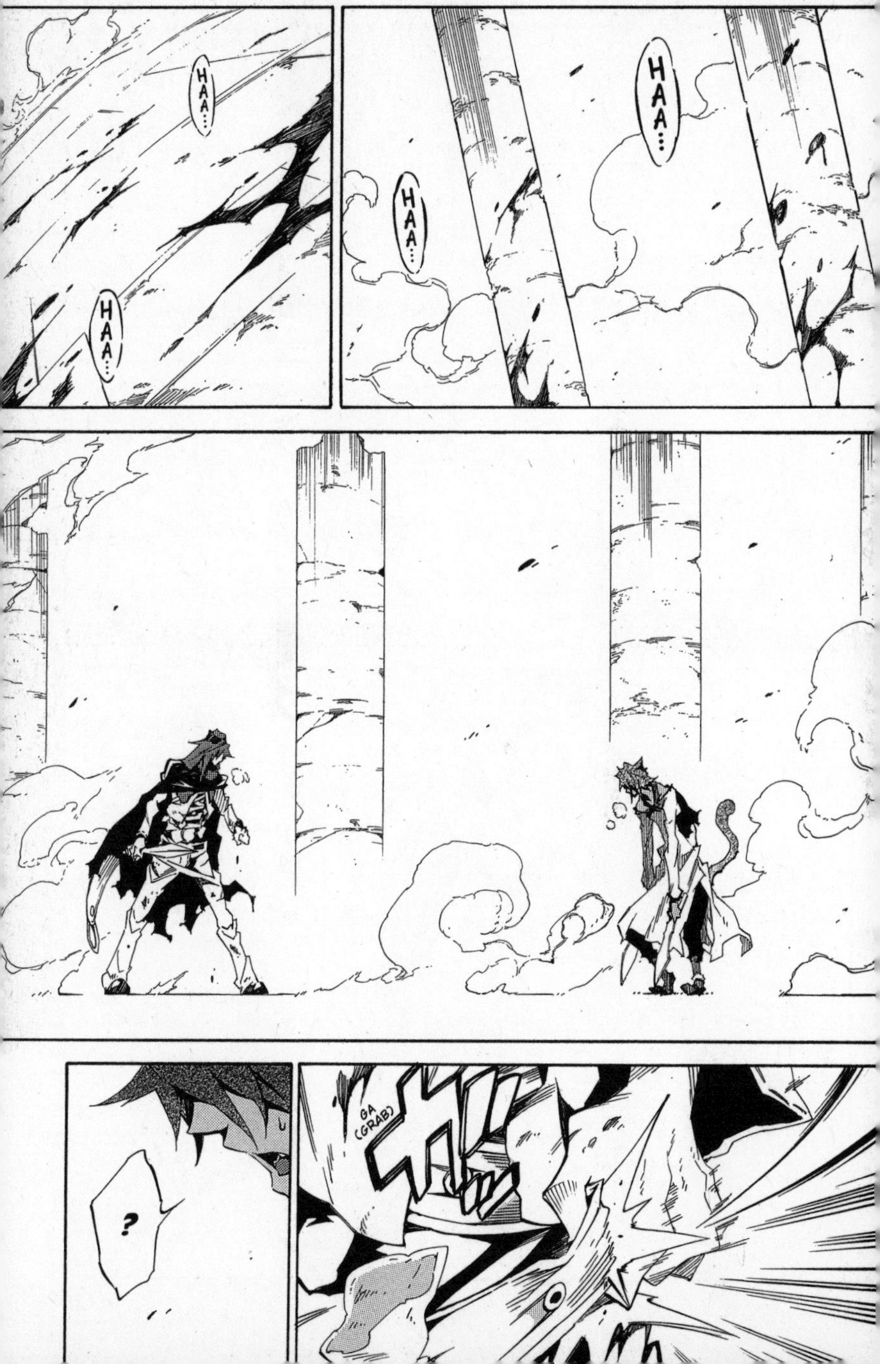

HAA...
HAA...
HAA...
HAA...
GA (GRAB)
?

BA

BASA

DOSA
(THUMP)

BASA
(TOSS)

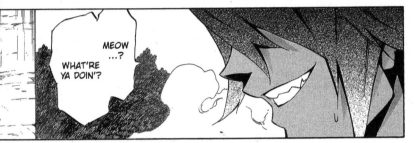

MEOW
...?

WHAT'RE
YA DOIN'?

COME
AT ME!

I DON'T
NEED ANY
MORE
FANCY
TOOLS.

I CAN
BEAT YOU
FAIR AND
SQUARE!!

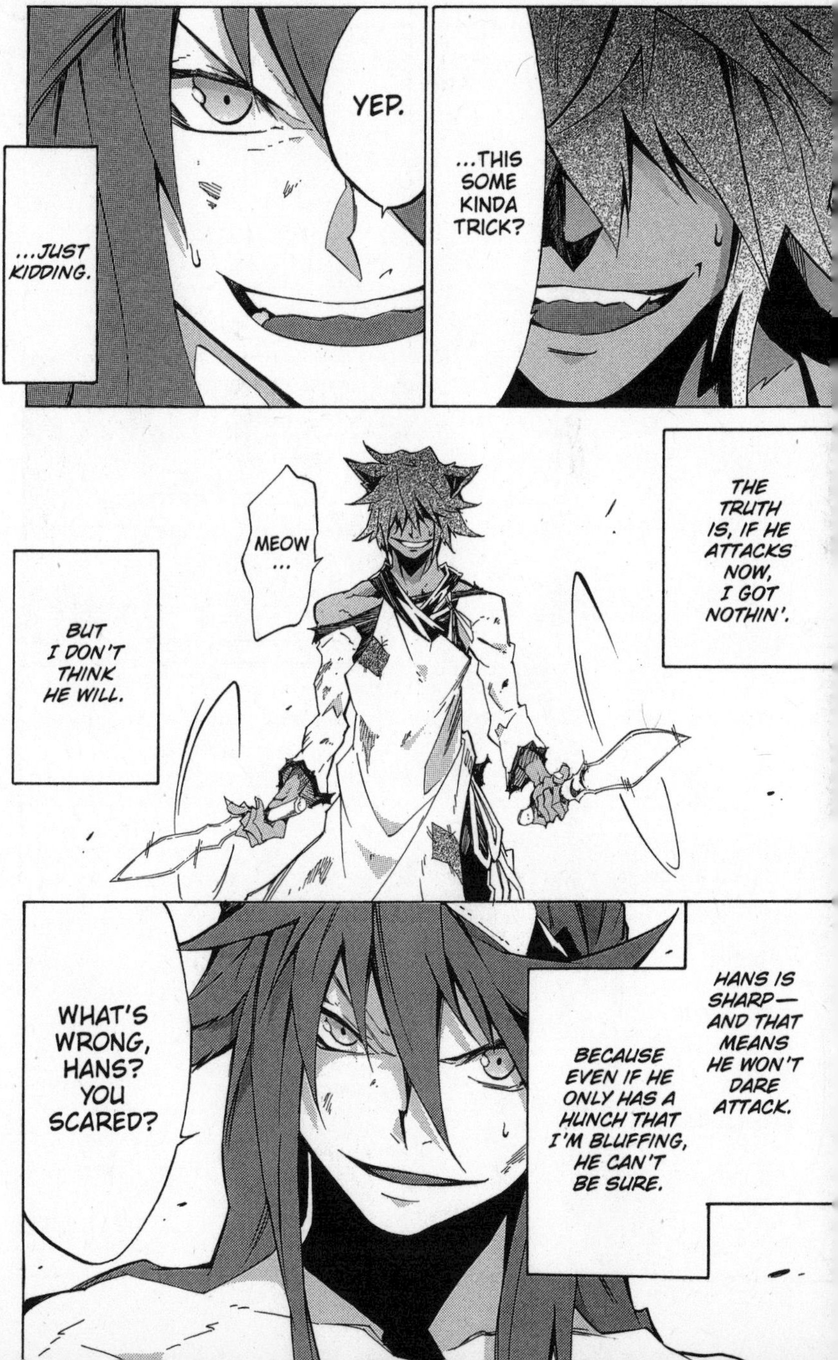
...THIS SOME KINDA TRICK?
YEP.
...JUST KIDDING.
THE TRUTH IS, IF HE ATTACKS NOW, I GOT NOTHIN'.
MEOW...
BUT I DON'T THINK HE WILL.
HANS IS SHARP—AND THAT MEANS HE WON'T DARE ATTACK.
BECAUSE EVEN IF HE ONLY HAS A HUNCH THAT I'M BLUFFING, HE CAN'T BE SURE.
WHAT'S WRONG, HANS? YOU SCARED?

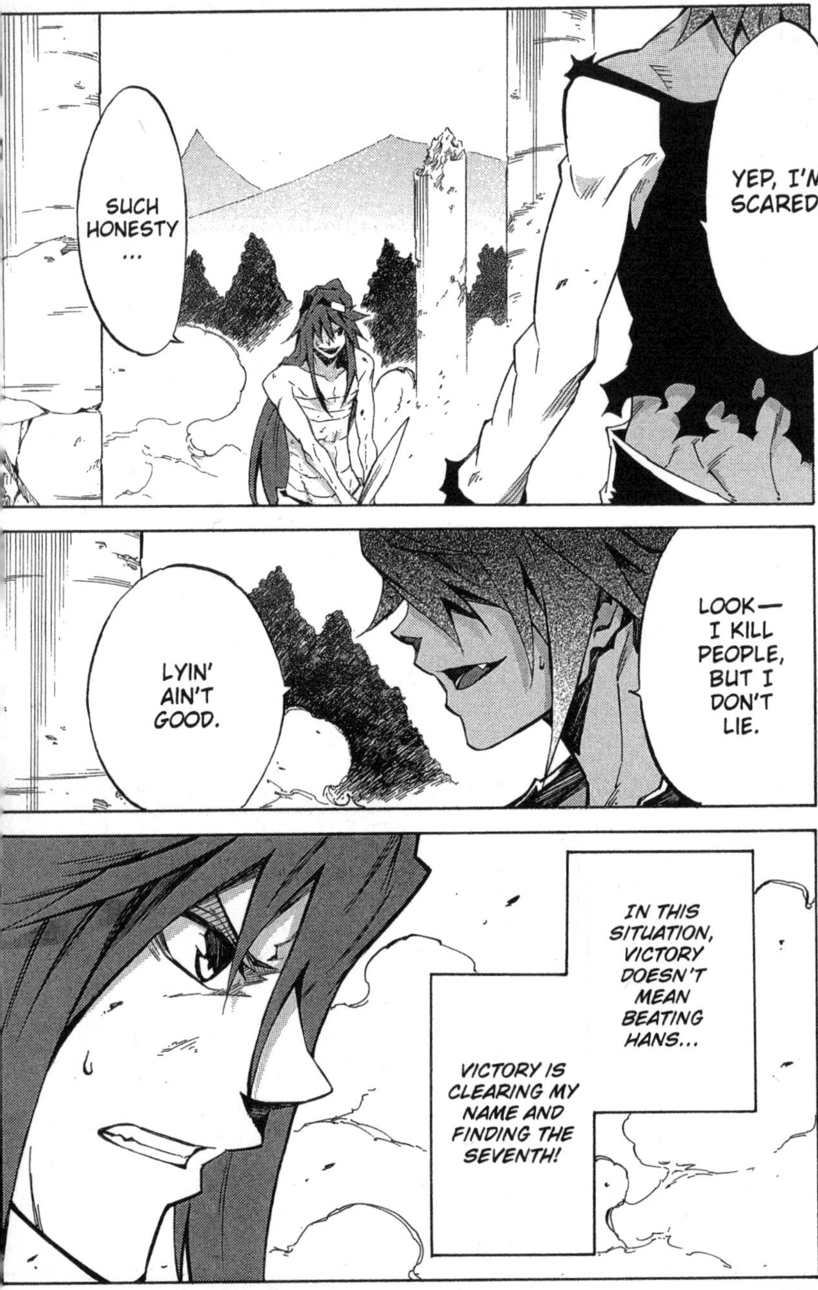
YEP, I'M SCARED.
SUCH HONESTY...
LOOK— I KILL PEOPLE, BUT I DON'T LIE.
LYIN' AIN'T GOOD.
IN THIS SITUATION, VICTORY DOESN'T MEAN BEATING HANS...
VICTORY IS CLEARING MY NAME AND FINDING THE SEVENTH!

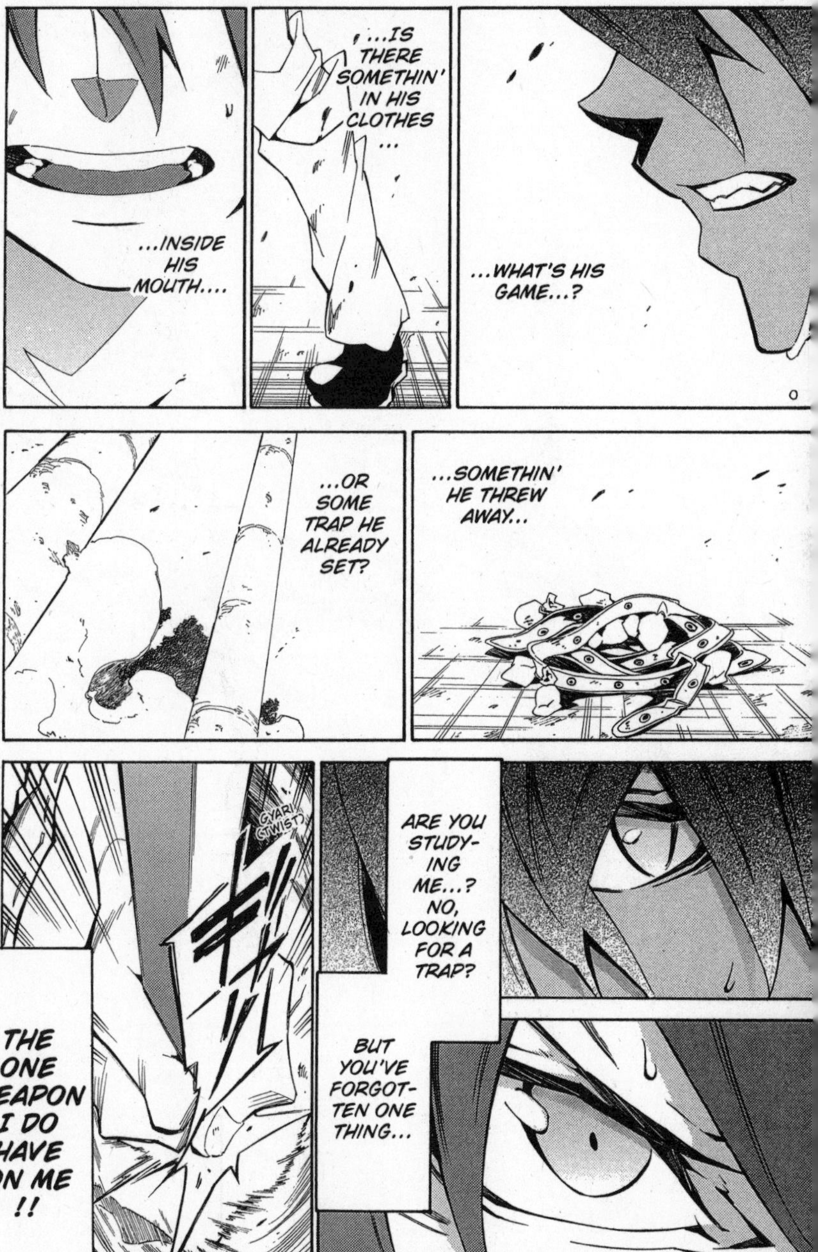
...WHAT'S HIS GAME...?
...IS THERE SOMETHIN' IN HIS CLOTHES...
...INSIDE HIS MOUTH....
...SOMETHIN' HE THREW AWAY...
...OR SOME TRAP HE ALREADY SET?
ARE YOU STUDYING ME...? NO, LOOKING FOR A TRAP?
BUT YOU'VE FORGOTTEN ONE THING...
GYARI (TWIST)
THE ONE WEAPON I DO HAVE ON ME!!

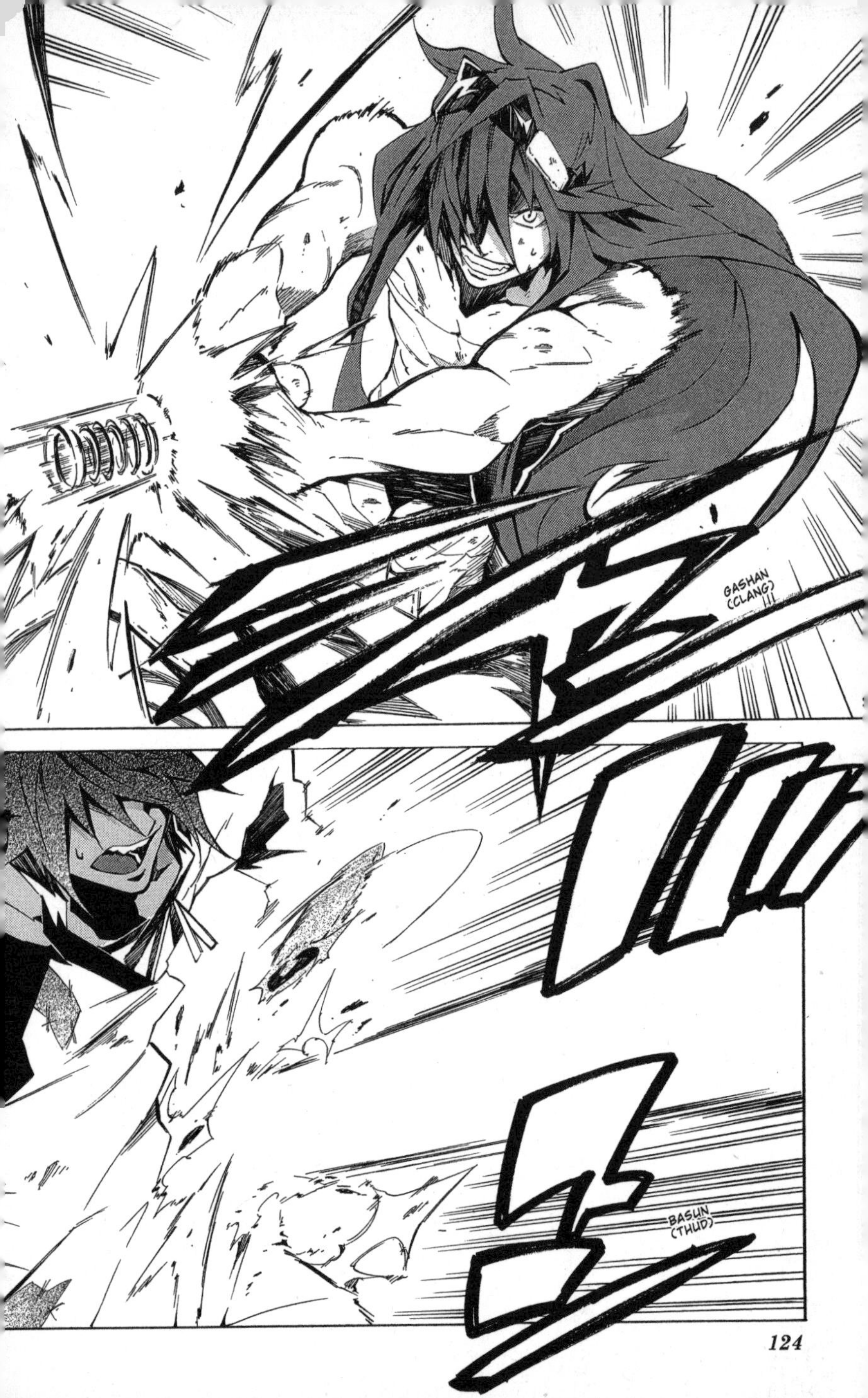
GASHAN
(CLANG)
BASUN
(THUD)

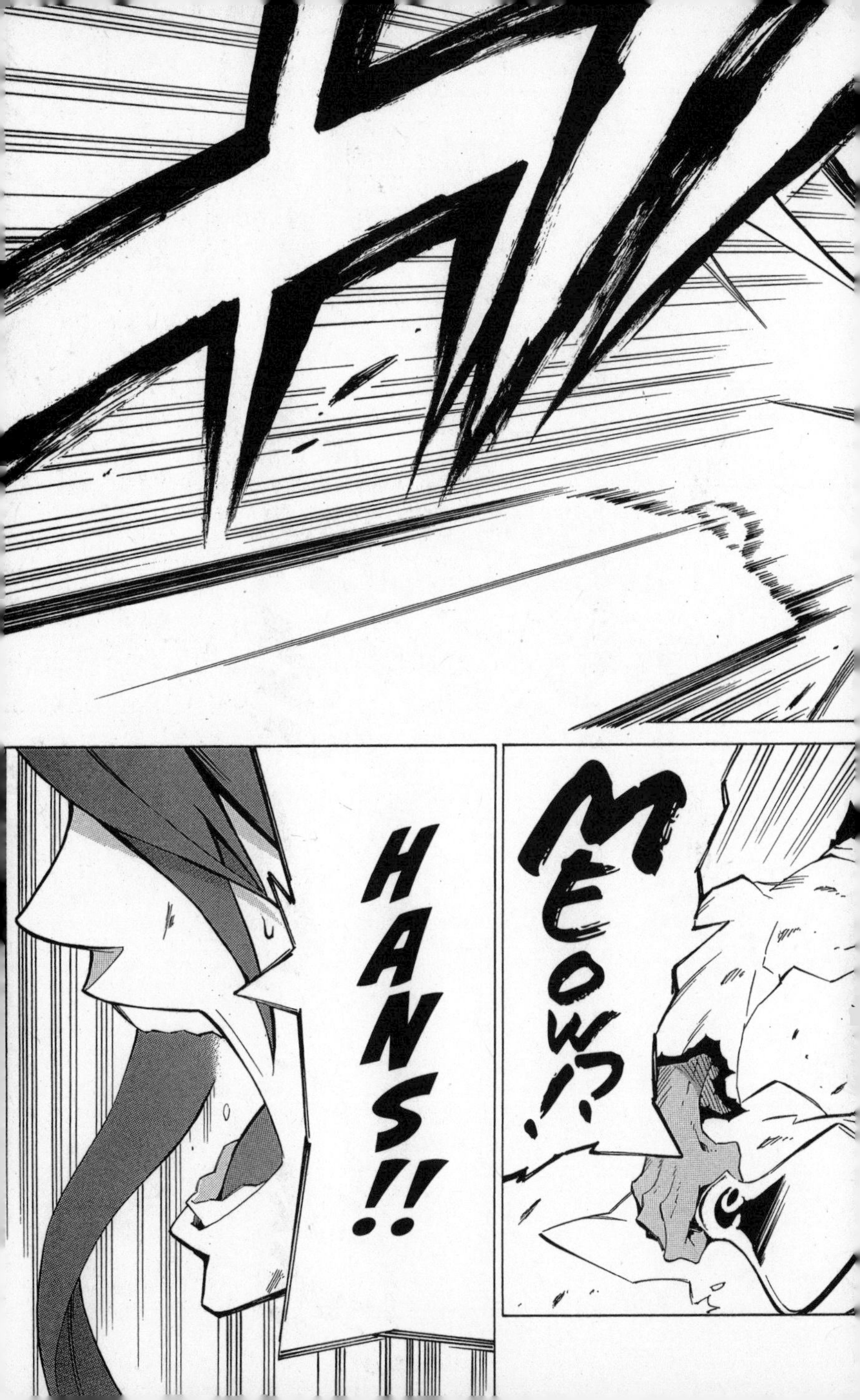
MEOW!?
HANS!!

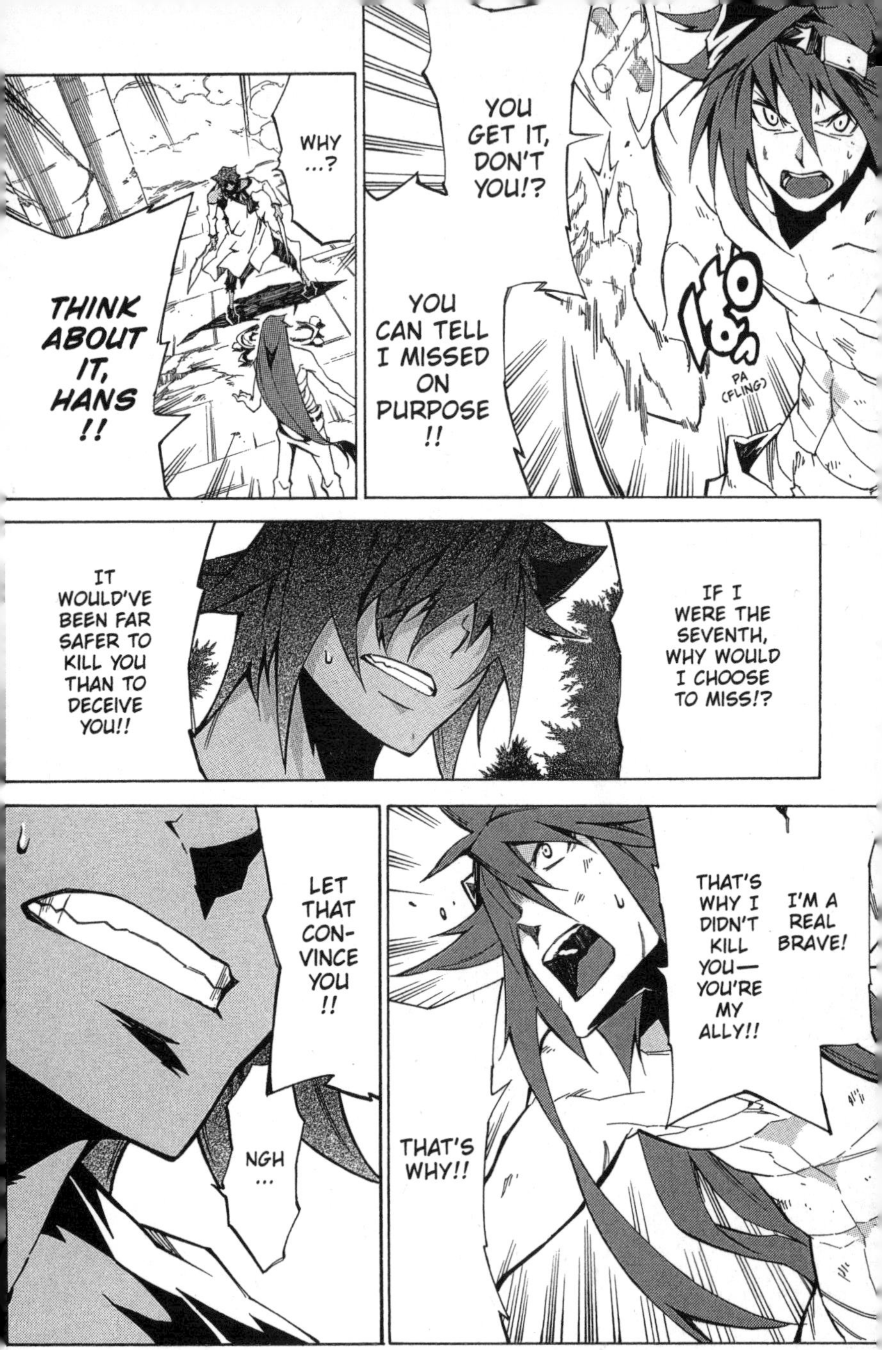
YOU GET IT, DON'T YOU!?
YOU CAN TELL I MISSED ON PURPOSE!!
PA (FLING)
WHY ...?
THINK ABOUT IT, HANS!!
IF I WERE THE SEVENTH, WHY WOULD I CHOOSE TO MISS!?
IT WOULD'VE BEEN FAR SAFER TO KILL YOU THAN TO DECEIVE YOU!!
I'M A REAL BRAVE!
THAT'S WHY I DIDN'T KILL YOU—YOU'RE MY ALLY!!
THAT'S WHY!!
LET THAT CONVINCE YOU!!
NGH ...

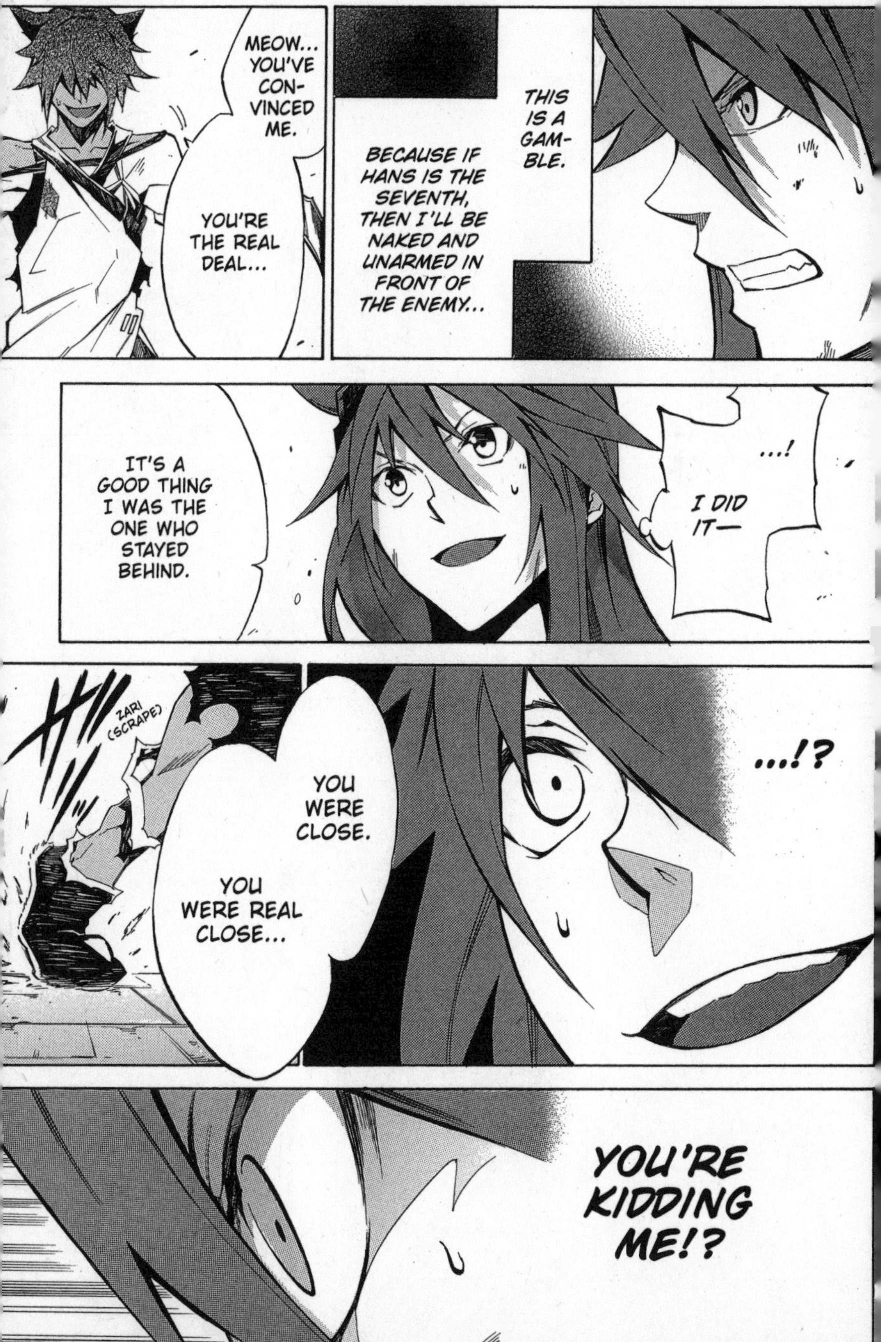
THIS IS A GAMBLE.
BECAUSE IF HANS IS THE SEVENTH, THEN I'LL BE NAKED AND UNARMED IN FRONT OF THE ENEMY...
MEOW... YOU'VE CONVINCED ME.
YOU'RE THE REAL DEAL...
...!
I DID IT—
IT'S A GOOD THING I WAS THE ONE WHO STAYED BEHIND.
YOU WERE CLOSE.
YOU WERE REAL CLOSE...
...!?
ZARI (SCRAPE)
YOU'RE KIDDING ME!?

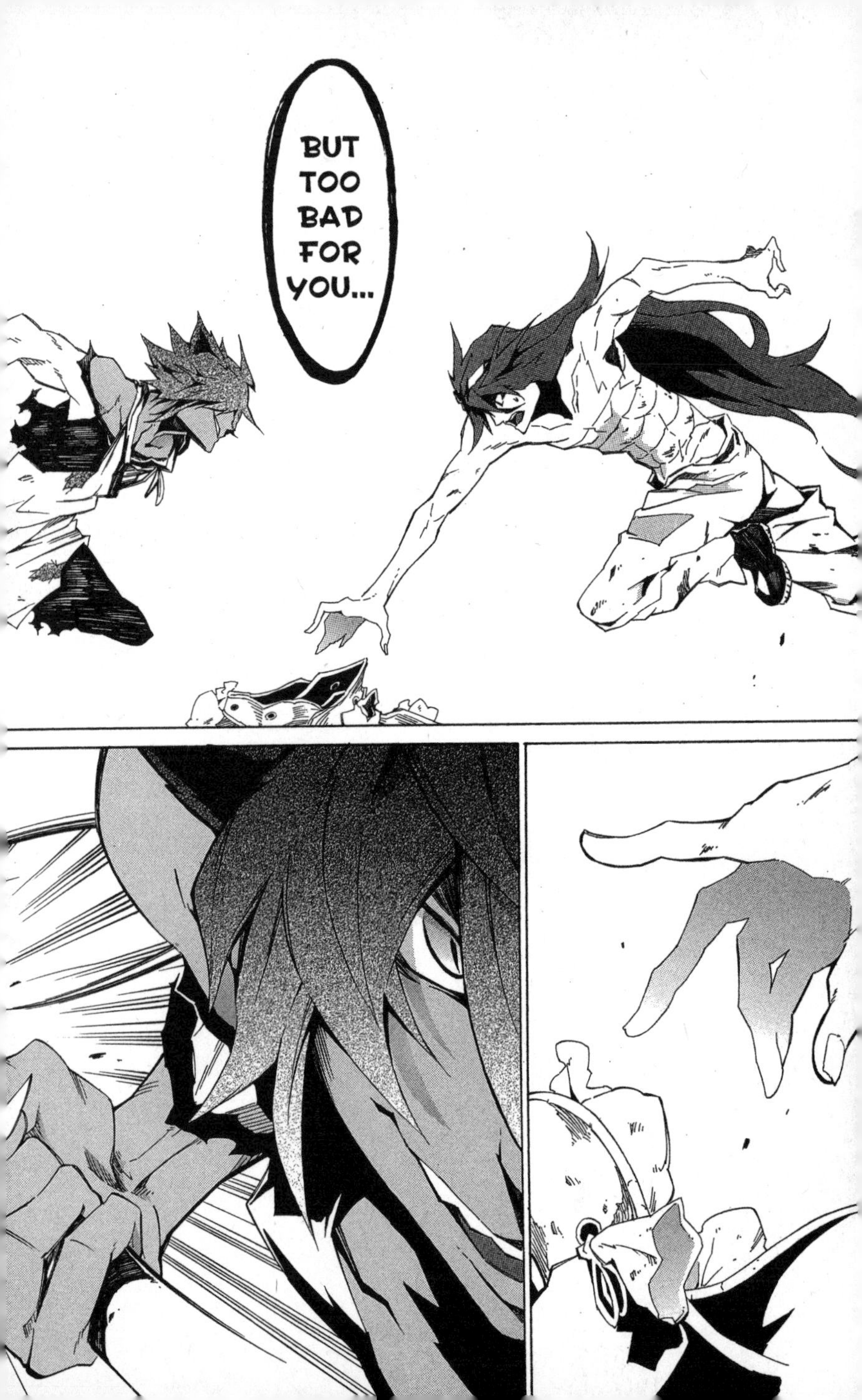
BUT TOO BAD FOR YOU...

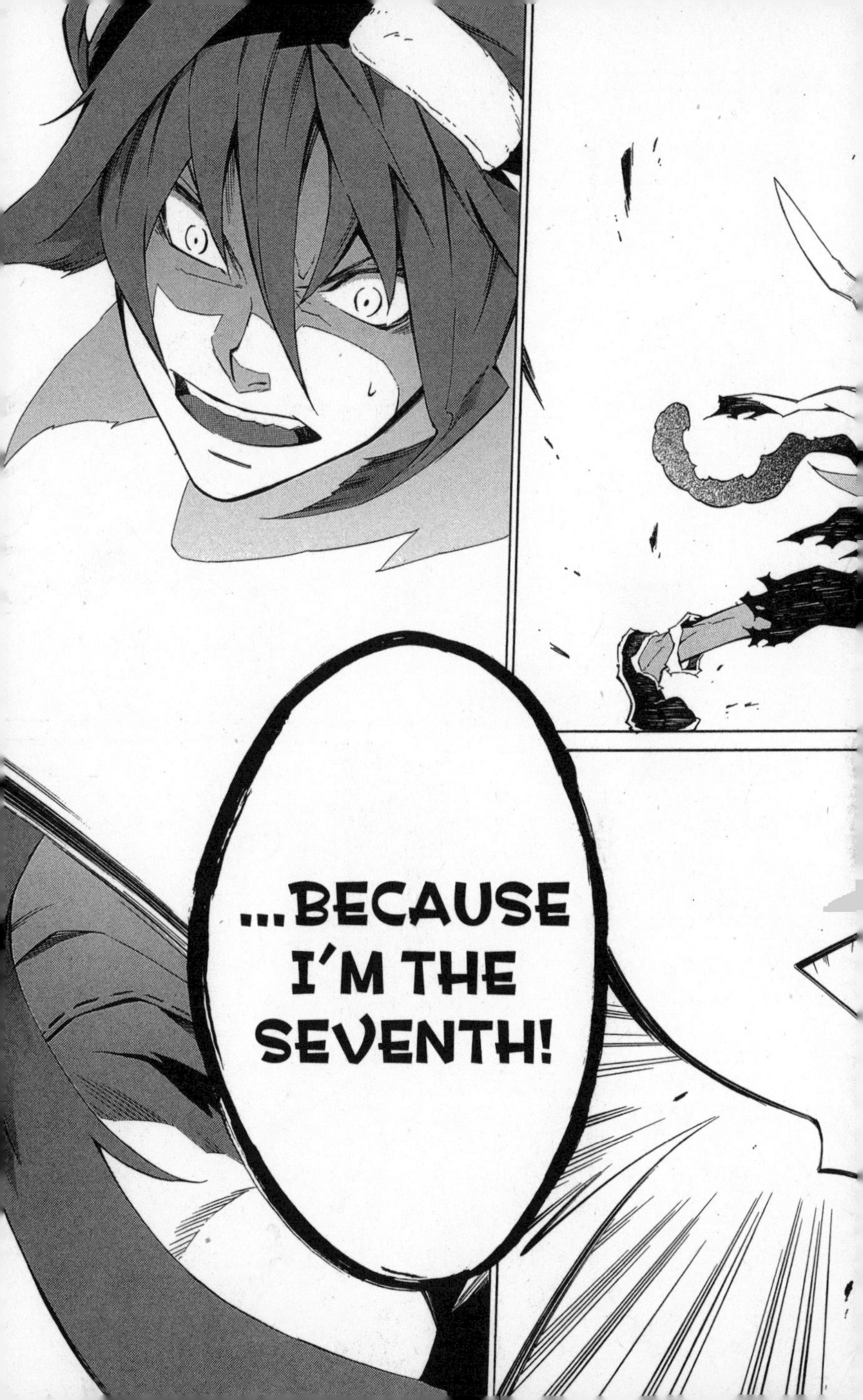
...BECAUSE I'M THE SEVENTH!

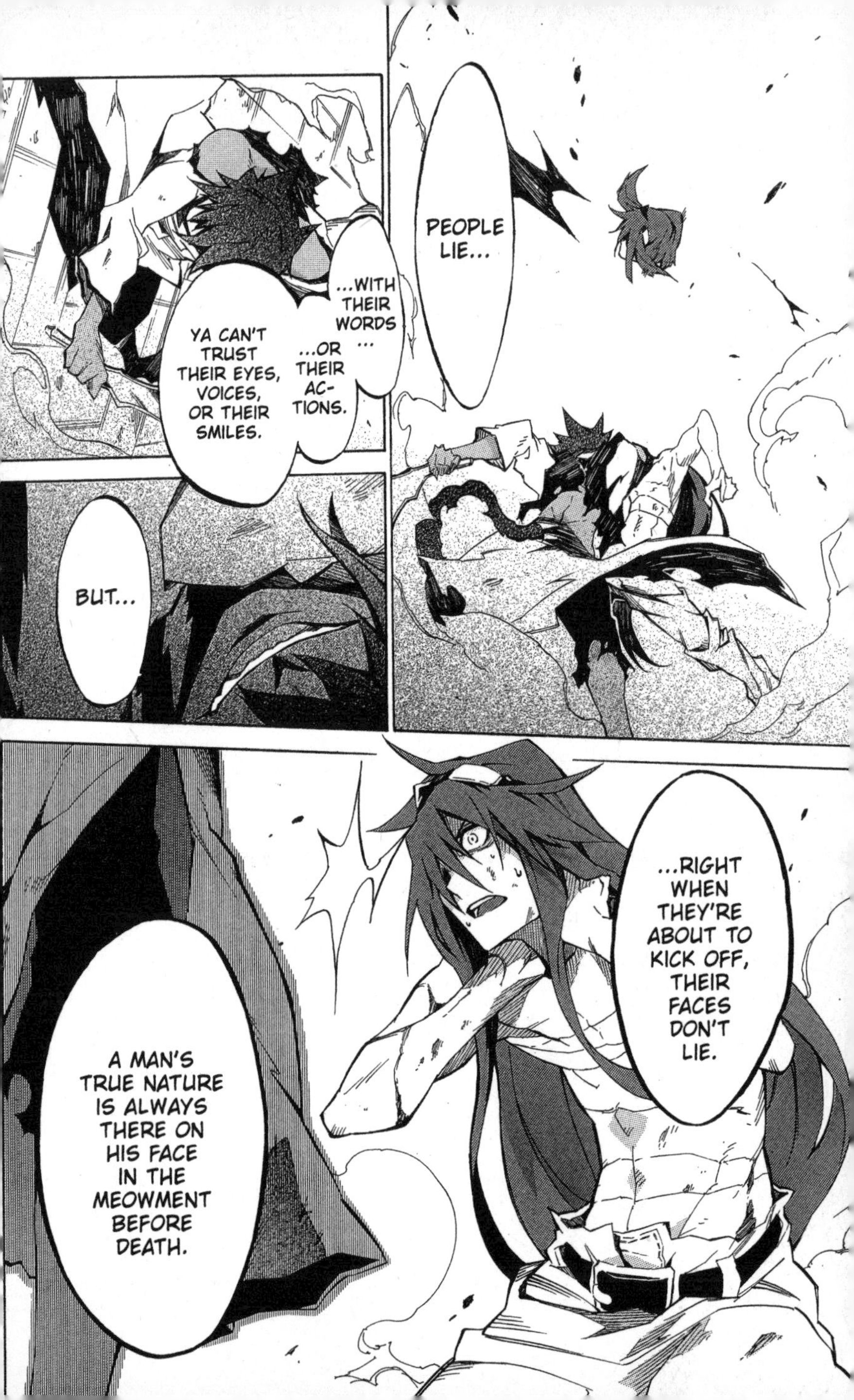
PEOPLE LIE...
...WITH THEIR WORDS...
...OR THEIR AC-TIONS.
YA CAN'T TRUST THEIR EYES, VOICES, OR THEIR SMILES.
BUT...
...RIGHT WHEN THEY'RE ABOUT TO KICK OFF, THEIR FACES DON'T LIE.
A MAN'S TRUE NATURE IS ALWAYS THERE ON HIS FACE IN THE MEOWMENT BEFORE DEATH.

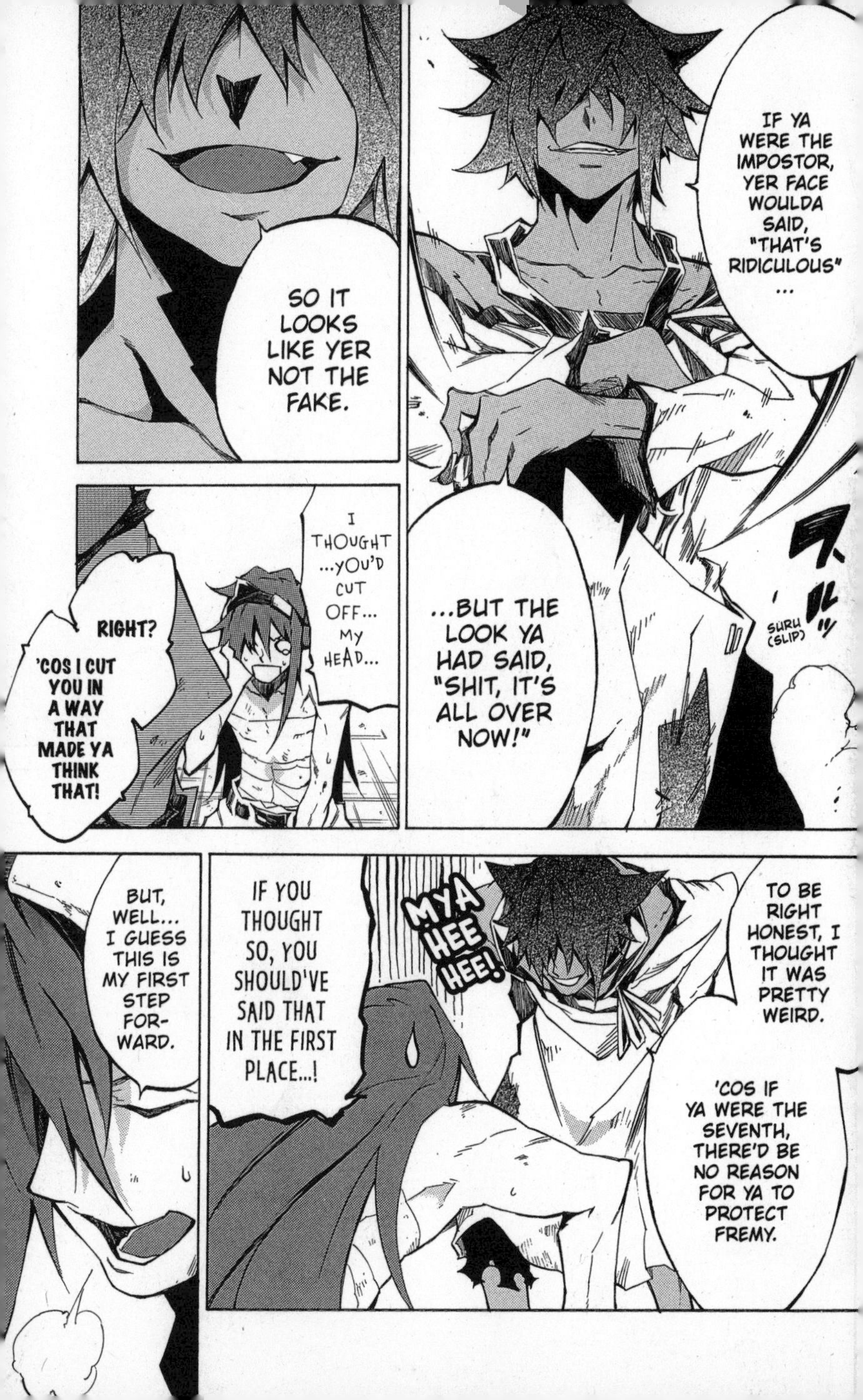
IF YA WERE THE IMPOSTOR, YER FACE WOULDA SAID, "THAT'S RIDICULOUS"...
...BUT THE LOOK YA HAD SAID, "SHIT, IT'S ALL OVER NOW!"
SURU (SLIP)
SO IT LOOKS LIKE YER NOT THE FAKE.
I THOUGHT ...YOU'D CUT OFF... MY HEAD...
RIGHT?
'COS I CUT YOU IN A WAY THAT MADE YA THINK THAT!
TO BE RIGHT HONEST, I THOUGHT IT WAS PRETTY WEIRD.
'COS IF YA WERE THE SEVENTH, THERE'D BE NO REASON FOR YA TO PROTECT FREMY.
MYA HEE HEE!
IF YOU THOUGHT SO, YOU SHOULD'VE SAID THAT IN THE FIRST PLACE...!
BUT, WELL... I GUESS THIS IS MY FIRST STEP FOR-WARD.

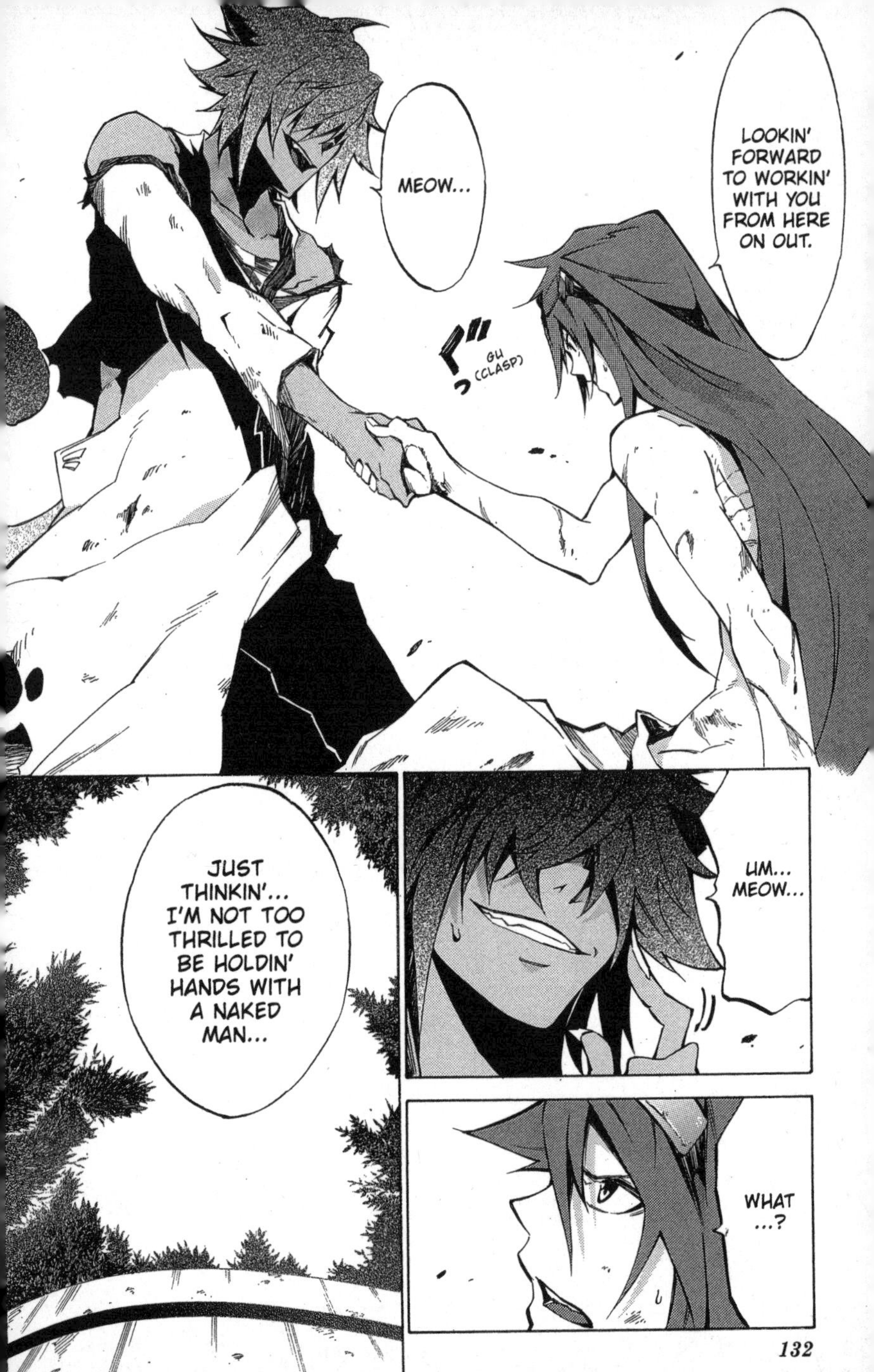
LOOKIN' FORWARD TO WORKIN' WITH YOU FROM HERE ON OUT.
MEOW...
GU (CLASP)
UM... MEOW...
WHAT ...?
JUST THINKIN'... I'M NOT TOO THRILLED TO BE HOLDIN' HANDS WITH A NAKED MAN...

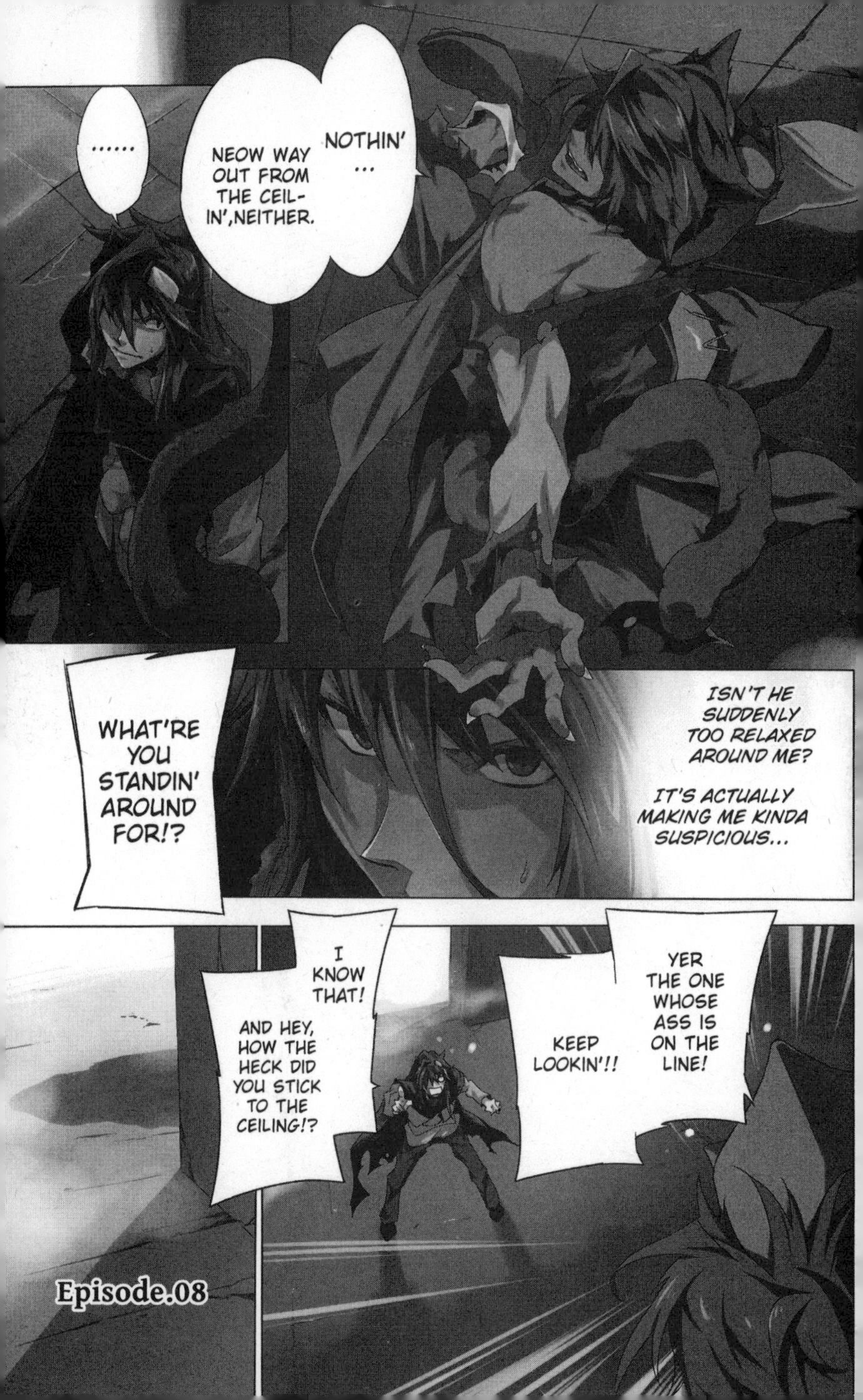
NOTHIN' ... NEOW WAY OUT FROM THE CEIL-IN', NEITHER.
......
ISN'T HE SUDDENLY TOO RELAXED AROUND ME?
IT'S ACTUALLY MAKING ME KINDA SUSPICIOUS...
WHAT'RE YOU STANDIN' AROUND FOR!?
YER THE ONE WHOSE ASS IS ON THE LINE!
KEEP LOOKIN'!!
I KNOW THAT!
AND HEY, HOW THE HECK DID YOU STICK TO THE CEILING!?
Episode.08

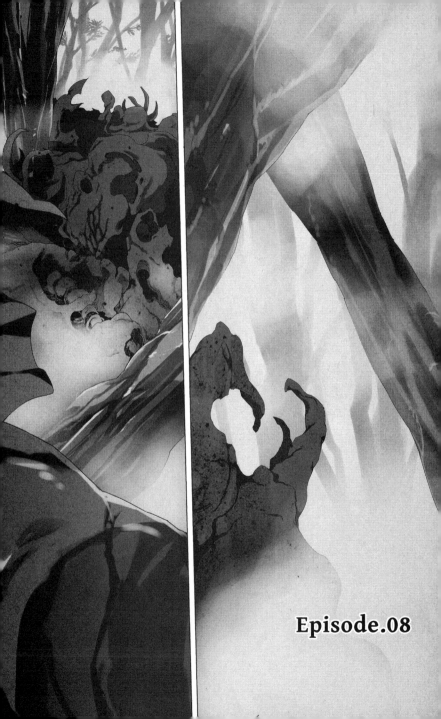

Episode.08

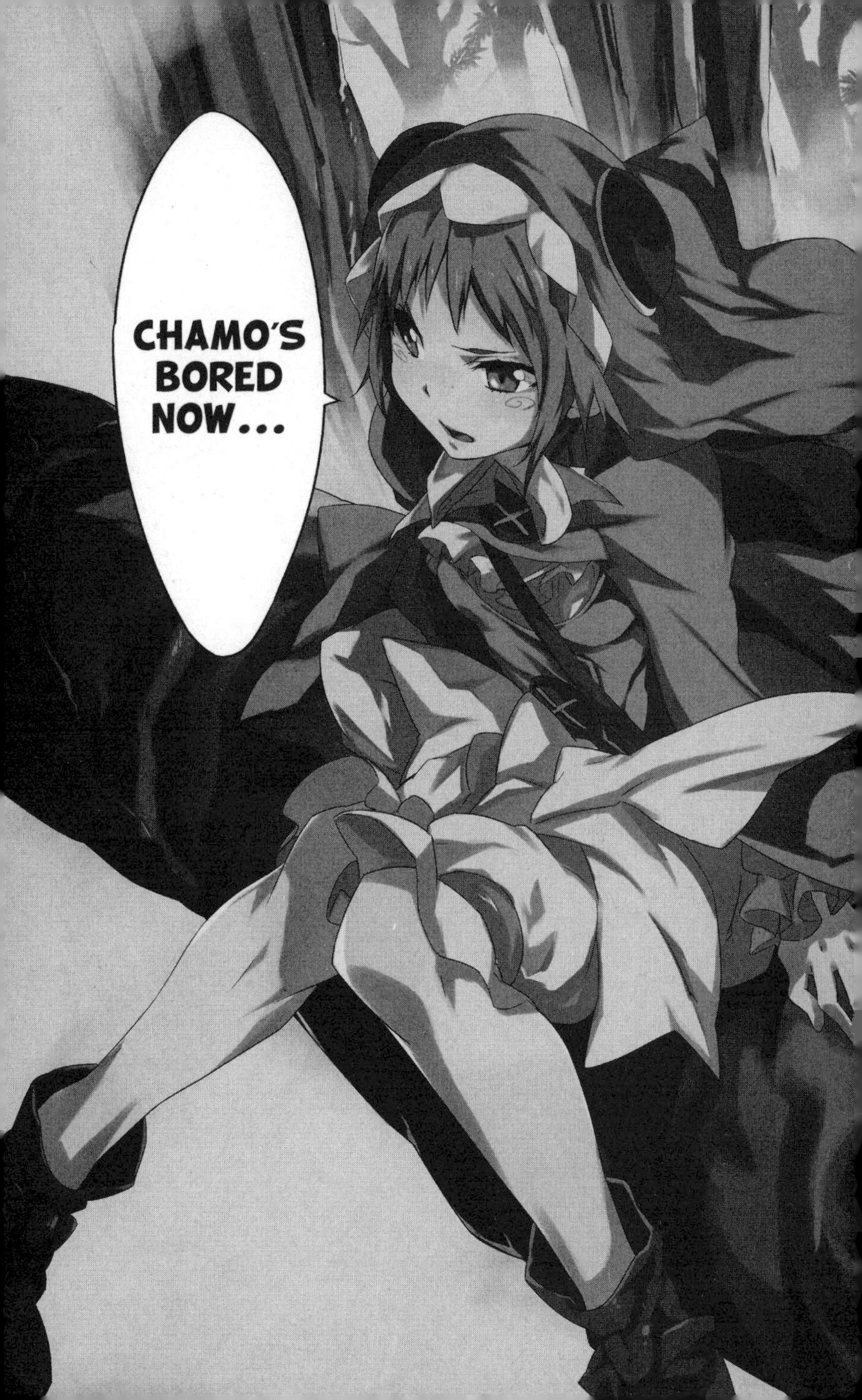
CHAMO'S BORED NOW...

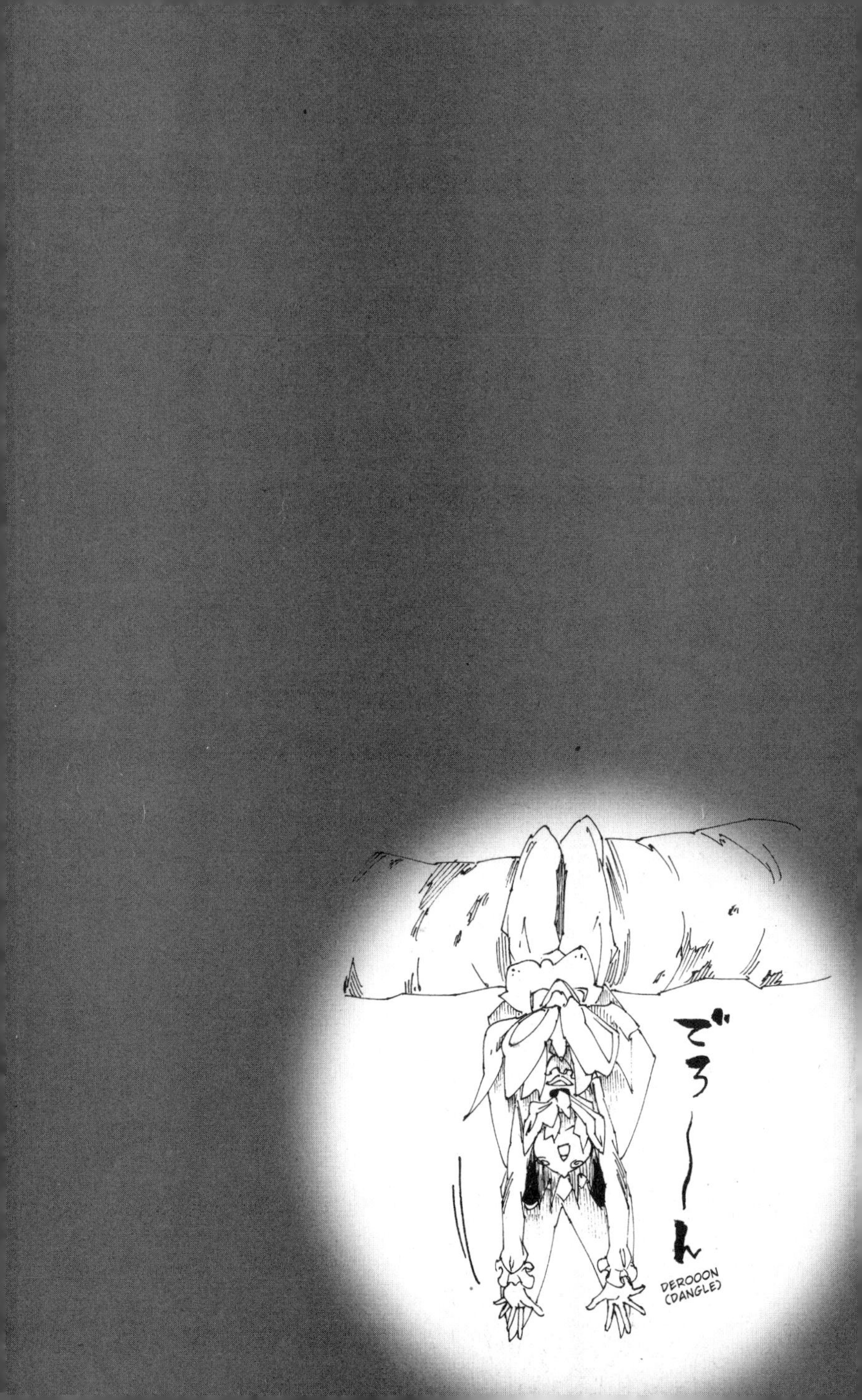
でろ〜〜ん
DEROOON
(DANGLE)

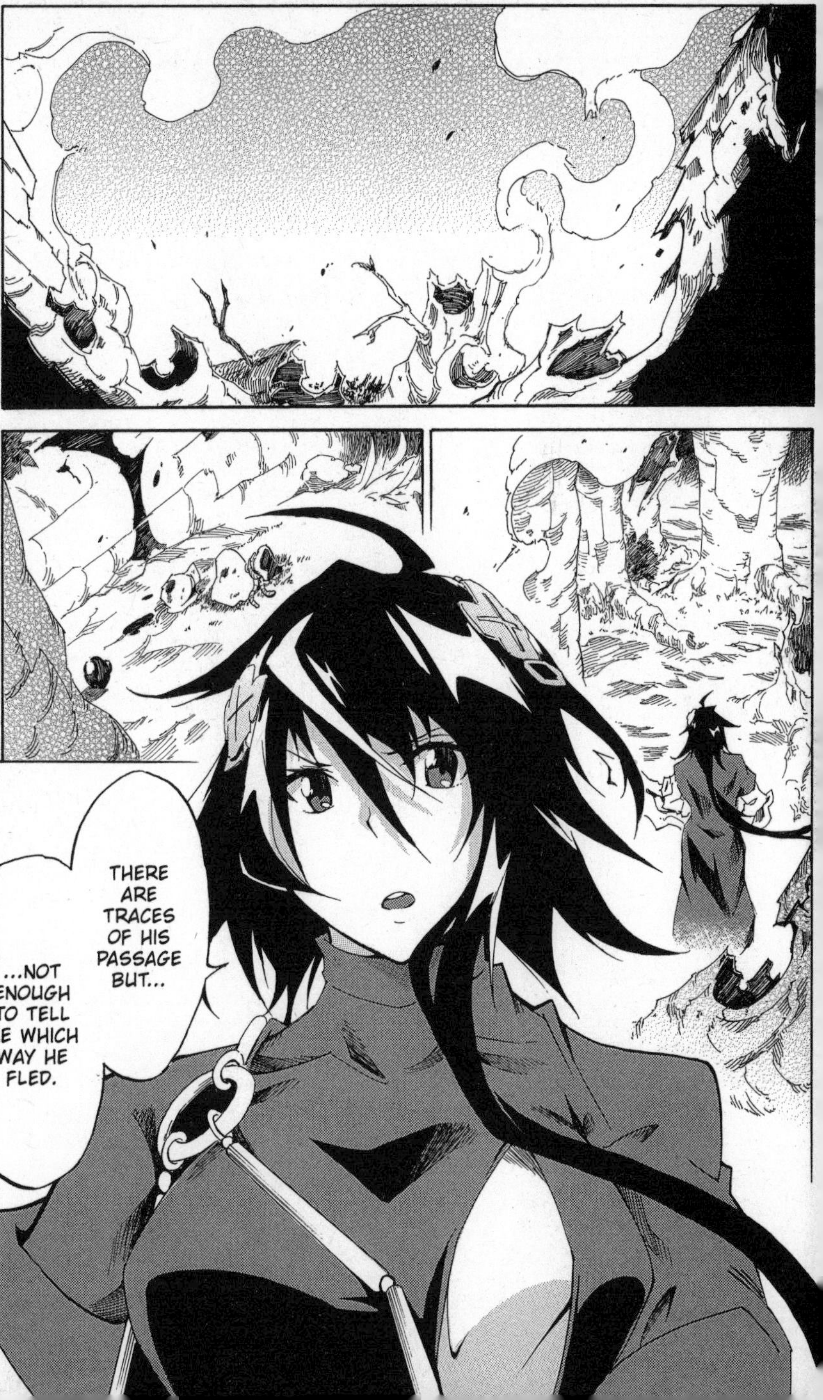
THERE ARE TRACES OF HIS PASSAGE BUT...
...NOT ENOUGH TO TELL ME WHICH WAY HE FLED.

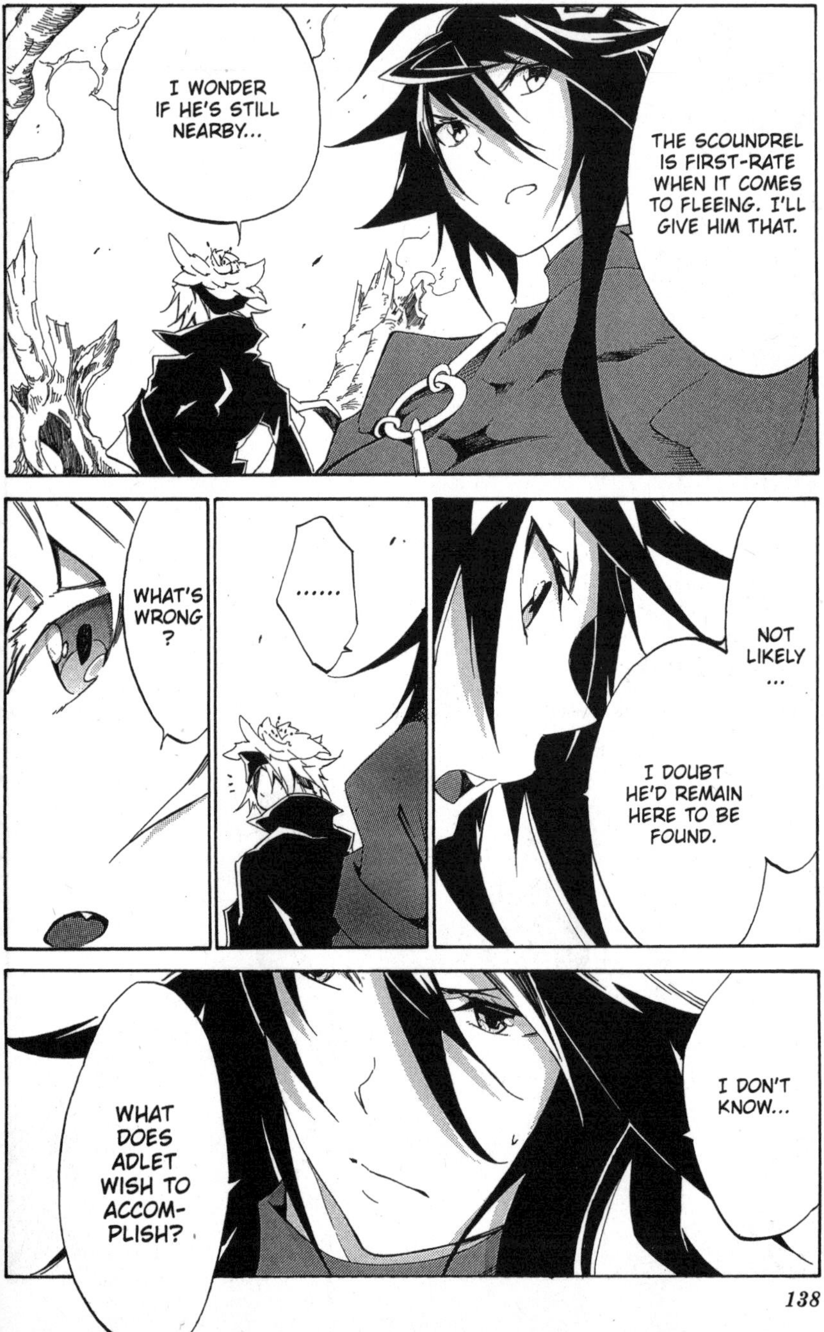
THE SCOUNDREL IS FIRST-RATE WHEN IT COMES TO FLEEING. I'LL GIVE HIM THAT.
I WONDER IF HE'S STILL NEARBY...
NOT LIKELY...
I DOUBT HE'D REMAIN HERE TO BE FOUND.
......
WHAT'S WRONG?
I DON'T KNOW...
WHAT DOES ADLET WISH TO ACCOMPLISH?

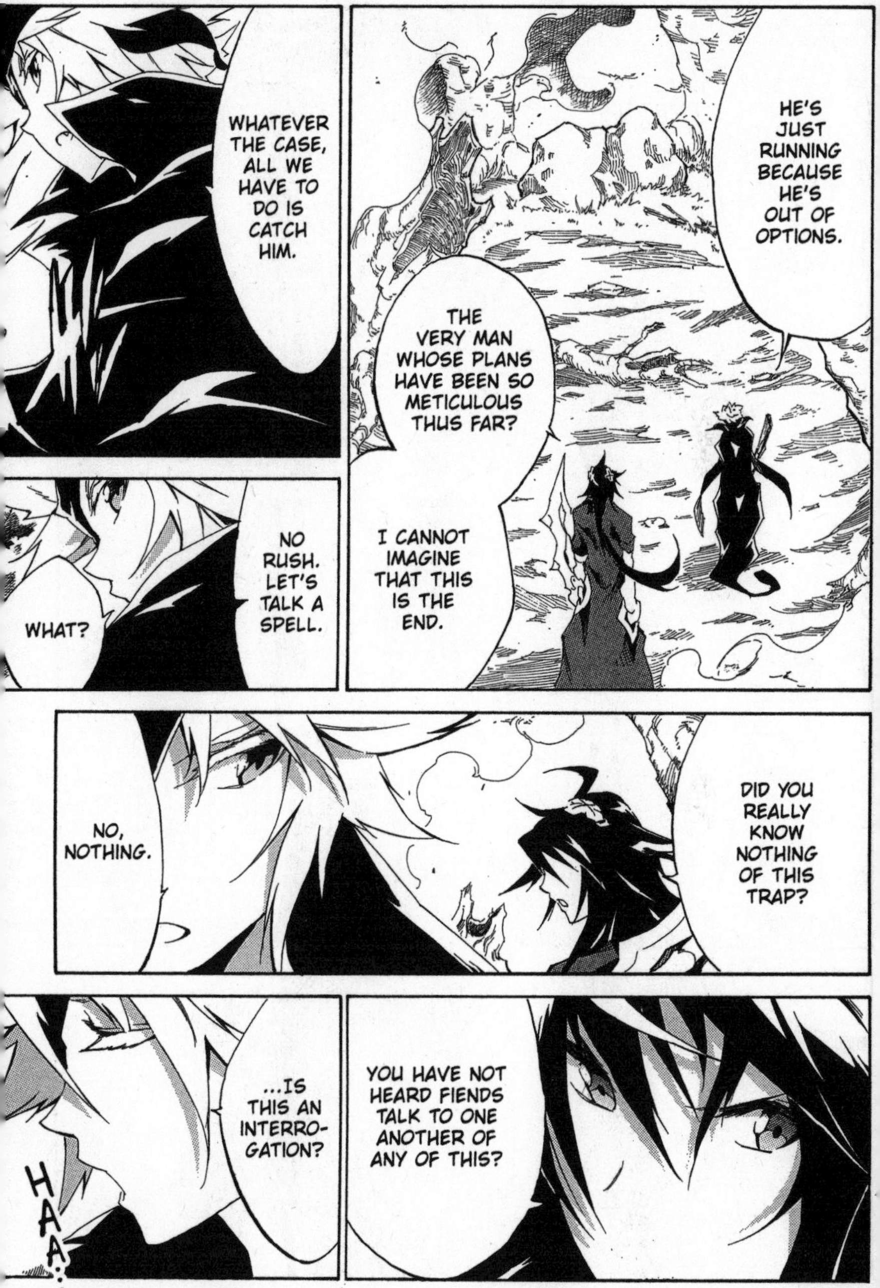
HE'S JUST RUNNING BECAUSE HE'S OUT OF OPTIONS.
THE VERY MAN WHOSE PLANS HAVE BEEN SO METICULOUS THUS FAR?
I CANNOT IMAGINE THAT THIS IS THE END.
WHATEVER THE CASE, ALL WE HAVE TO DO IS CATCH HIM.
NO RUSH. LET'S TALK A SPELL.
WHAT?
DID YOU REALLY KNOW NOTHING OF THIS TRAP?
NO, NOTHING.
YOU HAVE NOT HEARD FIENDS TALK TO ONE ANOTHER OF ANY OF THIS?
...IS THIS AN INTERROGATION?
HAA...

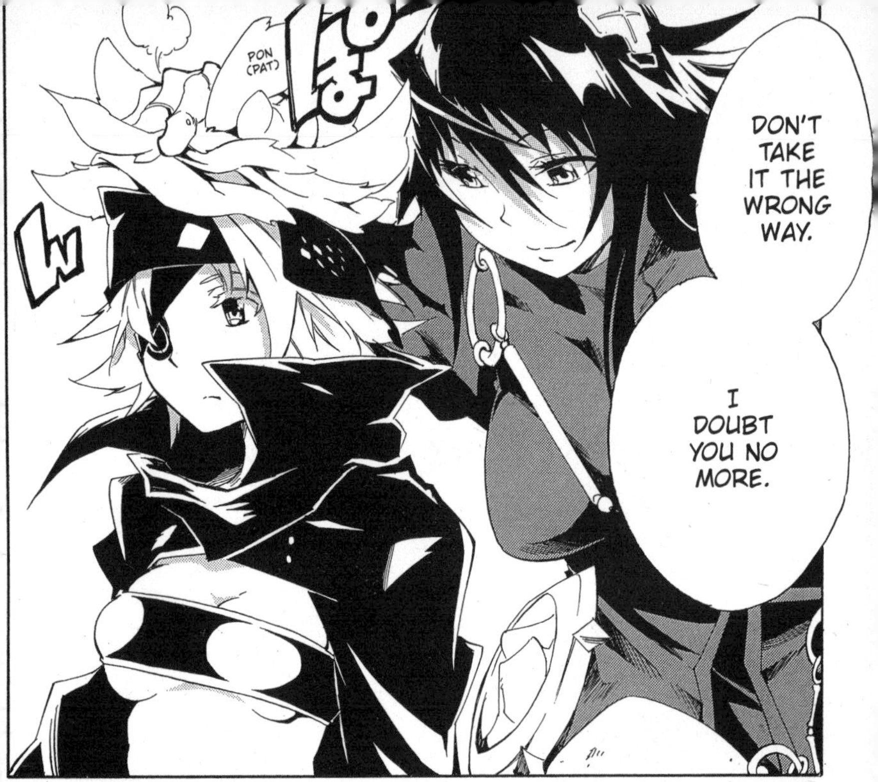
DON'T TAKE IT THE WRONG WAY.
I DOUBT YOU NO MORE.
PON (PAT)
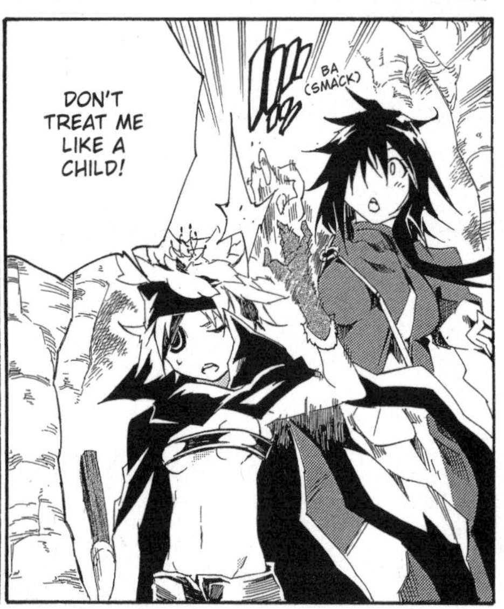
BA (SMACK)
DON'T TREAT ME LIKE A CHILD!
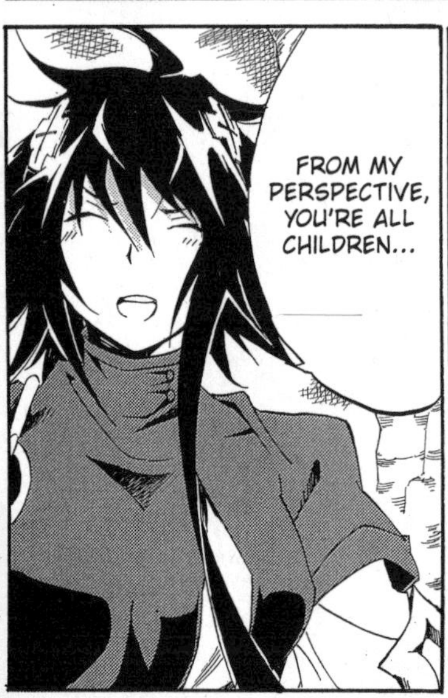
FROM MY PERSPECTIVE, YOU'RE ALL CHILDREN...

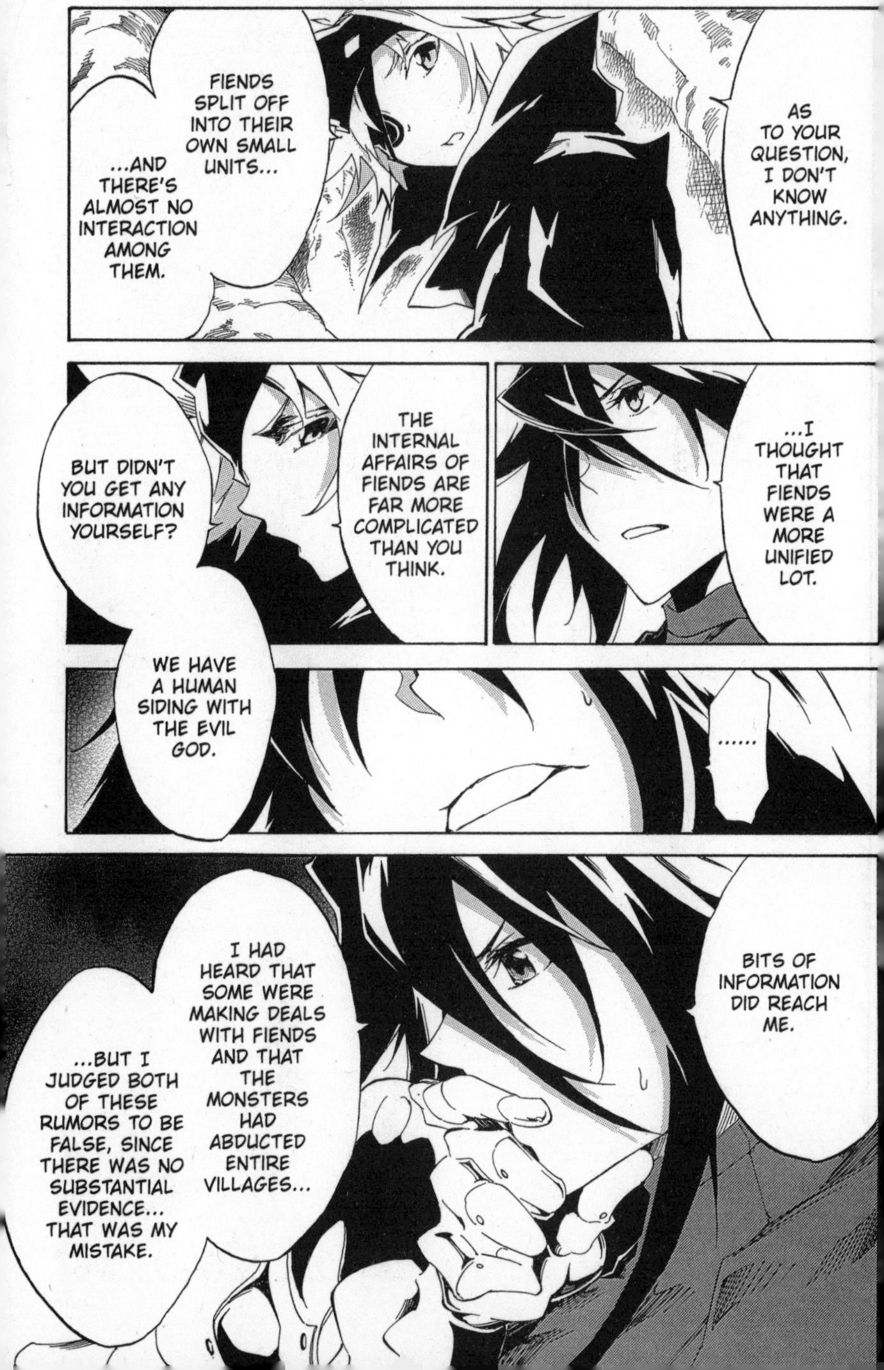
AS TO YOUR QUESTION, I DON'T KNOW ANYTHING.
FIENDS SPLIT OFF INTO THEIR OWN SMALL UNITS...
...AND THERE'S ALMOST NO INTERACTION AMONG THEM.
...I THOUGHT THAT FIENDS WERE A MORE UNIFIED LOT.
THE INTERNAL AFFAIRS OF FIENDS ARE FAR MORE COMPLICATED THAN YOU THINK.
BUT DIDN'T YOU GET ANY INFORMATION YOURSELF?
......
WE HAVE A HUMAN SIDING WITH THE EVIL GOD.
BITS OF INFORMATION DID REACH ME.
I HAD HEARD THAT SOME WERE MAKING DEALS WITH FIENDS AND THAT THE MONSTERS HAD ABDUCTED ENTIRE VILLAGES...
...BUT I JUDGED BOTH OF THESE RUMORS TO BE FALSE, SINCE THERE WAS NO SUBSTANTIAL EVIDENCE... THAT WAS MY MISTAKE.

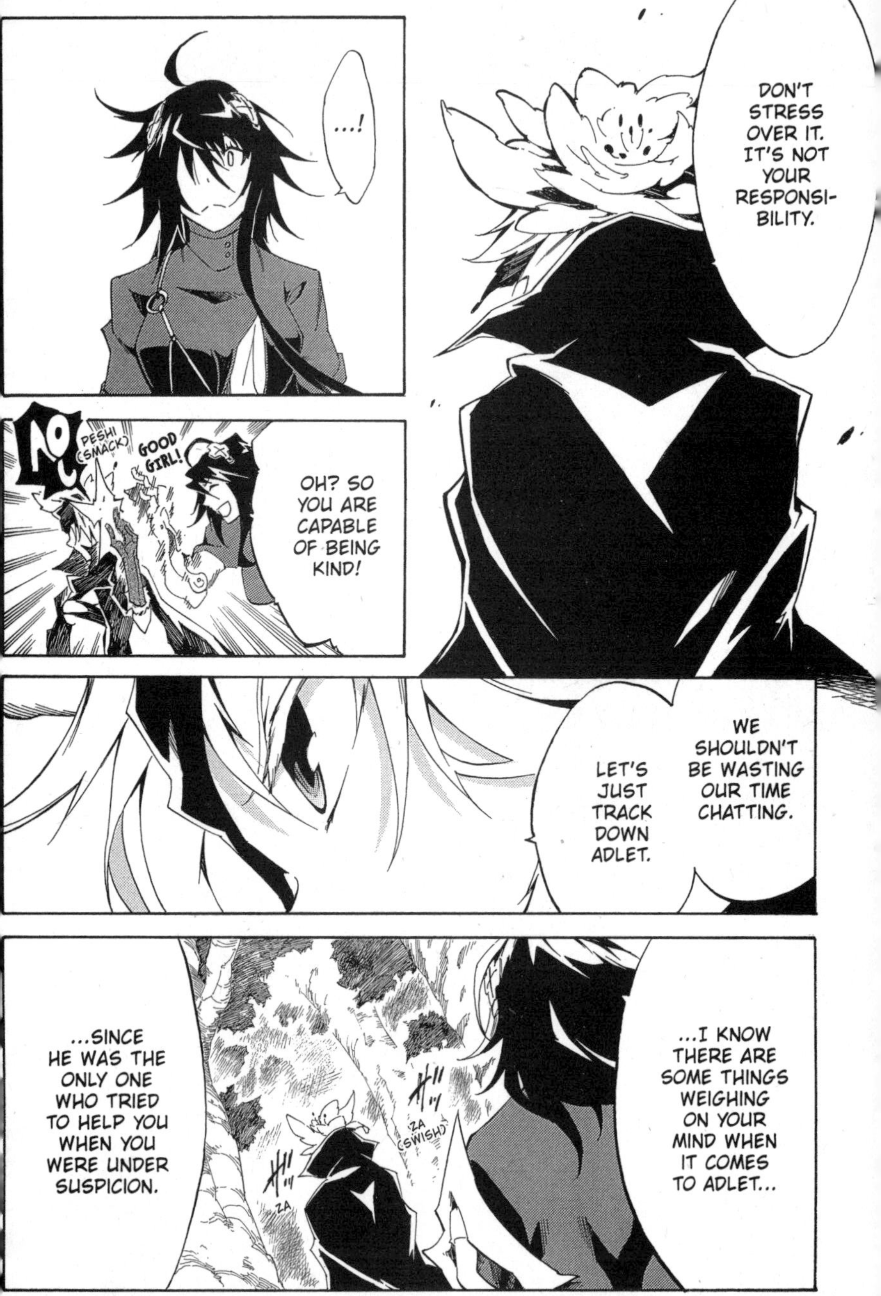
DON'T STRESS OVER IT. IT'S NOT YOUR RESPONSI-BILITY.
...!
OH? SO YOU ARE CAPABLE OF BEING KIND!
GOOD GIRL!
PESHI (SMACK)
WE SHOULDN'T BE WASTING OUR TIME CHATTING.
LET'S JUST TRACK DOWN ADLET.
...I KNOW THERE ARE SOME THINGS WEIGHING ON YOUR MIND WHEN IT COMES TO ADLET...
ZA (SWISH)
ZA
...SINCE HE WAS THE ONLY ONE WHO TRIED TO HELP YOU WHEN YOU WERE UNDER SUSPICION.

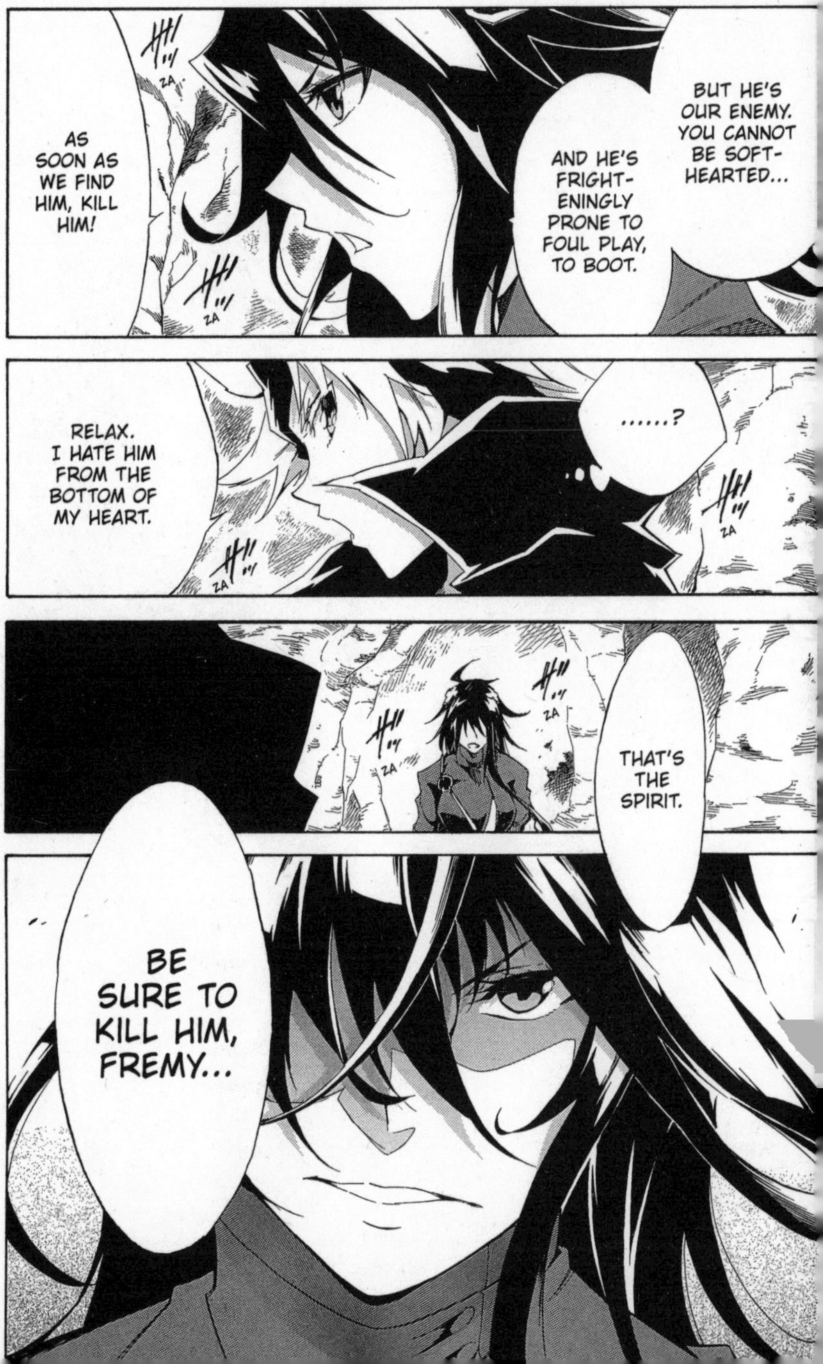
BUT HE'S OUR ENEMY. YOU CANNOT BE SOFT-HEARTED...
AND HE'S FRIGHT-ENINGLY PRONE TO FOUL PLAY, TO BOOT.
ZA
AS SOON AS WE FIND HIM, KILL HIM!
ZA
......?
ZA
RELAX. I HATE HIM FROM THE BOTTOM OF MY HEART.
ZA
ZA
THAT'S THE SPIRIT.
ZA
BE SURE TO KILL HIM, FREMY...

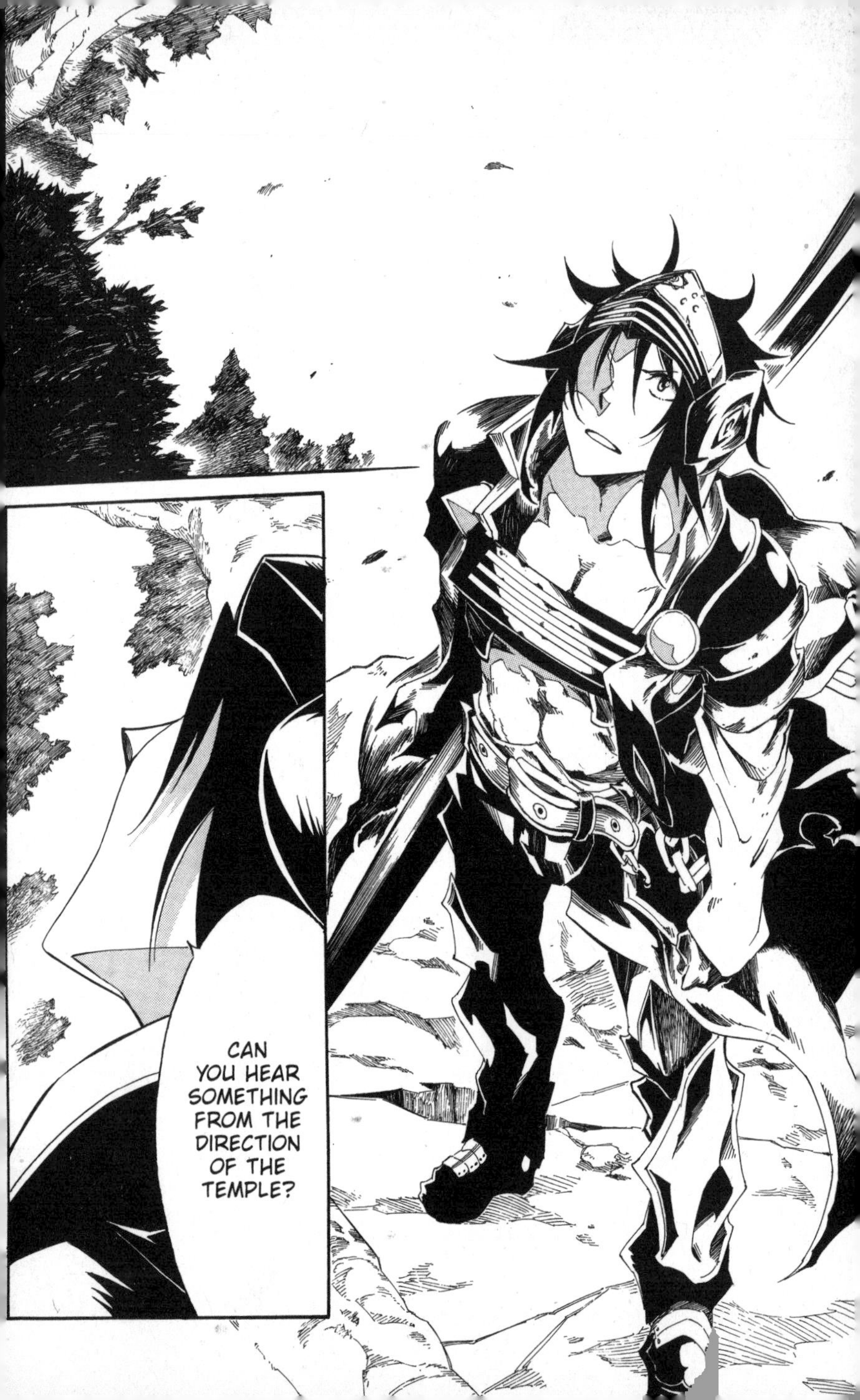
CAN YOU HEAR SOMETHING FROM THE DIRECTION OF THE TEMPLE?

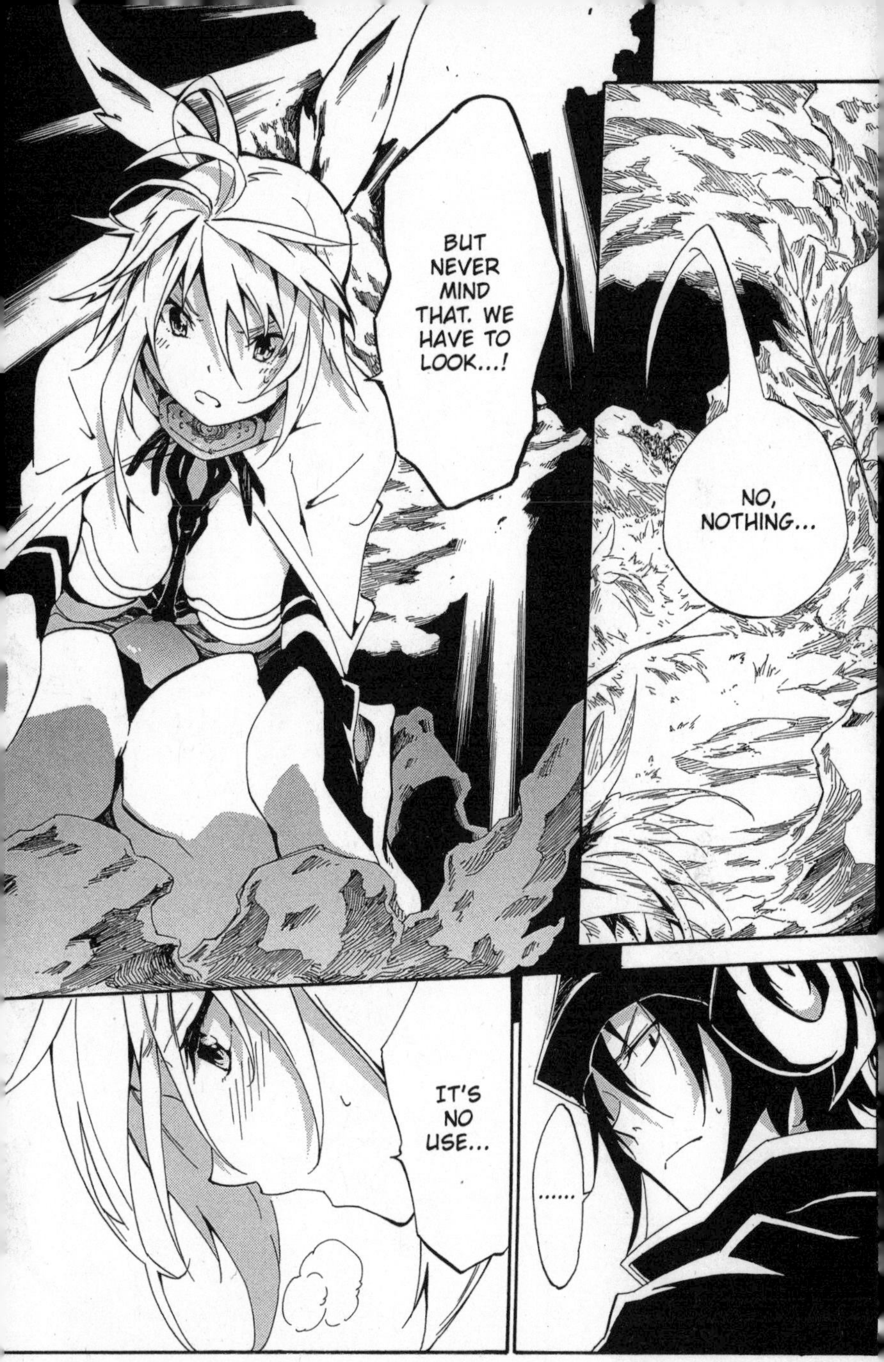
NO, NOTHING...
BUT NEVER MIND THAT. WE HAVE TO LOOK...!
......
IT'S NO USE...

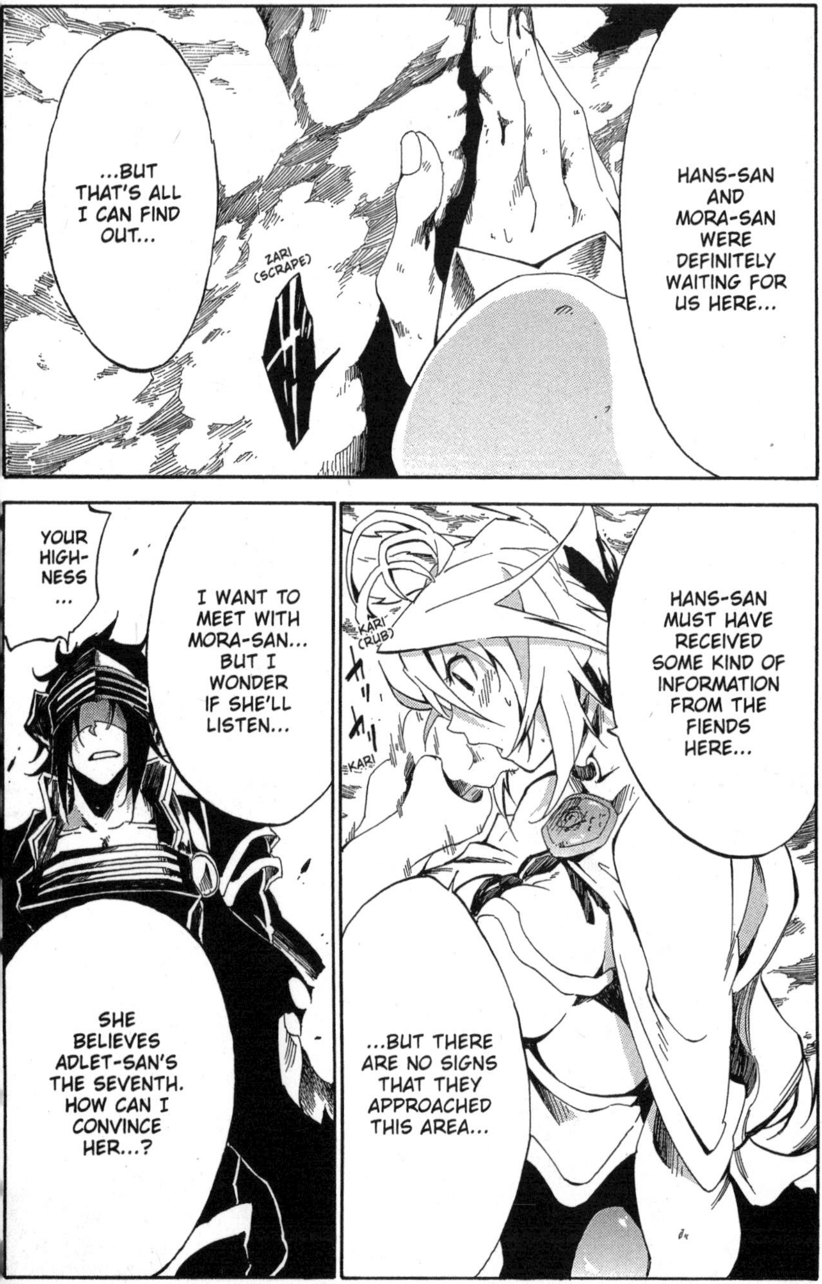
HANS-SAN AND MORA-SAN WERE DEFINITELY WAITING FOR US HERE...
ZARI (SCRAPE)
...BUT THAT'S ALL I CAN FIND OUT...
HANS-SAN MUST HAVE RECEIVED SOME KIND OF INFORMATION FROM THE FIENDS HERE...
KARI (RUB)
KARI
...BUT THERE ARE NO SIGNS THAT THEY APPROACHED THIS AREA...
I WANT TO MEET WITH MORA-SAN... BUT I WONDER IF SHE'LL LISTEN...
YOUR HIGH-NESS...
SHE BELIEVES ADLET-SAN'S THE SEVENTH. HOW CAN I CONVINCE HER...?

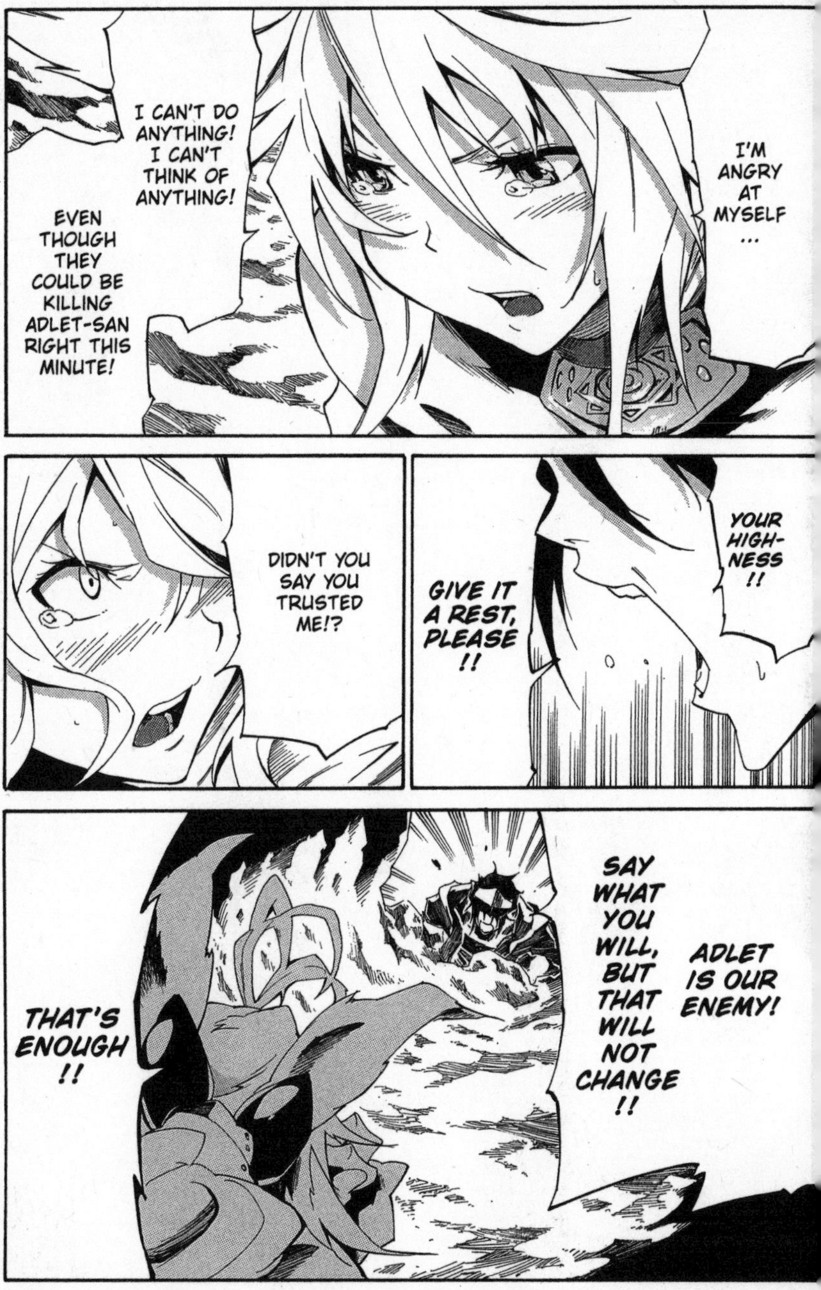

I'M ANGRY AT MYSELF ...
I CAN'T DO ANYTHING! I CAN'T THINK OF ANYTHING!
EVEN THOUGH THEY COULD BE KILLING ADLET-SAN RIGHT THIS MINUTE!
YOUR HIGHNESS !!
GIVE IT A REST, PLEASE !!
DIDN'T YOU SAY YOU TRUSTED ME!?
ADLET IS OUR ENEMY!
SAY WHAT YOU WILL, BUT THAT WILL NOT CHANGE !!
THAT'S ENOUGH !!

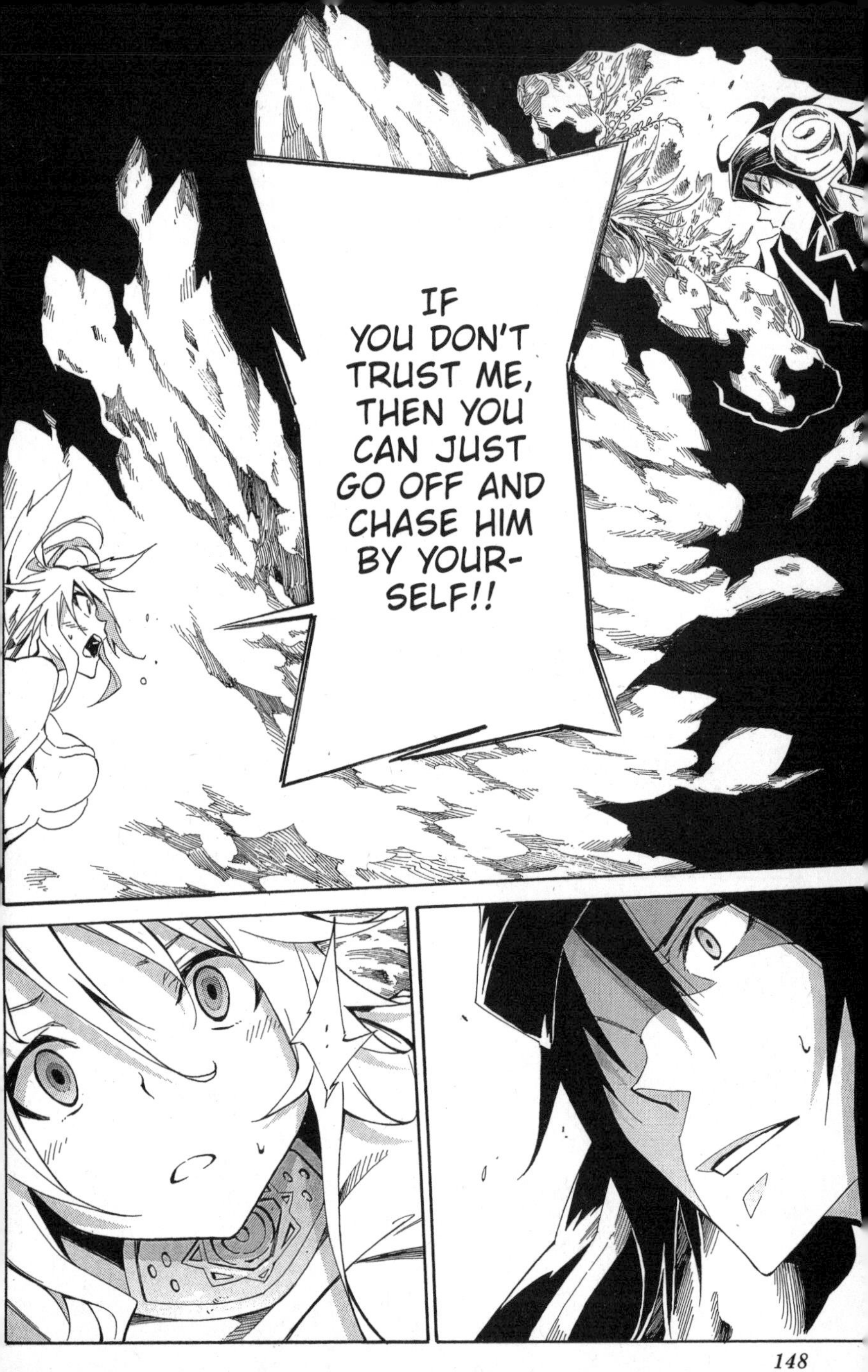
IF YOU DON'T TRUST ME, THEN YOU CAN JUST GO OFF AND CHASE HIM BY YOUR-SELF!!

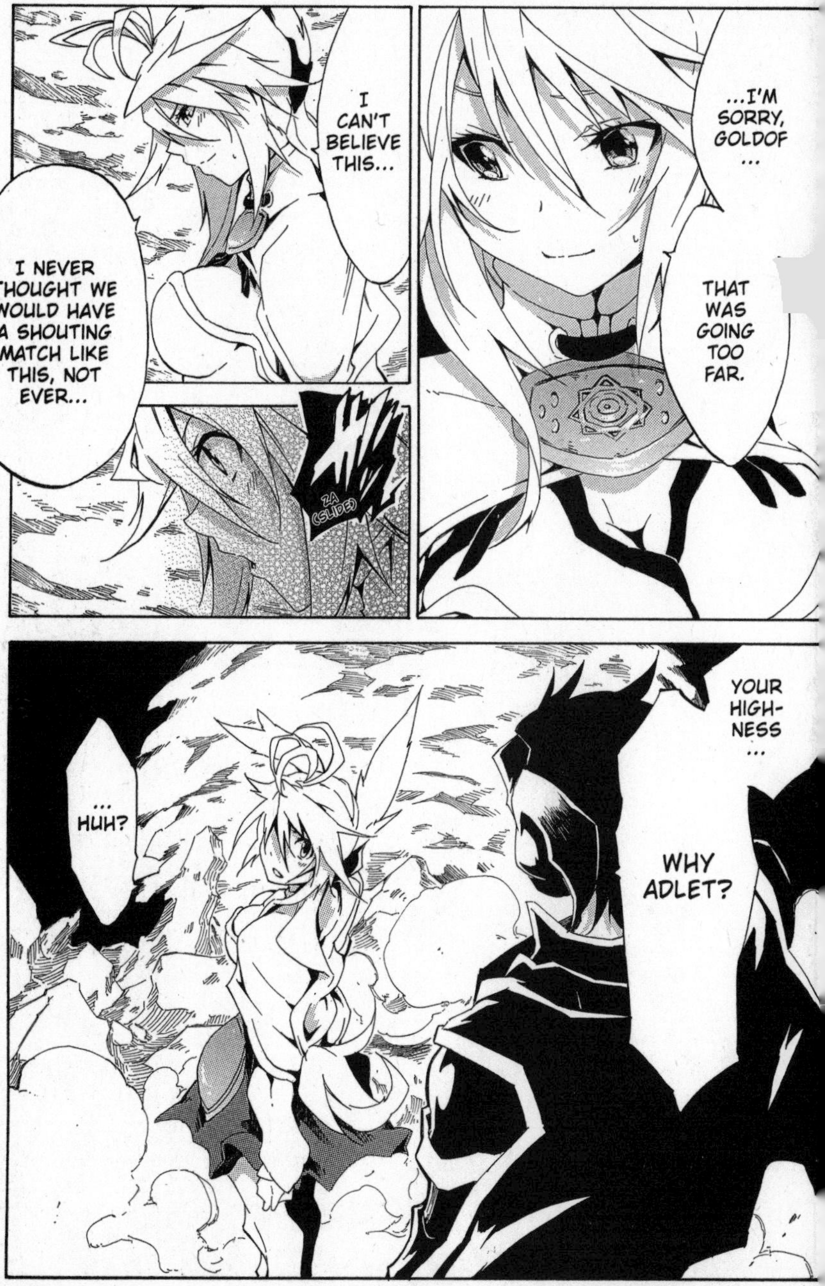
...I'M SORRY, GOLDOF ...
THAT WAS GOING TOO FAR.
I CAN'T BELIEVE THIS...
I NEVER THOUGHT WE WOULD HAVE A SHOUTING MATCH LIKE THIS, NOT EVER...
ZA (SLIDE)
YOUR HIGHNESS ...
WHY ADLET?
... HUH?

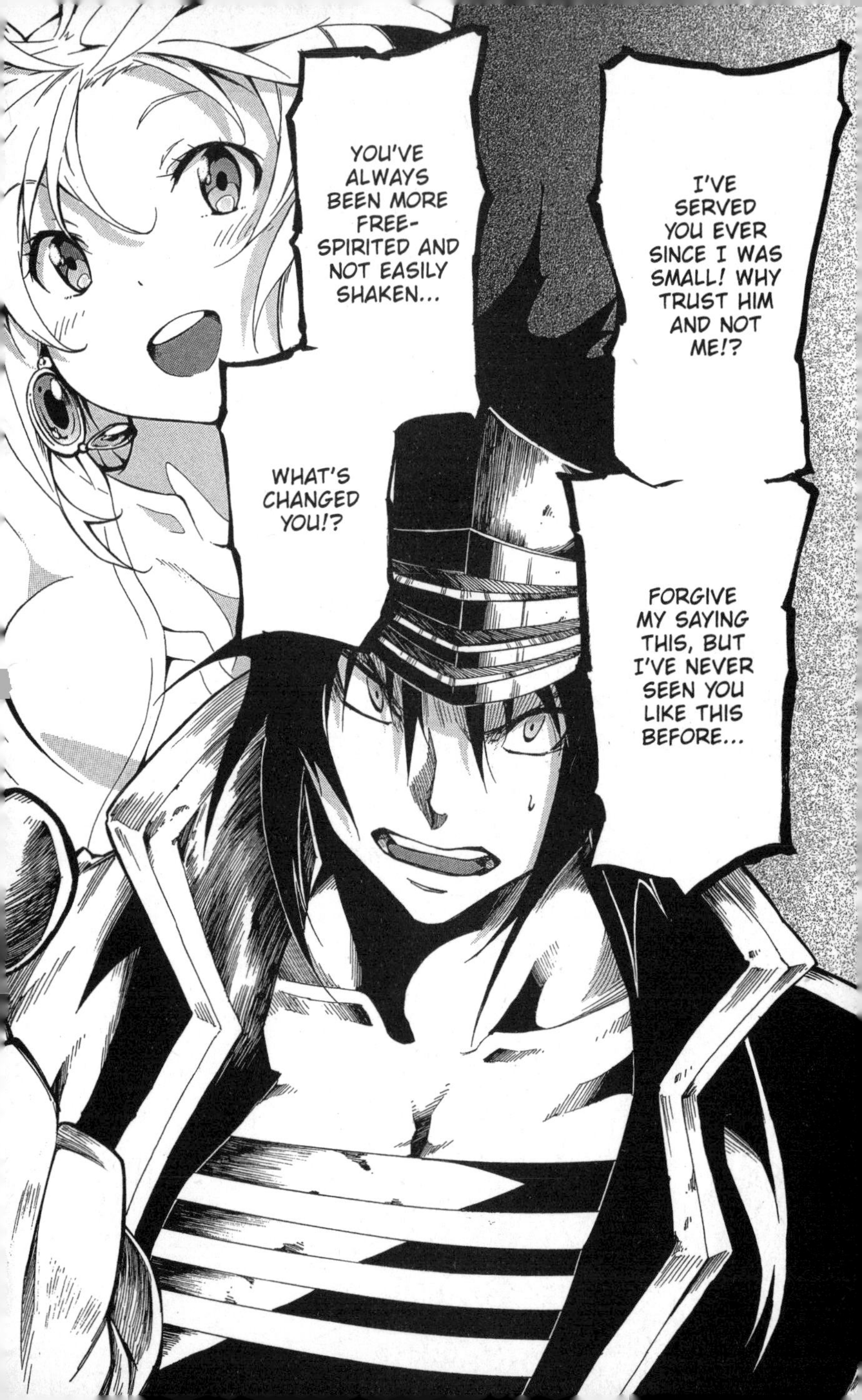
I'VE SERVED YOU EVER SINCE I WAS SMALL! WHY TRUST HIM AND NOT ME!?
YOU'VE ALWAYS BEEN MORE FREE-SPIRITED AND NOT EASILY SHAKEN...
WHAT'S CHANGED YOU!?
FORGIVE MY SAYING THIS, BUT I'VE NEVER SEEN YOU LIKE THIS BEFORE...

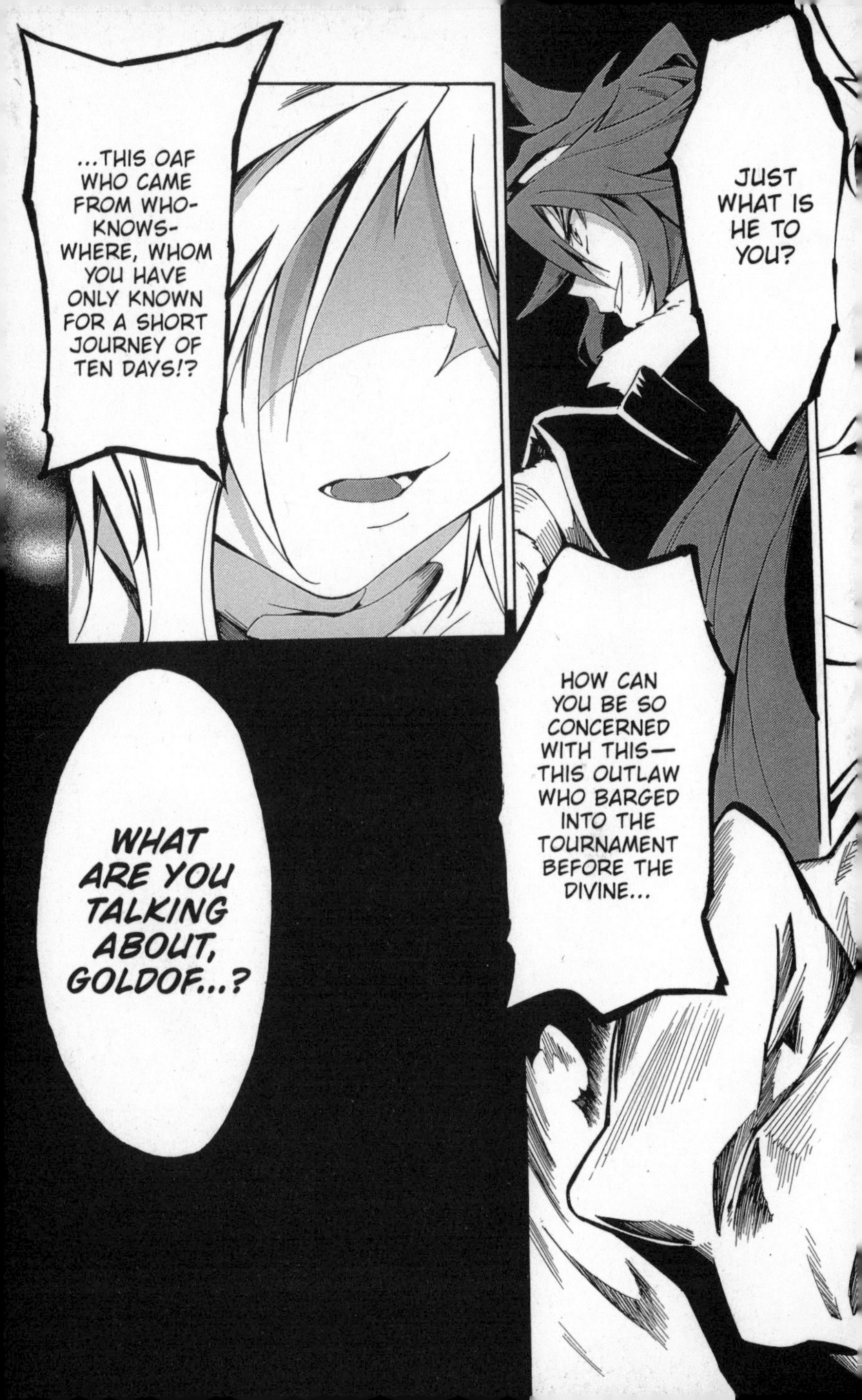
JUST WHAT IS HE TO YOU?
HOW CAN YOU BE SO CONCERNED WITH THIS—THIS OUTLAW WHO BARGED INTO THE TOURNAMENT BEFORE THE DIVINE...
...THIS OAF WHO CAME FROM WHO-KNOWS-WHERE, WHOM YOU HAVE ONLY KNOWN FOR A SHORT JOURNEY OF TEN DAYS!?
WHAT ARE YOU TALKING ABOUT, GOLDOF...?

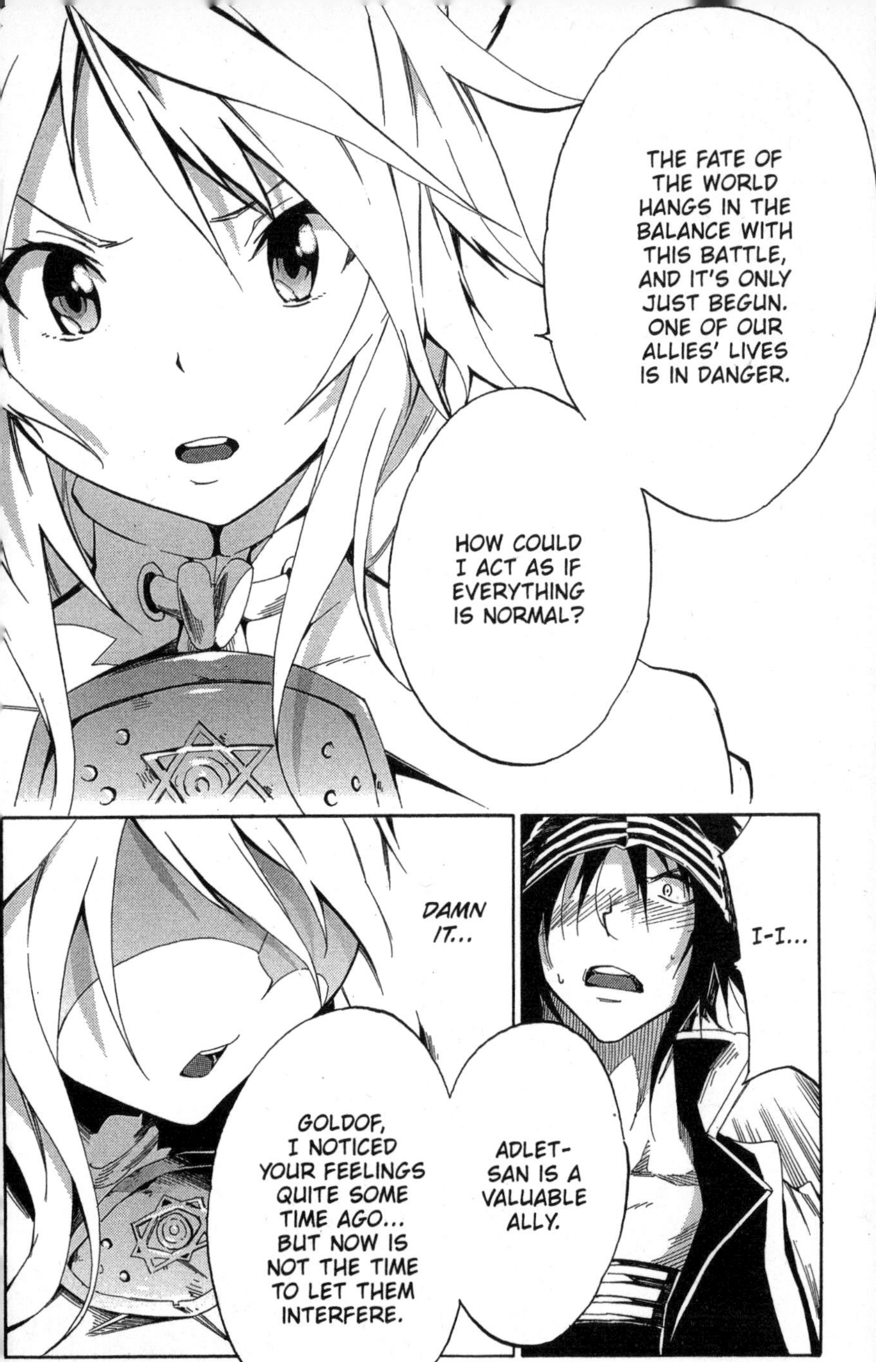
THE FATE OF THE WORLD HANGS IN THE BALANCE WITH THIS BATTLE, AND IT'S ONLY JUST BEGUN. ONE OF OUR ALLIES' LIVES IS IN DANGER.
HOW COULD I ACT AS IF EVERYTHING IS NORMAL?
I-I...
ADLET-SAN IS A VALUABLE ALLY.
DAMN IT...
GOLDOF, I NOTICED YOUR FEELINGS QUITE SOME TIME AGO... BUT NOW IS NOT THE TIME TO LET THEM INTERFERE.

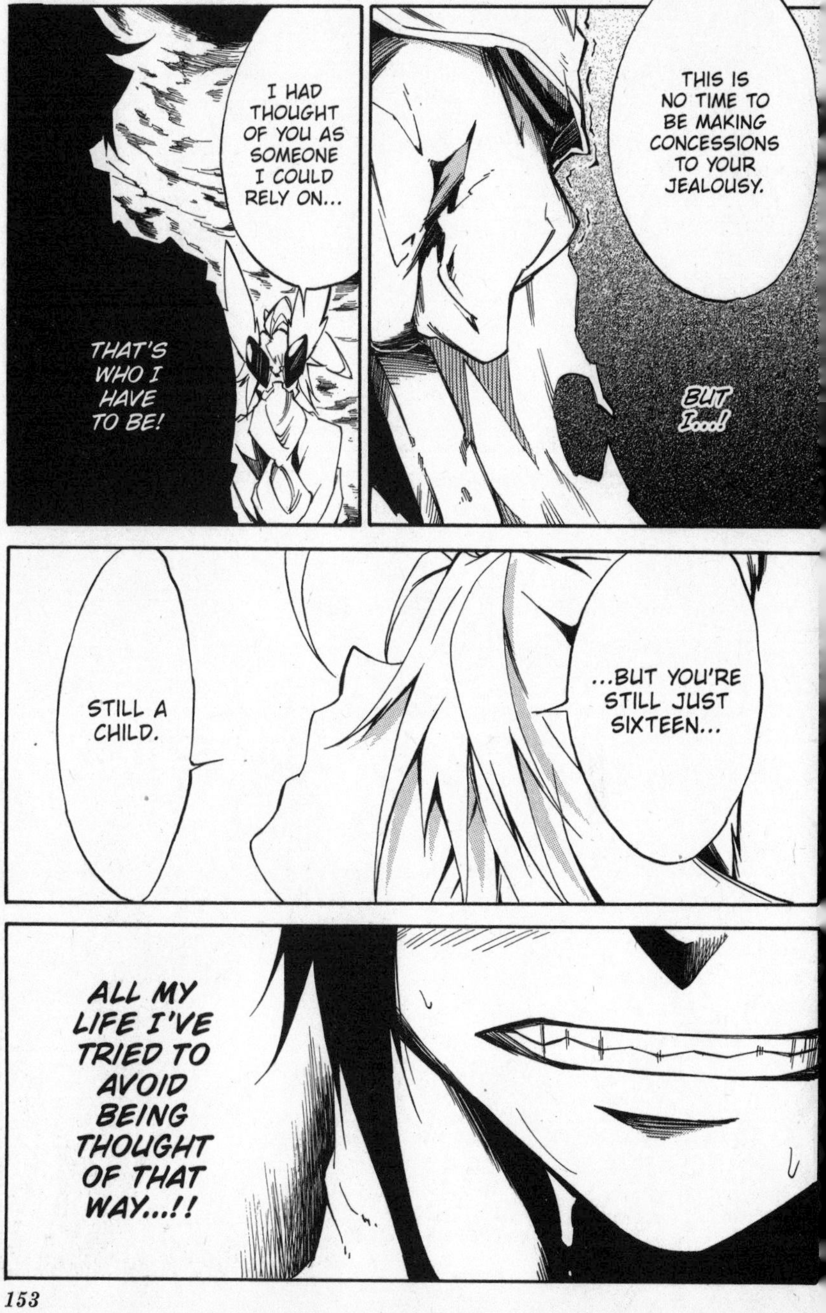
THIS IS NO TIME TO BE MAKING CONCESSIONS TO YOUR JEALOUSY.
BUT I...!
I HAD THOUGHT OF YOU AS SOMEONE I COULD RELY ON...
THAT'S WHO I HAVE TO BE!
...BUT YOU'RE STILL JUST SIXTEEN...
STILL A CHILD.
ALL MY LIFE I'VE TRIED TO AVOID BEING THOUGHT OF THAT WAY...!!

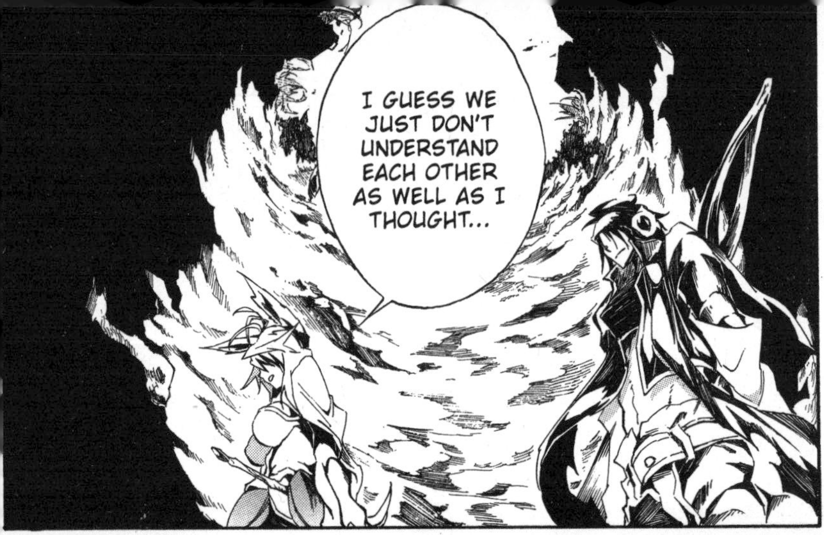
I GUESS WE JUST DON'T UNDERSTAND EACH OTHER AS WELL AS I THOUGHT...
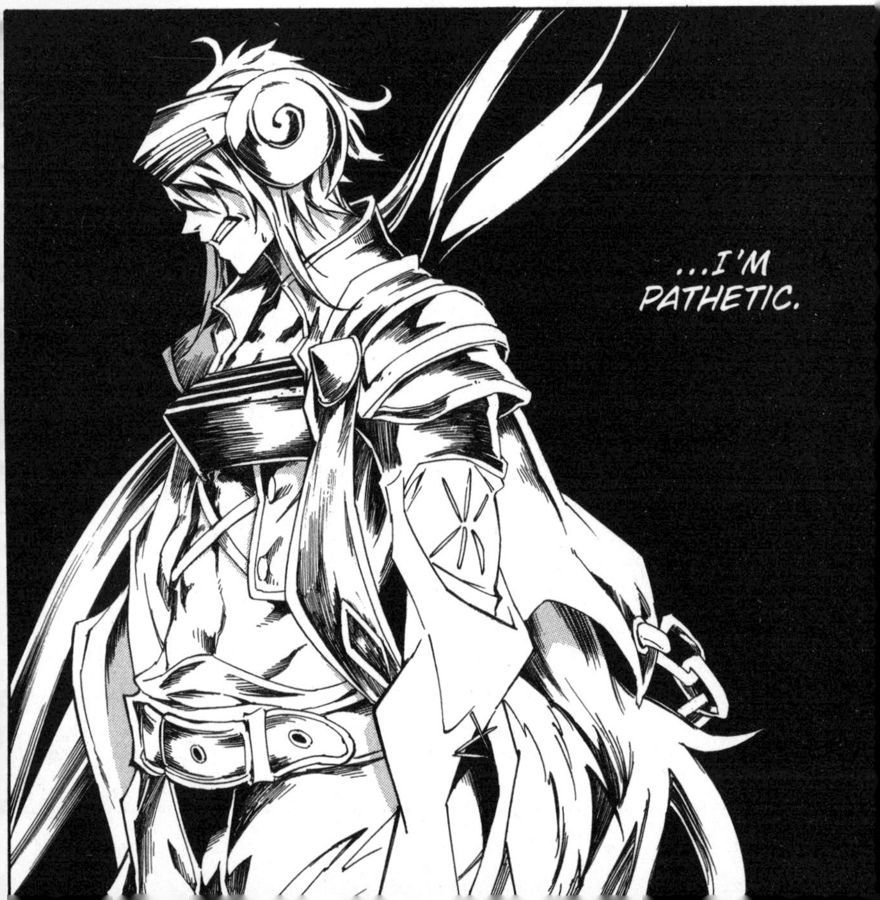
...I'M PATHETIC.

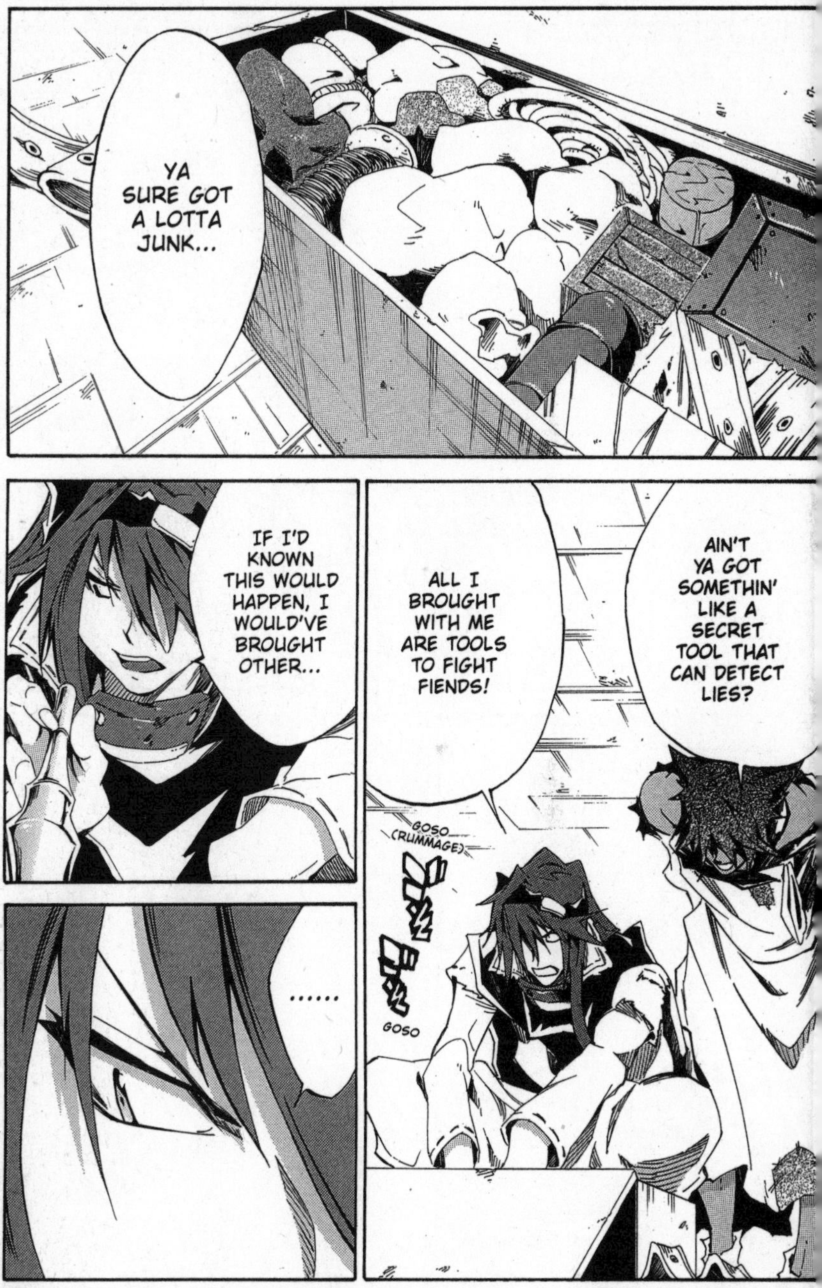
YA SURE GOT A LOTTA JUNK...
AIN'T YA GOT SOMETHIN' LIKE A SECRET TOOL THAT CAN DETECT LIES?
ALL I BROUGHT WITH ME ARE TOOLS TO FIGHT FIENDS!
GOSO (RUMMAGE)
GOSO
IF I'D KNOWN THIS WOULD HAPPEN, I WOULD'VE BROUGHT OTHER...
......

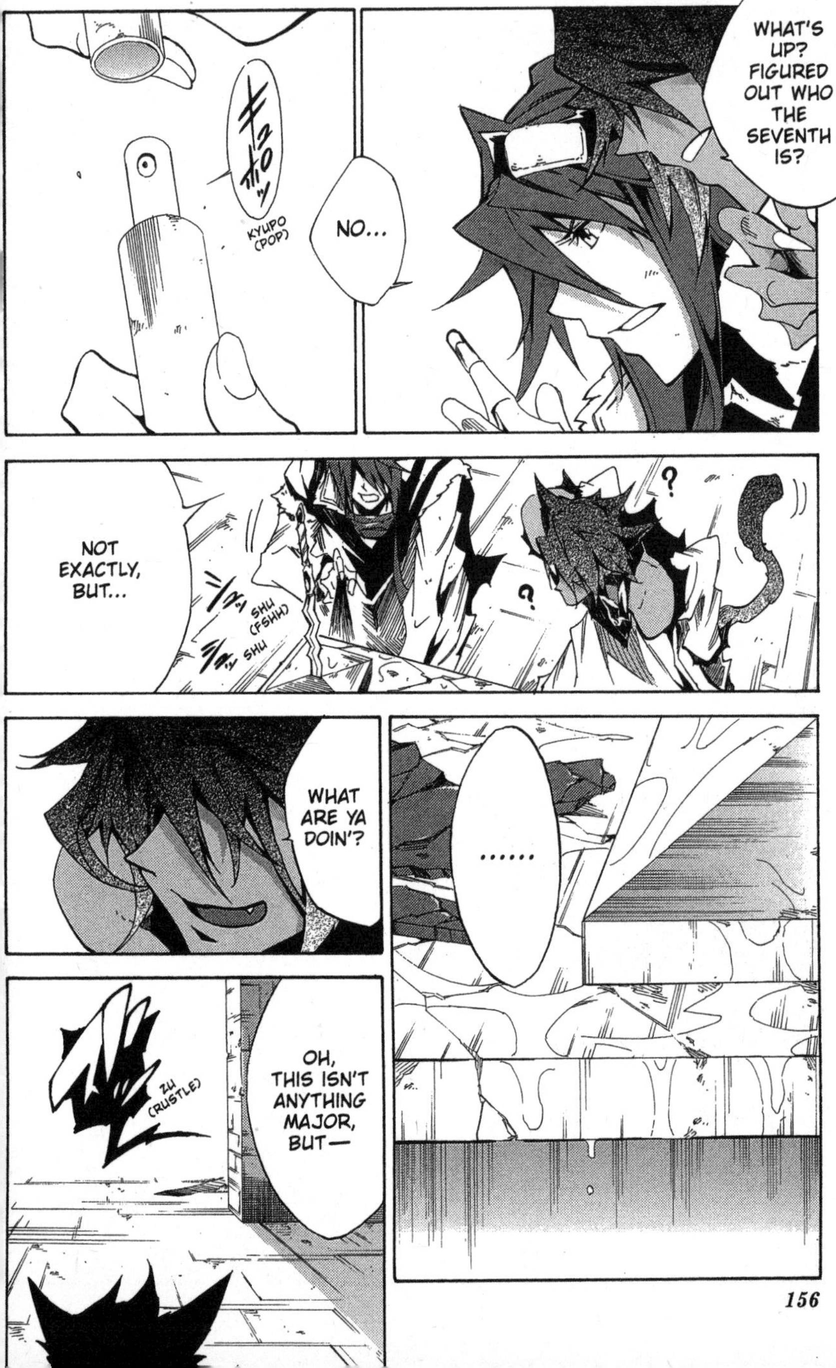
WHAT'S UP? FIGURED OUT WHO THE SEVENTH IS?
NO...
KYUPO (POP)
NOT EXACTLY, BUT...
SHU (FSHH)
SHU
?
?
......
WHAT ARE YA DOIN'?
ZU (RUSTLE)
OH, THIS ISN'T ANYTHING MAJOR, BUT—

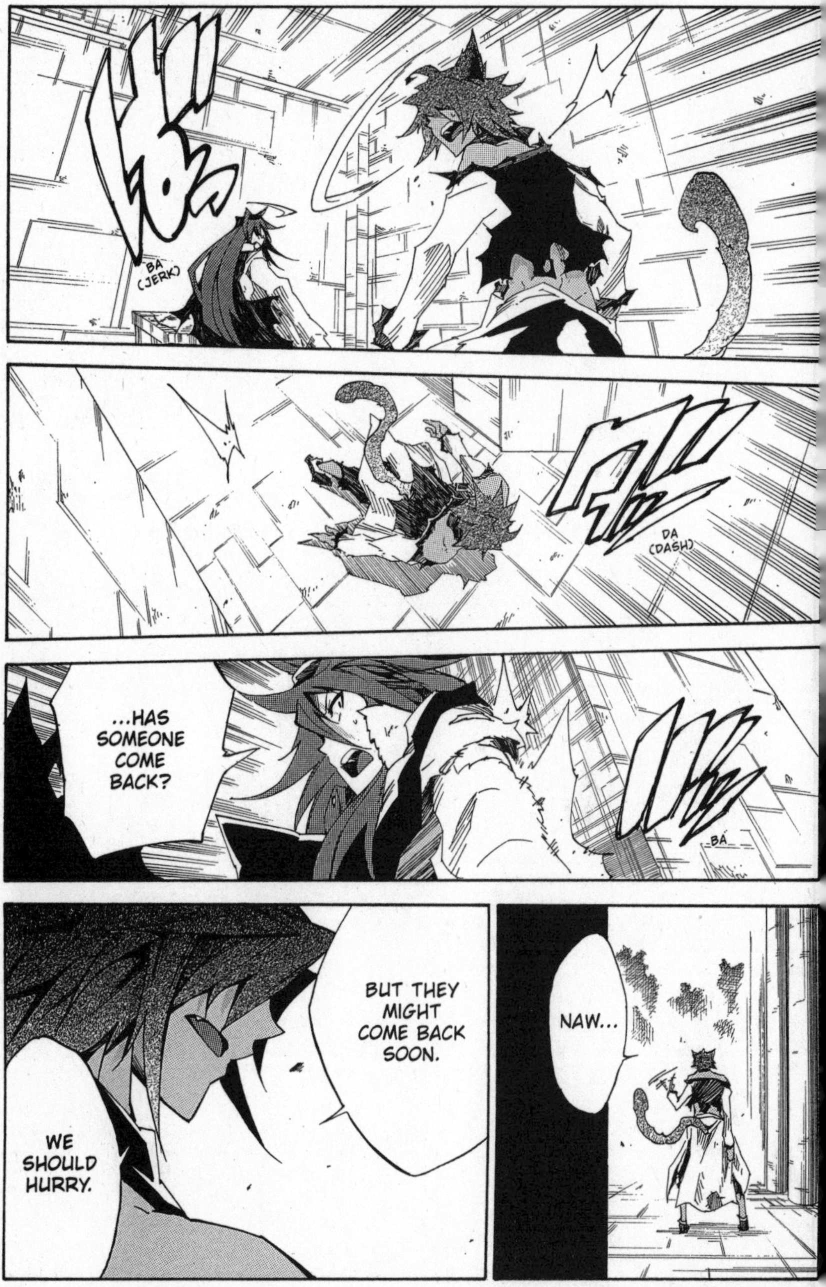
BA (JERK)
DA (DASH)
...HAS SOMEONE COME BACK?
BA
NAW...
BUT THEY MIGHT COME BACK SOON.
WE SHOULD HURRY.

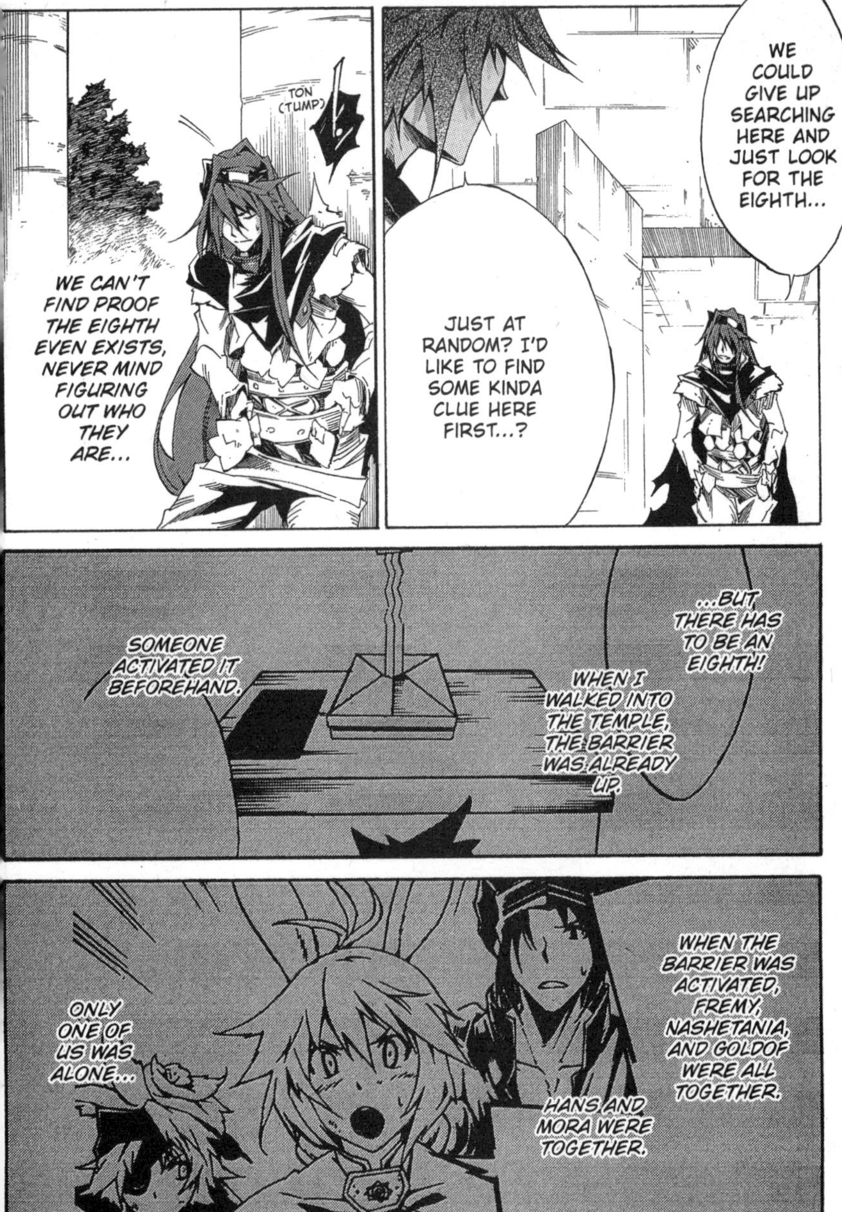
WE COULD GIVE UP SEARCHING HERE AND JUST LOOK FOR THE EIGHTH...
JUST AT RANDOM? I'D LIKE TO FIND SOME KINDA CLUE HERE FIRST...?
TON (TUMP)
WE CAN'T FIND PROOF THE EIGHTH EVEN EXISTS, NEVER MIND FIGURING OUT WHO THEY ARE...
...BUT THERE HAS TO BE AN EIGHTH!
WHEN I WALKED INTO THE TEMPLE, THE BARRIER WAS ALREADY UP.
SOMEONE ACTIVATED IT BEFOREHAND.
WHEN THE BARRIER WAS ACTIVATED, FREMY, NASHETANIA, AND GOLDOF WERE ALL TOGETHER.
HANS AND MORA WERE TOGETHER.
ONLY ONE OF US WAS ALONE...

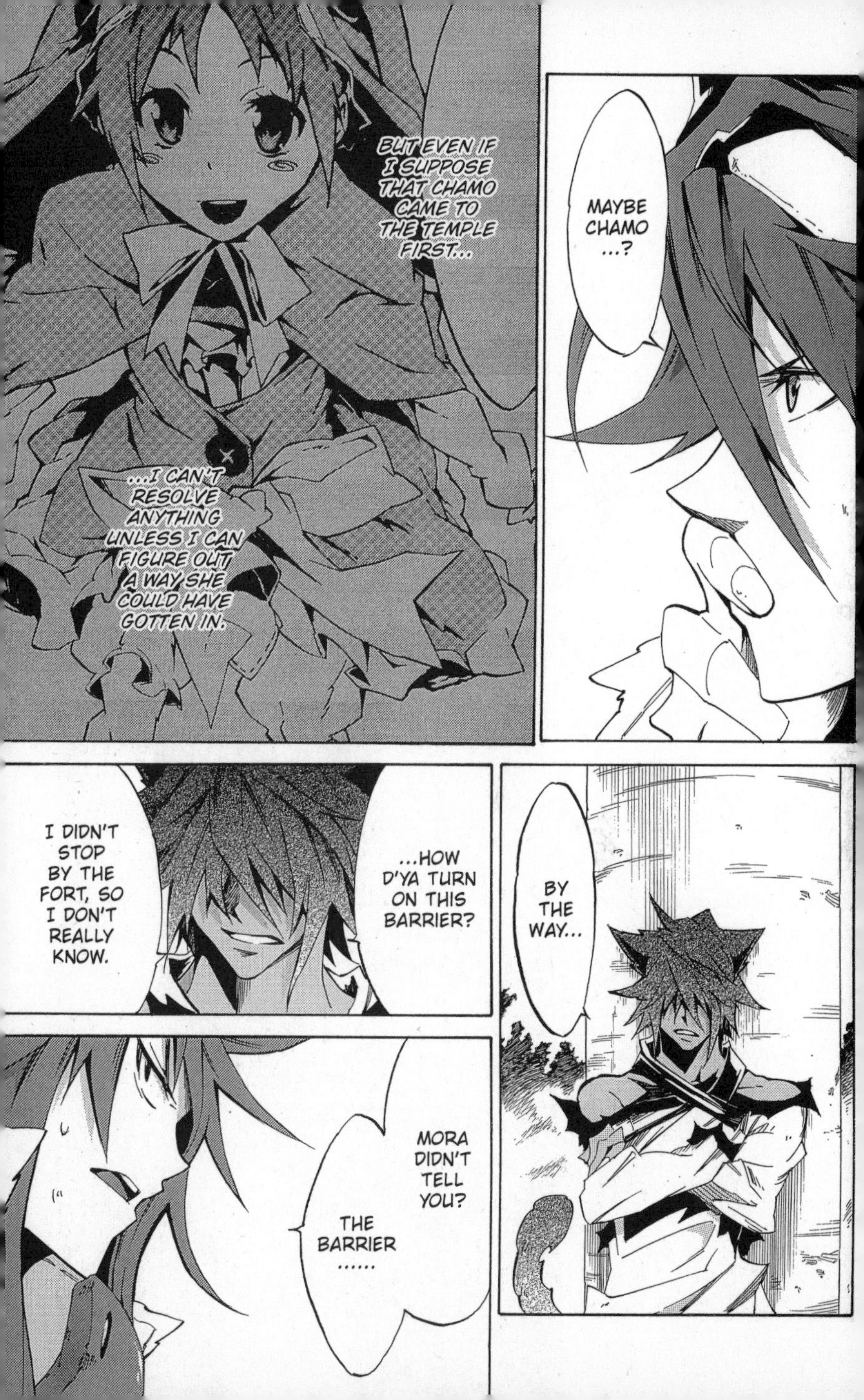
MAYBE CHAMO ...?
BUT EVEN IF I SUPPOSE THAT CHAMO CAME TO THE TEMPLE FIRST...
...I CAN'T RESOLVE ANYTHING UNLESS I CAN FIGURE OUT A WAY SHE COULD HAVE GOTTEN IN.
BY THE WAY...
...HOW D'YA TURN ON THIS BARRIER?
I DIDN'T STOP BY THE FORT, SO I DON'T REALLY KNOW.
MORA DIDN'T TELL YOU?
THE BARRIER ......

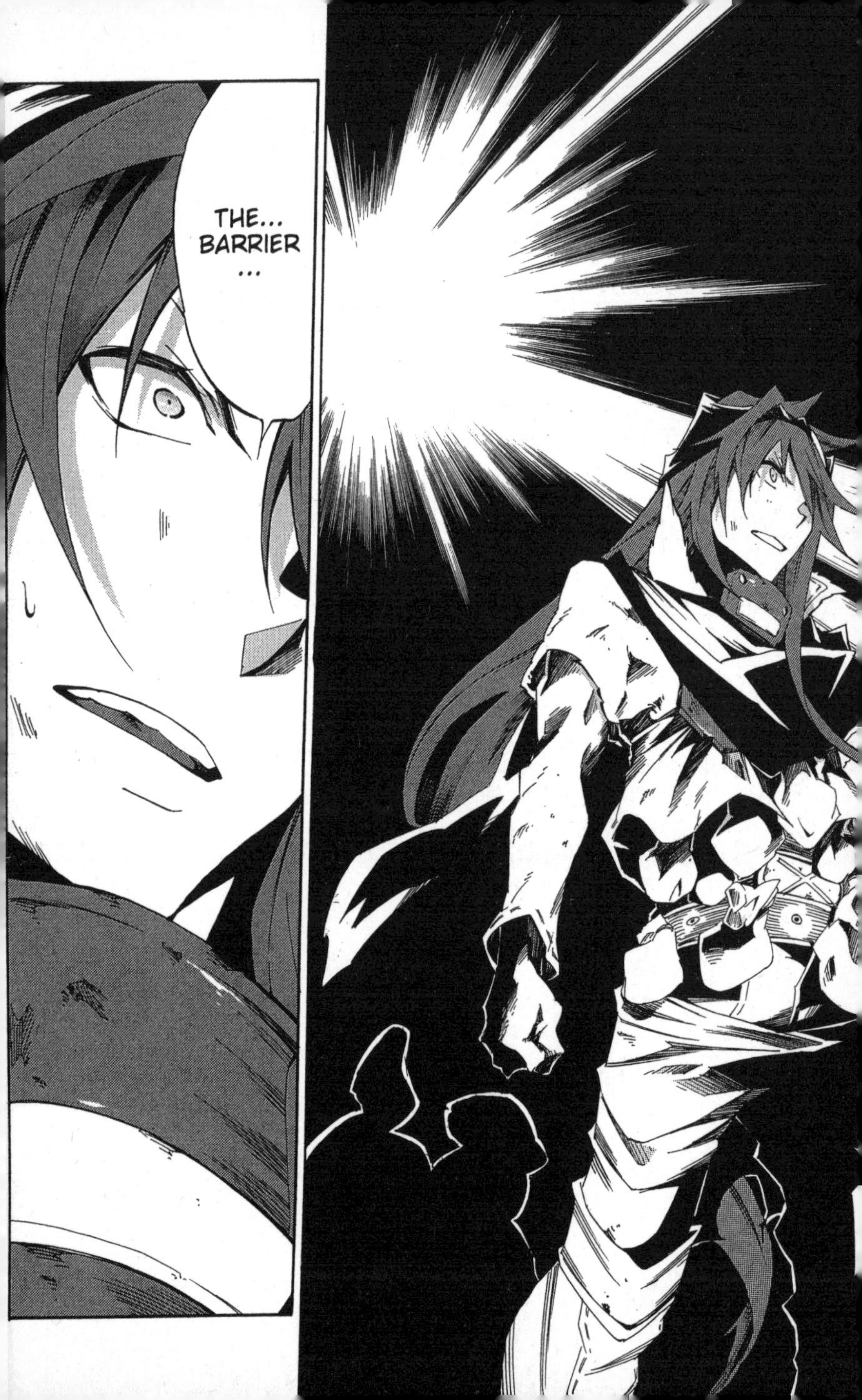
THE... BARRIER ...

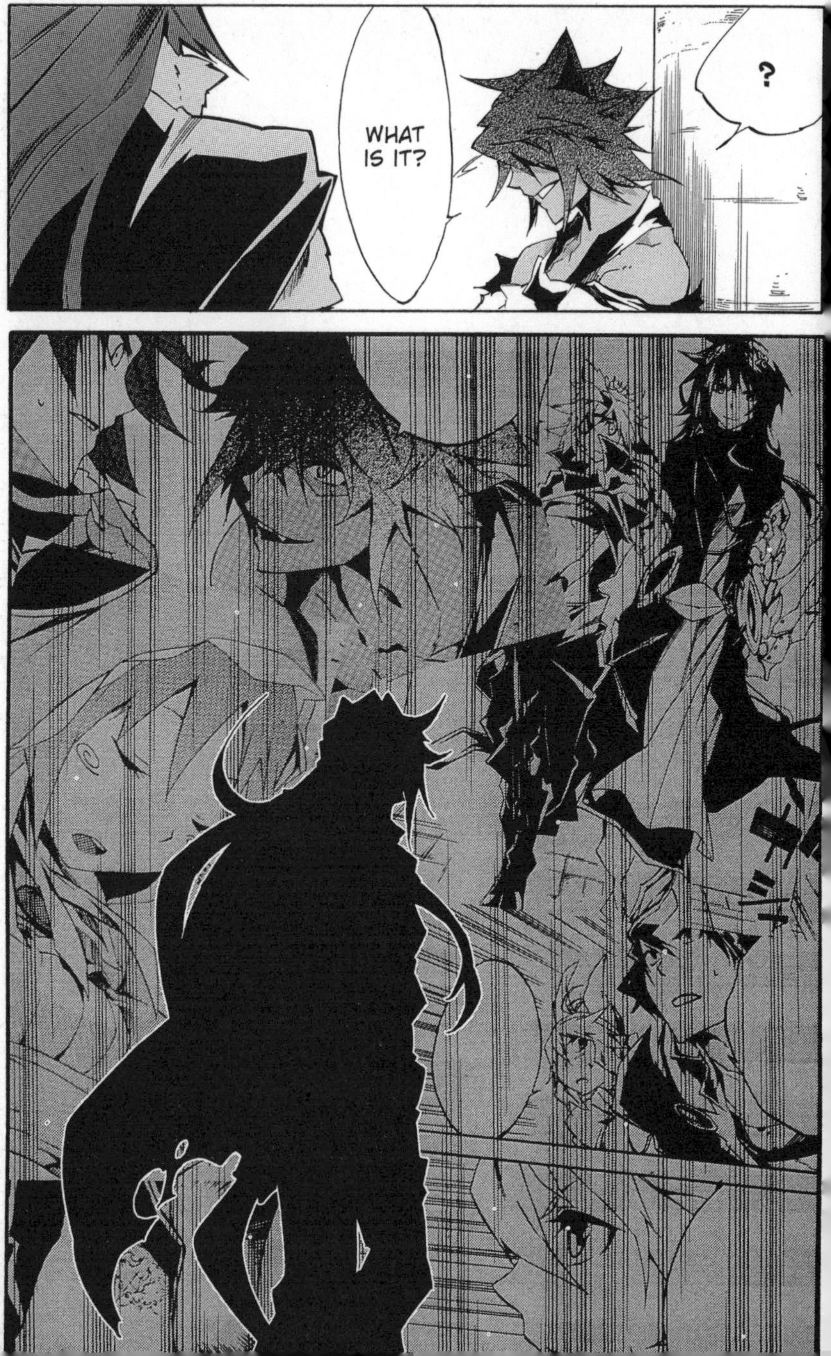
?
WHAT IS IT?

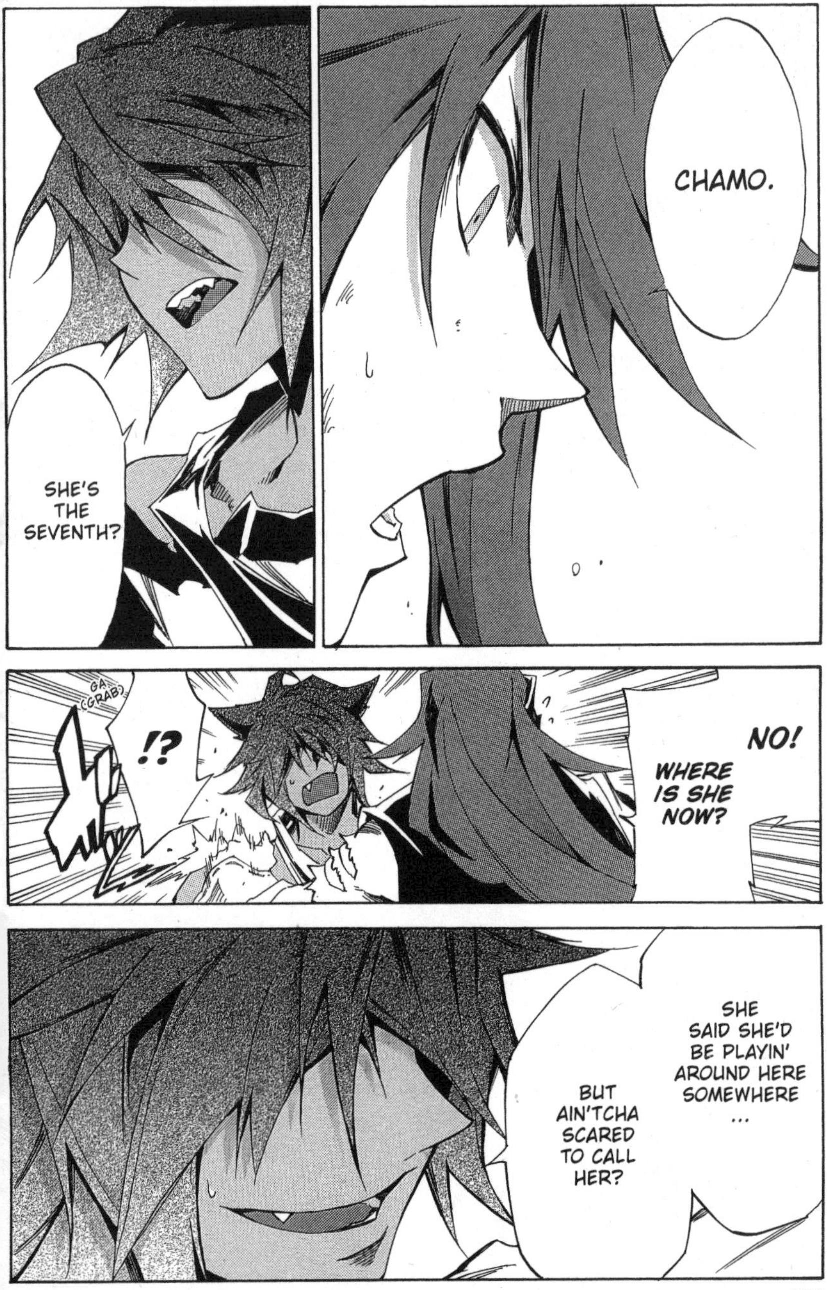
CHAMO.
SHE'S THE SEVENTH?
NO!
WHERE IS SHE NOW?
!?
GA (GRAB)
SHE SAID SHE'D BE PLAYIN' AROUND HERE SOMEWHERE ...
BUT AIN'TCHA SCARED TO CALL HER?

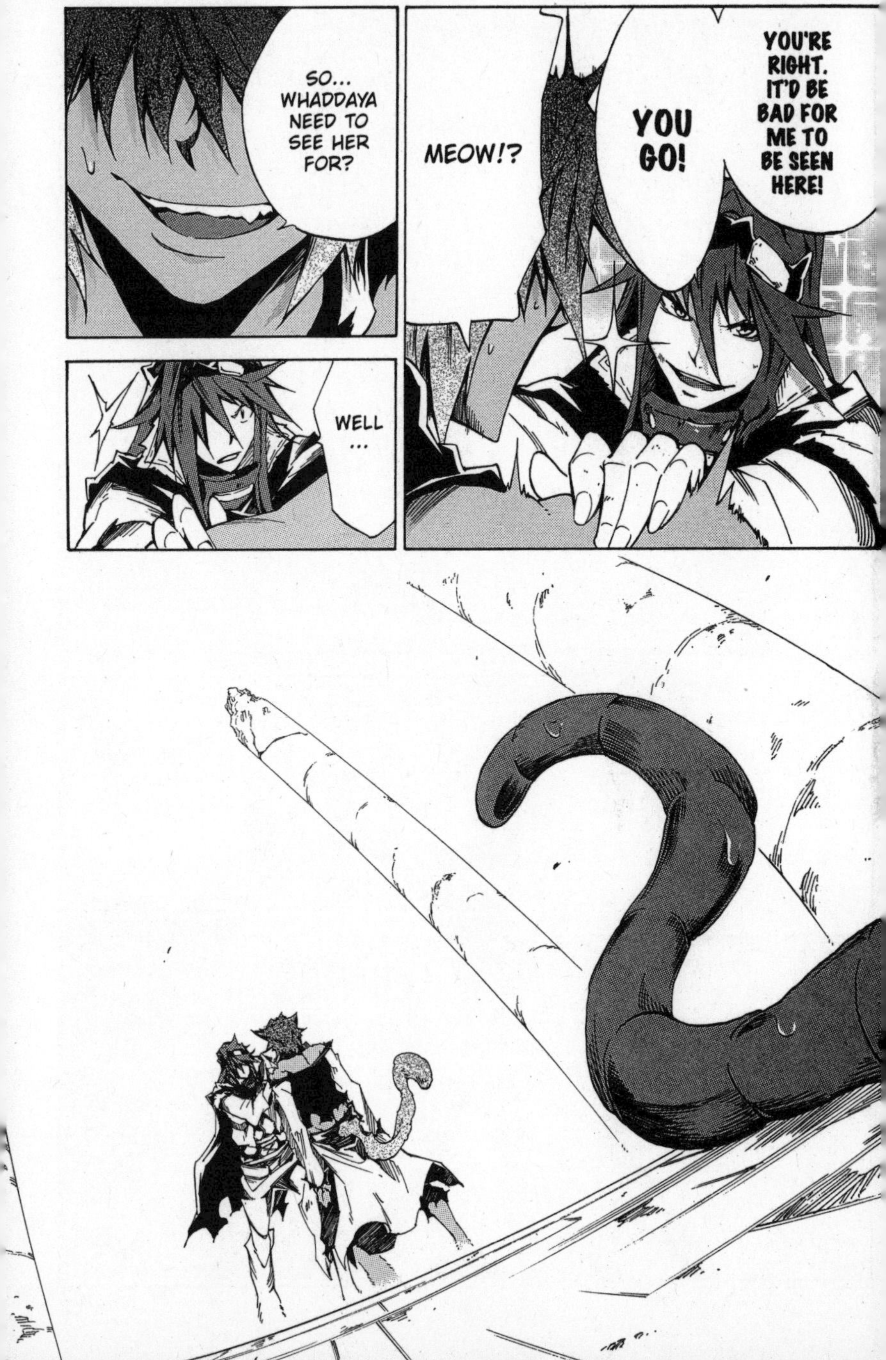
YOU'RE RIGHT. IT'D BE BAD FOR ME TO BE SEEN HERE!
YOU GO!
MEOW!?
SO... WHADDAYA NEED TO SEE HER FOR?
WELL ...

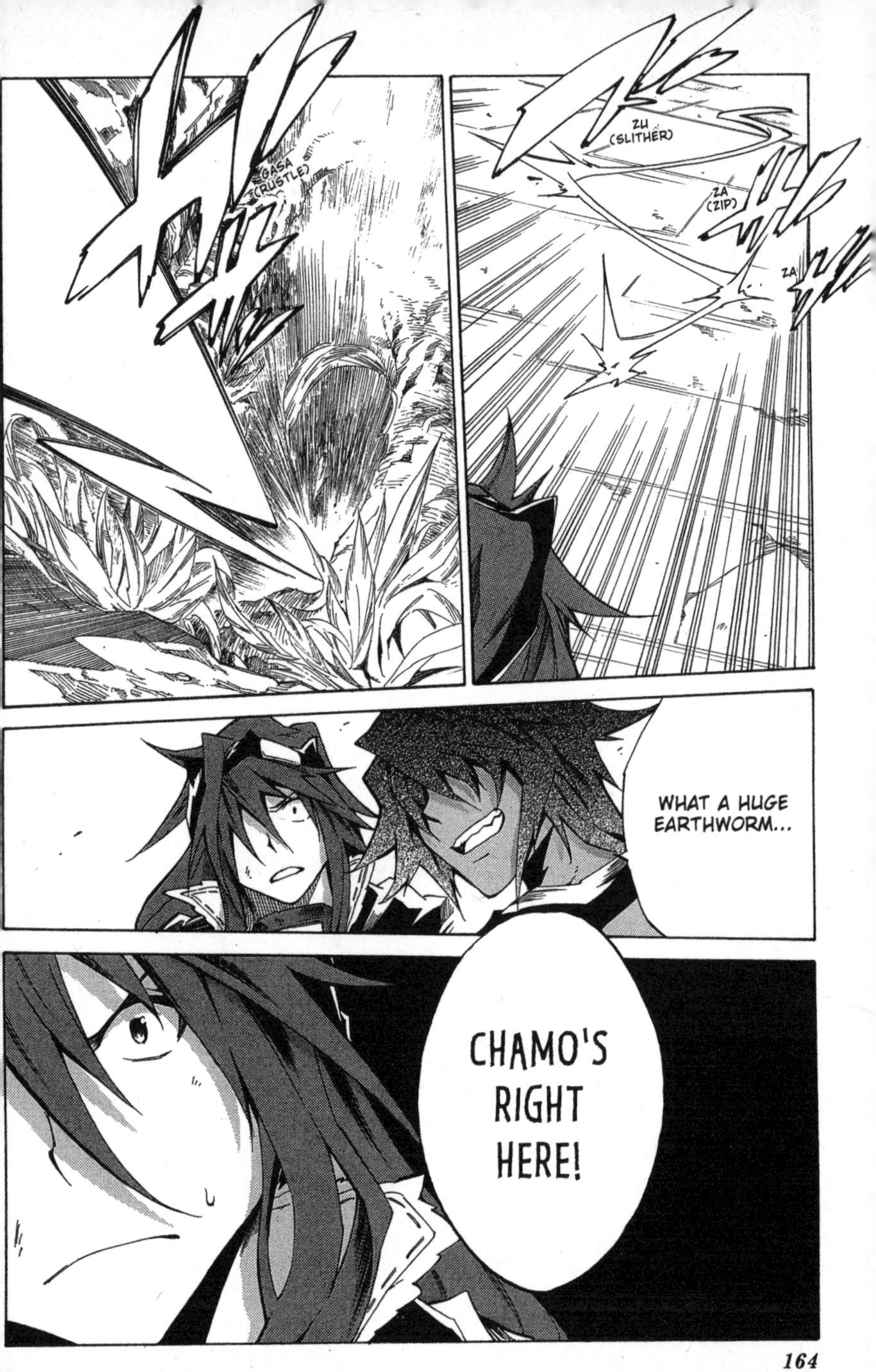
GASA
(RUSTLE)
ZU
(SLITHER)
ZA
(ZIP)
ZA
WHAT A HUGE EARTHWORM...
CHAMO'S RIGHT HERE!

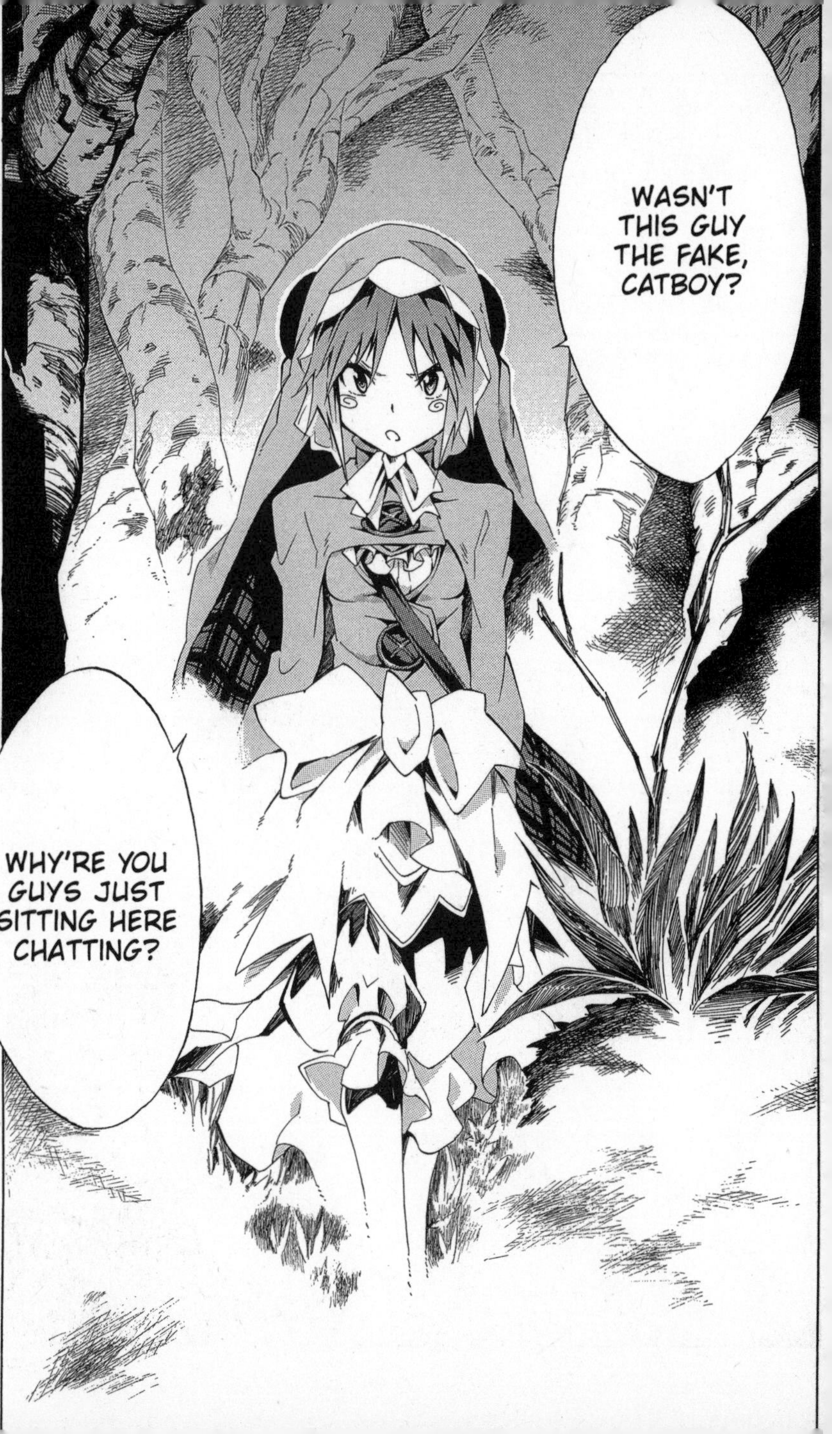
WASN'T THIS GUY THE FAKE, CATBOY?
WHY'RE YOU GUYS JUST SITTING HERE CHATTING?

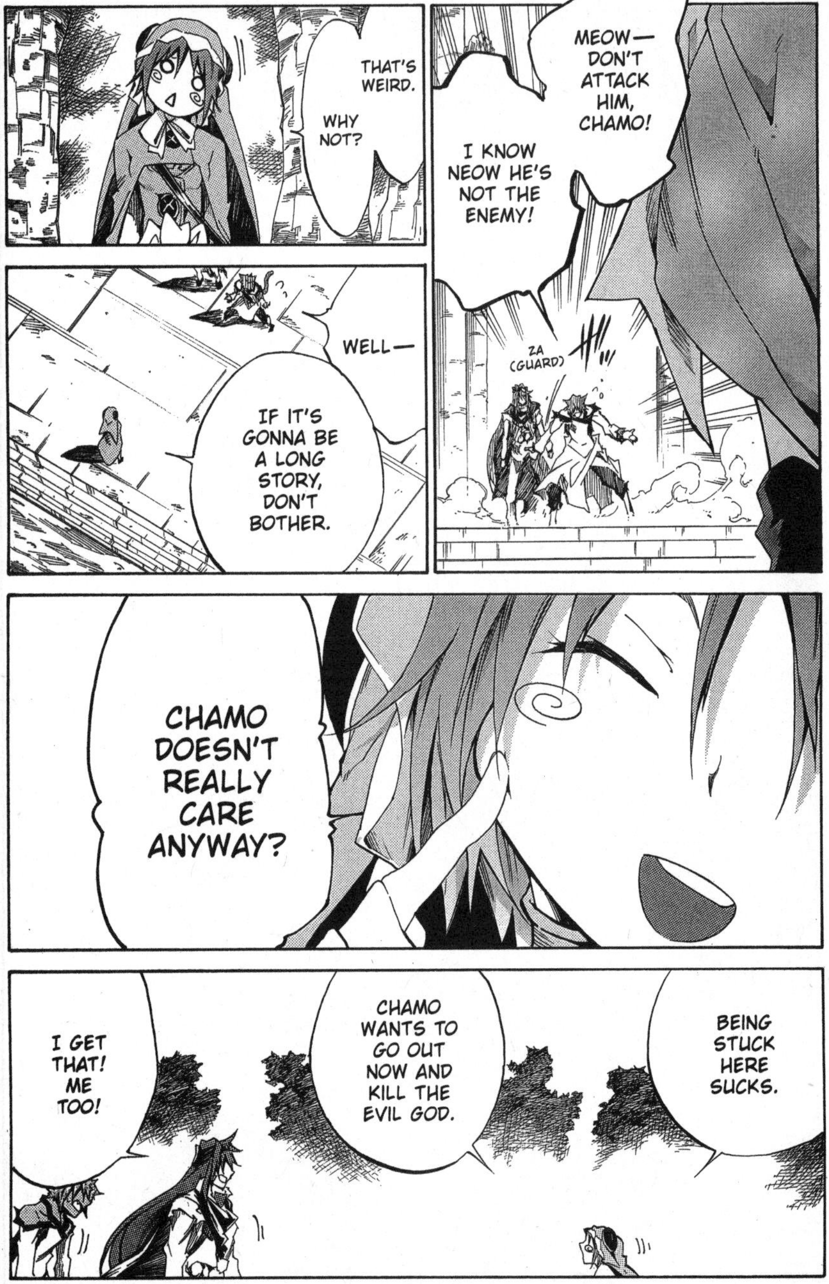
MEOW— DON'T ATTACK HIM, CHAMO!
I KNOW NEOW HE'S NOT THE ENEMY!
ZA (GUARD)
THAT'S WEIRD.
WHY NOT?
WELL—
IF IT'S GONNA BE A LONG STORY, DON'T BOTHER.
CHAMO DOESN'T REALLY CARE ANYWAY?
BEING STUCK HERE SUCKS.
CHAMO WANTS TO GO OUT NOW AND KILL THE EVIL GOD.
I GET THAT! ME TOO!

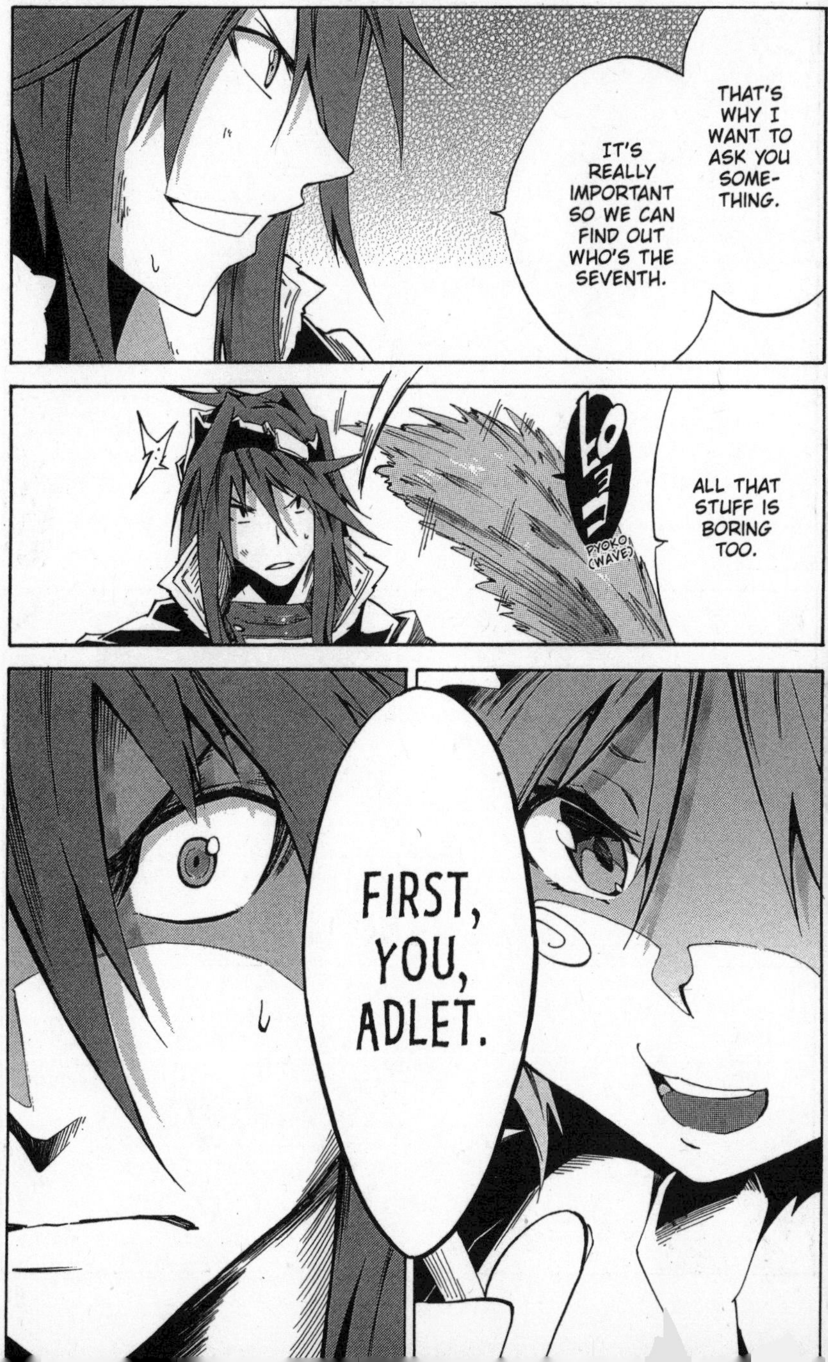
THAT'S WHY I WANT TO ASK YOU SOME-THING.
IT'S REALLY IMPORTANT SO WE CAN FIND OUT WHO'S THE SEVENTH.
ALL THAT STUFF IS BORING TOO.
PYOKO (WAVE)
FIRST, YOU, ADLET.

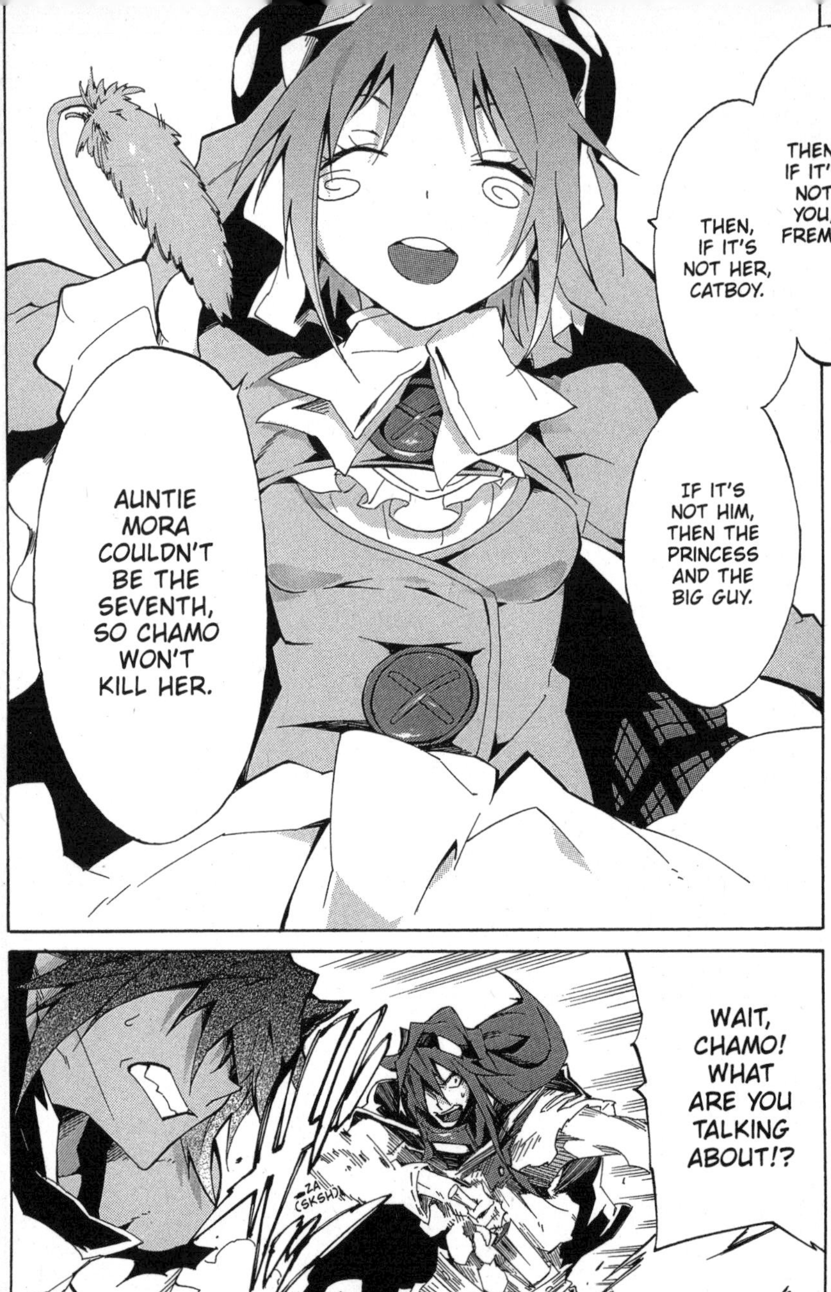
THEN, IF IT'S NOT YOU, FREMY.
THEN, IF IT'S NOT HER, CATBOY.
IF IT'S NOT HIM, THEN THE PRINCESS AND THE BIG GUY.
AUNTIE MORA COULDN'T BE THE SEVENTH, SO CHAMO WON'T KILL HER.
WAIT, CHAMO! WHAT ARE YOU TALKING ABOUT!?
ZA (SKSH)

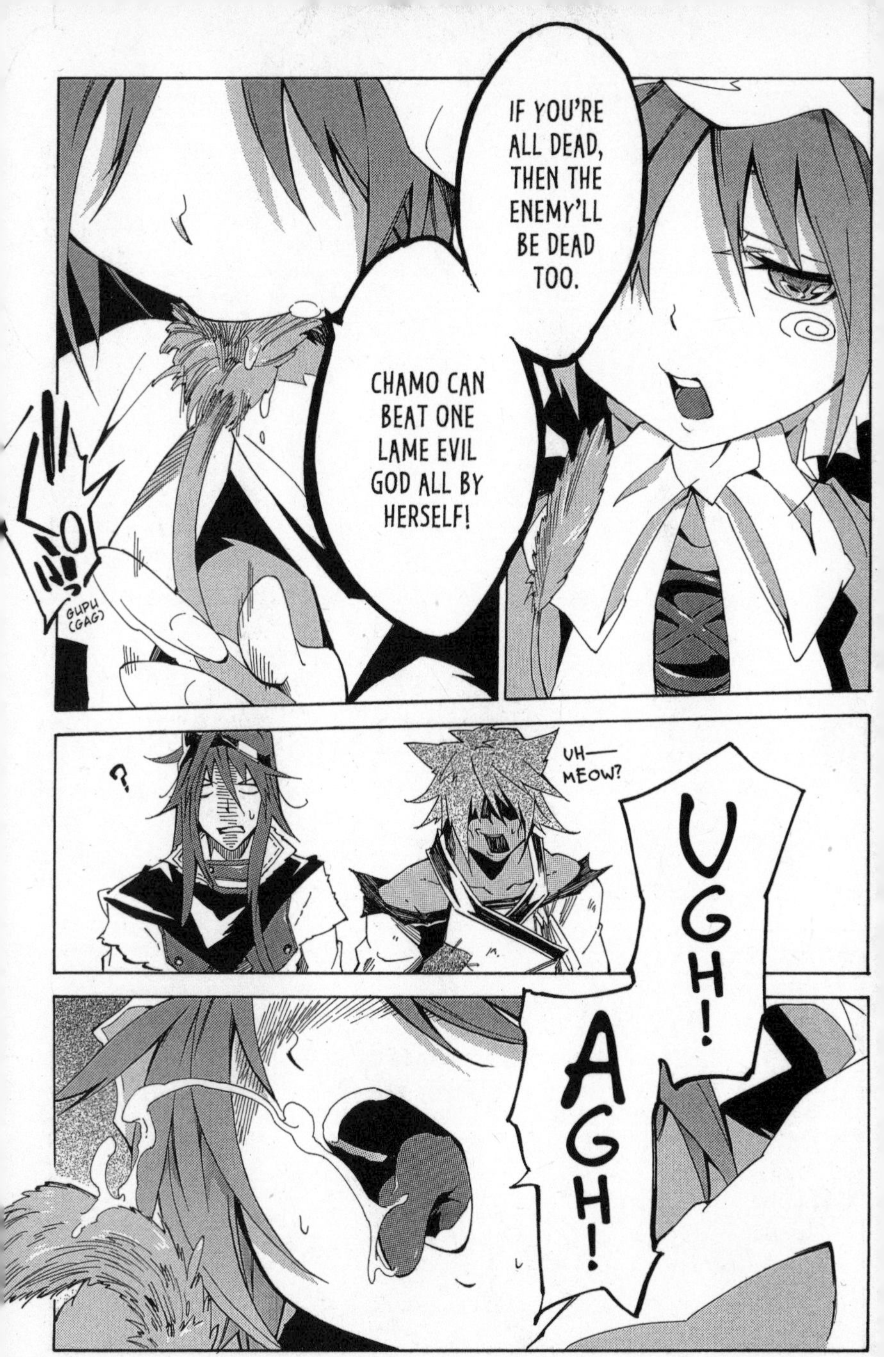
IF YOU'RE ALL DEAD, THEN THE ENEMY'LL BE DEAD TOO.
CHAMO CAN BEAT ONE LAME EVIL GOD ALL BY HERSELF!
GUPU (GAG)
UH— MEOW?
?
UGH! AGH!

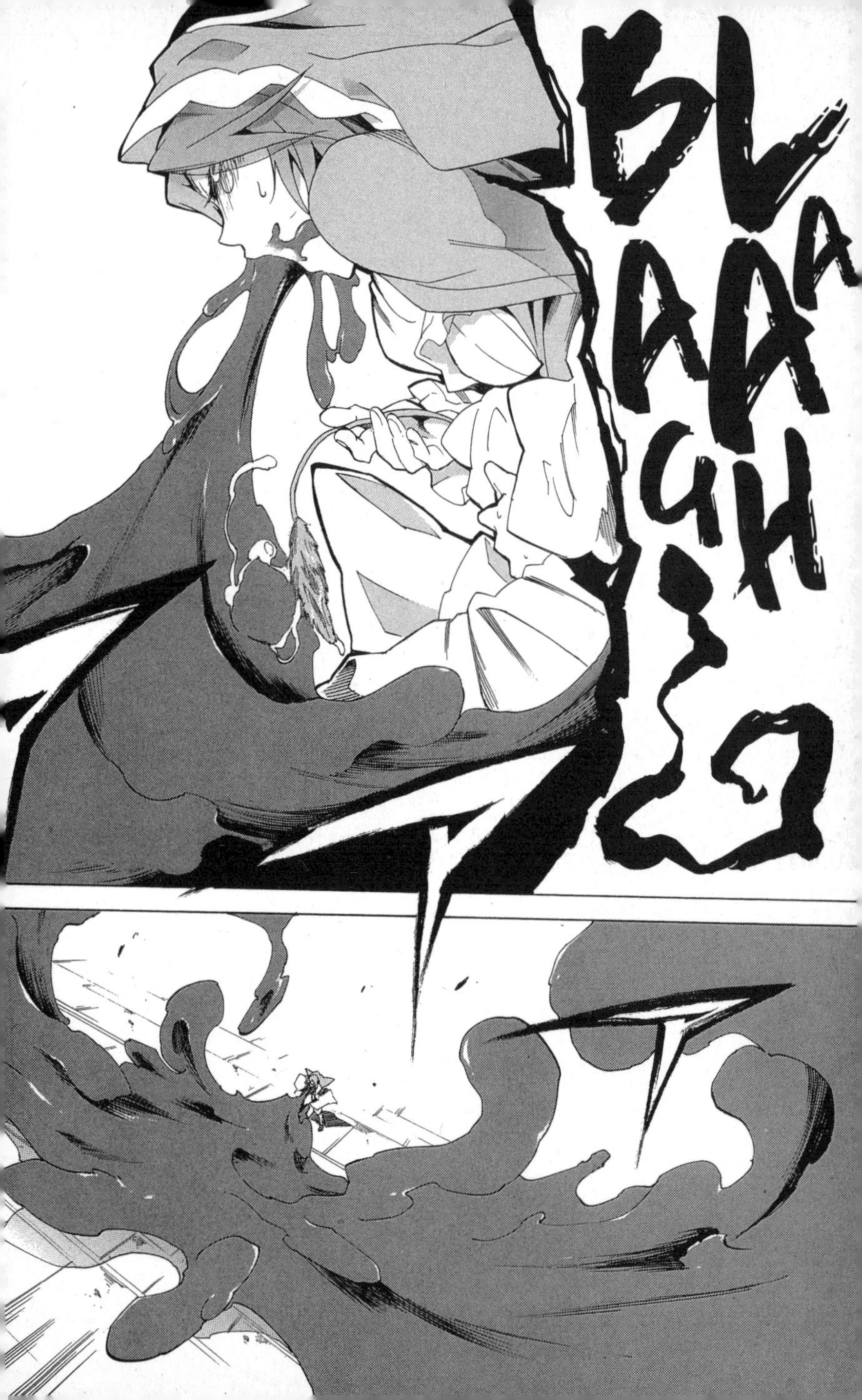
BLAAAAAAGH!

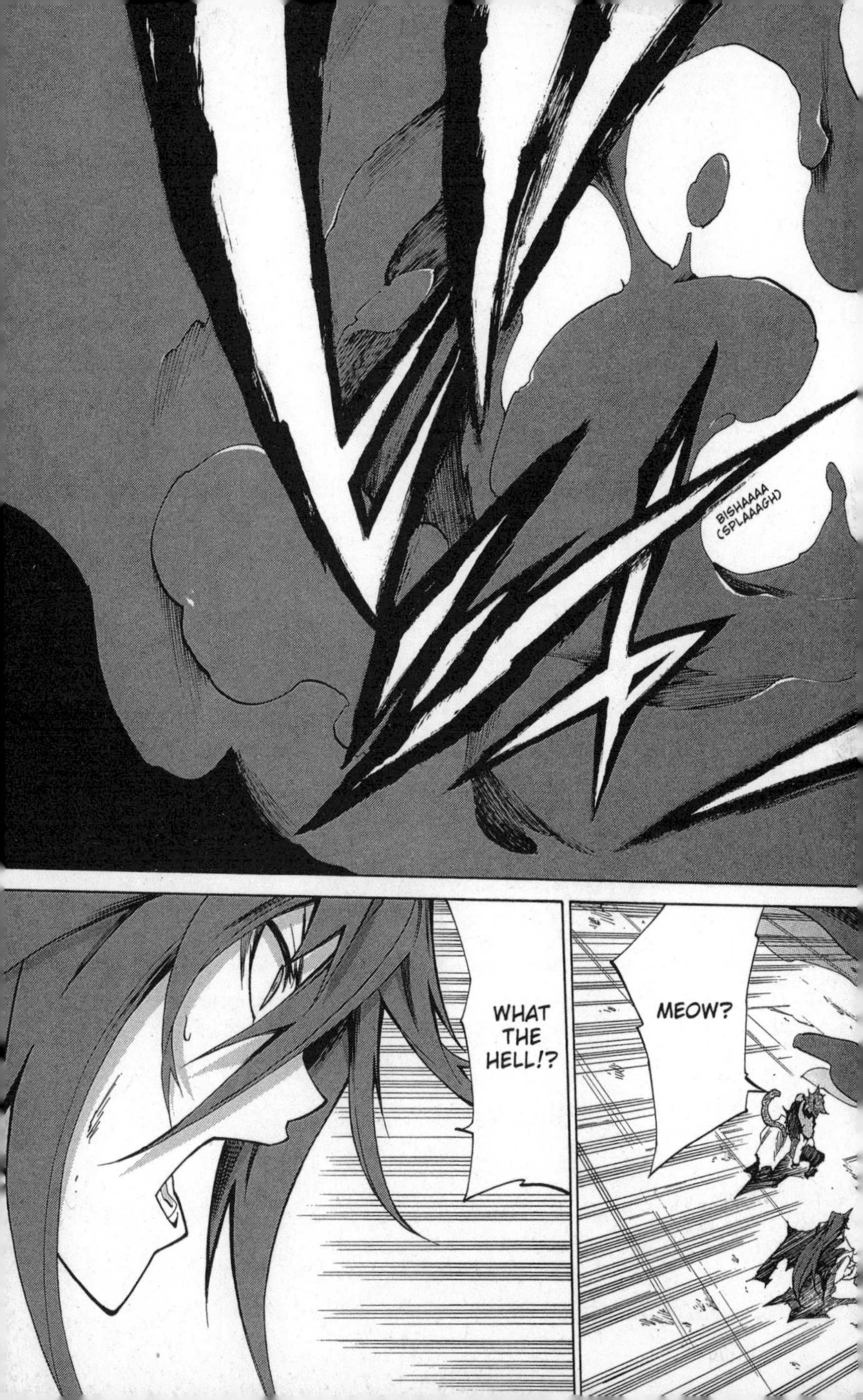
BISHAAAA (SPLAAAGH)
MEOW?
WHAT THE HELL!?

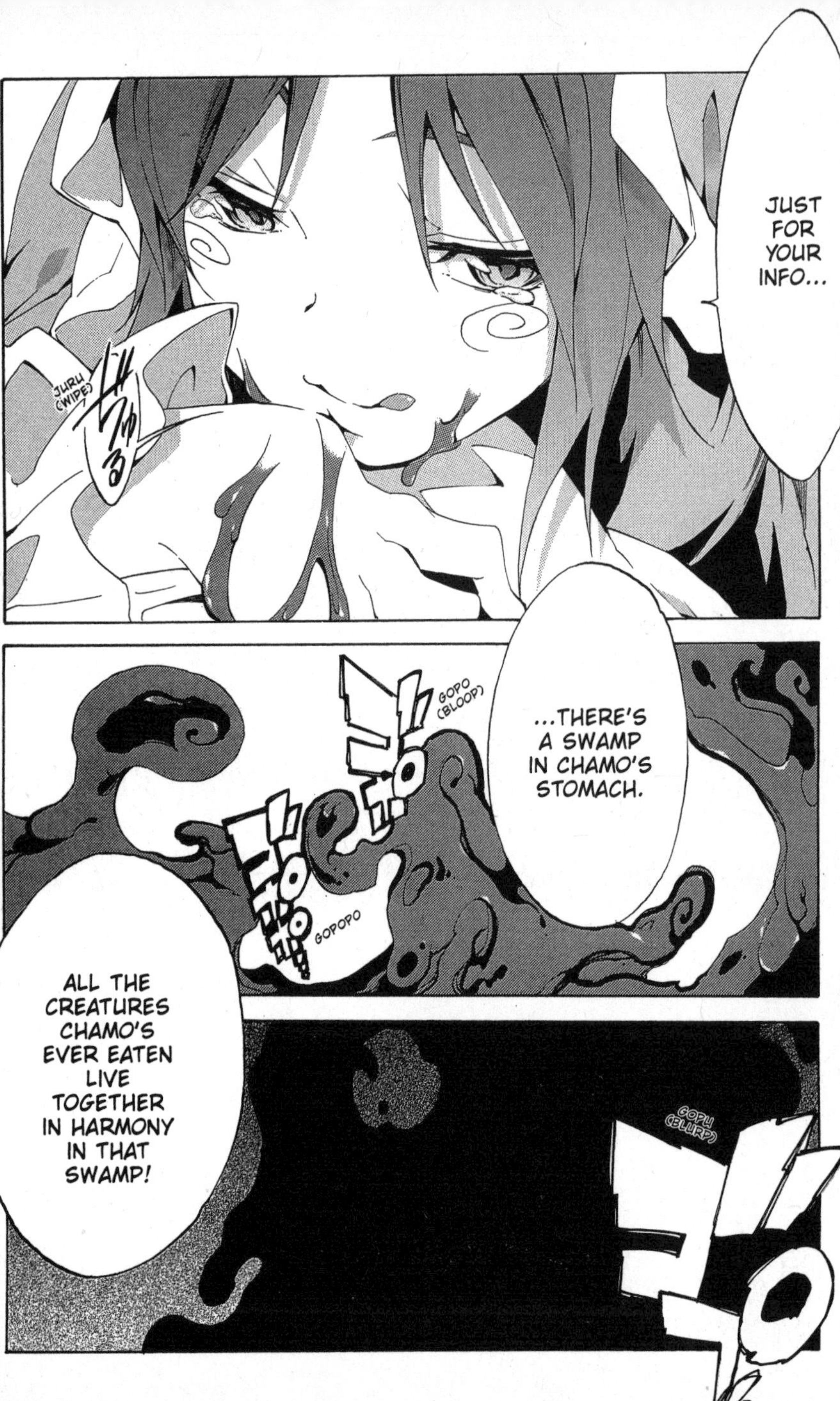
JUST FOR YOUR INFO...
JURU (WIPE)
...THERE'S A SWAMP IN CHAMO'S STOMACH.
GOPO (BLOOP)
GOPOPO
ALL THE CREATURES CHAMO'S EVER EATEN LIVE TOGETHER IN HARMONY IN THAT SWAMP!
GOPU (BLURP)

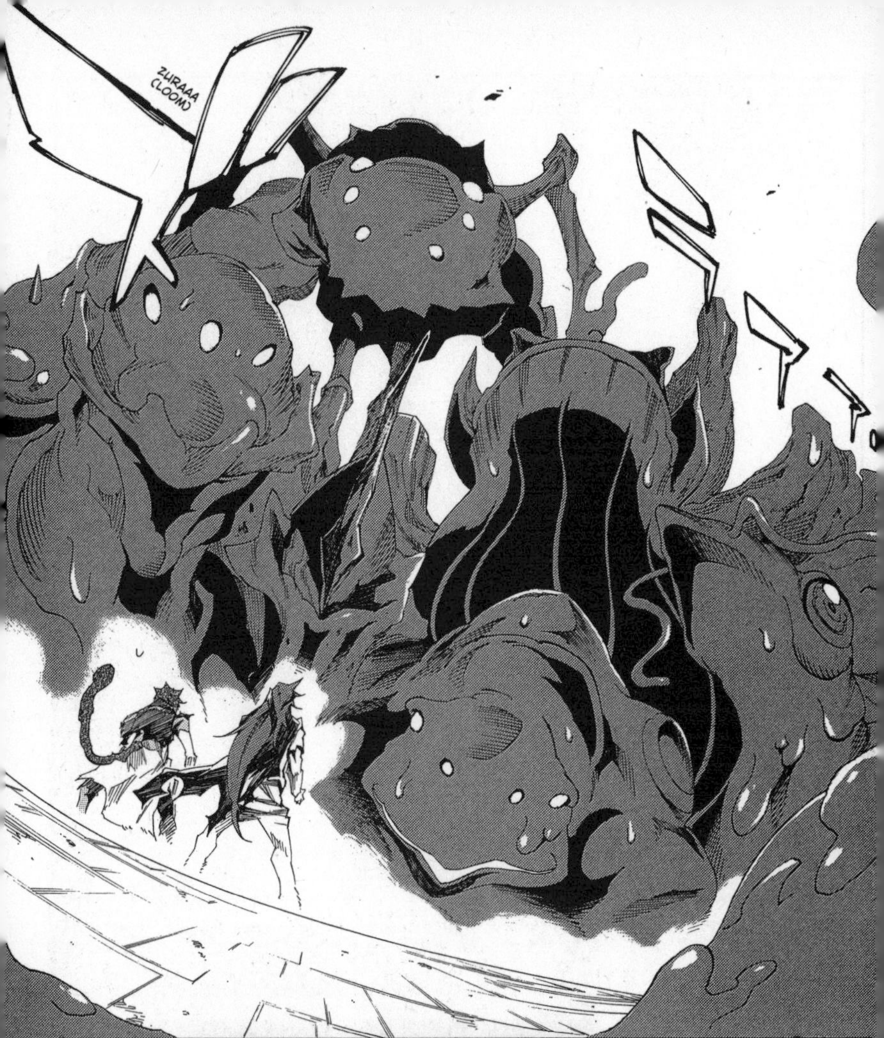
ZURAAA (LOOM)

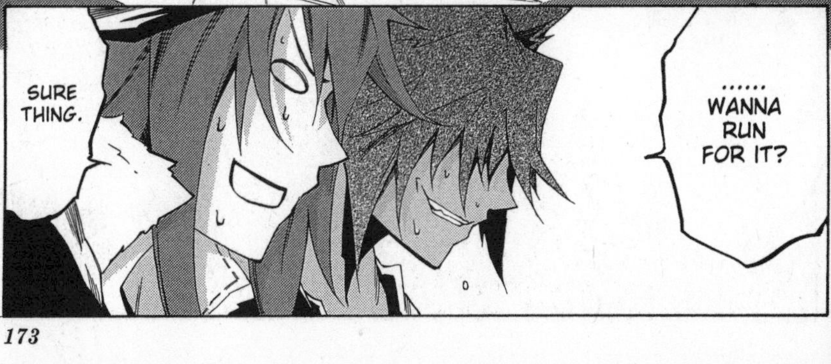
...... WANNA RUN FOR IT?
SURE THING.

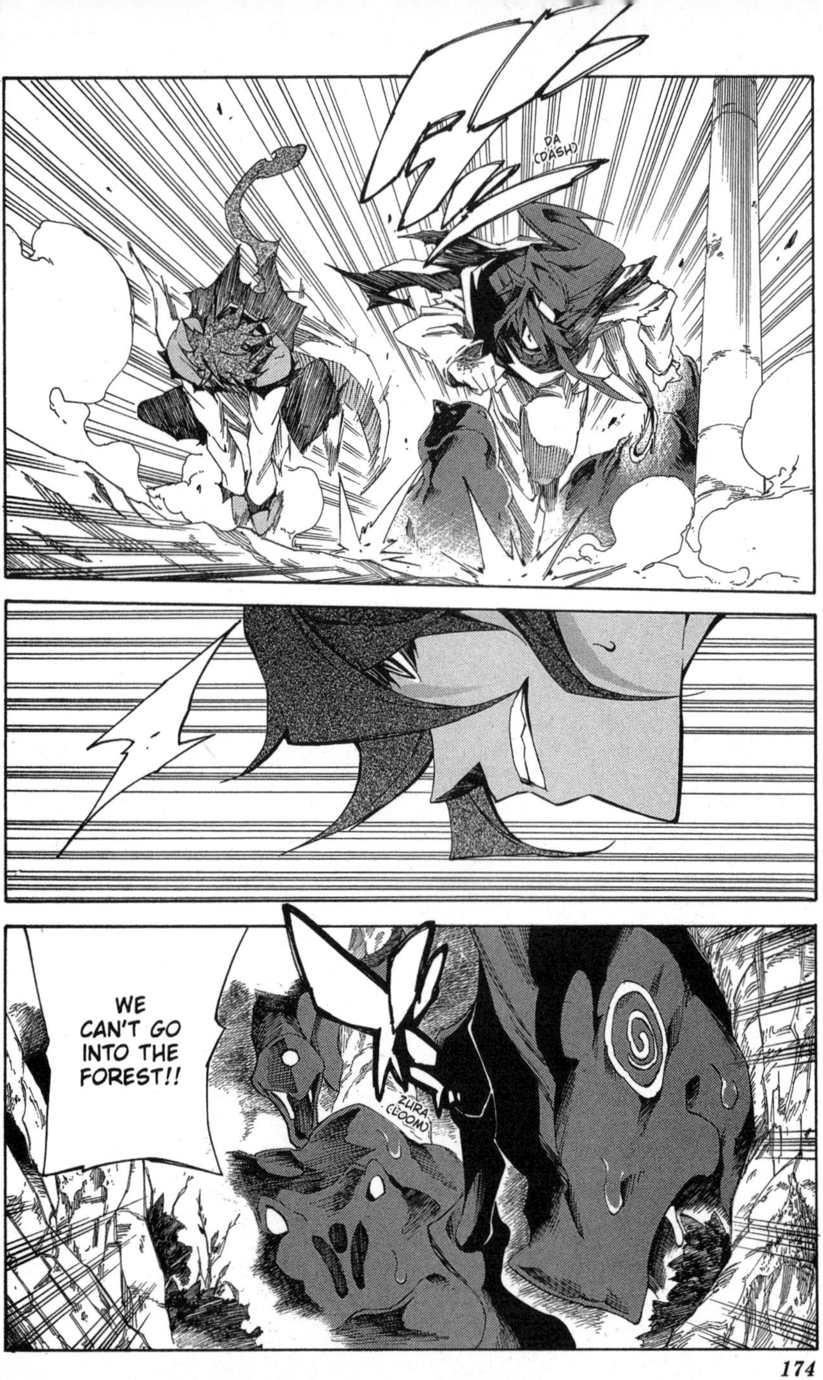
DA (DASH)
WE CAN'T GO INTO THE FOREST!!
ZURA (LOOM)

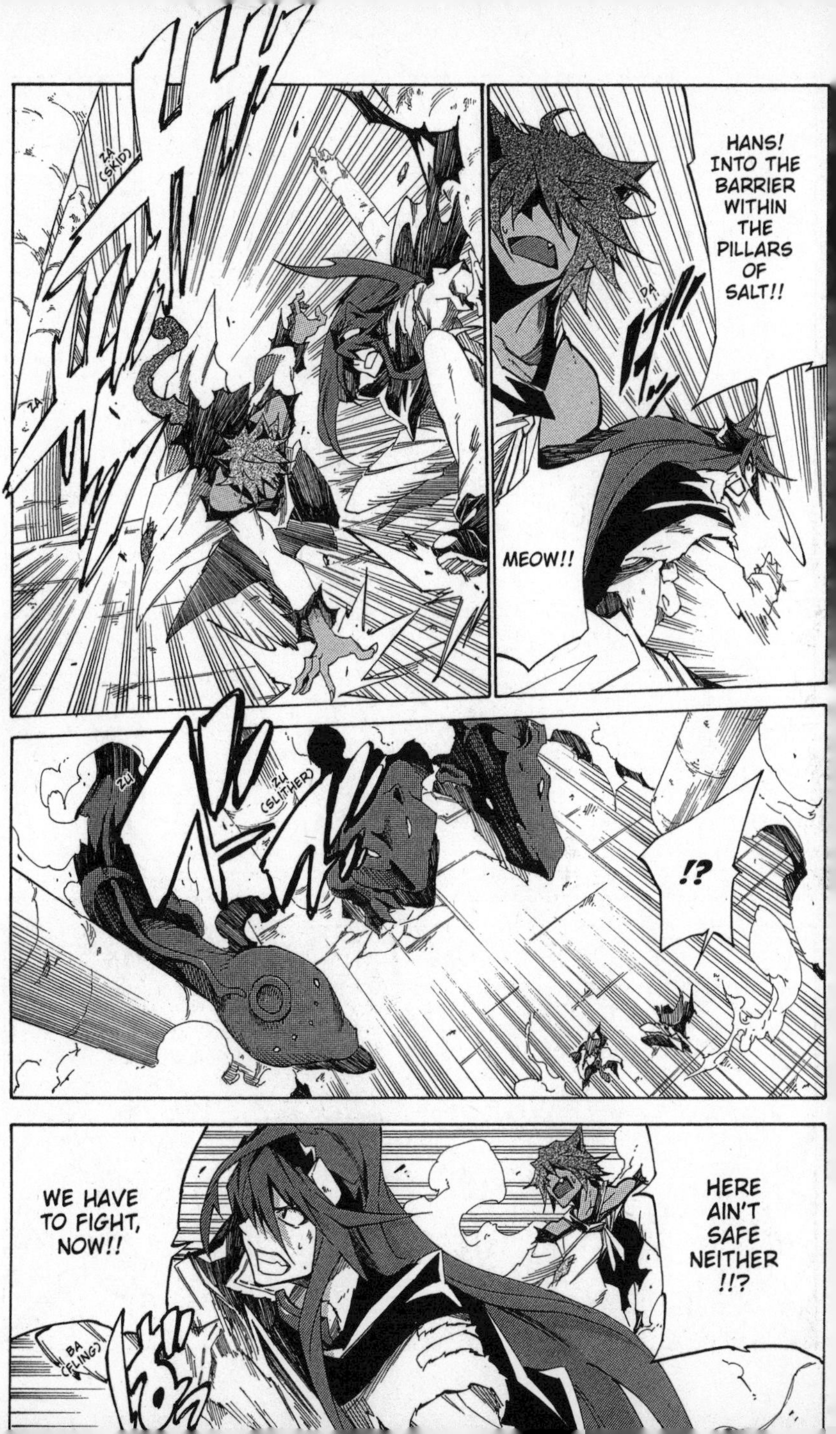
HANS! INTO THE BARRIER WITHIN THE PILLARS OF SALT!!
DA
MEOW!!
ZA (SKID)
ZA
!?
ZU (SLITHER)
ZU
HERE AIN'T SAFE NEITHER!!?
WE HAVE TO FIGHT, NOW!!
BA (FLING)

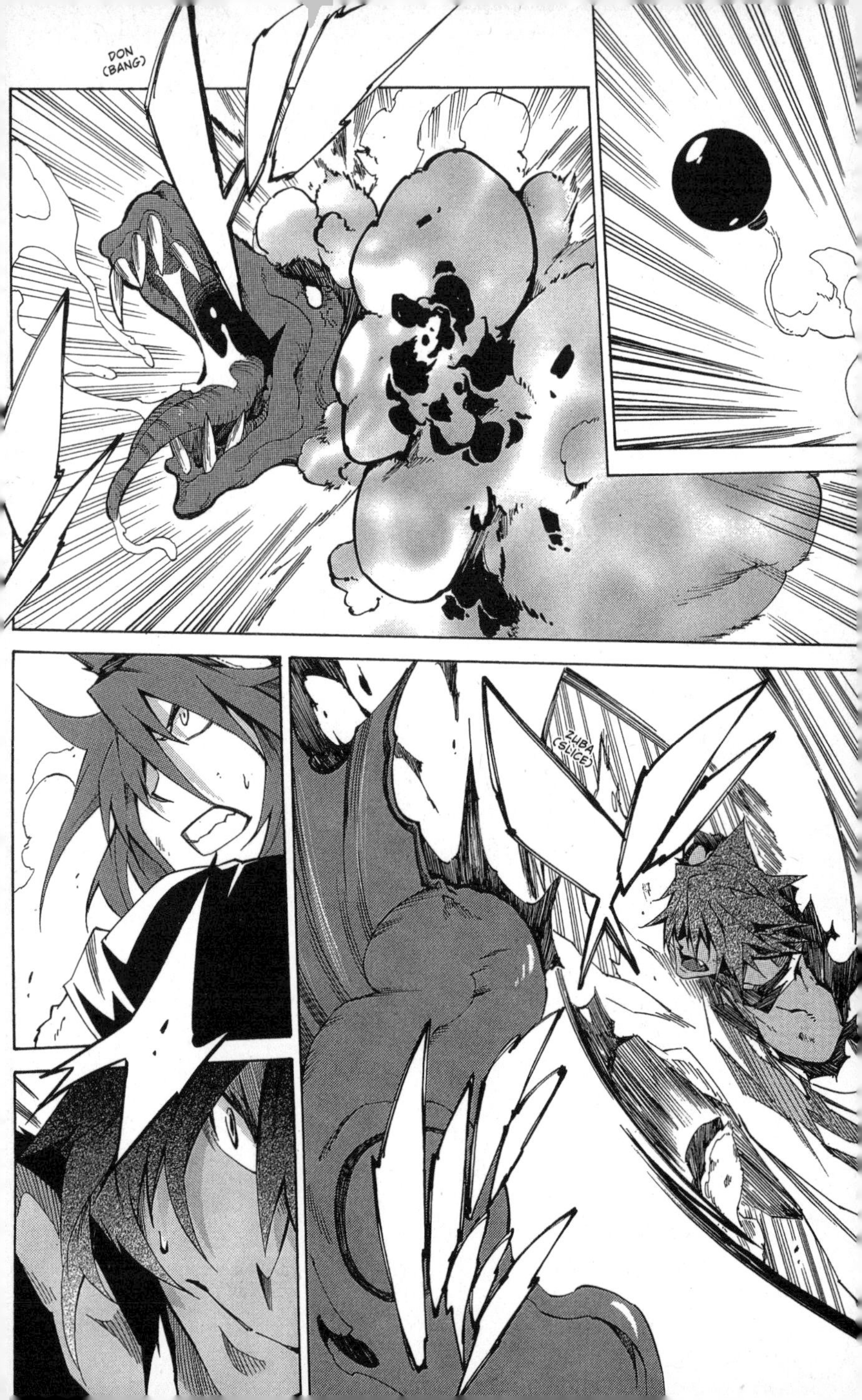
DON (BANG)
ZUBA (SLICE)

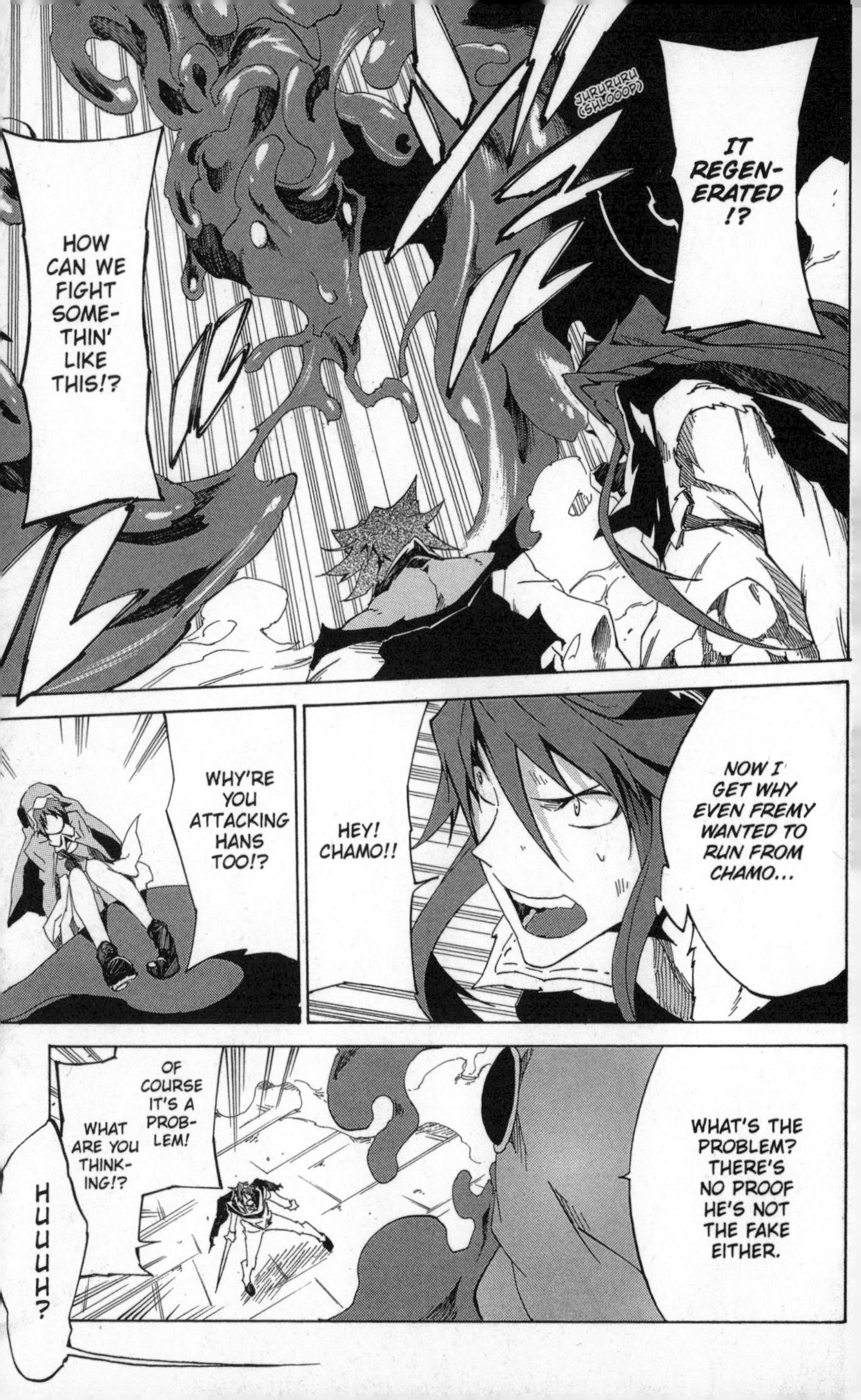
IT REGENERATED!?
JURURURU (SHLOOOP)
HOW CAN WE FIGHT SOMETHIN' LIKE THIS!?
NOW I GET WHY EVEN FREMY WANTED TO RUN FROM CHAMO...
HEY! CHAMO!!
WHY'RE YOU ATTACKING HANS TOO!?
WHAT'S THE PROBLEM? THERE'S NO PROOF HE'S NOT THE FAKE EITHER.
OF COURSE IT'S A PROBLEM!
WHAT ARE YOU THINKING!?
HUUUUH?

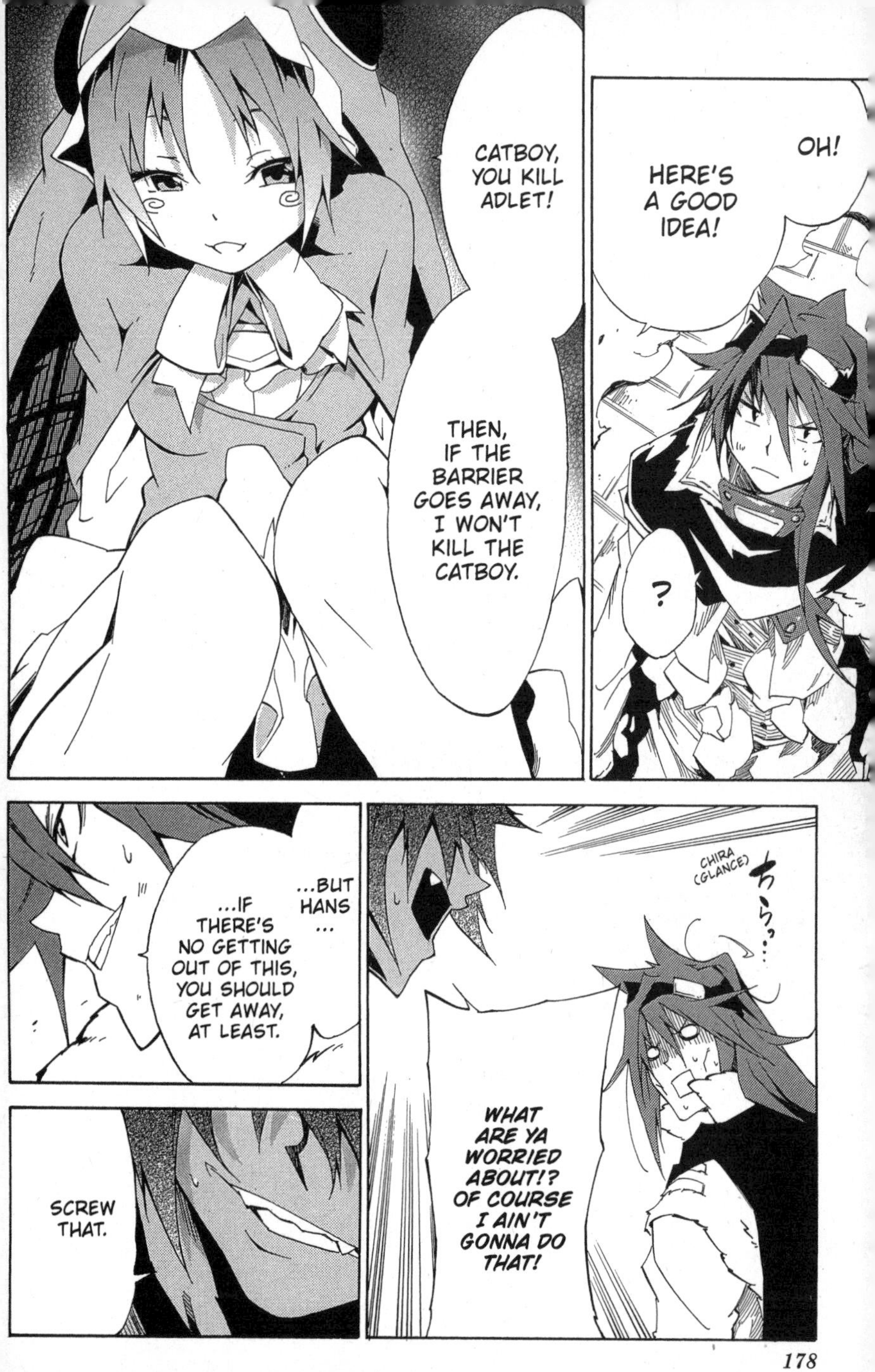
OH!
HERE'S A GOOD IDEA!
?
CATBOY, YOU KILL ADLET!
THEN, IF THE BARRIER GOES AWAY, I WON'T KILL THE CATBOY.
CHIRA (GLANCE)
ちらっ…
WHAT ARE YA WORRIED ABOUT!? OF COURSE I AIN'T GONNA DO THAT!
...BUT HANS...
...IF THERE'S NO GETTING OUT OF THIS, YOU SHOULD GET AWAY, AT LEAST.
SCREW THAT.

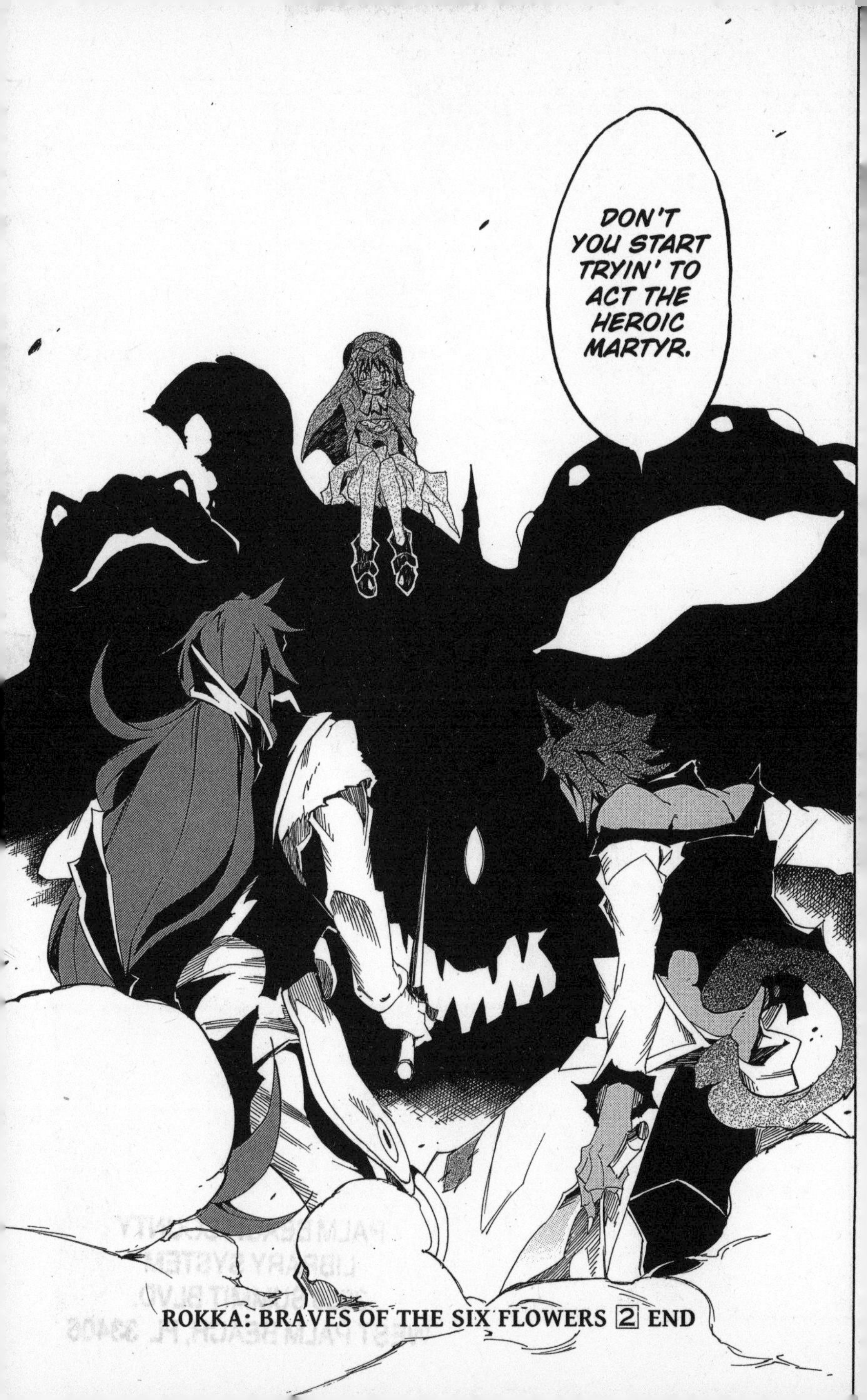
DON'T YOU START TRYIN' TO ACT THE HEROIC MARTYR.

ROKKA: BRAVES OF THE SIX FLOWERS 2 END

ROKKA: Braves of the Six Flowers 2

STORY **ISHIO YAMAGATA**
ART **KEI TORU**
CHARACTER DESIGN **MIYAGI**

Translation: Nicole Wilder
Lettering: Rochelle Gancio

This book is a work of fiction. Names, characters, places, and incidents are the product of the author's imagination or are used fictitiously. Any resemblance to actual events, locales, or persons, living or dead, is coincidental.

ROKKA NO YUSHA - COMIC EDITION- © 2012 by Kei Toru, Ishio Yamagata, Miyagi
All rights reserved. First published in Japan in 2012 by SHUEISHA, Inc. English translation rights arranged with SHUEISHA, Inc. through Tuttle-Mori Agency, Inc., Tokyo.

English translation © 2017 by Yen Press, LLC.

Yen Press
1290 Avenue of the Americas
New York, NY 10104

Visit us at yenpress.com
facebook.com/yenpress
twitter.com/yenpress
yenpress.tumblr.com
instagram.com/yenpress

First Yen Press Edition: May 2017

Yen Press is an imprint of Yen Press, LLC.
The Yen Press name and logo are trademarks of Yen Press, LLC.

The publisher is not responsible for websites (or their content) that are not owned by the publisher.

Library of Congress Control Number: 2016958577

ISBN: 978-0-316-55625-5

10 9 8 7 6 5 4 3 2 1

BVG

Printed in the United States of America